Commodity Modeling and Pricing

Founded in 1807, John Wiley & Sons is the oldest independent publishing company in the United States. With offices in North America, Europe, Australia and Asia, Wiley is globally committed to developing and marketing print and electronic products and services for our customers' professional and personal knowledge and understanding.

The Wiley Finance series contains books written specifically for finance and investment professionals as well as sophisticated individual investors and their financial advisors. Book topics range from portfolio management to e-commerce, risk management, financial engineering, valuation and financial instrument analysis, as well as much more.

For a list of available titles, please visit our Web site at www.WileyFinance.com.

Commodity Modeling and Pricing

Methods for Analyzing Resource Market Behavior

PETER V. SCHAEFFER

John Wiley & Sons, Inc.

Published by John Wiley & Sons, Inc., Hoboken, New Jersey.
Published simultaneously in Canada.

For general information on our other products and services or for technical support, please contact our Customer Care Department within the United States at (800) 762-2974, outside the United States at (317) 572-3993 or fax (317) 572-4002.

Wiley also publishes its books in a variety of electronic formats. Some content that appears in print may not be available in electronic books. For more information about Wiley products, visit our web site at www.wiley.com.

Library of Congress Cataloging-in-Publication Data:

Schaeffer, Peter V.
Commodity modeling and pricing : methods for analyzing resource market behavior / Peter V. Schaeffer.
p. cm. – (Wiley finance series)
Includes index.
ISBN 978-0-470-31723-5 (cloth)
1. Commodity exchanges–Mathematical models. 2. Primary commodities–Prices. 3. Prices–Mathematical models. I. Title.
HG6046.S353 2008
332.64′4–dc22

2008022839

Printed in the United States of America

10 9 8 7 6 5 4 3 2 1

In Memoriam

Daniel J. Gijsbers and Thomas F. Torries

Contents

Preface

Resource commodity markets are extremely important to agricultural producers, processors, consumers, foresters, and the wood processing industry and in the mineral and energy industries. They play a central role in economic development, international trade, and global economic and political stability. Globalization and the spectacular growth and industrial development of China, India, and other Southeast Asian countries have significantly added to total resource commodity demands and caused price increases. Additional pressures on prices have come from an increased use of agricultural commodities, particularly corn and sugar, for ethanol production, a recent development that has had significant impacts on food prices. In general, the closer integration of resource markets has been accompanied by growing economic and financial instability.

Resource-producing countries need export revenues: Brazil, from Amazon timber; Chile, from copper; Iraq, from crude oil; South Africa, from diamonds; and Argentina and the United States, from wheat. Resource-consuming countries need imports for industry: China, India, and Japan for raw materials and energy, the United States for crude oil. Because of cycles in consumption and production, these markets face high price instability. More than 60 commodity futures markets exist to ameliorate this problem. World commodity markets are again under scrutiny, and the economic analysis and modeling of these markets is as important as ever before.

This collection of chapters reflects the influence of Professor Walter C. Labys on the development of econometric methods for forecasting commodity prices. The contributors are former students and collaborators, ranging from practitioners in private industry, public sector and nongovernmental organizations, to scholars in higher education. They are from Australia, China, France, Indonesia, the Ivory Coast, Luxembourg, Tunisia, and the United States. Some of them came together in Morgantown, West Virginia, on the occasion of Professor Labys's retirement from West Virginia University for a symposium showcasing the current state of the art in commodity price modeling and forecasting, while the others joined them later to produce this volume.

During his career, which spanned over 40 years, Professor Labys published 15 books, 150 research articles, and gave 130 invited lectures. His many honors and recognitions include being appointed the first Gunnar Myrdal Scholar by the United Nations in Geneva, receiving a Master Knighthood in the Brotherhood of the Vine in California, being named a Benedum Distinguished Scholar at West Virginia University, and garnering the William H. Miernyk Award for Career Scholarly Achievement by the Regional Research Institute at West Virginia University.

Professor Labys grew up in southwest Pennsylvania. He received his undergraduate education at Carnegie Tech, now Carnegie Mellon University, where he studied engineering and also took courses in painting and sculpture. He then earned a master's degree in Economics at Harvard University. While attending a seminar presentation there, he met Professor Clive W.J. Granger, who would later become the 2003 Nobel laureate in economics. When Professor Granger moved to the University of Nottingham, Professor Labys followed him to complete a Ph.D. in Economics under his direction.

Shortly after receiving his Ph.D., he started work as a consultant for the Commodities Division at the World Bank, where a chance encounter with Alfred Maizels led to an invitation to join the United Nations Conference on Trade and Development in Geneva as a commodities specialist. At the time, the United Nations in Geneva was a virtual whirlwind of economic activity and research, and Professor Labys encountered many eventual Nobel laureates in Economics. He was coached through his first commodity model by Lawrence Klein, and made the acquaintance of Harry Johnston, Robert Mundell, James Meade, and Richard Stone.

Eventually Professor Labys moved back to the United States, opting for West Virginia University in Morgantown to be near his parents, rather than joining his doctoral advisor, Professor Granger, at the University of California in San Diego. His work continued to take him back to Europe, where he consulted with the United Nations in Geneva, the Food and Agriculture Organization in Rome, and the International Institute for Applied Systems Analysis in Vienna while maintaining academic affiliations with several French universities.

During his long career, Professor Labys served as advisor to many students both in the United States and abroad. His relationship with his doctoral students was characterized by strong support, with a willingness to help at any time and in any way possible. This collection of chapters is in part the result of such relationships.

W. Paul Labys
CRA International, Salt Lake City, Utah

Peter V. Schaeffer
West Virginia University, Morgantown, West Virginia

Acknowledgments

The Division of Resource Management and the Regional Research Institute financially supported the symposium that brought together the initial core of speakers and papers that led to the idea for this book. My West Virginia University colleagues Jerald J. Fletcher and Tim T. Phipps provided organizational support for the symposium, as did our secretary, Lisa Lewis. Randall W. Jackson, director of the Regional Research Institute, provided additional funding for technical support during the production of the manuscript. Walter Labys took pleasure and pride in this project and provided feedback and editorial advice on many issues and chapters. I benefited greatly from the advice and guidance of John Wiley & Sons' Debra W. Englander, Executive Editor, Stacey Small, Editorial Assistant, Kelly O'Connor, Development Editor, and Michael Lisk, Senior Production Editor. Jacquelyn Strager created the base map of Indonesia that served as the basis for Figure 11.1 and Gloria Nestor assisted with Figure 14.1. Ika Rahmawati helped with translating statistical information from Indonesian into English. Weslie Boyd's expert assistance was invaluable in getting the manuscript ready to meet the publisher's guidelines.

Editing this book was interesting and rewarding, but also time consuming and at times, it interfered with family life. I therefore very gratefully acknowledge my wife's love, support, and patience.

PETER V. SCHAEFFER

PART One

Dynamics of Commodity Price Behavior

At times the prices of many commodities display volatile behaviors. Since agricultural commodities and minerals, such as crude oil and metals, are among the fundamental inputs of our economies on the production and/or the consumption side, price volatility causes disruptions and can lead to crises. An improved understanding of the dynamics of price behavior is therefore highly desirable from a policy as well as from a consumer and supplier perspective.

Part One consists of four chapters, each written from a different point of view. In Chapter 1, the recently retired chief economist of Arcelor-Mittal and two colleagues from academia present a new method for estimating long memory processes from small samples, a common problem in industry, where forecasts frequently have to be made from very short series. This contribution provides a theoretically sound and interesting solution to a practical problem.

While the first chapter takes an industry and firm perspective, the second chapter analyzes time-series data to study the link between commodity price developments and business cycles. The question asked many times is whether commodity prices lead inflation or inflation leads commodity prices. The answer is not immediately visible from looking at the data, because trends can be obscured by short-run occurrences. This chapter's analysis offers a method to uncover the true trend and provides evidence that, on balance, commodity prices are procyclical. The exceptions are the price of gold, which is countercyclical, and the price of sugar, which is acyclical.

Chapter 3 also studies the connection between inflation and commodity prices. The author uses a recently developed procedure to test the possible presence of nonlinearity in the comovement of commodity prices and the consumer price index. The results reveal interdependences between the different price series, with policy implications, for example, on how to combat inflation.

Chapter 4 also is focused on macroeconomic issues, but the issue of interest turns from domestic policy to the world market. The chapter deals with the relationship between the dollar and the oil price. The real price of the oil in every currency depends on a variety of factors, including OPEC policy. The price of crude oil is in

U.S. dollars, but most of the imports of the largest oil-producing member countries originate in the euro zone or in Japan. Hence, the devaluation of the dollar lowers the purchase power of OPEC member countries, which they try to regain by adjusting the price of oil upward.

Together, these four chapters provide models, data, results, and insights that enhance our understanding of the dynamics of commodity price behavior. They use the most current models and techniques in time-series analysis and illustrate their application. The chapters complement each other by providing information at different levels of aggregation while dealing with the same general subject. Because of their mixed background in terms of professional experiences and geographic location, the authors also bring different perspectives to their respective tasks.

CHAPTER 1

Indirect Inference and Long Memory

A New Truncated-Series Estimation Method

Armand Sadler, Jean-Baptiste Lesourd and Vêlayoudom Marimoutou

INTRODUCTION

Long-memory processes are an important and even fundamental advance in time-series modeling. More precisely, the so-called autoregressive fractionally integrated moving average (ARFIMA) model has been introduced by Granger and Joyeux (1980) and Hosking (1981). It is a generalization of the ARIMA model, which is a short memory process, by allowing the differencing parameter d to take any real value. The goal of this specification is to capture *parsimoniously* long-run multipliers that decay very slowly, which amounts to modeling long memories in a time series. ARFIMA processes, however, are associated with hyperbolically decaying autocorrelations, impulse response weights, and spectral density function exploding at zero frequency. As noted by Brockwell et al. (1998), while a long memory process can always be approximated by an ARMA(p, q) process, the orders p and q required to achieve a good approximation may be so large as to make parameter estimation extremely difficult. In any case, this approximation is not possible with small samples.

ARFIMA processes are defined as follows in their canonical form:

$$\Phi(L)(1-L)^d y_t = \mu + \Theta(L)\varepsilon_t, \quad \varepsilon_t : iid(0, \sigma^2) \tag{1.1}$$

where $d \in (-0.5, 0.5)$ is the fractional difference operator and μ can be any deterministic function of time. If μ is zero, this process is called fractionally differenced autoregressive moving average (e.g., Fuller (1996)). The *iid* (independent and identically distributed) assumption is the strongest assumption; it implies mixing, that is, conditions on the dependence of the sequence. For a stationary sequence, mixing implies ergodicity (restrictions on the dependence of the sequence). Ergodic processes are not necessarily mixing; mixing conditions are stronger than ergodicity. For details, see White (1984) and Rosenblatt (1978).

For general overviews on long memory processes, surveys, and results, we refer the reader to Baillie (1996); Brockwell and Davis (1998); Fuller (1996); Gouriéroux and Monfort (1995); Gourieroux and Jasiak (1999); Hamilton (1994); Jasiak (1999, 2000); Lardic and Mignon (1999); Maddala and Kim (1998); and Sowell (1990) as well as to the discussions and comments by Bardet (1999), Bertrand (1999), Gourieroux (1999), Jasiak (1999), Lardic and Mignon (1999), Prat (1999), Renault (1999), Taqqu (1999), and Truong-Van (1999). Concerning recent research on the topic of long memory, we refer the reader to Andrews and Guggenberger (2003), Andrews and Sun (2004), and Davidson and Terasvirta (2002). Note also the presentation of a new stationarity test for fractionally integrated processes by Dolado, Gonzalo, and Mayoral (2002). Among the most important papers concerning estimation techniques for these ARFIMA model are Fox and Taqqu (1986), Geweke and Porter-Hudak (1983), Li and McLeod (1986), and Sowell (1992a). Tests for long memory across a variety of commodity spot and futures prices can be found in Barkoulas, Labys, and Onochie (1997, 1999) as well as in Cromwell et al. (2000).

The methods for estimating d, the long-range dependence parameter, can be summarized in three classes:

1. The heuristic methods [the Hurst (1951) method, the Lo (1989, 1991) method, the Higuchi (1988) method]
2. The semiparametric methods [Geweke and Porter-Hudak (GPH) (1983) method, the Robinson (1983, 1995a, 1995b) estimation methods]
3. The maximum likelihood methods [the exact maximum likelihood method, the Whittle (1951) approximate maximum likelihood method]

For a comparison of these classes of estimators, refer to Boutahar et al. (2005).

The estimation of fractional integration exponents leads to significant problems in some cases. In the case of small samples, as often encountered with industrial data, it is even impossible. Long-memory estimations often are performed with financial time series with large numbers of observations (5,000 observations and more are not uncommon). However, small samples of 50 to 100 observations are the order of magnitude usually encountered in industrial forecasting problems. In such cases the need for a consistent and precise estimation technique is of great interest. Thus, we motivate the need for a new estimator for the long-memory parameter by the small sample sizes often encountered in practice. Why should we care about long memory in those situations? For instance, one could argue that from a forecasting perspective, long memory starts to make a difference only when forecasting over long horizons. In situations when you only have a few observations available, you would not forecast too many steps ahead. The reply to this comment covers three aspects:

1. What really matters in time series analysis is the span, not the number of observations. Fifty yearly observations on apparent steel use in a region have another informational content than 5,000 real-time observations over a short period of time on some financial stock index.
2. Many industry sectors are producing medium- and long-range forecasts based on a relatively small number of yearly or quarterly observations. A steel producer planning to invest in a new rolling mill or a new greenfield facility can not wait for a long time series before making a decision but has to work with the actually available data.

3. We have come to believe from our past studies that for transfer function models (models with explanatory variables), long memory does not even exist. Detected long memory always followed some misspecification of the actual model. If a model is correctly specified, long memory should disappear. In this sense, we look at long memory as a specification test.

By using indirect inference to adjust for the bias, is the computational burden increasing? The answer is no. We suggest the use of our reference tables to correct for the bias. To our knowledge, since the work of Li and McLeod (1986), no new estimation techniques that are valid for small samples have been proposed in the econometric literature. Moreover, Li and McLeod developed an estimation technique based on truncating the power series defining the process after about 50 terms.

In this chapter, we propose a completely different approach based on low-order truncation (after about five terms). Li and McLeod considered their truncated model as approximating the true model, whereas we explicitly consider our low-order truncated model as an instrumental model that is necessarily biased. The bias is corrected by an indirect inference technique, through minimizing a distance function.

This chapter aims at defining an estimation technique of the fractional integration exponent d for comparatively small samples. Its asymptotical properties are based on a result established by Mira and Escribano (2000) about the almost sure consistency of a nonlinear least square (NLS) estimator. The hypotheses used by these authors are shown to apply to our particular case of truncated series. A new method for identification and estimation of these truncated series is developed and applied to steel consumption time series as well as to the analysis of atmospheric carbon dioxide (CO_2) concentrations derived from in situ air measurements at Mauna Loa Observatory, Hawaii.

ALMOST SURE CONSISTENCY OF THE NLS ESTIMATOR FROM OUR TRUNCATED MODEL

We consider the simplest ARFIMA process, also called fractionally differenced (or integrated) white noise (see, e.g., Fuller (1996) or Brockwell et al. (1998)):

$$(1 - L)^d \, y_t = e_t \tag{1.2}$$

with $e_t \sim iid$, or $y_t + \sum_{j=1}^{\infty} \kappa_j(d) y_{t-j} = e_t$.

$$\kappa_j(d) = [\Gamma(j+1)\Gamma(-d)]^{-1}\,\Gamma(j-d) = \prod_{i=1}^{j} i^{-1}(i-1-d)$$

Γ is the gamma function and $d \in (-0.5, 0.5)$. If ξ is not an integer, then $\xi = n + \phi$, $\phi \in (0,1)$: $\Gamma(\xi) = (\phi + n - 1)(\phi + n - 2)\ldots(\phi + 1)\,\phi\Gamma(\phi)$. We define the truncated version of this model by:

$$y_t + \sum_{j=1}^{r} \kappa_j\,(d) y_{t-j} = e_t \tag{1.3}$$

In addition, we relax the *iid* assumption for e_t and replace it by the less restrictive α-mixing assumption, thus allowing for some heteroscedasticity (see White (1984) for details). In the appendix we show that the parameter d of model (1.3) can be consistently estimated and that the true fractional parameter can be estimated by indirect inference.

In the next section, we show how to identify and estimate the truncated long memory process.

IDENTIFICATION AND ESTIMATION OF THE TRUNCATED LONG MEMORY PROCESS

We define the combined consumption model (CCM) as a transfer function model including long memory. The starting point is either a cointegration relationship between variables having a common stochastic trend or a stable relationship between stationarized variables. In the case of structural breaks, the break may be in level, in slope, or in both. Care has to be taken with the specification because, as pointed out by Diebold and Inoue (2001), long memory and structural breaks are easily confused.

The CCM is thus aiming at a parsimonious representation of reality by focusing on a few key explanatory variables, an ARMA part in order to take account of short memory and a fractional parameter representing long memory. With this definition, the estimated parameter d will always lie in the open interval (–0.5, 0.5). An estimated parameter d out of that range is an indication that the series have not been correctly stationarized because the process is only both stationary and invertible if $d < 10.51$.

If long memory is specified by a truncated version of the model, the CCM can be estimated easily. The next estimation procedure follows the outline proposed by Hosking (1981), except that we change the order of the steps and estimate the combined model. To illustrate the estimation procedure, let us start with the ARFIMA model

$$\Phi(L)\left[y_t + \sum_{j=1}^{r} \kappa_j(d)\, y_{t-j}\right] = \Theta(L)\,\varepsilon_t \tag{1.4}$$

or

$$F(L)\,\nabla^d y_t = \Theta(L)\,\varepsilon_t \tag{1.5}$$

Define

$$u_t = y_t + \sum_{j=1}^{r} \kappa_j(d) y_{t-j} \tag{1.6}$$

so that $\{u_t\}$ is an ARIMA $(p, 0, q)$ process.

$$\Phi(L)[u_t] = \Theta(L)\,\varepsilon_t \tag{1.7}$$

Let

$$x_t = \{\Theta(L)\}^{-1} \Phi(L) y_t \tag{1.8}$$

so that x_t is a truncated ARIMA (0, d, 0) process because

$$\nabla^d x_t = \{\Theta(L)\}^{-1} \Phi(L) \nabla^d y_t = \varepsilon_t \tag{1.9}$$

d is estimated in four steps:

1. Start the algorithm by setting $d = 0$ in (1.4) and estimating the ARMA parameters by the Gauss-Newton algorithm.
2. Take the residuals (z_t) from the equation in step 1 and check if the series displays long memory; in other words, estimate d.
3. Calculate u_t from equation 1.6 with the d estimated in step 2.
4. Reestimate the ARMA parameters from equation 1.7 and check for convergence. If not converged, reestimate d and go to step 3.

Adding additional exogenous explanatory variables poses no problem in this estimation procedure. There is generally no convergence problem in applying this procedure, except when the sample size is really too small.

INFORMAL PROOF OF THE CONVERGENCE OF THE ABOVE ESTIMATION PROCEDURE

In practice, we are running a conditional loop. The instructions in the loop are executed repeatedly until a specified condition is true. In our case, the condition is that the distance between successive values of the respective parameters in successive runs gets arbitrarily small (the Cauchy criterion of convergence of a sequence). Suppose the true DGP (data generating process) is given by formula 1.4 and that d is positive. By setting $d = 0$ in step 1, the ARMA parameters are capturing *partly* the impact of a missing explanatory variable and are distorted. But the ARMA specification cannot capture long memory. Thus, the residuals (z_t) in step 2 are not *iid* and the estimated d in this step is necessarily positive, given our assumption. In step 4, the reestimated ARMA parameters are closer to reality as we are taking into account the new estimated d. By proceeding further in this way, the distortions are becoming smaller and smaller. The procedure is converging.

Monte Carlo Simulation and Indirect Inference Estimation of an ARFIMA (0,*d*,0)

In this section, we use a methodology called indirect inference to demonstrate the usefulness of our approach. This methodology, introduced by Gouriéroux, Monfort, and Renault (1993), Smith (1993), and Gallant and Tauchen (1996) is nowadays largely used in applied econometric research. The idea is to draw a simulation-based inference on generally intractable structural models through an instrumental model, conceived as easier to handle. We refer the reader to Gouriéroux and Monfort (1997) for a detailed description of the methodology.

The initial model (M) is equation 1.2 and the approximated one (M^a) is equation 1.3. The estimator is obtained by minimizing equation A.1 (see appendix) by nonlinear least squares.

Equation A.1 may be written

$$Q_n(d) = n^{-1} \sum_{t=1}^{n} f^a(\underline{y_t}, d),$$

whereas the initial model is

$$Q_n(d) = n^{-1} \sum_{t=1}^{n} f(\underline{y_t}, d)$$

with $\underline{y_t}$ denoting the present and past values y_t, y_{t-1}, y_{t-2}, and so on, of the process y. Let d be the true value of the parameter and d^a the estimated parameter of the instrumental model. The estimated parameter d^a does not generally converge toward the true parameter d because $f(\underline{y_t}, d) \neq f^a(\underline{y_t}, d)$.

First we will show that the asymptotic bias is a function of d. We simulated different ARFIMA (0,d,0) models by using a RATS program written by Schoen (1997). The fractionally integrated parameter d (the true d) is estimated by considering the estimator d^a obtained by minimizing formula 1.3 with six lags and with large samples. d^a, reported in row 2 in Tables 1.1 to 1.5, is the arithmetic mean of 10,000 (respectively 50,000) parameters estimated from each simulation. We observe an important bias when approaching the nonstationary case for positive d. The gain in precision is significant for increasing n.

A visual representation of the relationship between the value of the true d and the estimated value d^2 is provided in Figure 1.1. It shows that the bias is a function of d.

We next test the sensitivity of estimates as a function of the lag, r. Table 1.5 shows simulation results when $r = 3$.

It follows from Tables 1.1 to 1.5 that the estimated fractional parameter d^a does not differ significantly from the true d, except for values of d approaching the extreme points of the open interval (–0.5,0.5). Nevertheless, the bias has to be

TABLE 1.1 Bias as a Function of d with 1,000 Observations and 10,000 Simulations

True d	–0.49	–0.4	–0.3	–0.2	–0.1	0.1	0.2	0.3	0.4	0.49
d^a	–.405	–0.345	–0.271	–0.188	–0.098	0.101	0.212	0.333	0.474	0.706
Std Error	0.035	0.036	0.036	0.037	0.037	0.037	0.037	0.036	0.035	0.029
Stat T	2.4	1.5	0.8	0.3	0.05	0.03	0.3	0.9	2.1	7.5

TABLE 1.2 Bias as a Function of d with 500 Observations and 50,000 Simulations

True d	−0.49	−0.4	−0.3	−0.2	−0.1	0.1	0.2	0.3	0.4	0.49
d^a	−0.405	−0.345	−0.271	−0.189	−0.101	0.099	0.208	0.329	0.467	0.70
Std Error	0.05	0.05	0.05	0.05	0.05	0.05	0.05	0.05	0.05	0.04
Stat T	1.7	1.1	0.6	0.2	−0.02	−0.02	0.2	0.6	1.3	5.3

TABLE 1.3 Bias as a Function of d with 100 Observations and 10,000 Simulations

True d	−0.49	−0.4	−0.3	−0.2	−0.1	0.1	0.2	0.3	0.4	0.49
d^a	−0.41	−0.35	−0.28	−0.20	−0.11	0.08	0.19	0.31	0.44	0.69
Std Error	0.12	0.12	0.12	0.12	0.12	0.12	0.12	0.12	0.12	0.10
Stat T	0.7	0.4	0.2	0.0	−0.1	−0.2	−0.1	0.1	0.3	2.0

TABLE 1.4 Bias as a Function of d with 50 Observations and 10,000 Simulations

True d	−0.49	−0.4	−0.3	−0.2	−0.1	0.1	0.2	0.3	0.4	0.49
d^a	−0.416	−0.360	−0.291	−0.213	−0.130	0.060	0.163	0.280	0.421	0.680
Std Error	0.18	0.19	0.19	0.19	0.19	0.19	0.19	0.19	0.18	0.15
Stat T	0.4	0.2	0.05	−0.07	−0.2	−0.2	−0.2	−0.1	0.1	1.3

TABLE 1.5 Estimates of d^a as a Function of Lag when $r = 3$

True d	−0.49	−0.4	−0.3	−0.2	−0.1	0.1	0.2	0.3	0.4	0.49
d^a	−0.379	−0.326	−0.262	−0.187	−0.104	0.088	0.200	0.326	0.478	0.751
Std Error	0.12	0.12	0.12	0.12	0.125	0.125	0.124	0.121	0.115	0.088
Stat T	0.9	0.6	0.3	0.1	−0.03	−0.1	0.0	0.2	0.7	3.0

n = number of observations = 100; 10,000 simulations.

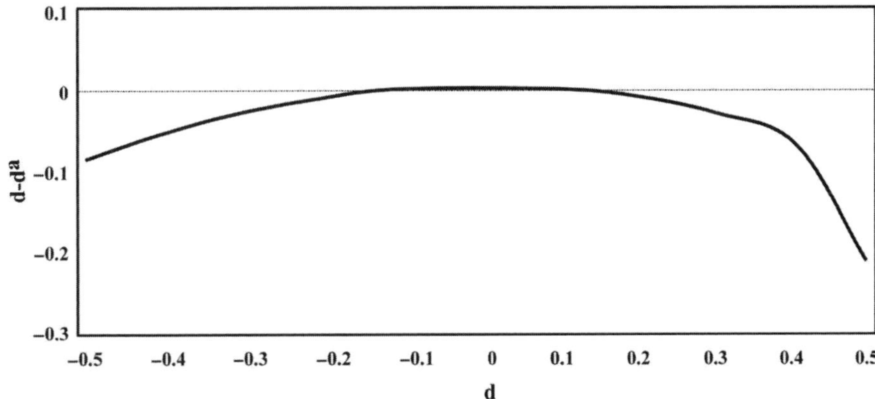

FIGURE 1.1 Bias of d^a as a Function of d

corrected. This is done by minimizing the following distance (Gouriéroux, Monfort and Renault (1993); Gouriéroux and Monfort (1997); and Smith (1993)):

$$d_{aSn}(\Omega) = \arg\min\,[d_{an} - d_{aSn}(d)]'\,\Omega\,[d_{an} - d_{aSn}(d)] \tag{1.10}$$

$$d \in (-0.5, 0.5) \quad \text{with} \quad d_{an} = \arg\min Q_n(d) = n^{-1}\sum_{t=1}^{n} f^a(y_t, d),$$

$$d_{aSn}(d) = (1/S)\sum_{s=1}^{S} d_{an}(d)$$

In short, d_{an} is the estimator of d obtained by maximizing the instrumental criterion in the case of a given sample of interest whereas $d_{aSn}(d)$ is the arithmetic mean of the maximization of the same instrumental criterion for the S simulated samples. So, $d_{aSn}(d)$ is what we report in Tables 1.1 to 1.5. In order to maximize the asymptotic covariance matrix of an M-estimator like $d_{aSn}(\Omega)$, Gouriéroux et al. have shown that the optimal choice of Ω is:

$$\Omega^* = J_0\,(I_0 - K_0)^{-1}\,J_0 \tag{1.11}$$

We use the notation proposed in Dridi and Renault (2000). In the absence of additional exogenous variables, as in the case here, $K_0 = 0$ (Gouriéroux et al., 1996). Gouriéroux et al. (1993) noted that the efficiency gain obtained by using the optimal estimator is negligible (and that for practical applications they) only consider the estimator based on $\Omega = Id'$. Thus, (10) is simplified to

$$d_{aSn}(\Omega) = \arg\min\,[d_{an} - d_{aSn}(d)]^2 \tag{1.12}$$

$$d \in (-0.5, 0.5)$$

Suppose the following simple analytical form for the relationship between the true d and $d_{aSn}(d)$: $d = d_{aSn}(d) - 0.1$.

$$d_{aSn}(\Omega) = \arg\min\left[d_{an}^2 - 2d_{an}(d + 0.1) + (d + 0.1)^2\right] \tag{1.13}$$

By minimizing the above distance with respect to d we obtain:

$$-2d_{an} + 2\,(d + 0.1) = 0 \text{ and } d = d_{an} - 0.1. \tag{1.14}$$

As the analytical form of the relationship is unknown, we correct on the basis of Tables 1.1 to 1.4.

We will show that this procedure works remarkably well by simulating different ARFIMA (0, *d*, *0*) series with $n = 500$ observations. The corresponding fractional parameter is then estimated by indirect inference (II) and by the method of Geweke and Porter-Hudak (GPH). The results are reported in Tables 1.6 and 1.7.

The results from the two simulations are presented in Figure 1.2. Note that the results diverge toward the endpoints of the (–0.5, +0.5) open interval and that the

TABLE 1.6 Estimation by Indirect Inference

True d	−0.49	−0.4	−0.3	−0.2	−0.1	0.1	0.2	0.3	0.4	0.49
Estimated d	−0.463	−0.379	−0.285	−0.191	−0.096	0.103	0.212	0.321	0.444	0.558
Std error	0.053	0.053	0.054	0.054	0.054	0.054	0.054	0.052	0.049	0.038
Bias	0.027	0.021	0.015	0.009	0.004	0.003	0.012	0.021	0.044	0.068

n = number of observations = 500; 1000 replications.

TABLE 1.7 Estimation by GPH

True d	−0.49	−0.4	−0.3	−0.2	−0.1	0.1	0.2	0.3	0.4	0.49
Estimated d	−0.387	−0.352	−0.267	−0.197	−0.107	0.106	0.217	0.317	0.49	0.79
Std Error	0.17	0.17	0.17	0.17	0.17	0.17	0.17	0.16	0.17	0.17
Bias	0.1	0.05	0.03	0.003	−0.07	0.006	0.017	0.017	0.09	0.30

n = number of observations = 500; 1000 replications.

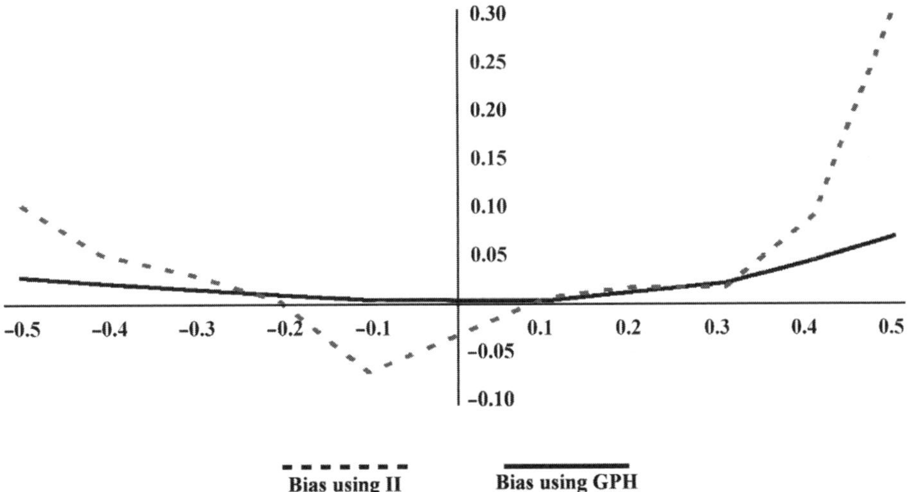

FIGURE 1.2 Bias of d^a for the Two Methods

indirect inference (II) method generates better estimates than the method suggested by GPH. The standard error and the bias are much smaller for the II method.

APPLICATIONS

In this section, we apply the estimation procedure described in the previous section to the analysis of apparent steel consumption (ASC) in the European Union 15, North America, Japan, and China.

Apparent Steel Consumption and Industrial Production

The starting point is the demand equation from the traditional standard commodity model (SCM) (see G. Adams (1996)). This demand equation is obtained from the first-order conditions of cost minimization by the firm. The explicit demand function for factor x_i for a given firm may be written:

$$x_i = h_i\,(p_1, p_2, \ldots, p_i, \ldots, p_n, q) \tag{1.15}$$

where x_i = demand of commodity i
q = the production of the firm
p_i = price of commodity i

By aggregating over the total number of firms in a country, the demand function of commodity i may be written:

$$D_t = D(P_t, PS_t, Y_t) \tag{1.16}$$

where P = price of commodity i
PS = price of competing commodities
Y = production of the sectors consuming commodity i

The commodity steel (x_i) is widely used in most production sectors so that it is reasonable to replace Y with the index of industrial production (IP) of the country. This approach has been taken by Afrasiabi, Moallem, and Labys (1991) in their study of the demand for copper, zinc, and lead. The properties of the global demand function of a given production factor are generally:

$$\partial D/\partial P < 0, \partial D/\partial/PS > 0, \ \partial D/\partial Y > 0 \tag{1.17}$$

For this exercise, prices have been removed from the equations, mainly because of a common stochastic trend in the aluminum price and steel price series. Table 1.8 summarizes the descriptive statistics of the endogenous and exogenous series. Figures 1.3 and 1.4 show the growth patterns of these series over the period 1974 to 2006.

Data come from three sources: Global Insight, Inc., the European Commission, and the International Iron and Steel Institute (IISI). The period studied were the years

TABLE 1.8 Descriptive Statistics, 1974–2006

Series	Obs	Mean	Std Error	Minimum	Maximum	$H_0 = I(1)$
LEU15	33	4.78	0.13	4.5	5.0	accept
LAMERNOR	33	4.75	0.15	4.4	5.0	accept
LJAPAN	33	4.28	0.13	3.9	4.5	accept
LCHINE	33	4.23	0.82	2.8	5.8	accept
IPEU15	33	1.6	2.6	−6.3	6.9	reject
IPAMNOR	33	2.6	3.7	−8.7	9.1	reject
IPJAPAN	33	2.0	5.0	−11.0	11.1	reject
IPCHINE	33	12.1	4.7	0.7	21.6	reject

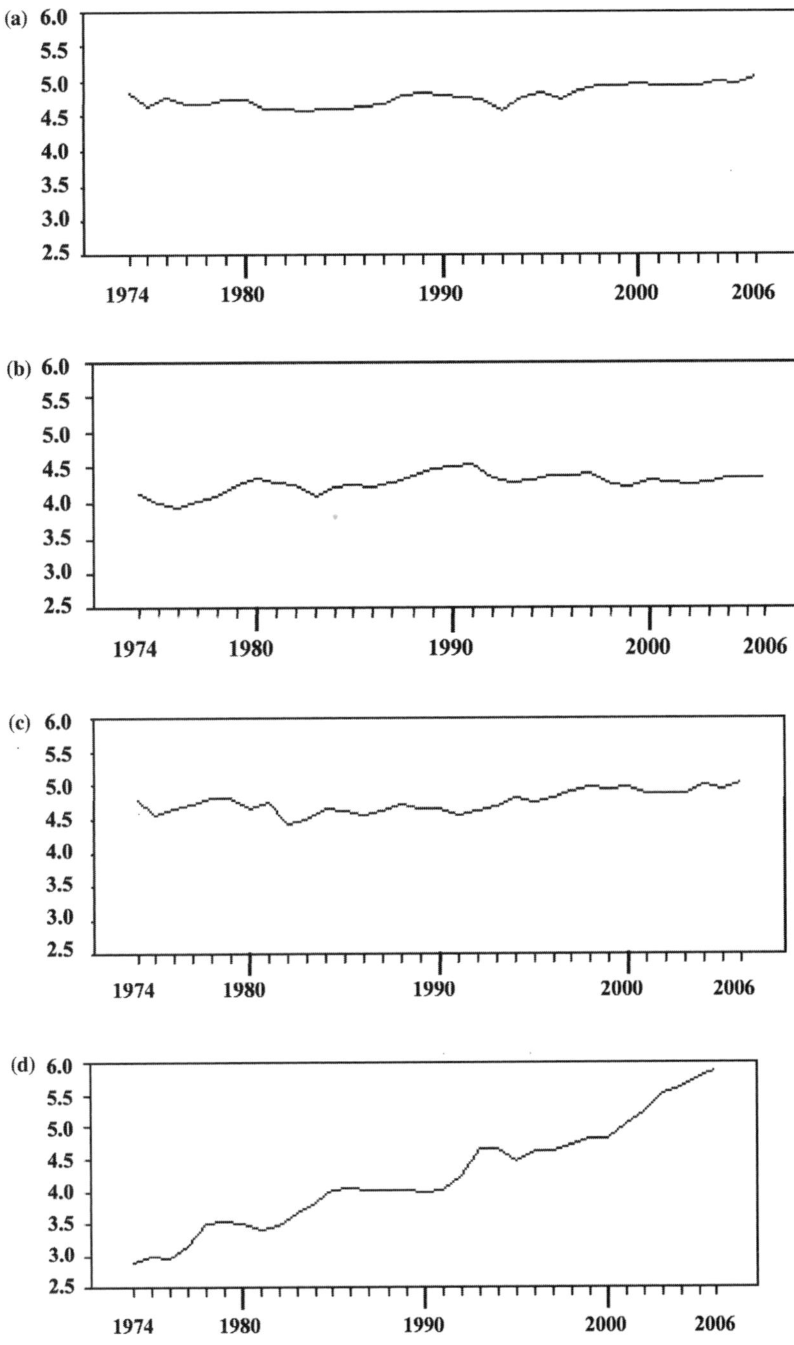

FIGURE 1.3 (a) ASC in EU15 (in logs, LEU15), 1974–2006. (b) ASC in Japan (in logs, LJAPAN), 1974–2006. (c) ASC in North America (in logs, LAMERNOR), 1974–2006. (d) ASC in China (in logs, LCHINE), 1974–2006

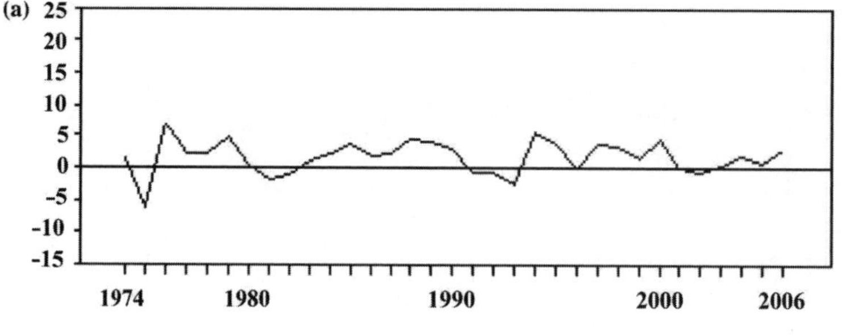

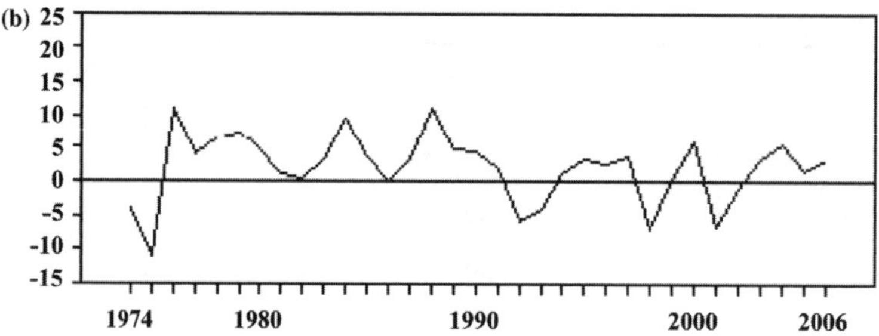

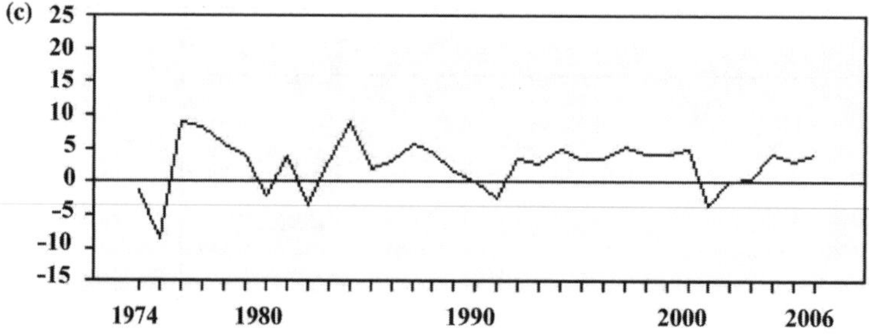

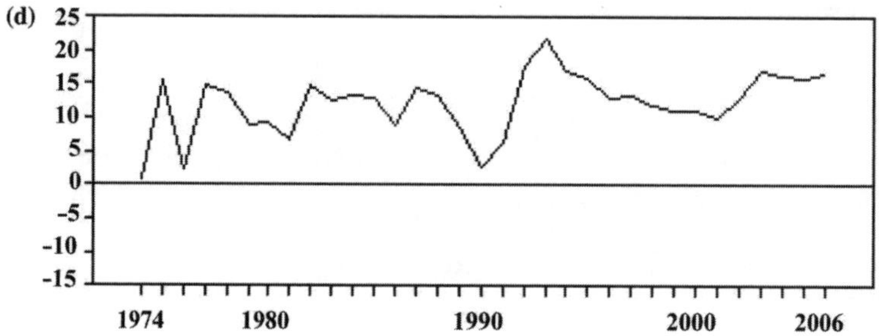

FIGURE 1.4 (a) Industrial Production in EU15 (IPEU15), 1974–2006. (b) Industrial Production in Japan (IPJAPAN), 1974–2006. (c) Industrial Production in North America (IPAMNOR), 1974–2006. (d) Industrial Production in China (IPCHINE), 1974–2006

1974 to 2006, and the data were obtained for each year. For this study we defined these variables:

- EU15 = apparent steel consumption in the European Union 15, in million metric tons
- AMERNOR = apparent steel consumption in North America (US, Canada, and Mexico), in million metric tons
- JAPAN = apparent steel consumption in Japan, in million metric tons
- CHINE = apparent steel consumption in China, in million metric tons
- LEU15 = log(EU15)
- LAMERNOR = log(AMERNOR)
- LJAPAN = log(JAPAN)
- LCHINE = log(CHINE)
- D = (1 − L); e.g., DLEU15 = (1 − L)∗LEU15 = $LEU15_t - LEU15_{t-1}$
- IP = industrial production growth rate, year on year; e.g., IPEU15 = industrial production growth rate in the EU15

Figures 1.3a to 1.3d show the apparent steel consumption in the European Union (EU15), North America, Japan, and China from 1974 to 2006. The difference in trend between China and the other three economies stands out, with consumption in the latter growing rapidly to support the growth and development of its economy, whereas the other economies were growing at a slower pace and becoming less dependent on manufacturing; hence the flatter curves.

The trend differences shown in Figures 1.3a to 1.3d are also reflected in Figures 1.4a to 1.4d, which show industrial production in the same economies, but the differences are not as striking. Whereas the ASC trend lines are relatively smooth, the production trend lines have pronounced peaks and valleys.

The most important stylized facts of these series are:

- The ASC (apparent steel consumption) series (in logs) are I(1) whereas the growth rates of IP are I(0).
- All series display highly stochastic cycles. *Real* steel consumption (RC) equals ASC +/– stocks movements and is unobserved. The stochastic cycles in RC follow closely those in the IP series. ASC cycles, however, have much larger amplitude due to the speculative behavior on inventories held by the steel consumers (merchants, steel service centers, and final consumers, e.g., automotive, construction, mechanical engineering, domestic appliances, metal ware and tubes).

The specification of the statistical model, together with the constraints imposed by economic theory, raises some identification problems. The latter are solved by the rigorous modeling strategy proposed in the previous sections, taking into account exogenous explanatory variables, short-memory ARMA components, as well as a long-memory parameter.

Tables 1.9 to 1.12 show the results by running the CCM by country or region.

It follows from Tables 1.9 to 1.12 that the fractional parameter d is not significantly different from zero, so that the formulas can be simplified (see Tables 1.13 to 1.16). All processes are characterized by the property of short memory. Additional specifications not reproduced in this chapter show that price variables of steel and aluminium were not significant.

TABLE 1.9 European Union (EU15)

1975–2006	CONSTANT	N_IPEU15{0}	*d*
DLEU15	–0.0341	0.0258	–0.1067
(Significance)	(0.0005)	(0.0000)	(0.4623)
$\overline{R}^2 = 0.72$		Q(8-0) = 2.34	
		(0.97)	

TABLE 1.10 North America

1979–2006	CONSTANT	N_IPAMNOR{0}	Dummy (1982)	*d*
DLAMERNOR	–0.042	0.023	–0.192	–0.124
(Significance)	(0.005)	(0.000)	(0.001)	(0.503)
$\overline{R}^2 = 0.76$		(7-0) = 8.82		
		(0.26)		

TABLE 1.11 Japan

1979–2006	CONSTANT	N_IPJAPAN{0}	AR{1}	MA{1}	MA{2}	*d*
DLJAPAN	−0.018	0.015	−0.369	0.521	0.514	−0.004
(Significance)	(0.213)	(0.000)	(0.337)	(0.142)	(0.011)	(0.976)
$\overline{R}^2 = 0.63$		Q(7-3) = 3.02				
		(0.55)				

TABLE 1.12 China

1979–2006	CONSTANT	N_IPCHINE{0}	Dummy (1994–1995)	*d*
DLCHINE	–0.133	0.020	–0.254	–0.082
(Significance)	(0.027)	(0.000)	(0.001)	(0.586)
$\overline{R}^2 = 0.49$		Q(7-0) = 11.74		
		(0.109)		

TABLE 1.13 Reestimated Combined Consumption, European Union (EU15)

1975–2006	CONSTANT	N_IPEU 15{0}
DLEU15	–0.036	0.026
(Significance)	(0.0004)	(0.0000)
$\overline{R}^2 = 0.72$	Q(8-0) = 1.46	
	(0.99)	

JB = 1.67, Hansen (1992) = 0.32, DF = –5.8.

TABLE 1.14 Reestimated Combined Consumption, North America

1975–2006	CONSTANT	N_IPAMNOR{0}	Dummy (1982)
DLAMERNOR	−0.040	0.020	−0.210
(Sign)	(0.003)	(0.000)	(0.001)
$\bar{R}^2 = 0.75$		Q(8-0) = 11.3	
		(0.19)	

JB = 1.40, Hansen (1992) = 0.21, DF = −6.5.

TABLE 1.15 Reestimated Combined Consumption, Japan

1976–2006	CONSTANT	N_IPJAPAN{0}	AR{1}	MA{1}	MA{2}
DLJAPAN	−0.036	0.015	−0.570	0.637	0.510
(Sign)	(0.0211)	(0.000)	(0.044)	(0.02)	(0.009)
$\bar{R}^2 = 0.50$		Q(7-3) = 8.50			
		(0.07)			

JB = 6.91, Hansen (1992) = 0.10, DF = −6.5.

TABLE 1.16 Reestimated Combined Consumption, China

1975–2006	CONSTANT	N_IPCHINE{0}	Dummy (1994–1995)
DLCHINE	−0.117	0.018	−0.278
(Sign)	(0.034)	(0.000)	(0.000)
$\bar{R}^2 = 0.46$		Q(8-0) = 20.36	
		(0.009)	

JB = 0.167, Hansen (1992) = 0.05, DF = −4.3.

Tables 1.13 to 1.16 show the reestimated equations with the fractional parameter dropped and the analysis of the residuals from these equations as well as a test of the stability of the parameter linked to industrial production.

The results of this model are compatible with economic theory. For the EU15, North America, and China, the stochastic cycle in the ASC series seems to be entirely captured by the cyclical pattern of the explanatory variable. In Japan, however, additional ARMA parameters are needed to explain the cycle in ASC. The analysis of the residuals shows that the latter are *iid* normal, except in the case of Japan.

Steel Intensity Curve (SI Curve)

The so-called SI curve is part of the rich history of studies related to materials use in economic systems. Main references to this literature are found in Sadler (2003). The first SI curve was constructed in the late 1960s by the Committee on Economic Studies of the IISI (International Iron and Steel Institute). It relates the evolution of SI (the ratio of apparent steel consumption to gross domestic product [GDP]) to the level of economic development of a country as measured by GDP per capita (IISI 1974).

There are five stages in the development of SI:

1. Very low level before economic takeoff
2. Rapid rise
3. Leveling-off stage
4. Decline
5. Stabilization

The development at the first two stages of SI is due to changes in the economic structure of a country, mainly increases in the shares of investments and manufacturing production.

The decline at the fourth stage results from the changes in the relative importance of activity of steel-using sectors in total economic activity (Swip [Steel Weighted Industrial Production Index]/GDP) and a decline of specific steel consumption defined as "apparent steel consumption/Swip."

Apparent steel consumption (ASC) of a country A is defined as production + imports – exports. So ASC equals real steel consumption +/– stock movements. Production and trade figures are based on a broad definition of steel industry products as compiled by the IISI, including ingots and semifinished products, tubes and tube fittings, single-strand wire, railway wheels, tires, and axles.

The IISI and the Organization for Economic Cooperation and Development (OECD) (H. Duisenberg 1985) proposed the following formula to estimate the SI curve:

$$SI = f - (a - bx)\, e^{-cx},$$

where $x = \text{GDP/capita}$ with $SI > 0$, $x > 0$, and $b > 0$

The formula above largely reproduces the theoretical SI curve.

Figures 1.5 to 1.7 show the SI patterns over the period 1960 to 2005. The results are in Table 1.17.

The long memory parameter is not significant. We conclude that there is no (additional) long memory. In other words, no important "other" explanatory variables are omitted in the above-specified models.

Atmospheric Concentrations

In this application, we test for the presence of a long memory parameter in a series of atmospheric CO_2 concentrations (*ppmco*2) derived from in situ air measurements at Mauna Loa Observatory, Hawaii. The period covers monthly data from March 1958 to January 2007 (Keeling et al. 2005).

Figure 1.8 shows the growth pattern of CO_2 concentrations over the period March 1958 to January 2007.

The Hodrick-Prescott filter was used to extract the trend. Further, the series *ppmco*2 is stationarized by taking logs and applying a seasonal differencing filter to the latter. The series tested for long memory is labeled *lppm*1. The spectrum (Figure 1.9) suggests the presence of long memory.

FIGURE 1.5 Steel Intensity Curve, EU15

We use our instrumental model with six lags to estimate the long memory parameter. The results are reported in Table 1.18.

From Table 1.2, we correct for bias and derive an estimated d of about 0.46. Testing for structural change in the first and second half of the sample revealed an unstable parameter. The Chow test for the Gauss-Newton regression is $F(6{,}563) = 2.58$ with significance level 0.017. Splitting the sample in two halves, we estimated with the instrumental model a d of 0.578 for the first half and a d of 0.641 for the second half. We test the model by running intrasample forecasts over the observations 451 to 588 on the basis of an estimate of d, using the first 450 observations. Figure 1.10 shows that the model forecasts well.

FIGURE 1.6 Steel Intensity Curve, Japan

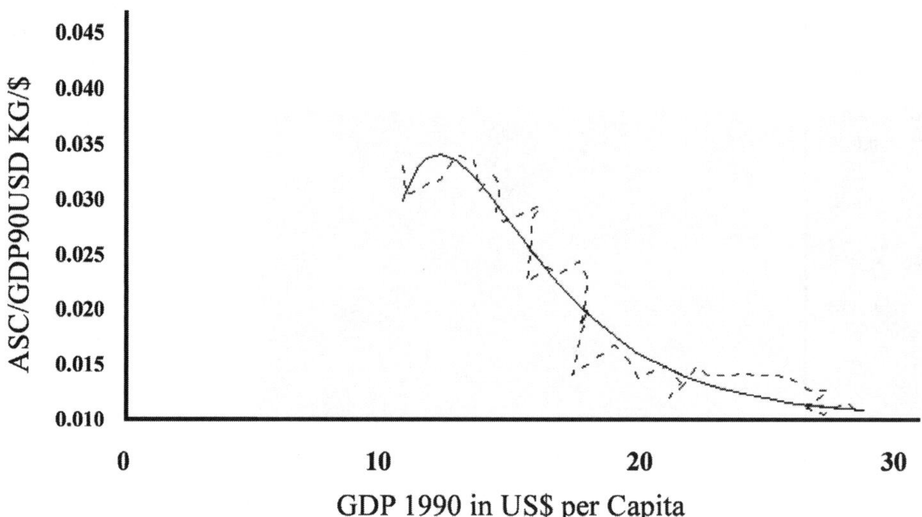

FIGURE 1.7 Steel Intensity Curve, USA

TABLE 1.17 SI Curve

	f	a	b	c	d
EU15	0.011	3.423	0.434	0.435	0.129
(Significance)	(0.000)	(0.31)	(0.28)	(0.000)	(0.35)
Japan	0.010	37.880	3.24	0.438	0.116
(Significance)	(0.000)	(0.35)	(0.34)	(0.000)	(0.441)
USA	0.013	0.187	0.029	0.199	0.154
(Significance)	(0.000)	(0.247)	(0.153)	(0.000)	(0.314)

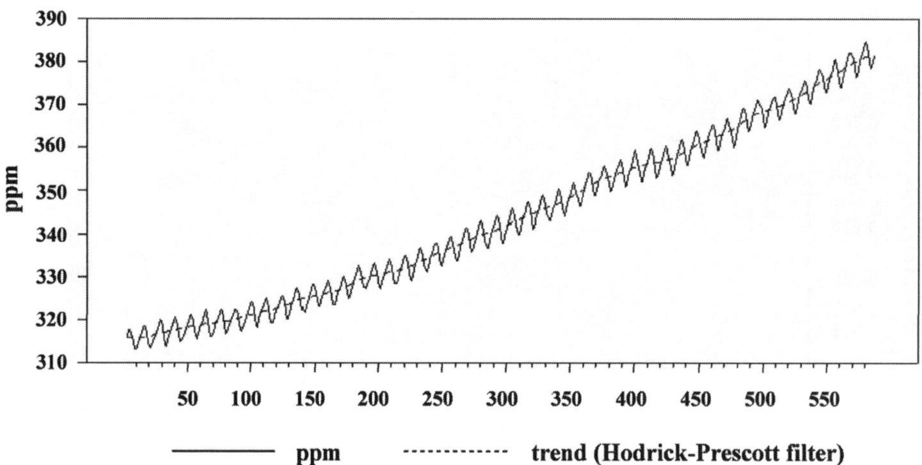

FIGURE 1.8 CO_2 Concentrations (Parts per Million, ppm)

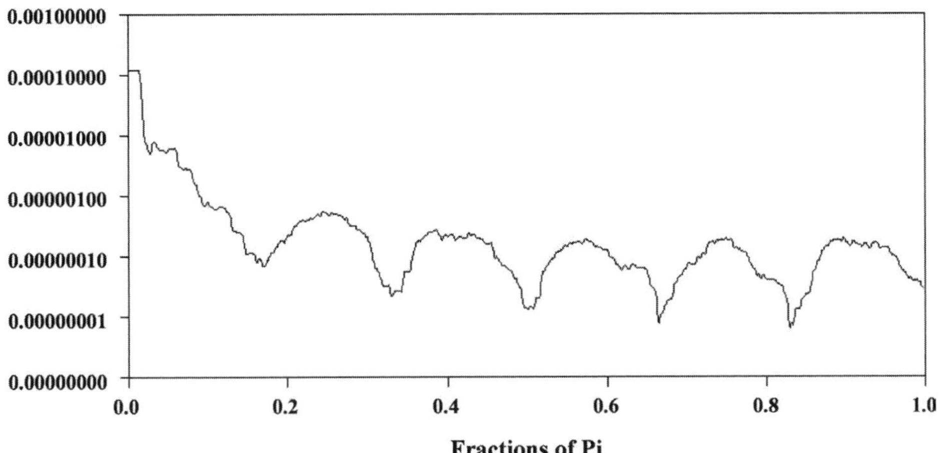

FIGURE 1.9 Long Memory Test, Spectrum lppm1

TABLE 1.18 CO_2 Concentrations, 1958(3)–2007(1)

	c	d
Lppm1	0.0005 (0.00000000)	0.626 (0.00000000)
$\overline{R}^2 = 0.67$, *Log Likehood* = 3071		

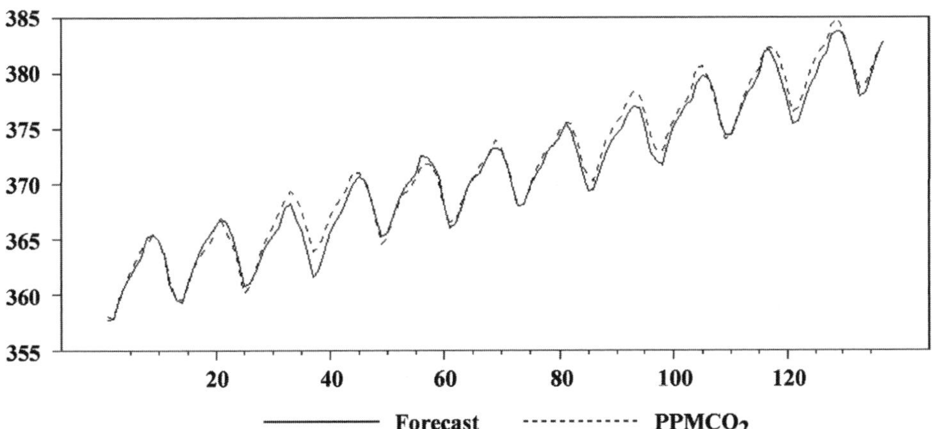

FIGURE 1.10 PPMCO2 Intrasample Forecast 451–588

CONCLUSIONS

Fractional integration is an important issue in modern time-series analysis. Traditional ARMA models, insofar as they are parsimonious, do not accurately describe situations where the long memory component of the impulse-response coefficients is predominant. Of course, long memory could be approximated arbitrarily well with a suitably large-order ARMA representation, but this is of little help in the case of small samples. Care must be taken to correctly stationarize the original time series. Long memory and structural change are easily confused. The concept of long memory leads in a natural way to the detection of stable relationships for stationary series, the so-called copersistence.

The problem with fractional integration, however, lies in the estimation techniques of the parameters. In order to simplify these techniques, we propose a truncated version of the fractionally integrated model that has the advantage of being easy to estimate and that captures parsimoniously the growth pattern of processes displaying impulse-response coefficient decaying at a much slower rate than those for stationary ARMA processes.

In this chapter we show that the number of autoregressive lags in this truncation can be chosen in the short range, from 2 to 6. We derived two results. First, under the assumption that the truncated model is the true model, the NLS estimator d^* of the parameter d of this model is consistent. This result is obtained under rather general assumptions. Specifically, we relax the *iid* assumption for e_t and replace it with the less restrictive α-mixing assumption. Second, using Monte Carlo experiments, we show that the fractional parameter (of the nontruncated model) can be consistently estimated by NLS and indirect inference on the basis of the simple truncated model. In our applications related to apparent steel consumption (annual data), we found no evidence for the presence of long memory. However, we found stochastic cycles and a significant impact of IP, particularly in the EU15, North America, and Japan, confirming economic theory. In the case of China, the exogenous variable IP has less explanatory power. Concerning the SI curves in the EU15, the United States, and Japan, there was no evidence for long memory, so that we conclude that there is no misspecification, in other words, no important explanatory variables are missing in the specification.

For a series of atmospheric CO_2 concentrations derived from in situ air measurements at Mauna Loa Observatory, Hawaii, we found a high persistence with a significant positive long memory parameter.

APPENDIX: PROOF OF CONSISTENCY OF THE ESTIMATOR D^*

We assume that model 1.3 is the true model and show that the NLS estimator d^* of the parameter d from model 1.3 is consistent.

First, we justify the choice of the NLS estimator. It follows from assumption OP (optimand) in Gallant and White (1988) that the methodology proposed hereafter in order to prove almost sure consistency allows us to consider the class of M estimators, which are defined as solutions to an optimization problem, such as NLS estimators, maximum likelihood (ML) estimators, and generalized method of moments (GMM) estimators. The unified theory of these estimators was developed originally in Hansen (1982). We use the NLS estimator for the following reasons.

The ML approach is primarily a large-sample approach (see Davidson and Mackinnon (1993), p. 247). The same argument holds for the GMM approach. As claimed by Bates (1990), the method of instrumental variables is inherently a large-sample estimation method based as it is on the law of large numbers and the central limit theorem. Of course, the GMM allows us to deal efficiently with heteroskedasticity if the latter is of a known form. This however is generally not the case. So we rely only on NLS. However, we propose to correct for heteroskedasticity by computing a consistent estimate of the covariance matrix as in White (1980). This correction does not affect the coefficients themselves, only their standard errors. Of course, if the form of heteroskedasticity is known, this latter approach will not be as efficient as weighted least squares.

Note that the robust errors approach is also a way to check the quality of the Monte Carlo simulation of ARFIMA processes. For example, we simulated an ARFIMA (0, 0.2, 0) with *iid* errors and estimated the fractional parameter d on the basis of the truncated model 1.3 with $r = 6$ lags. The estimated d was 0.206 with a standard error of 0.009 without the robust errors correction of the covariance matrix, while the standard error was 0.0091 if this correction is taken into account.

Let $\{y_t\}_{t=1}^{n}$ be a process generated by equation 1.3, and we desire an estimator of d. Consider $\hat{d}$ solution of

$$\hat{d} = \arg\min Q_n(d) = n^{-1}\sum_{t=1}^{n}\left[y_t + \sum_{j=1}^{r}\kappa_j(d)y_{t-j}\right]^2 \tag{A.1}$$

r is a constant that may be chosen in practice.

We specify the nonlinear autoregressive distributed lag model 1.3 in companion form. Let us define the p vectors $Y_t = [y_t, \ldots, y_{t-p+1}]'$, $V_t = [e_t, 0, \ldots, 0]'$, and the p^2 matrix $\boldsymbol{B}^*$ by

$$B^* = \begin{pmatrix} 0 & 0 & \vdots & 0 & 0 \\ 1 & 0 & \vdots & 0 & 0 \\ \cdots & \cdots & \ddots & 0 & \cdots \\ 0 & 0 & \vdots & 1 & 0 \end{pmatrix} \tag{A.2}$$

Define also the p vector $F\,(Y_{t-1}, d^*) = [\,f(y_{t-1}, \ldots, y_{t-p}, d^*), 0, \ldots, 0]'$. Thus, (3) can be rewritten as

$$Y_t = B^* Y_{t-1} + F\,(Y_{t-1}, d^*) + V_t \tag{A.3}$$

We will now prove the almost sure (a.s.) consistency of the nonlinear least squares estimator d^*. To do this, we apply theorem 3.5 from Mira and Escribano (2000) by checking that the assumptions (*MD, MX, CT, LR,* and *LN*) they used to derive the consistency result are satisfied in the case of model 1.3. Their approach is based on Gallant and White (1988), the seminal paper on estimation of and inference for nonlinear dynamic models, with the main advantage that they are able to write explicit assumptions related to a nonlinear model, such as moment conditions and conditions on the nonlinear function. They show (lemma 3.4) that assumptions *MD* to *LN* imply *near epoch dependence*, *r-integrability uniformly in t*, *s-domination* and the *Lipschitz-L_1 condition a.s.*, and thus consistency.

These assumptions are called *Lipschitz-type* assumptions. Consistency can be proved also on the basis of an *equicontinuity* assumption of the underlying functions (see Pötscher and Prucha 1991). The latter paper also provides a set of modules that can readily be used to prove consistency of a variety of M-estimators. Mira's and Escribano's (2000) assumptions are:

Assumption MD: Model 1.3 is the true model in the sense that

$$E\left(y_t | y_{t-1}, \ldots, y_{t-p}\right) \equiv f\left(y_{t-1}, \ldots, y_{t-p}, d^*\right) \tag{A.4}$$

Assumption MX (mixing): The sequence $\{V_t\}$ is strong mixing with $\{a_n\}$ of size $-v/(v-2)$ with $v > 2$.

By this assumption, we allow for some heterogeneity (some nonstationarity).

Assumption CT:

(i) For some fixed value $\varepsilon > 0$ and for all matrices $\boldsymbol{B}\nabla \boldsymbol{F}$ given by $\boldsymbol{B}\nabla\boldsymbol{F} \equiv \boldsymbol{B} + \nabla_y \boldsymbol{F}(\boldsymbol{Y}, d)$, with $\theta \in \Theta$, we have that $\rho\left(\boldsymbol{B}\nabla\boldsymbol{F}\right) < 1 - \varepsilon < 1$ *where* $\rho\left(\boldsymbol{B}\nabla\boldsymbol{F}\right)$ is the spectral radius of $\boldsymbol{B}\nabla\boldsymbol{F}$, i.e., the largest eigenvalue of the matrix $\boldsymbol{B}\nabla\boldsymbol{F}$.

Notice that for each specific matrix $\boldsymbol{B}\nabla\boldsymbol{F}$, its associated norm $\|.\|_S$ will verify that

$$\|\boldsymbol{B}\nabla\boldsymbol{F}\|_S \equiv \delta_{BY} < 1 - \varepsilon \tag{A.5}$$

$$\|.\|_s \equiv \left(E\left(\|.\|_s^r\right)\right)^{1/r} \equiv E^{1/r}\left(\|.\|_s^r\right) \tag{A.6}$$

(ii) For the norms $\|.\|_S$ and $\|.\|_2$ we have $\|B\| \leq \delta_{CB}$.

(iii) The compact parametric space Θ is such that the Jordan decomposition of the matrix $\mathbf{B\nabla F}$ given in part (i), $J = M^{-1}\left(\mathbf{B\nabla F}\right)M$, verifies $\|M^{-1}\|_\infty < \Delta^{-1}$ and $\|M\|_\infty < \Delta$ for some fixed values Δ and Δ^{-1}.

Assumption CN: $f\left(y_{t-1}, \ldots, y_{t-p}, d\right)$ is continuously differentiable in each argument, and its second-order derivatives with respect to d are continuous functions.

Assumption LR: For $r = 6$ we have

$$\mathrm{E}\,\|V_t\|_S^r \leq \Delta_V^{(r)} \tag{A.7}$$

$$E\,\|V_t\|_S^r\,\|V_s\|_S^r \leq \Delta_{VV}^{(r)} \tag{A.8}$$

Assumption LN: For the norms$\|.\|_S$ and $\|.\|_2$:

The following inequality holds a.s.:

$$\|F\ (Y_t, d)\|_S \leq \delta_{CF}\ (\|Y_t\|_S) \tag{A.9}$$

The following inequality holds a.s.:

$$\|\nabla_d F\ (Y_{t-1}, d)\|_s^2 \leq \left\|\nabla_d f\left(y_{t-1,\dots,} y_{t-p}, d\right)\right\|_s^2 \leq \delta_L\left(\|Y_{t-1}\|_S\right)^2 \tag{A.10}$$

We will now check these assumptions in the case of model 3.

Assumption MD: Assumption *MD* is satisfied because of the specification of model 1.3.

Assumption MX (mixing): α-mixing sequences are called *strong mixing*. The quantity $\alpha\ (m)$ measures how much dependence exists between events separated by at least m time periods. By definition, y_t is a stationary time series where all ARMA components have been removed. It is therefore reasonable to assume that assumption *MX* is satisfied for the sequence $\{V_t\}$ because e_t may effectively be interpreted as an innovation.

Assumption CT(i):

$$\begin{aligned} y_t = {} & dy_{t-1} + d(1-d)/2y_{t-2} + d(1-d)(2-d)/6y_{t-3} \\ & + d(1-d)(2-d)(3-d)/24y_{t-4} + d(1-d)(2-d)(3-d)(4-d)/120y_{t-5} \\ & + d(1-d)(2-d)(3-d)(4-d)(5-d)/720y_{t-6} + e_t \\ \equiv {} & f(.) \end{aligned} \tag{A.11}$$

$$\begin{array}{ll} \partial f(.)/\partial y_{t-1} = d & = \kappa_1 \\ \partial f(.)/\partial y_{t-2} = d\ (1-d)/2 & = \kappa_2 \\ \quad\vdots & \ \vdots \\ \partial f(.)/\partial y_{t-6} = d\ (1-d)\ (2-d)\ (3-d)\ (4-d)\ (5-d)/720 & = \kappa_6 \end{array} \tag{A.12}$$

$$B^* = \begin{pmatrix} 0&0&0&0&0&0 \\ 1&0&0&0&0&0 \\ 0&1&0&0&0&0 \\ 0&0&1&0&0&0 \\ 0&0&0&1&0&0 \\ 0&0&0&0&1&0 \end{pmatrix} \nabla F = \begin{pmatrix} \kappa_1&\kappa_2&\kappa_3&\kappa_4&\kappa_5&\kappa_6 \\ 0&0&0&0&0&0 \\ 0&0&0&0&0&0 \\ 0&0&0&0&0&0 \\ 0&0&0&0&0&0 \\ 0&0&0&0&0&0 \end{pmatrix} \tag{A.13}$$

$$B\nabla F = \begin{pmatrix} \kappa_1&\kappa_2&\kappa_3&\kappa_4&\kappa_5&\kappa_6 \\ 1&0&0&0&0&0 \\ 0&1&0&0&0&0 \\ 0&0&1&0&0&0 \\ 0&0&0&1&0&0 \\ 0&0&0&0&1&0 \end{pmatrix} \tag{A.14}$$

Figure A.1 shows the growth pattern of the spectral radius of the matrix $B\nabla F = B + \nabla F$ as a function of d.

As the spectral radius is less than 1 for $-0.5 < d < 0.5$, we conclude that assumption CT is satisfied.

Assumption LR are restrictions as moment conditions on V_t.

Assumption LN(i):

$$|f(y_{t-1}, \ldots y_{t-6}, d)| = |dy_{t-1} + \ldots + d(1-d)(2-d)(3-d)(4-d)(5-d)/720 y_{t-6}|$$
$$\leq |d|\, |y_{t-1}| + \ldots + |d(1-d)(2-d)(3-d)(4-d)(5-d)/$$
$$720|\, |y_{t-6}| < \sum_{i=1}^{6} |y_{t-i}| \qquad \text{(A.15)}$$

The last inequality follows from $-0.5 < d < 0.5$.

Assumption LN(ii):

$$\left|\frac{\partial f(y_{t-1}, \ldots, y_{t-6}, d)}{\partial d}\right| = \left|y_{t-1} + \frac{(1-2d)}{2} y_{t-2} + \frac{3d^2 - 6d + 2}{6} y_{t-3} \cdots\right|$$
$$\leq |y_{t-1}| + \left|\frac{1-2d}{2}\right| |y_{t-2}| + \cdots \qquad \text{(A.16)}$$
$$< \sum_{i=1}^{6} |y_{t-i}|$$

Again, the last inequality follows from $-0.5 < d < 0.5$. Thus, assumption LN is satisfied.

The next theorem proves the consistency of the NLS estimator d that minimizes equation A.1.

- **Theorem 1:** Under assumptions *MD, MX, CT, CN, LR* and *LN* and the identification condition stated below, the nonlinear least squares estimator for model 1.3 converges a.s. to the true value of the parameter.
- **Proof:** See Mira and Escribano (2000).

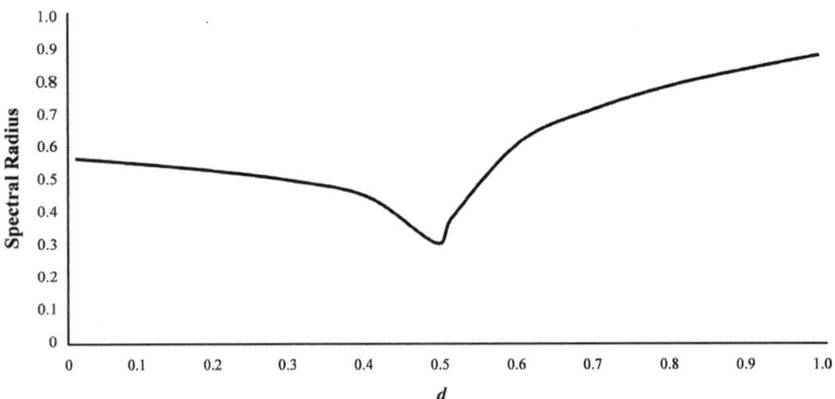

FIGURE A.1 Growth Pattern of Spectral Radius of Matrix $B\nabla F = B + \nabla F$

In our case, the identification assumption is: Since the mean square error has a unique minimum at the conditional mean, and since model 1.3 is the conditional mean from assumption *MD*, the identification condition is that

$$F\,(Y_{t-1}, d^*) \neq F\,(Y_{t-1}, d) \text{ for } d^* \neq d \tag{A.17}$$

REFERENCES

Adams, F.G. (1996). *Modeling Commodity Markets: New Needs and New Methods*, The State of Art in Applied Econometrics, 50th Conference, Association d'Econométrie Appliquée.

Afrasiabi, A., M. Moallem, and W.C. Labys. (1991). *Spectral Interpretation of Stock Adjustment Processes in Mineral Markets. International Commodity Market Models.* London, UK: Chapman and Hall.

Andrews, D.W.K., and P. Guggenberger. (2003). "A Bias-Reduced Log-Periodogram Regression Estimator for the Long-Memory Parameter," *Econometrica* 71.2: 675–712.

Andrews, D.W.K., and Y. Sun. (2004). "Adaptive Local Polynomial Whittle Estimation of Long-Range Dependence," *Econometrica* 72.2: 569–614.

Baillie, R.T. (1996). "Long Memory Processes and Fractional Integration in Econometrics," *Journal of Econometrics* 73: 5–59.

Bardet, J.M. (1999). "La mémoire longue en économie, discussion et commentaires," *Journal de la Société Française de Statistique* 140.2: 49–54.

Barkoulas, J., W.C. Labys, J. Onochie. (1997). "Fractional Dynamics in International Commodity Prices," *Journal of Futures Markets* 17: 161–189.

Bates, Ch.E. (1990). "Instrumental Variables."In J. Eatwell, M. Milgate, and P. Newman, eds., *Econometrics, The New Palgrave*, pp. 113–117. New York: Norton.

———. (1999). "Long Term Memory in Commodity Futures Prices," *Financial Review* 34: 91–100.

Bertrand, P. (1999). La mémoire longue en économie, discussion et commentaires, *Journal de la Société Française de Statistique* 140.2: 55–60.

Boutahar, M., V. Marimoutou, and L. Nouira (2005). *Estimation Methods of the Long Memory Parameter: Monte Carlo Analysis and Application*, GREQAM, Université de la Méditerranée, Working paper.

Brockwell, P.J., and R.A. Davis. (1998). *Time Series: Theory and Methods.* New York: Springer Verlag.

Cromwell, J.B., W.C. Labys, and E. Kouassi. (2000). "What Color Are Commodity Prices? A Fractal Analysis." *Empirical Economics* 25: 563–580.

Davidson, J., and T. Terasvirta, eds. (2002). *Long Memory and Nonlinear Time Series*, special issue of *Journal of Econometrics* 110. 2.

Davidson, R., and J. Mackinnon. (1993). *Estimation and Inference in Econometrics.* New York: Oxford University Press.

Diebold, F.X., and A. Inoue. (2001). "Long Memory and Regime Switching," *Journal of Econometrics* 105: 131–159.

Dolado, J.J., J. Gonzalo, and L. Mayoral. (2002). "A Fractional Dickey-Fuller Test for Unit Roots," *Econometrica* 70.5: 1963–2006.

Dridi, R., and E. Renault. (2000). "Semi-Parametric Indirect Inference," *STICERD/ Econometrics*, Discussion paper No. EM/00/392.

Duisenberg, H. (1985) "Long-Term Forecasting Models for Steel Demand," Communication, 12th International Conference of the Applied Econometric Association, Saragoza, Spain.

Fox, R., and M.S. Taqqu. (1986). "Large Sample Properties of Parameter Estimates for Strongly Dependent Stationary Gaussian Time Series," *Annals of Statistics* 14: 517–532.

Fuller, W.A. (1996). *Introduction to Statistical Time Series*. New York: Wiley-Interscience.

Gallant, A.R., and Tauchen, G. (1996). "Which Moments to Match?" *Econometric Theory* 12: 657–681.

Gallant, A.R., and H. White. (1988). *A Unified Theory of Estimation and Inference for Nonlinear Dynamic Models*. Oxford, UK: Basil Blackwell.

Geweke, J., and S. Porter-Hudak. (1983). "The Estimation and Application of Long Memory Time Series Models," *Journal of Time Series Analysis* 4: 221–238.

Gourieroux, C. (1999). "La mémoire longue en économie, discussion et commentaires," *Journal de la Société Française de Statistique* 140.2: 61–64.

Gourieroux, C., and J. Jasiak. (1999). *Nonlinear Persistence and Copersistence,* Research paper, http://dept.econ.yorku.ca/~jasiakj.

Gourieroux, C., and A. Monfort. (1995a). *Series Temporelles et Modèles Dynamiques*. Paris, France: Economica.

———. (1997). *Simulation-Based Econometric Methods*. Oxford, UK: Oxford University Press.

Gourieroux, C., A. Monfort, and E. Renault. (1993). "Indirect Inference," *Journal of Applied Econometrics* 8: S85–S118.

Granger, C.W.J., and R. Joyeux. (1980). "An Introduction to Long-Memory Models and Fractional Differencing," *Journal of Time Series Analysis* 1: 15–39.

Hamilton, J. D. (1994). *Time Series Analysis*. Princeton, NJ: Princeton University Press.

Hansen, B. E. (1992). "Testing for Parameter Instability in Linear Models," *Journal of Policy Modeling*, 14: 517–533

Hansen, L.P. (1982). "Large Sample Properties of Generalized Method of Moments Estimators," *Econometrica* 50: 1029–1054.

Higuchi, T. (1988). "Approach to an Irregular Time Series on the Basis of the Fractal Theory," *Physica D*, 31: 277–283.

Hosking, J.R.M. (1981). "Fractional Differencing," *Biometrika* 68: 165–176.

Hurst, H.E. (1951). "Long-Term Storage Capacity of Reservoirs," *Transactions of the American Society of Civil Engineers* 116: 770–799.

IISI. (1974). *Steel Intensity and GNP Structure*. Brussels, Belgium: International Iron and Steel Institute.

Jasiak, J. (1999). "La mémoire longue en économie, discussion et commentaires," *Journal de la Société Française de Statistique* 140.2: 65–70.

———. (1999). *Persistence in Intertrade Durations*. Research paper, http://dept.econ.yorku.ca/~jasiakj.

———. (2000). *Long Memory in Economics: A Comment*, Research paper, http://dept.econ.yorku. ca/~jasiakj/.

Keeling, C.D., T.P. Whorf, and the Carbon Dioxide Research Group. (2005). "Atmospheric CO_2 Concentrations (Ppmv) Derived from in situ Air Samples Collected at Mauna Loa Observatory, Hawaii." Scripps Institution of Oceanography (SIO) University of California La Jolla, California USA 92093-0444, May 2005 http://cdiac.ornl.gov/ftp/trends/co2/maunaloa.co2.

Lardic, S., and V. Mignon. (1999). "La mémoire longue en économie: Une revue de la littérature," *Journal de la Société Française de Statistique* 140.2: 5–48

———. (1999). "La mémoire longue en économie: Une revue de la littérature, réponse aux intervenants," *Journal de la Société Française de Statistique* 140.2: 103–108.

Li, W. K., and A. I. McLeod. (1986). "Fractional Time Series Modelling," *Biometrica* 73: 217–221.

Lo, A. (1991). "Long-Term Memory in Stock Market Prices," *Econometrica* 59: 1279–1313.

Lo, A., and C. Mackinlay. (1989). "The Size and Power of the Variance Ratio Test in Finite Samples: A Monte Carlo Investigation," *Journal of Econometrics* 40: 203–238.

Maddala, G.S., and I.M. Kim. (1998). *Unit Roots, Cointegration, and Structural Change.* Cambridge, UK: Cambridge University Press.

Mandelbroth, B.B. (1977). *Fractals: Form, Chance and Dimension.* San Francisco, CA: W.H. Freeman.

Mayoral, L. (2000). *A New Minimum Distance Estimation Procedure of ARFIMA Processes,* Working Paper Series No. 00-17, Universidad Carlos III de Madrid. Revised version (2002). Available upon request.

Mira, S., and A. Escribano. (2000). "Nonlinear Time Series Models: Consistency and Asymptotic Normality of NLS under New Conditions."In W. Barnett et al., eds., *Nonlinear Econometric Modeling in Time Series Analysis*: 119–164 New York: Cambridge University Press.

Pötscher, B.M., and I.R. Prucha. (1991). "Basic Structure of the Asymptotic Theory in Dynamic Nonlinear Econometric Models, Part I: Consistency and Approximation Concepts," *Econometric Reviews* 10.2: 125–216.

Prat, G. (1999). "La mémoire longue en économie, discussion et commentaires," *Journal de la Société Française de Statistique* 140.2: 71–77.

Renault, E. 1999, "La mémoire longue en économie, discussion et commentaires," *Journal de la Société Française de Statistique* 140.2: 79–89

Robinson, P.M. (1994). "Semiparametric Analysis of Long-Memory Time Series," *Annals of Statistics* 22: 515–539.

———. (1995). "Gaussian Semiparametric Estimation of Log Range Dependence," *Annals of Statistics* 23: 1630–1661.

———. (1995). "Log-Periodogram Regression of Time Series with Long Range Dependence," *Annals of Statistics* 23: 1048–1072.

Rosenblatt, M. (1978). "Dependence and Asymptotic Independence for Random Processes."In M. Rosenblatt, ed., *Studies in Probability Theory.* Washington, DC: Mathematical Association of America: 24–25

Sadler, A. (2003), *Demande Internationale de Produits Sidérurgiques, Croissance et Développement,* Ph.D. dissertation, Université de la Méditerranée. Marseille, France.

Smith, A.A. Jr. (1993). "Estimating Nonlinear Time-Series Models Using Simulated Vector Autoregressions," *Journal of Applied Econometrics* 8: S63–S84.

Sowell, F. (1990). "The Fractional Unit Root Distribution," *Econometrica* 58: 495–505.

———. (1992). "Maximum Likelihood Estimation of Stationary Univariate Fractionally Integrated Time Series Models," *Journal of Econometrics* 53: 165–188.

———. (1992). "Modeling Long Run Behavior with the Fractional ARIMA Model," *Journal of Monetary Economics* 29: 277–302.

Taqqu, M.S. (1999). "La mémoire longue en économie, discussion et commentaires," *Journal de la Société Française de Statistique* 140.2: 91–96.

Truong-Van, B. (1999). "La mémoire longue en économie, discussion et commentaires," *Journal de la Société Française de Statistique* 140.2: 97–102.

White, H. (1980). "A Heteroskedasticity-Consistent Covariance Matrix Estimator and Direct Test for Heteroskedasticity." *Econometrica* 48: 817–838.

———. (1984). *Asymptotic Theory for Econometricians.* New York: Academic Press.

Whittle, P. (1951). *Hypothesis Testing in Time Series Analysis.* New York: Hafner Publishing Company.

CHAPTER 2

Procyclicality of Primary Commodity Prices

A Stylized Fact?

A. Behrooz Afrasiabi

INTRODUCTION

Since the pioneering work by Burns and Mitchell (1946), numerous economic time series have been analyzed for their cyclical characteristics using the methodologies employed in that study. The collection of these studies has created a body of facts that underlie much of today's business cycle theory. With the advent of newer methodologies and theoretical perspectives, reliance on these stylized facts still provides a starting point for business cycle research. As stated by Blackburn and Ravn (1992), these new methodologies place two basic demands on business cycle research: "The complete and systematic characterization of the cyclical phenomena in the form of stylized facts, and the construction of fully articulated model economies which can be evaluated both quantitatively and qualitatively in terms of their ability to replicate these facts."

Research on stylized facts is an important and integral part of business cycle research. After Lucas (1977), research has mostly focused on sample moments. Among these, probably the most important are the sample comovements of the output with other time series. For example, a rich and at times controversial literature on real wages attempts to establish the positive comovements of real wages with output as a stylized fact (Abraham and Haltiwanger 1995). The relative efficacy of competing business cycle theories is then judged by their abilities to simulate these positive comovements (Abraham and Haltiwanger 1995). For example, the simple Keynesian model predicts that real wages are countercyclical, based on assumptions of a shifting labor supply and a stable labor demand curve over the business cycle. Alternatively, models that incorporate shifts in the labor demand curve, such as real business cycle models, predict procyclical real wages. For a review of this literature, see Stadler (1994) and Cooley (1995). Numerous extensions of either of these models, such as allowing for price markups (Hanes 1996) or adjustment costs (Chiarini 1998), change the predicted cyclicality.

Primary commodities, such as petroleum and metals, as well as certain agricultural commodities are widely used as inputs to the production process throughout the economy. As stylized facts, the cyclical comovements of the prices of these commodities with the output have the same significance for business cycle research as does the procyclicality of wages. In other words, alternative business cycle theories can be evaluated in light of their capacity to predict these comovements correctly. Unfortunately, although much has been written about the cyclicality of many commodity prices (see the next section), there is no unified literature that documents the procyclicality of these prices as stylized facts for further research in the field of business cycles. The purpose of many of these studies is to research the cyclical phenomena in individual markets rather than the relation of those cycles with the business cycles at large. The relationship between commodity prices and the macroeconomy has received some attention. For example, Bosworth and Lawrence (1982), Cristini (1999), and Labys et al. (1999) studied the relationship between commodity prices and inflation, unemployment, and industrial production, respectively. The latter study, in particular, focused attention on issues such as the timing of turning points and phase relationships.

The purpose of this study is to document the procyclicality of primary commodity prices. We do this both for aggregate commodity price indexes and for the individual prices of a select group of commodities. These include important commodities such as petroleum and metals such as copper, lead, zinc, aluminum, and gold.

There are many empirical issues in establishing stylized facts. The literature on wages can serve as a guide in tackling these issues. As noted by Afrasiabi and Nonnenmacher (2005), "historical evidence concerning the cyclicality of real wages is based largely upon the measurements of contemporaneous comovements of real wages and cyclical indicators, such as output or employment." Needless to say, this simple, contemporaneous, and unconditional correlation is not meant to be interpreted as a structural relation, but only as one stylized fact that the subsequently developed models of business cycles is required to replicate. In the case of real wages, while some studies find a negative covariance between real wages and output, others show a positive relationship, and still others claim no relationship at all. "The divergence of empirical findings is in part explained by the choice of the deflator, detrending technique, sample period, and measure of aggregate wages and cyclical indicators" (Afrasiabi and Nonnenmacher 2005).

A number of other reasons can explain the differences in empirical findings that are important to the present study. Neftci (1977), in a study employing distributed lag methods, finds that while the contemporaneous comovements are positive, lagged relations can be negative and significant. He concludes that an important reason for the empirical divergence is the ignoring of the dynamics of the problem. In another critique, also related to the ignoring of the dynamics, Cushing (1990) and den Haan (1996, 2000) indicate that an important source of disagreement is the fact that the comovements are not measured at business cycle frequencies. Cushing claims that the strong positive or strong negative unconditional correlation between real wages and cyclical indicators may be a relic of the influence of variations too long or too short in duration to be related to the business cycles. He concludes that the "true business cycle relationship is quite different from that revealed by simple regressions of real wages on employment." Similarly, den Haan (2000) argues that "an important source of disagreement in the literature is the focus on only one correlation coefficient."

As with wages, business cycle theory must also correctly predict the comovements of output with energy and material input prices. Simple economic theory holds that the expansion of demand for commodities in boom periods will cause the prices to increase when the supplies of the commodity are relatively fixed. So, over the business cycle, one may observe procyclical prices. However, a growing body of literature holds that price markups are countercyclical (e.g., Bils 1987; Rotemberg and Woodford 1991; Hanes 1996). When the gap between price and marginal cost is large, then a positively sloped supply curve is, strictly speaking, not defined. There is thus no guarantee that an upward shift in the demand for a commodity will lead to a rise in its price. There is evidence that producers, especially at the retail level, tend to reduce their markups during the boom periods (e.g., Barsky and Warner 1995). When markups are large, the cyclical behavior of prices can be determined by these markups and consequently prices can become countercyclical. Hanes (1996) holds that prices of finished goods that are farther along the production process include a large proportion of markups and thus are more likely to be countercyclical. Indeed, he holds that the consumer price index (CPI) is more likely to be countercyclical than the producer price index (PPI) since the former contains more finished goods. Importantly, wages and prices deflated by the PPI then will be more likely to be countercyclical.

COMMODITY PRICES AND BUSINESS CYCLES

Next we review the relationship between primary commodity prices and business cycle phenomena. The primary purpose of many previous studies was not to establish stylized facts for business cycle research but to understand and explain commodity price movements and their relationship with different aspects of the business cycles. However, in doing so, they also established many facts that are useful for business cycle research and provide a background for this study.

Studies that analyze the volatility, persistence, and amplitude of primary commodity price cycles include Labys (2006) and Labys et al. (1998, 2000). The linkages between cycles in industrial production and commodity prices have received attention by Labys et al. (1999). Borensztein and Reinhart (1994) and Chu and Morrison (1984) reviewed the importance of the interactions between national economies and commodity markets. Borensztein and Reinhart (1994) specifically examine the effects of various macroeconomic determinants on commodity markets and, in turn, on commodity prices. Their goal is to "identify the main economic fundamentals behind the behavior of commodity prices ... and to quantify how the relative importance of each of these factors has evolved over time." In an effort to determine the causes for price declines among nonoil commodities, Borensztein and Reinhart focused mainly on supply changes as aided by international trade and analyzed the effects of technology, politics, and economic conditions, concentrating on the effects of inelastic demand shifts and economic crises. Such supply changes can reflect how globalization might lead to a dynamic expansion in import volumes and a fall in commodity prices.

Chu and Morrison (1984) also analyzed the commodity market impacts of macroeconomic variables as contained in supply—and demand—side representations in both the short and medium run. They evaluated the relationship between "current prices [and] future supplies via the impact of current prices on investments in productive capacity, and the effect of capacity changes on commodity prices." Their results explain how commodity price fluctuations can increase or decrease consumer price inflation and how these prices, in turn, are influenced by other macroeconomic variables, such as exchange rates and industrial production. Turning to time-series analysis, Labys and Maizels (1993) focused on causality and feedback effects between commodity prices and macroeconomic variables by employing Granger-causality tests to compare the results of a large number of studies dealing with macroeconomic and commodity market interactions. The relationship between industrial production and commodity prices was found to be particularly important.

At the individual commodity level, Liu et al. (1990) evaluated the relationship between business cycles and agricultural prices, and Labys, Achouch and Terraza (1999) analyzed the impacts of business cycles on metal prices. The direct influence of industrial production on prices was found to be paramount, particularly in the case of France, Italy, Japan, and the OECD (Organization for Economic Cooperation and Development) as a whole. Borensztein and Reinhart (1994), Chu and Morrison (1984), Bosworth and Lawrence (1982), Darby (1982), Fama and French (1988), Grilli and Yang (1980), and Moore (1988) also report on some relationships between business cycles and metals prices. More specifically, fluctuations in global industrial production and financial variables have been shown to influence the industrial demand for metals. Given the short-term price inelasticity of metal supplies, the resulting demand fluctuations tend to influence the related metal prices. Financial variables influence the formation of expectations of agents who deal in the demand, supply, and stocking of metals less directly. Changes in industrial production may have also been associated with changes in the prices of crude oil. Labys (2000) and Mork, Mysen, and Olsen (1994) provide further evidence on linkages between crude oil prices and inflation.

There has been some consideration in the previously mentioned studies regarding whether commodity prices lead or lag business cycles. Falling commodity prices imply recessionary behavior and precede downturns in industrial activity. Rising industrial activity increases demand pressure on primary commodities and raises their prices. Rising commodity prices seem to lead to increased inflation. As can be surmised, both causal and feedback effects can be detected.

EMPIRICAL PROCEDURE

The empirical procedure relies on the calculation of regression coefficients of detrended and filtered commodity prices on the U.S. Federal Reserve Board index of industrial activity. In similar studies concerning procyclicality of wages, Abraham and Haltiwanger (1995) have shown that the uses of different detrending methods have been an important source of disagreement in the literature. The more popular methods of detrending are variate differencing for the removal of the stochastic trend and the Hodrick-Prescott filter. The latter is the method we employ to remove the trend from price and output data.

Several points concerning the properties of these detrending methods need to be discussed. The adequacy of both the Hodrick-Prescott filter and first differencing to detrend data has been questioned. For example, Cogley and Nason (1992) and Jaeger (1994) show that the Hodrick-Prescott filter can produce spurious cyclicalities and comovements if the data are nonstationary. It is also easy to show that over- (under-) differencing of data (including differencing of trend-stationary time series) can produce spurious time-series properties. Koopmans (1974) showed that as a filter, the difference operator has a gain function that smoothly rises from 0 to 2 as the frequency increases from 0 to π, becoming equal to 1 at frequency $\pi/3$. This means that while frequencies below $\pi/3$ (longer than six periods) will be attenuated, higher frequencies can become $w_{kj} = \exp(2pijk/T)$ amplified up to two times. As such, the frequency response function of the difference operator deviates significantly from that of an ideal high pass filter.

The procedure that we use for filtering unwanted frequencies is similar to that used in band spectrum regression developed by Engle (1974). All variables are filtered in the frequency domain prior to running the regression. The filtering procedure masks (sets to zero) the unwanted frequency components of the Fourier transform of the series, and the results are inverse-transformed back to the time domain. As with Cushing (1990), we start with a baseline case where all frequency components are included, and we use this baseline for comparison. Each time the series are filtered, one additional high (or low) frequency component is excluded. Formally, assume **X** is a time-series vector of length T that is to be filtered. Define a T × T complex matrix **W** with elements w_{kj} defined as

$$w_{kj} = \exp\left(2pijk/T\right)$$

where $i^2 = -1$

$$j, k = 0, 1, \ldots, T-1 \tag{2.1}$$

Further, if $N = (T/2) + 1$, define S as a $T \times N$ matrix of ones with zeroes inserted in each column corresponding to the frequencies that are to be masked. Since the Fourier transform ordinates are complex conjugates about frequency π, the ordinates are masked in a pair-wise symmetric fashion, such that for every ordinate corresponding to a frequency $\pi - \delta$, we also set the ordinate corresponding to $\pi + \delta$ equal to zero. We do not include zeroes in the first column of S (the baseline estimate), the second column has a zero in row N corresponding to frequency π, the third column has zeros in rows $N-1$ to $N+1$, and so on. The last pair that is set to zero and must correspond to rows 3 and $T-1$. This is because if we continue to set the pair 2 and T equal to zero, then the only nonzero element of the Fourier transform will be the ordinate at frequency zero (mean of the observations). In this case the inverse transform will yield a constant since all sources of variation will have been removed. Recursively filtered versions of X are given by the columns of matrix $\widetilde{X}$ defined as

$$\widetilde{X} = T^{-1} W^H \widehat{WX} S \tag{2.2}$$

where W^H = conjugate transpose of W

$\hat{}$ = diagonalization of vector WX

We define Y and X as time series representing the detrended real price and industrial activity respectively. If $\widetilde{X}_m$ and $\widetilde{Y}_m$ are the mth columns of matrices $\widetilde{X}$ and $\tilde{Y}$ defined according to equation (2.2, the model to be estimated is

$$\widetilde{Y}_m = \widetilde{X}_m \beta_m + u_m \quad m = 1, \ldots, N-1 \tag{2.3}$$

where u_m = vector of disturbances associated with the mth regression

Let $\hat{\beta}_{m\pi}$ be the ordinary least squares estimate of equation 2.3. $\hat{\beta}_1$ represents the least square estimate of the coefficient of the regression of Y on X, that is, the simple unfiltered (unconditional) measure of procyclicality often used in the literature. $\hat{\beta}_2, \hat{\beta}_3, \ldots, \hat{\beta}_{N-1}$ correspond to regression coefficients where higher frequencies are recursively and cumulatively removed from the data. Similarly, by defining matrix S appropriately, we can obtain an alternative set of coefficients $\hat{\beta}'_m$, $m = 1, \ldots, N-1$, representing estimates of the regression coefficients where lower frequencies are recursively and cumulatively filtered. Removing frequencies in this order will show whether the sign and magnitude of the baseline are impacted by lower frequency variations. The residual sums of squares from these regressions are calculated as in Engle (1974) and are used to find standard errors of the estimated coefficients in the usual manner with the exception that the degrees of freedom used in calculation of the residual variance is $T' - 2$ rather than $T - 2$, where T' is the number of included frequencies.

EMPIRICAL EVIDENCE

Aggregate Price Series

The baseline results for the four aggregate price measures are given in Table 2.1. These aggregate measures include the Bureau of Labor Statistics' index of all primary commodities prices, the all-fuel price index, the metals price index, and the agricultural price index. The data are monthly, and the sample period is from January 1960 to April 2007. The measure of output is the Federal Reserve Board's index of industrial production and all time series are logarithmic and not seasonally adjusted. As already pointed out, the data were filtered by the Hodrick-Prescott filter to separate their cyclical components. Table 2.1 shows that at the baseline the coefficients of the all-commodities price index and the agricultural price index are positive and significant. In other words, these two time series are procyclical in nature. The same, however, cannot be said of the aggregate metals and the aggregate fuels price

TABLE 2.1 Baseline Estimates for Aggregate Price Measures

Aggregate Price Index	Coefficient	t-stat	P-value
All Primary Commodities	0.783	9.535	0.000
Fuel	−0.021	−0.208	0.835
Metals	0.039	1.006	0.3157
Agricultural	0.396	5.453	0.000

index. While the former has a positive and insignificant coefficient, the coefficient of the latter is negative and insignificant. At the baseline level, one might conclude that these two aggregate price indexes are acyclical. Fuels and metals are widely used in the industrial process, and, as already discussed, one expects them to be procyclical.

As mentioned, the baseline coefficients are a weighted average of coefficients from all frequency bands. Before any further interpretation of these results, it is necessary to study the contributions of different frequency bands to the baseline estimates. It is entirely possible that the results are caused by very low or very high frequencies.

Unlike Cushing (1990), who used a band pass filter to find the contributions of the "business cycle frequency band," we use a series of recursive high-pass and low-pass filters to avoid strong assumptions regarding the period of the business cycles. This approach generates numerous tables, which are time-consuming to view. The results can be shown more quickly and intuitively through diagrams. Therefore, for each time series, we present one diagram for high-pass and one for low-pass filtering, respectively. Results for all primary commodities combined are in Figure 2.1.

Figure 2.1 has two panels representing the high and low pass filtering diagrams for combined commodities series. The horizontal axes on these diagrams show the period of the components that have been filtered out. Each point on a diagram corresponds to the regression coefficient when all components up to and including the value indicated by the horizontal axis are removed. The coefficients that are statistically significant are represented by a solid square and the first point on both diagrams corresponds to the baseline estimate. Thus, Figure 2.1a shows what happens to the baseline coefficient as low frequency components are removed and Figure 2.1b shows what happens to the baseline coefficient when the higher frequency components are removed.

Figure 2.1a shows that while the baseline coefficient is positive and significant, the removal of low-frequency variations reduces the size of the coefficient. Eventually, if we remove all components with periods above 20 months, the coefficient will not be statistically significant. This suggests that the positive sign and the significance of the baseline coefficient are not due to common seasonal components. Figure 2.1b also indicates that the removal of seasonal frequencies does not have an appreciable impact on the size or the significance of the baseline coefficient. In interpreting these diagrams, keep in mind that the degrees of freedom of the regressions are reduced by 2 each time a frequency component is removed. Therefore, points at the right end of the diagrams are estimates based on too few degrees of freedom to be trusted.

The conclusion from this analysis is that the sign, size, and significance of the baseline coefficients are strongly affected by lower-frequency components. Now, since our data are monthly, these "lower-frequency components" correspond to variations with periods higher than 20 months. This is well inside the range of period of normal business cycles.

The baseline coefficient for the aggregate fuel price index was negative and insignificant. Figure 2.2a shows that this is caused by very low frequencies. After removing the components with periods higher than 60 months, the relation becomes positive and significant. This means that the negative sign of the baseline coefficient is caused by variations that are longer in period than five years. When we remove all components lengthier than 20 months, the relation becomes insignificant again. Once

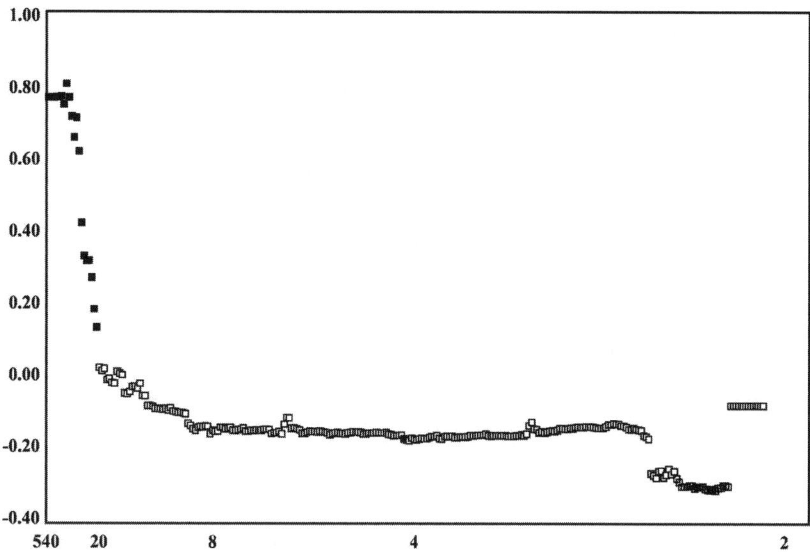

FIGURE 2.1a All Primary Commodities, High-Pass Filtering

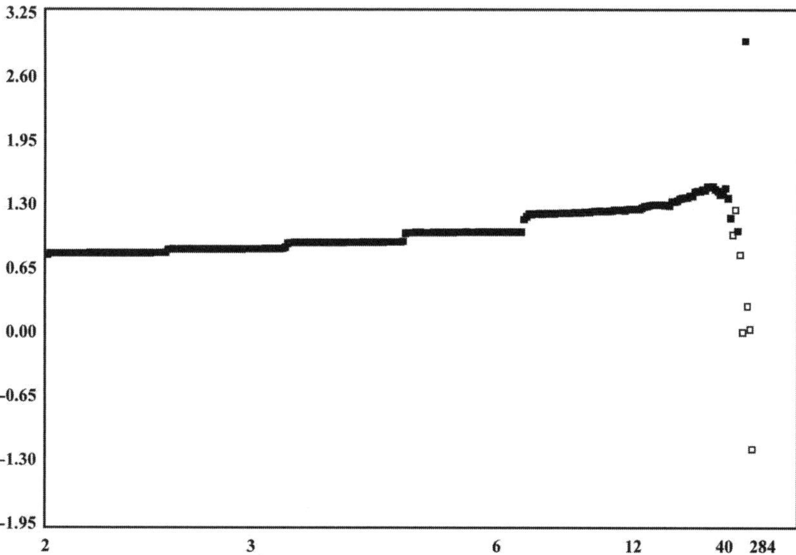

FIGURE 2.1b All Primary Commodities, Low-Pass Filtering

again, this implies variations with period less than 2 years do not account for the positive relation observed. Figure 2.2b confirms that the removal of higher-frequency components does not have much effect on the baseline coefficients.

Figures 2.3a and 2.3b show that the same is true for the aggregate metals price index. In other words, after removing the very low frequency components, the co-movements become positive and significant.

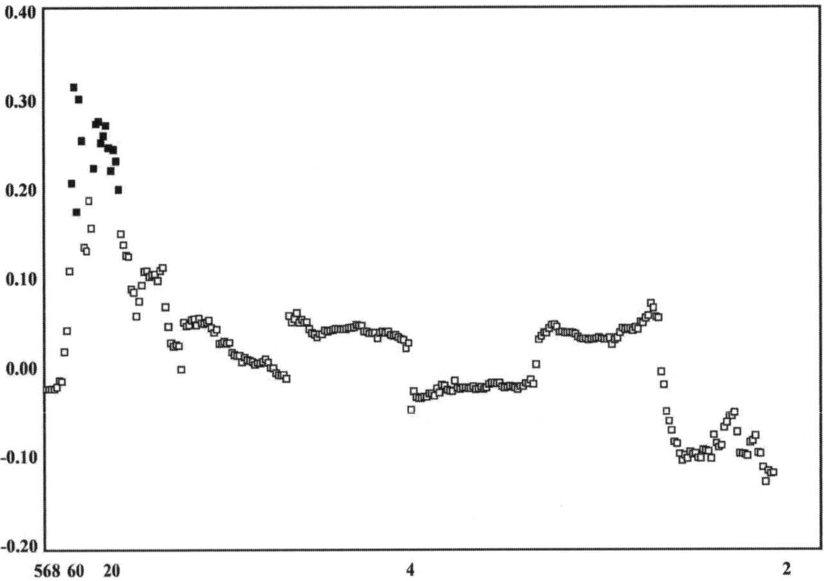

FIGURE 2.2a Aggregate Fuel Price Index, High-Pass Filtering

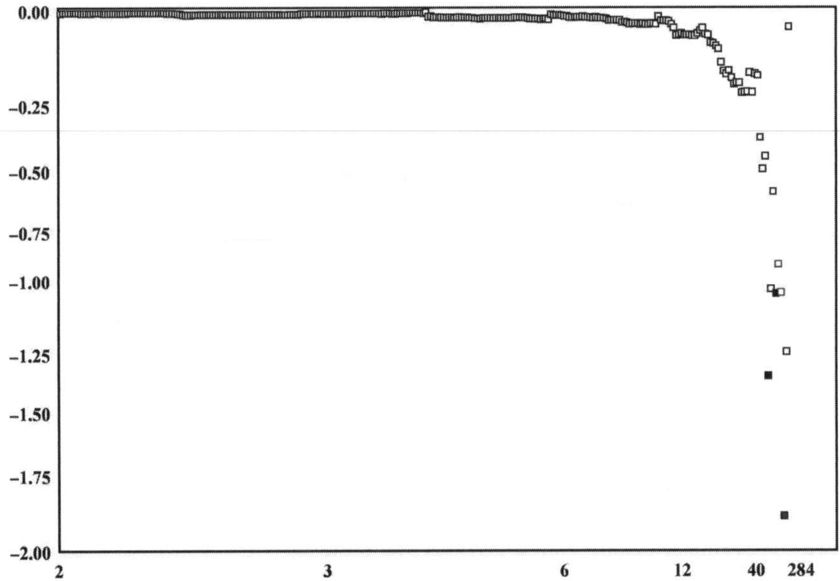

FIGURE 2.2b Aggregate Fuel Price Index, Low-Pass Filtering

In Figure 2.4 we observe a somewhat different situation. Here the baseline coefficient is positive and significant. If we remove the components with period longer than 5 years, the relation remains positive and significant. However, if we continue removing the components longer than 4 years (47 months), the relation will no longer be significant. Again this indicates that components less than 4 years

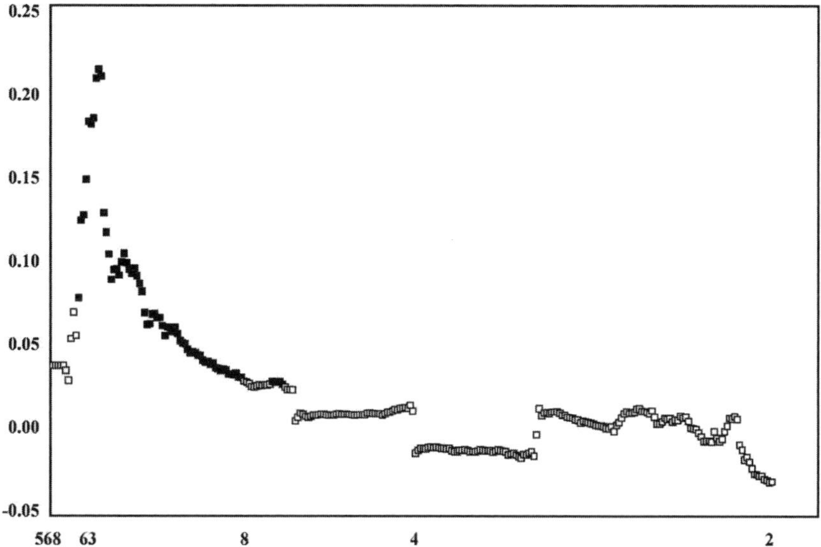

FIGURE 2.3a Aggregate Metal Price Index, High-Pass Filtering

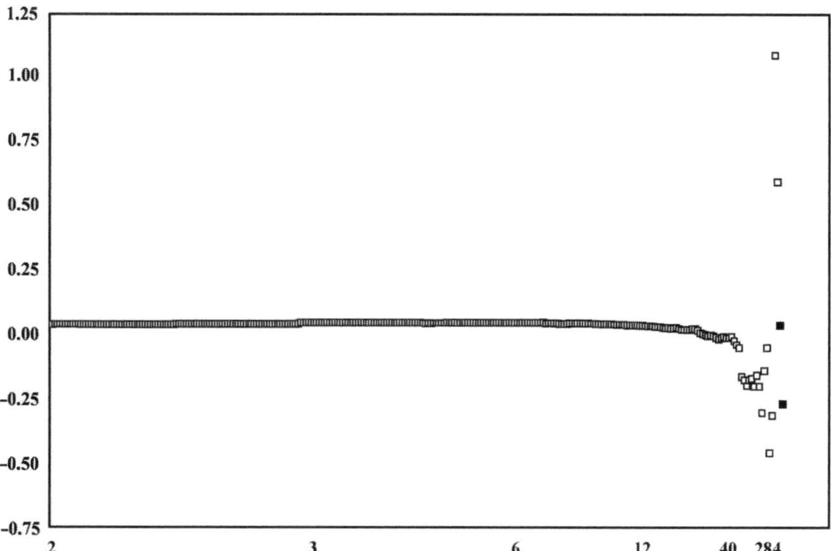

FIGURE 2.3b Aggregate Metal Price Index, Low-Pass Filtering

do not account for the procyclicality of agricultural prices. Our conclusion is that over the 2- to 5-year variations, these aggregate price series are procyclical. In other words, after filtering out the impacts of variations at either end of the spectrum, the aggregate series have a positive comovement with industrial activity. In general, we find no evidence of countercyclical price markups for these aggregate measures of primary commodities prices.

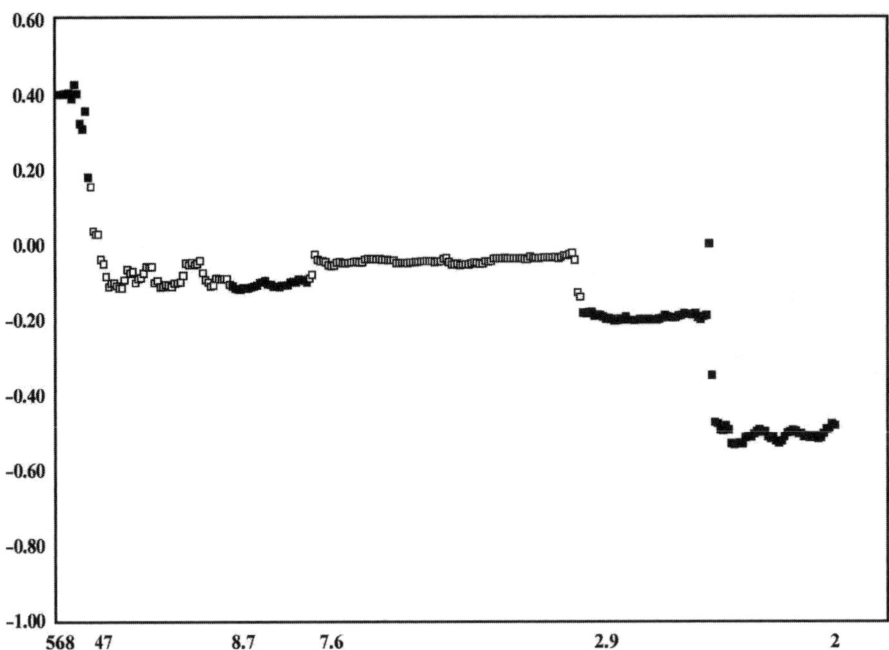

FIGURE 2.4a Agricultural Price Index, High-Pass Filtering

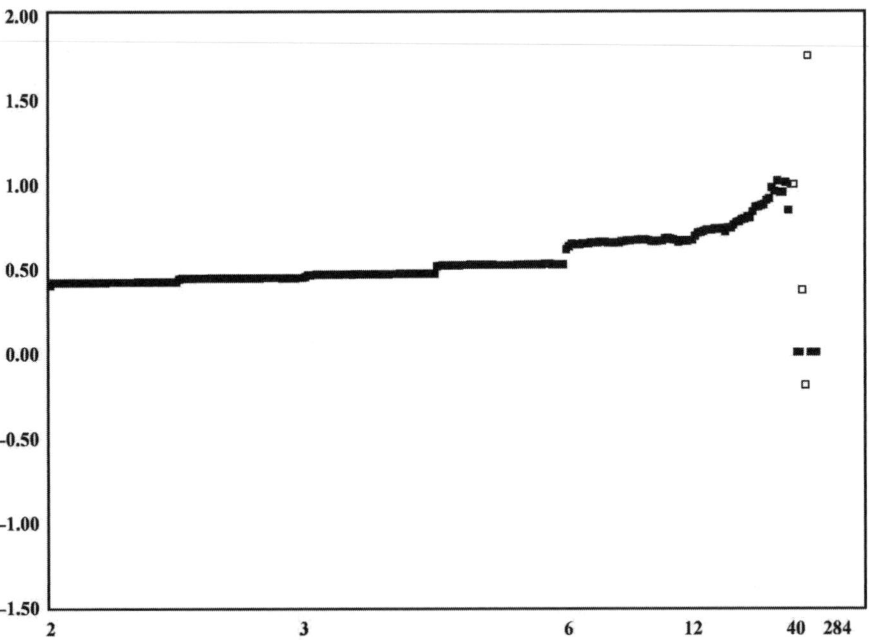

FIGURE 2.4b Agricultural Price Index, Low-Pass Filtering

Individual Price Series

Table 2.2 presents the baseline results for 14 individual commodity price series. Figures 2.5 to 2.12 present the high- and low-pass filtering diagrams for each commodity. A quick inspection of the diagrams indicates that with few exceptions, the conclusions reached for the aggregate price measures also hold for individual commodity prices

In almost all cases, the high-pass filtering diagrams show that by removing the lower-frequency components, the observed positive comovements lose their statistical significance. The exact frequency at which the loss of significance occurs varies, but they are all in the 2- to 5-year range. Notable exceptions to this rule are the cases of gold, silver, and sugar (Table 2.2). In the case of gold, after dropping only a few components, the relationship becomes countercyclical and significant (Figure 2.5). This suggests that very low frequency components were the cause of the insignificant comovements.

Unlike gold, silver becomes procyclical when variations above 4 years are filtered out. Sugar remains insignificant even after removing the low-frequency components (Figure 2.7). Thus the only evidence for countercyclical price movements that we found is that of gold. Primary commodity prices for metals, agricultural products, and petroleum are generally procyclical.

Except for gold and sugar, the prices of all other commodities have positive coefficients. That is, they have a procyclical character. Furthermore, except for gold, silver, and sugar, all other comovements are statistically significant. This means that none of the countercyclical findings is statistically significant. We observe this in the case of industrial metals, such as aluminum, copper, zinc, and tin. Figures 2.8 and 2.9 show the results for aluminum and copper, two major industrial metals.

It is interesting to note that the procyclicality of prices that holds for industrial metals, such as aluminum and copper, also applies to agricultural commodities, such as beef, rice, wheat, tea, and wool. Figures 2.10 to 2.12 show the results for beef, rice, and wheat, three major agricultural commodities.

TABLE 2.2 Baseline Estimates for Individual Commodities

Commodity	Coefficient	t-stat	P-value
Aluminum	1.5901017	5.2618763	0000002
Beef	0.77577961	5.39926829	0.00000010
Coffee	0.82381045	3.1893101	0.00075466
Copper	1.8609939	8.5546887	0.00000000
Gold	−0.18237775	−0.85774022	0.39152280
Petroleum	0.74740081	2.1587040	0.03144857
Rice	1.1142740	5.5845706	000000018
Silver	0.30859353	1.2653107	0.10315437
Sugar	−0.35931293	−0.91033649	0.81847325
Tea	0.84818777	3.9229454	00004.9413
Tin	0.86039792	5.2272102	0.0000001
Wheat	0.53274323	3.1867116	0.0007613
Wool	2.1674305	10.362116	0.0000000
Zinc	1.5416939	7.0444626	0.00000002

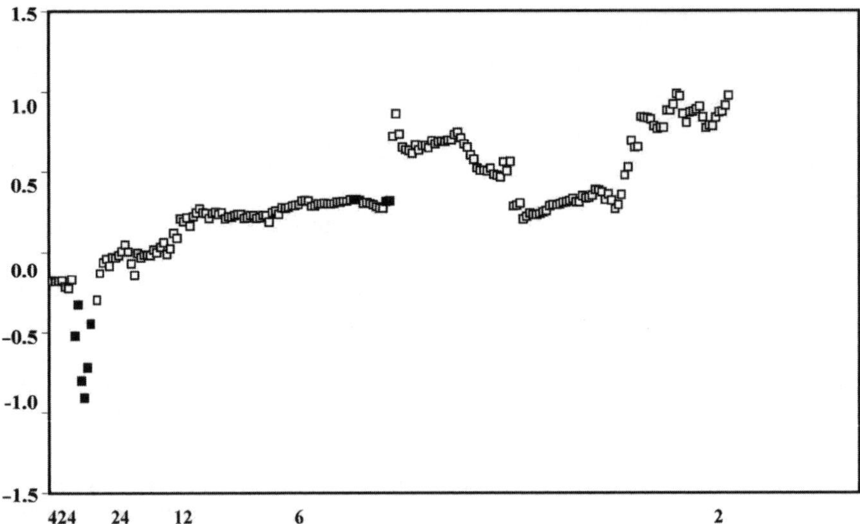

FIGURE 2.5a Price of Gold, High-Pass Filtering

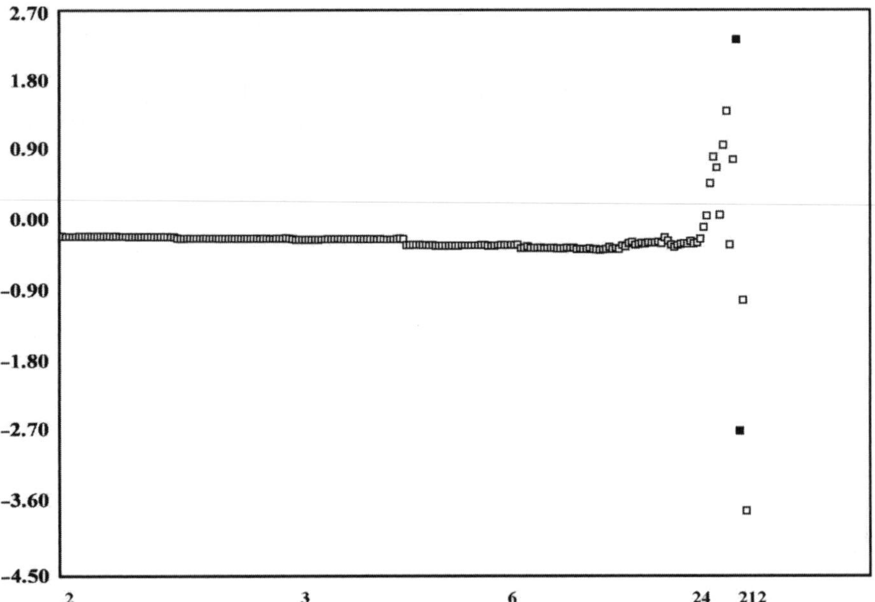

FIGURE 2.5b Price of Gold, Low-Pass Filtering

We did not display the results for all commodities studied (see Table 2.2) because doing so would yield no additional insights into their qualitative behaviors due to their similarities to the commodities shown. As noted, the only commodities that did not display procyclical behaviors are gold, silver, and sugar.

Therefore, based on the primary commodities used, our study does not support the existence of countercyclical price markups. One reason may be that because

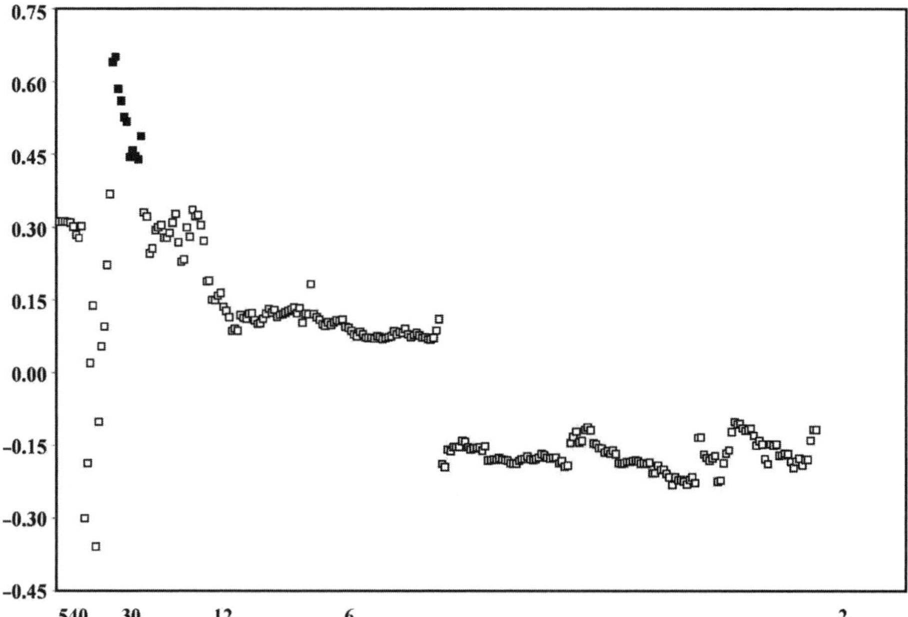

FIGURE 2.6a Price of Silver, High-Pass Filtering

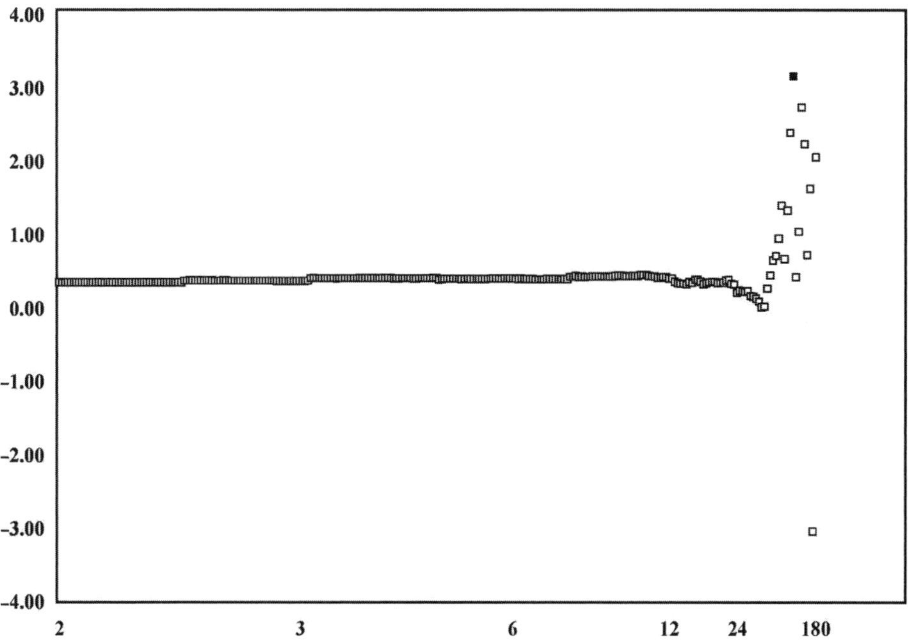

FIGURE 2.6b Price of Silver, Low-Pass Filtering

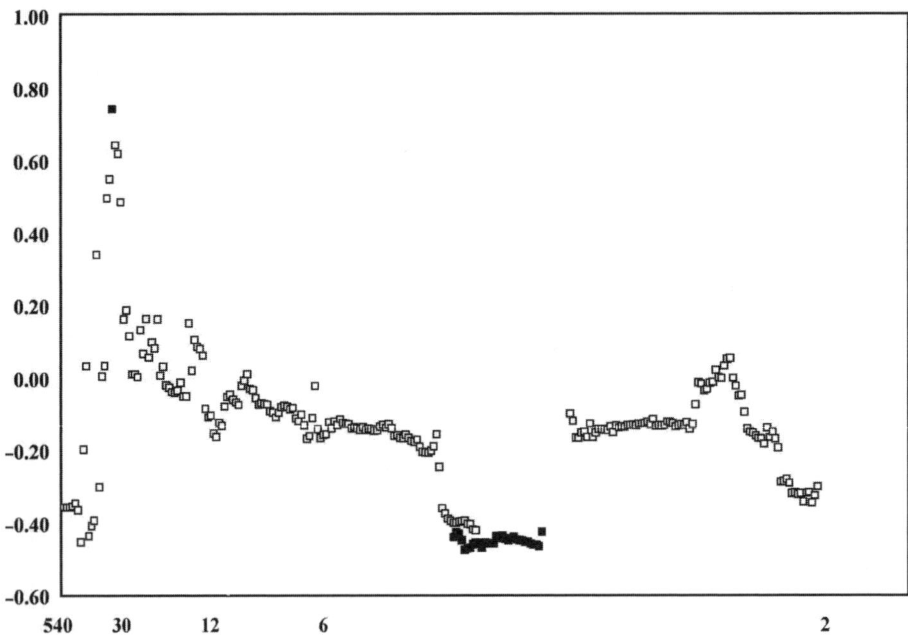

FIGURE 2.7a Price of Sugar, High-Pass Filtering

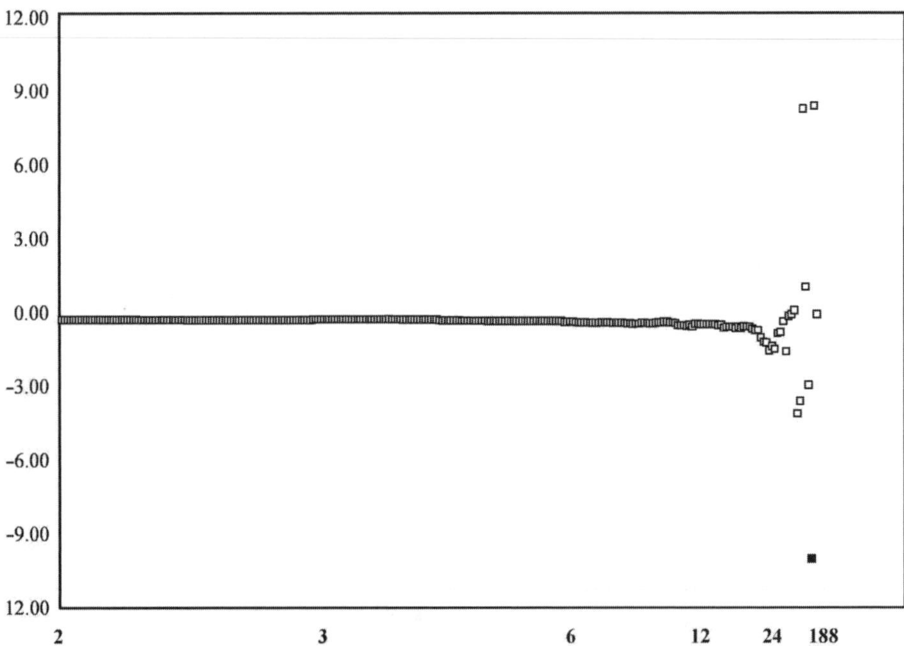

FIGURE 2.7b Price of Sugar, Low-Pass Filtering

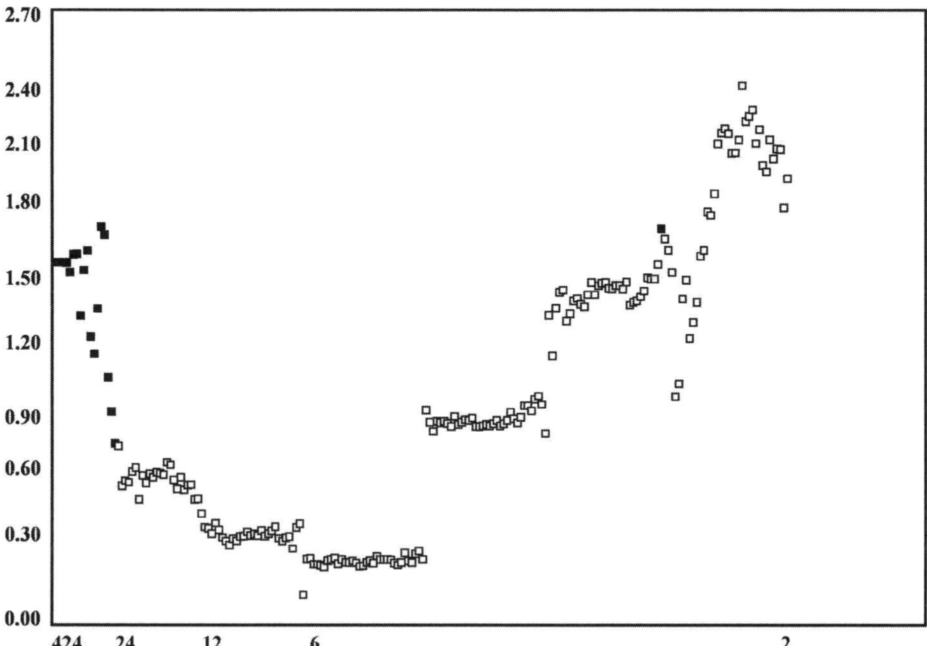

FIGURE 2.8a Aluminum Price, High-Pass Filtering

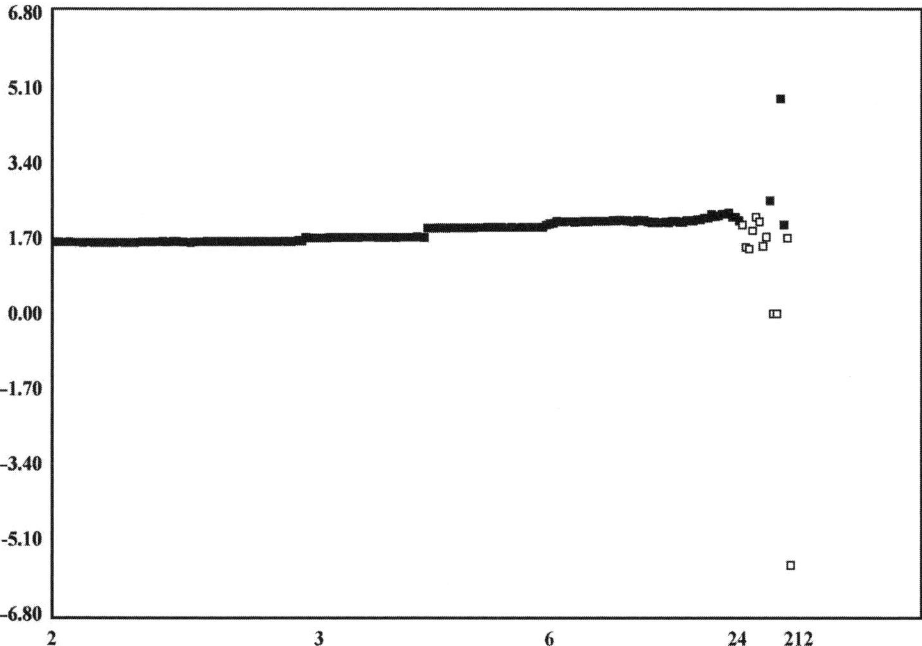

FIGURE 2.8b Aluminum Price, Low-Pass Filtering

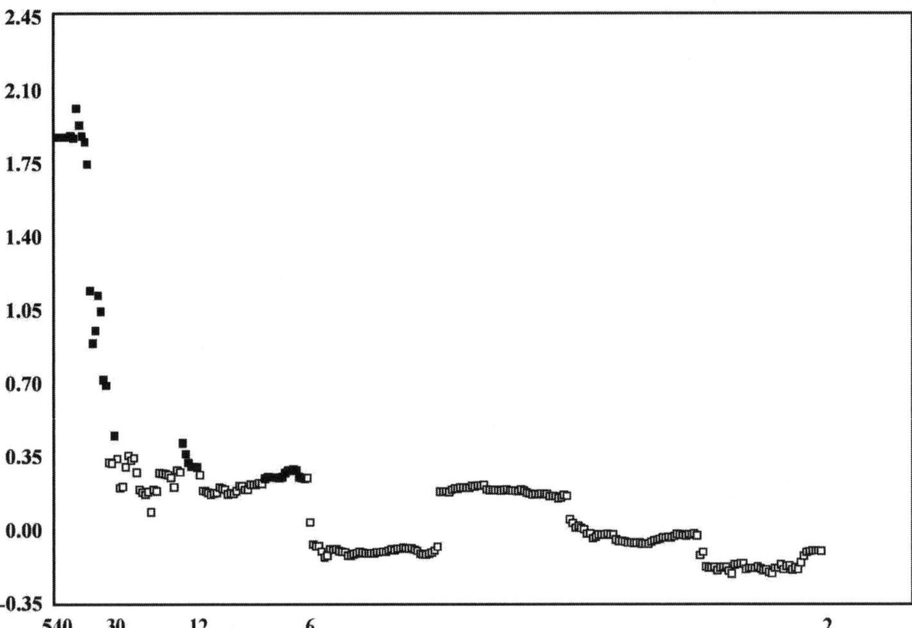

FIGURE 2.9a Price of Copper, High-Pass Filtering

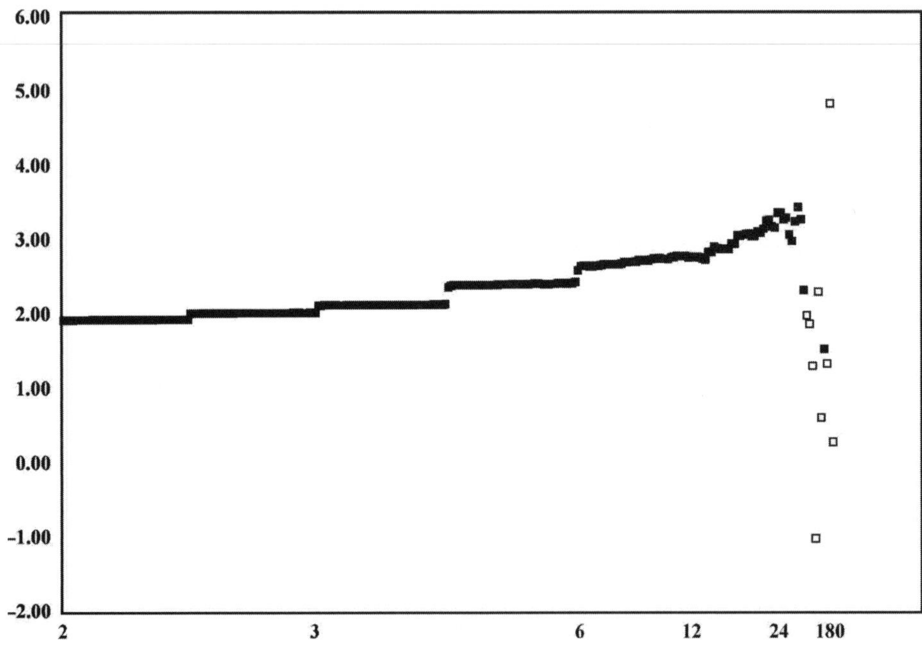

FIGURE 2.9b Price of Copper, Low-Pass Filtering

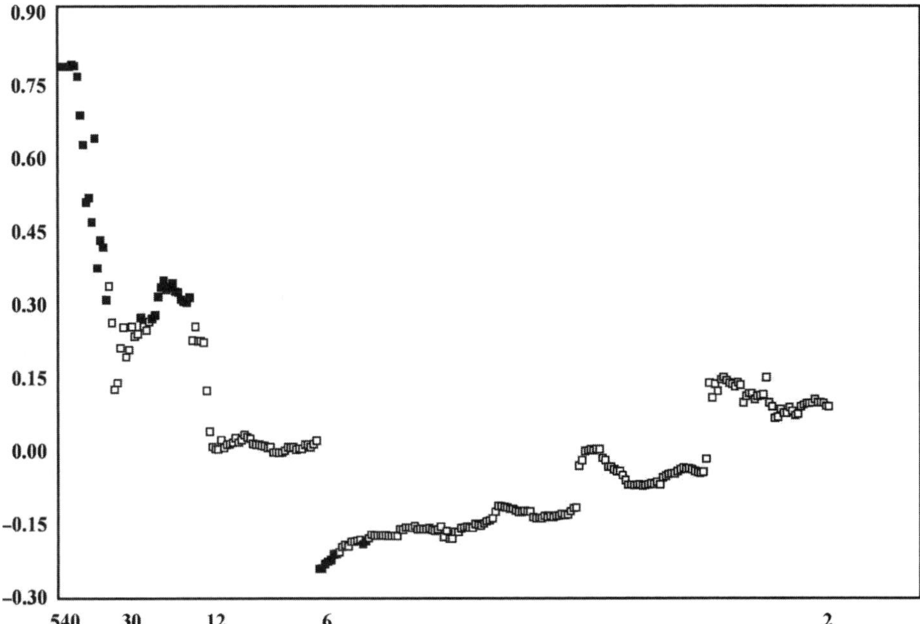

FIGURE 2.10a Price of Beef, High-Pass Filtering

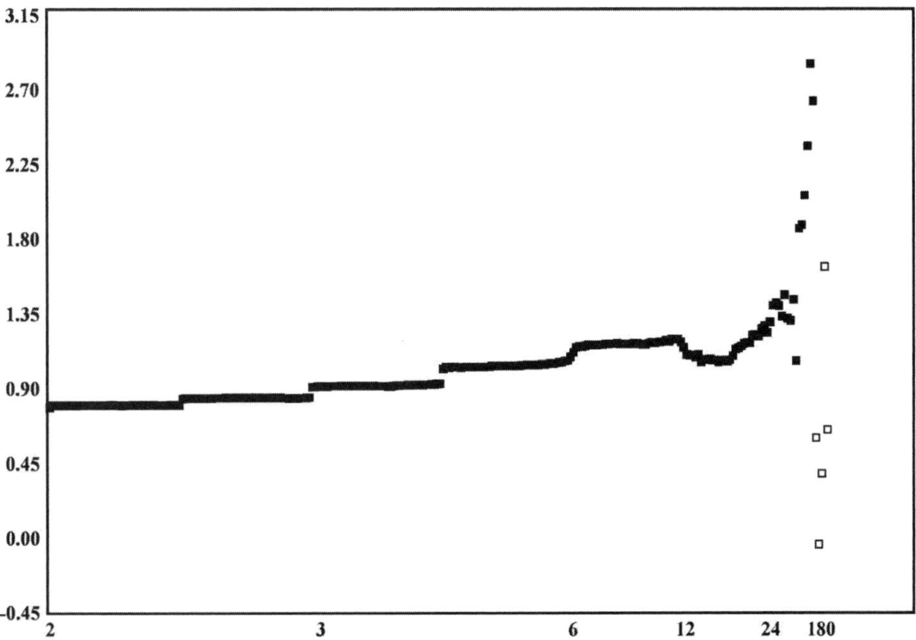

FIGURE 2.10b Price of Beef, Low-Pass Filtering

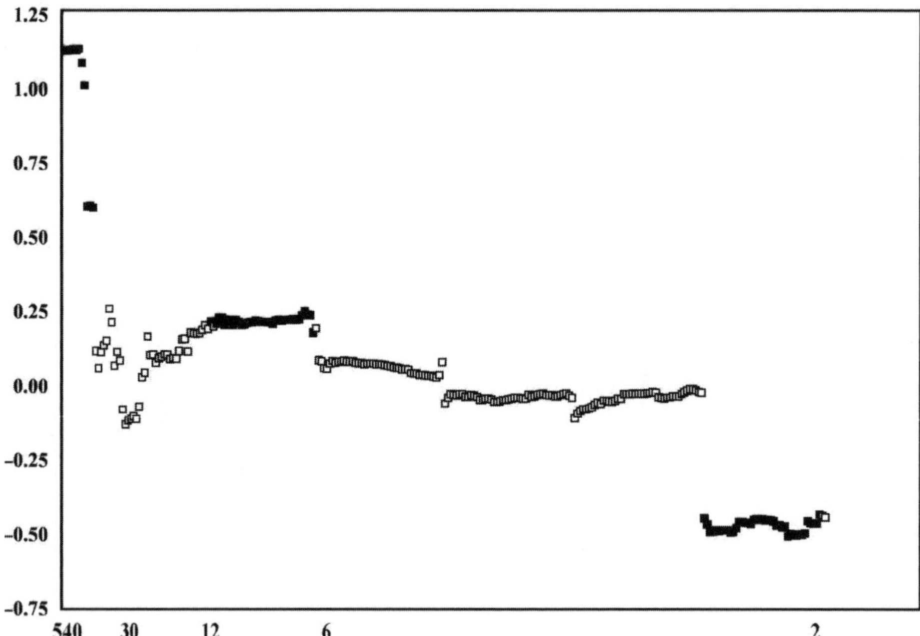

FIGURE 2.11a Price of Rice, High-Pass Filtering

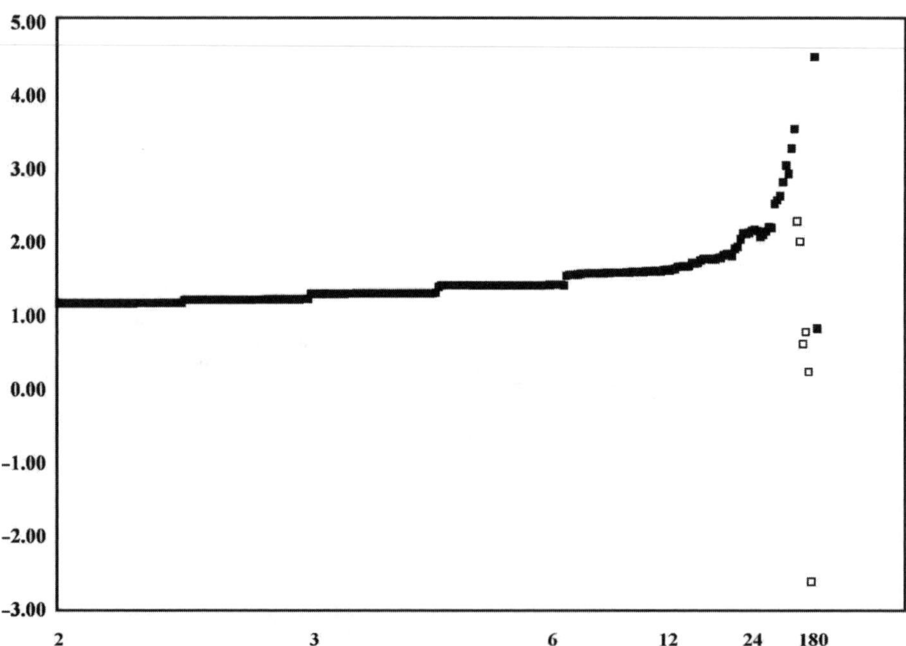

FIGURE 2.11b Price of Rice, Low-Pass Filtering

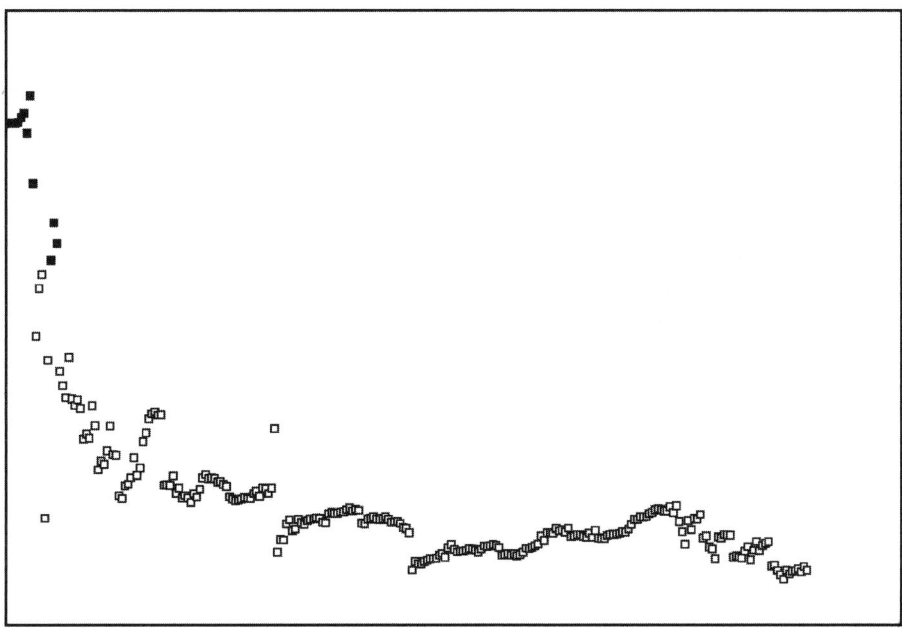

FIGURE 2.12a Price of Wheat, High-Pass Filtering

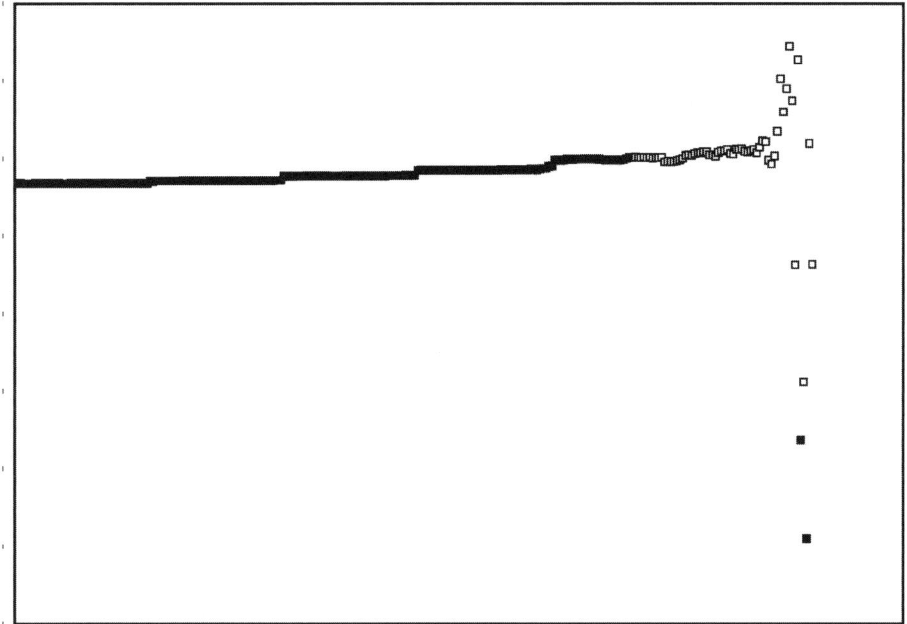

FIGURE 2.12b Price of Wheat, Low-Pass Filtering

primary commodities do not go through an extensive production process and are not sold at the retail level, markups constitute a smaller portion of their prices. Thus, countercyclical markups do not have an appreciable impact on their prices.

CONCLUSIONS

Over what we have termed the business cycle frequencies, commodity prices are generally procyclical. With few exceptions, this holds true for aggregate as well as individual price series. Even though the baseline coefficients in some cases are negative or insignificant, removal of longer-term variations (often longer than the durations of typical business cycles), turns the coefficients positive and significant. The sole exceptions are the price of gold, which is countercyclical, and the price of sugar, which is acyclical.

REFERENCES

Abraham, K.G., and J.C. Haltiwanger. (1995). "Real Wages and the Business Cycle," *Journal of Economic Literature* 33: 1215–1264.

Afrasiabi, A.B., and T.W. Nonnenmacher. (2005). "High and Low Frequency Variations and the Cyclical Behavior of Real Wages," *Applied Economics* 37: 571–579.

Barsky, R., and E. Warner. (1995). "The Timing and Magnitude of Retail Stores Markdowns: Evidence from Weekends and Holidays," *Quarterly Journal of Economics* 104: 699–718.

Bils, M. (1987). "The Cyclical Behavior of Marginal Cost and Price," *American Economic Review* 77: 838–855.

Borensztein, E., and C.M. Reinhart. (1994). "The Macroeconomic Determinants of Commodity Prices," WP/94/9. Research Department, International Monetary Fund, Washington, DC.

Bosworth, B., and R.Z. Lawrence. (1982). *Commodity Prices and the New Inflation.* Washington, DC: The Brookings Institution.

Burns, A.F., and W.C. Mitchell. (1946). *Measuring Business Cycles.* New York: National Bureau of Economic Research.

Chiarini, B. (1998). "Cyclicality of Real Wages and Adjustment Costs," *Applied Economics* 30: 1239–1250.

Chu, K.Y., and T.K. Morrison. (1984). "World Non-Oil Commodity Markets," *Staff Papers, International Monetary Fund*, 33 (March): 139–184.

Cogley, T., and J.M. Nason. (1992). "Effects of the Hodrick-Prescott Filter on Trend and Difference Stationary Time Series." Discussion paper, University of British Columbia Department of Economics.

Cooley, T.F. (1995). *Frontiers of Business Cycle Research.* Princeton, NJ: Princeton University Press.

Cristini, A. (1999). *Unemployment and Primary Commodity Prices.* London, Great Britain: Macmillan.

Cushing, M. (1990). "Real Wages over the Business Cycle: A Band Spectrum Approach," *Southern Economic Journal* 56: 905–1017.

Darby, R. (1982). "The Price of Oil and World Inflation and Recession," *American Economic Review* 72: 738–751.

Den Haan, W.J. (1996). "The Comovements between Real Activity and Prices at Different Business Cycle Frequencies," National Bureau of Economic Research Working Paper, No. 5553.

Den Haan, W.J. (2000). "The Comovement between Output and Prices," *Journal of Monetary Economics* 46: 3–30.

Engle, R. (1974). "Band Spectrum Regression," *International Economic Review* 15: 1–11.

Fama, E.F., and K.R. French. (1988). "Business Cycles and the Behavior of Metal Prices," *Journal of Finance* 43: 1075–1088.

Grilli, R.E., and C.M. Yang. (1981). "Real and Monetary Determinants of Non-Oil Commodity Price Movements," CDWP 1981-6. Washington, DC: World Bank.

Hanes, C. (1996). "Changes in the Cyclical Behavior of Real Wage Rates, 1870–1990," *Journal of Economic History* 56: 837–861.

Jaeger, A. (1994). "Mechanical Detrending by Hodrick-Prescott Filtering: A Note," *Empirical Economics* 19: 493–500.

Koopmans, L. (1974). *The Spectral Analysis of Time Series*. New York: Academic Press.

Labys, W.C. (2006). *Modeling and Forecasting Primary Commodity Prices*. London: Ashgate.

Labys, W.C. (2000). " Can World Market Volatility Upset the US Economy?" *Economic Directions*. Latrobe, PA: St. Vincent College.

Labys, W.C., and A. Maizels. (1993). "Commodity Price Fluctuations and Macroeconomic Adjustments in the Developed Economies," *Journal of Policy Modeling*, 15, no. 3: 335–352.

Labys, W.C., J.B. Lesourd, and D. Badillo. (1998). "The Existence of Metal Price Cycles," *Resources Policy* 24, no. 3: 147–155.

Labys, W.C., A. Achouch, and M. Terraza. (1999). "Metal Prices and the Business Cycle," *Resources Policy* 25: 229–238.

Lewis, W.A. (1949). *Economic Survey: 1919–1939*. London: Allen and Unwin.

Mork, K.A., H.T. Mysen, and O. Olsen. (1994). "Macroeconomic Responses to Oil Price Increases and Decreases in Seven OECD Countries." *Energy Journal* 15.4: 19–35.

Moore, G.H. (1988), "Inflation Cycles and Metals Prices," *Mineral Processing and Extracting Metallurgy Review* 3: 95–104.

Neftci, S.H. (1978). "A Time-Series Analysis of the Real Wages-Employment Relationship," *Journal of Political Economy* 86, no. 2: 281–291.

Reinhart, C., and P. Wickham. (1994). "Commodity Prices: Cyclical Weakness or Secular Decline?" *IMF Staff Paper* 41, no. 2: 175–213.

Rotemberg, J., and M. Woodford. (1991). Markups and the Business Cycle. In O.J. Blanchard and S. Fischer, eds., *NBER Macroeconomics Annual 1991, Vol. 6*. Cambridge, MA: MIT Press, 63–128.

Stadler, G.W. (1994). "Real Business Cycles," *Journal of Economic Literature* 32: 1750–1783.

UNCTAD. (1996 and earlier issues). *Commodity Price Bulletin*. Geneva: *United Nations*.

CHAPTER 3

Nonlinear Features of Comovements between Commodity Prices and Inflation

Catherine Kyrtsou

INTRODUCTION

This chapter further investigates the nonlinear feedback relationship found in Kyrtsou and Labys (2006) between U.S. inflation (Bureau of Labor Statistics consumer price index [BLS CPI]) and the primary commodity price index (the BLS producer price index [PPI] component for all primary commodity series). Our goal is to disaggregate the index to the individual commodity level for a group of raw materials prices, including crude oil. Assuming that a nonlinear feedback relationship exists between U.S. inflation and the commodity price index, we examine if individual primary commodity prices also nonlinearly cause inflation and vice versa. We improve on our previous research by employing a new test for nonlinear feedback causality recently developed by Hristu-Varsakelis and Kyrtsou (2006).

BACKGROUND

Why are primary commodity prices so volatile, and why does this volatility affect inflation? For agricultural commodities whose demand is relatively constant (price-inelastic), fluctuations in production resulting from weather variations cause fluctuations in prices. For mineral and energy commodities where supply is relatively fixed (capacity is price inelastic in the short term), fluctuations in international business cycles tend to destabilize commodity demand and hence prices. In the case of the crude oil market, policies designed to decrease or increase production or to allocate market shares can also induce price disturbances. For markets where futures exchanges also exist, excessive speculation (relative to actual production) can amplify any price swings already started. Underlying this view of "market fundamentals" is the assumption that traders have "rational expectations" and thus incorporate available information concerning these "fundamentals" in their decisions. However, random information or noise often distorts such price formation, and price behavior will deviate from efficiency, often being cyclic or even chaotic.

The volatility of commodity prices can affect the economy and inflation as well as vice versa. Commodity producers and consumers, whether they are individuals or vast multinational organizations, suffer from price fluctuations. For example, sudden high crude oil prices can cause consumers to reduce purchases and to reallocate their budgets. Transportation becomes restrictive with gasoline prices rising and supplements added to normal passenger fares and freight rates. Elderly persons on fixed incomes can no longer afford normal heating bills. Manufacturers not capable of rapid energy substitution face costly disruptions in order to avoid final product price increases.

When the latter occurs, we have the beginnings of inflation. A strong case has been made for the relations between commodity prices and inflation by Bosworth and Lawrence (1982), Beckerman and Jenkinson (1986), Cooper and Lawrence (1975), and Moore (1988). An important extension of this work by Boughton and Branson (1988), Durand and Blondal (1988), and Mahdavi and Zhou (1997) is determining whether commodity prices constitute leading indicators of inflation. Since then the study of this relationship has received more critical attention. See, for example, Hua (1998), Kyrtsou and Labys (2006, 2007), and Malliaris (2005). Inflation can be caused by the expectations about the future of consumers, producers, and investors. "In an overheated economy, increased futures trading activity on the part of speculators can amplify already rising commodity prices" (Labys 2000). In this case, if speculators expect demand for a good to rise, the price for that good will lead the increase in demand, thus leading to higher consumer prices. Conversely, if there is an increase in commodity production due to speculation such that production exceeds commodity demand, then there will be a surplus that causes exports to rise and imports to fall.

Because a rise in inflation will lower profits for many producers, they may reduce the workforce, thus increasing the level of unemployment. A rise in unemployment will reduce disposable income, which will lower commodity demand and thus cause a surplus if there is not a reduction in commodity production. Cristini (1999), for example, shows an influence of commodity prices on employment in Organization for Economic Cooperation and Development (OECD) countries. The combination of lower wages, higher unemployment and an increased CPI will amplify a recessionary cycle: decreased commodity demand in addition to overall demand, fall in industrial activity, further decline in disposable income, increased decline in elastic goods demand, inventory surplus, increased exports coupled with decreased imports, worsened trade imbalance, and so on.

Turning to econometric analysis, Labys and Maizels (1993) focused on causality and feedback effects between commodity prices and macroeconomic variables by employing Granger-causality tests to compare the results of a large number of studies dealing with macroeconomic and commodity market interactions. They found a direct relationship between commodity prices and industrial production. When commodity prices rise, especially at an accelerated rate, consumers and often the government react strongly. Today, high prices are causing some consumers to cut back on expenditures and are thus offsetting producers' expected profit. Simultaneously, the Federal Reserve is looking to adjust interest rates, to cool down the economy and to temper inflation. Labys and Maizels conclude that the highest degree of causality exists between "international primary commodity prices and national prices, selected macroeconomic indicators including industrial production, and monetary variables in the major OECD countries than was previously believed." The practical implications of their findings rest in incorporating commodity price fluctuations in determining effective stabilization policies.

Borensztein and Reinhart (1994), Bosworth and Lawrence (1982), Chu and Morrison (1984), Darby (1982), Fama and French (1988), Grilli and Yang (1980), and Moore (1988) report on relationships between business cycles and metals prices. More specifically, fluctuations in global industrial production and financial variables have been shown to influence the industrial demand for metals. Given the short-term price inelasticity of metal supplies, the resulting demand fluctuations tend to influence the related metal prices. The influence of the financial variables may come less directly in the forming of expectations of agents who deal in the demand, supply, and stocking of metals. As evidence for such phenomena, Kyrtsou and Labys (2007) in particular have found a relationship between primary metals prices and inflation.

A final linkage comes from the extent to which the U.S. economy relies on imports of primary commodities such as crude oil to sustain its own production, consumption and services. There is no doubt of the importance of crude oil prices on inflation, since these prices influence just about all sectors of a national economy. Considerable efforts have been made to demonstrate this interaction. See, for example, studies by Darby (1982), Ferderer (1996), Labys (2000), and Mork et al. (1994).

HRISTU-VARSAKELIS AND KYRTSOU NONLINEAR GRANGER CAUSALITY TEST (2006)

This test is constructed on the basis of a special type of nonlinear structure, known as the bivariate noisy Mackey-Glass model (Kyrtsou and Labys 2006, 2007). The nonlinear causality test was implemented in MATLAB®. The code is available from the author upon request. The asymmetric version of the test can be found in Hristu-Varsakelis and Kyrtsou (2007).The model is given in equation 3.1:

$$X_t = \alpha_{11}\frac{X_{t-\tau_1}}{1+X_{t-\tau_1}^{c_1}} - \delta_{11}X_{t-1} + \alpha_{12}\frac{Y_{t-\tau_2}}{1+Y_{t-\tau_2}^{c_2}} - \delta_{12}Y_{t-1} + \varepsilon_t \quad \varepsilon_t \sim N(0,1),$$

and (3.1)

$$Y_t = \alpha_{21}\frac{X_{t-\tau_1}}{1+X_{t-\tau_1}^{c_1}} - \delta_{21}X_{t-1} + \alpha_{22}\frac{Y_{t-\tau_2}}{1+Y_{t-\tau_2}^{c_2}} - \delta_{22}Y_{t-1} + u_t \quad u_t \sim N(0,1),$$

where X and Y = a pair of related time-series variables
α_{ij}, and δ_{ij} = parameters to be estimated
τ_i = delays
c_i = constants

The best model (3.1) is that allowing the maximum Log Likehood value and minimum Schwarz information criterion. Erroneous conclusions about the pair of parameters c_i and τ_i used for estimating model 3.1 can lead to misleading interpretations of the underlying dynamics causing nonlinear comovements. As mentioned in Kyrtsou and Labys (2006, 2007), Kyrtsou and Vorlow (2007), and Kyrtsou and Malliaris (2007), the principal advantage of (1) over simple value at risk (VAR) alternatives is that the nonlinear Mackey-Glass (hereafter M-G) terms are able to capture more complex dependent dynamics in a time series. The identification of significant M-G terms in a pair of series reveals the nonlinear feedback law between X and Y and elucidate qualitative features of this law.

The Hristu-Varsakelis and Kyrtsou causality test aims to capture whether past samples of a variable Y have a significant nonlinear effect (of the type $Y_{t-\tau_2}/1 + Y_{t-\tau_2}^{c2}$) on the current value of another variable X. Algorithmically, the test is similar to the linear Granger causality test, except that the two models fitted to the series are M-G processes. The test procedure begins with estimating the parameters of an M-G model that best fits the given series, using ordinary least squares. To test reverse causality (i.e., *from Y to X)*, a second M-G model is estimated, under the constraint $\alpha_{12} = 0$. The latter equation represents our *null hypothesis*. Let $\hat{\varepsilon}_t, \hat{\theta}_t$ be the residuals produced by the unconstrained and constrained best-fit M-G models, respectively. We compute and compare the sums of squared residuals $S_c = \sum_{t=1}^{N} \hat{\theta}_t$ and $S_u = \sum_{t=1}^{N} \hat{\varepsilon}_t$. Let $n_{free} = 4$ be the number of free parameters in our M-G model and $n_{restr} = 1$ be the number of parameters set to zero when estimating the constrained model. If the test statistic

$$S_F = \frac{(S_c - S_u)/n_{restr}}{S_u/(N - n_{free} - 1)} \sim F_{n_{restr}, N-n_{free}-1} \tag{3.2}$$

is greater than a specified value, then we reject the null hypothesis that Y causes X. The p-value for the test is computed from

$$p = 1 - F^{cdf}_{n_{restr}, N-n_{free}-1}(S_F, n_{restr}, N - n_{free} - 1), \tag{3.3}$$

where $F^{cdf}_{a,b}$ = cumulative distribution function for the $F_{a,b}$ distribution

It is worth noting that the Hristu-Varsakelis and Kyrtsou test is implemented in order to filter specific nonlinear structures, such as the M-G framework, providing useful information on the particularity of feedback between economic time series. The presence of nonlinear feedback can be the precursor of instability and inherent unpredictably. The nonproportionality in the response of one variable to a shock on a second or even an entire set of variables mirrors profound characteristics of the overall economic system where this mechanism is observed. Evidence for the applicability of conclusions from the use of the M-G model in financial market analysis can be found in Kyrtsou and Terraza (2003), Kyrtsou et al. (2004), Kyrtsou (2005), and Kyrtsou and Serletis (2006).

DATA DESCRIPTION AND EMPIRICAL RESULTS

The consumer price index is from the U.S. Bureau of Labor Statistics. The price data are monthly price series for a set of individual primary commodities, namely aluminum, copper, gold, lead, nickel, crude oil (petrol), platinum, silver, tin, tungsten, and zinc. Raw materials or metal and energy prices were selected rather than agricultural prices because the former prices have a more profound impact on manufacturing activities and hence inflation.

These prices are drawn from the United Nations Conference on Trade and Development (UNCTAD) *Commodity Price Bulletin*. Definitions and sources of each price series appear in the appendix. Following the rationale of Kyrtsou and Labys (2006), these series are compared to the BLS CPI—all urban consumers (CUUROOOOAA0) index. The sample period for all series extends from January 1970 through December 2004. Data are not seasonally adjusted as the aim is to preserve possibly intrinsic structures. First differences of the logarithms of price series are employed to obtain returns series: dlcpi for CPI, dlalum for aluminum, dlcop for copper, dlgold for gold, llead for lead, dlnic for nickel, dlpetr for crude oil, dlplat for platinum, dlsilv for silver, dltin for tin, dltun for tungsten ore, and dlzin for zinc. Figure 3.1 describes the behavior of the return series of dlcpi (consumer price index).

Figures 3.2 to 3.12 show the behaviors of the return series of individual commodities, starting with aluminum (Figure 3.2).

Aluminum (dlalum) shows the typical pattern of the commodities studied in this chapter. The return series is centered about zero but has significant positive and negative spikes. Its behavior looks qualitatively similar to that of copper (dlcop, Figure 3.3), lead (dllead, Figure 3.4), platinum (dlplat, Figure 3.5), tin (dltin, Figure 3.6), tungsten (dltun, Figure 3.7), and zinc (dlzin, Figure 3.8). Of course, only statistical tests can reliably differentiate behaviors (Table 3.1).

Nickel (dlnic, Figure 3.9) follows the same general pattern but appears to experience greater volatility towards the second half of the series than in the first, which does not seem to be the case for other commodities.

Gold (dlgold, Figure 3.10), crude oil (dlpetr, Figure 3.11), and, to lesser degree, silver (dlsilv, Figure 3.12) also follow the general pattern of the other commodities, but they have fewer large spikes. This is particularly true in the case of gold, which

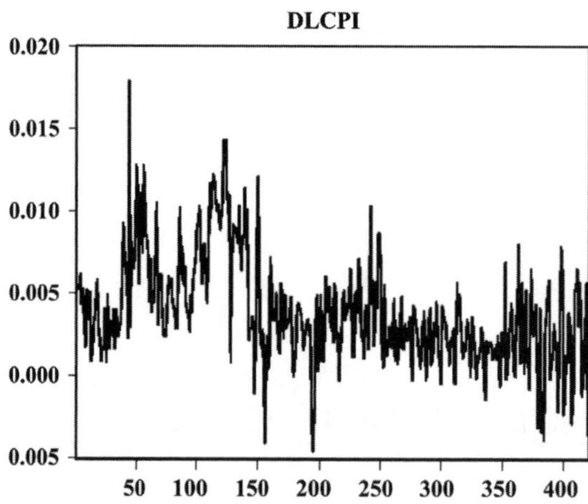

FIGURE 3.1 U.S. Inflation Series, CPI

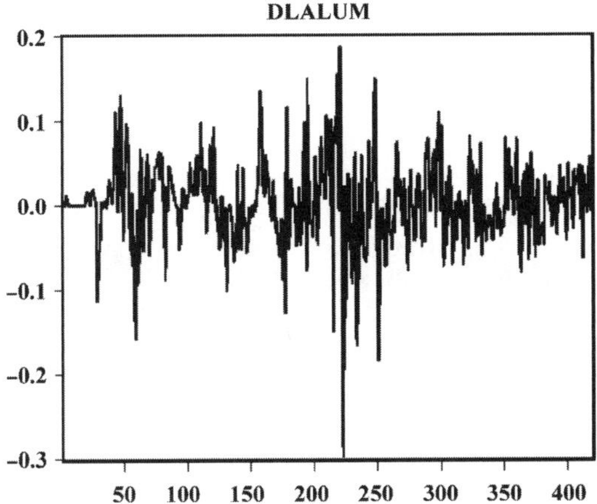

FIGURE 3.2 Commodity Price Returns Series, Aluminum

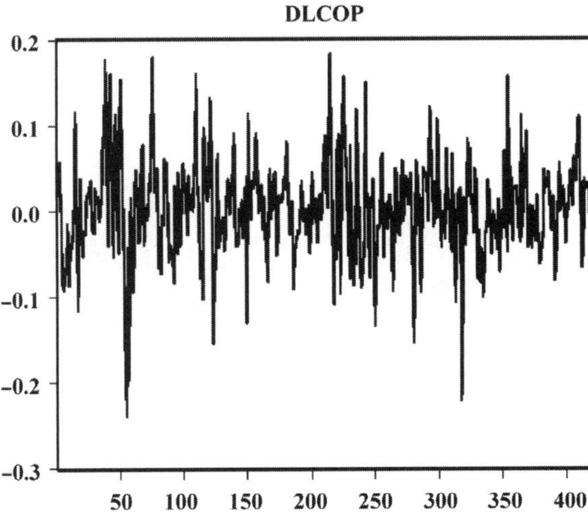

FIGURE 3.3 Commodity Price Returns Series, Copper

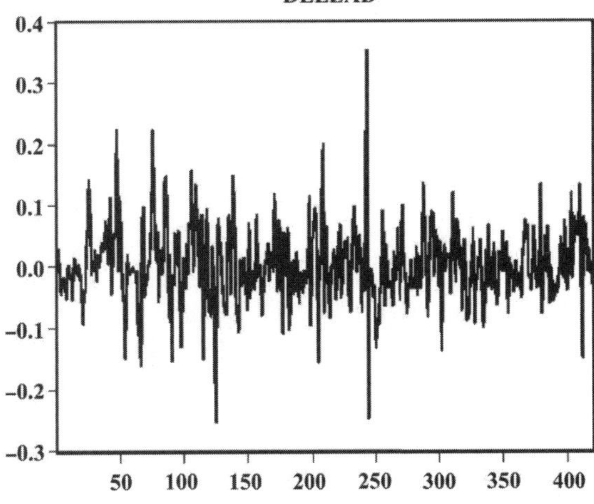

FIGURE 3.4 Commodity Price Returns Series, Lead

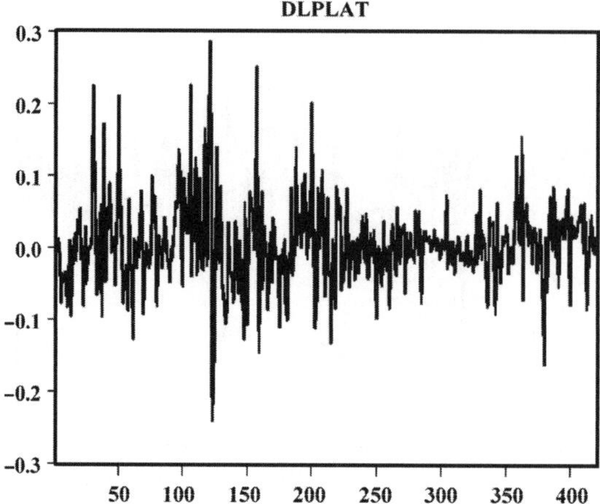

FIGURE 3.5 Commodity Price Returns Series, Platinum

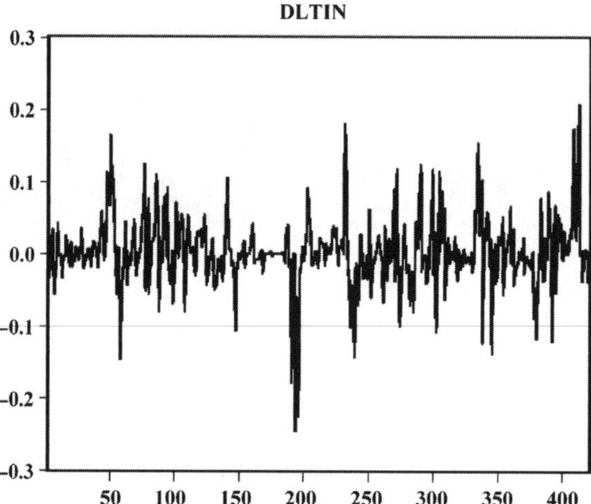

FIGURE 3.6 Commodity Price Returns Series, Tin

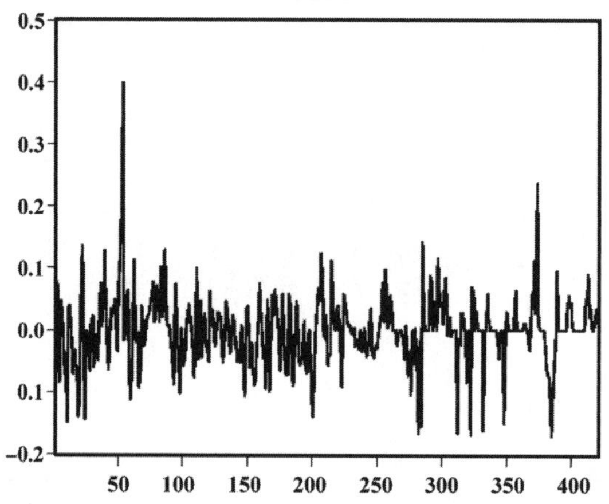

FIGURE 3.7 Commodity Price Returns Series, Tungsten

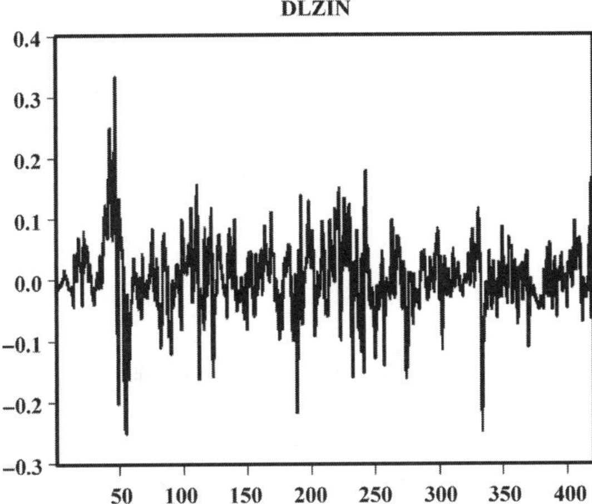

FIGURE 3.8 Commodity Price Returns Series, Zinc

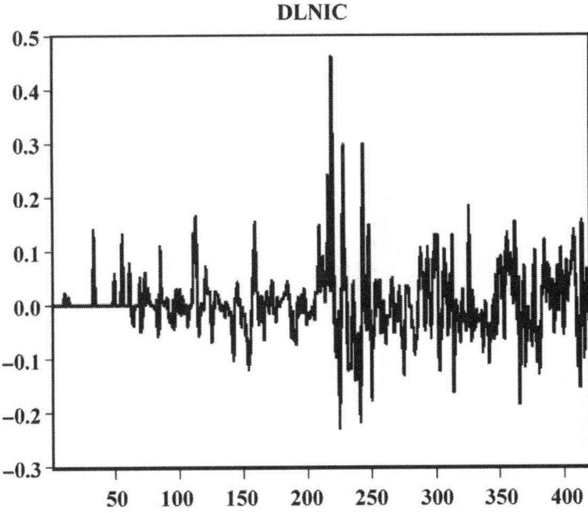

FIGURE 3.9 Commodity Price Returns Series, Nickel

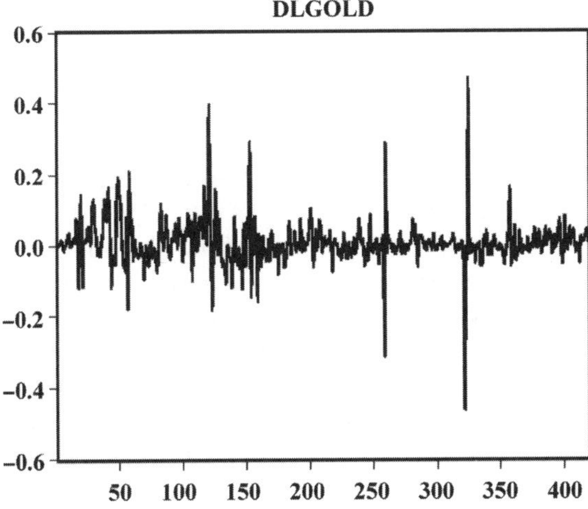

FIGURE 3.10 Commodity Price Returns Series, Gold

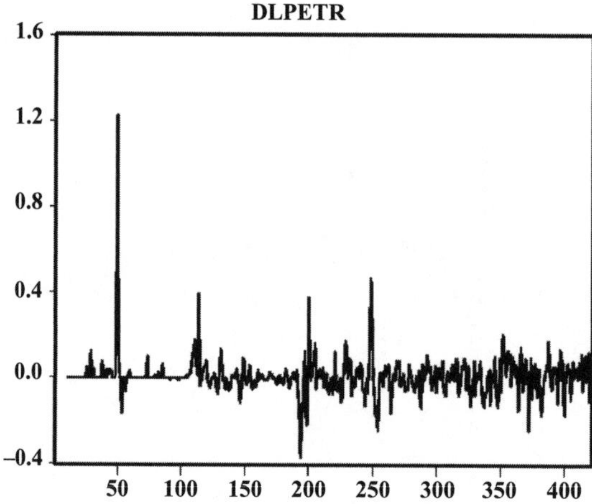

FIGURE 3.11 Commodity Price Returns Series, Crude Oil

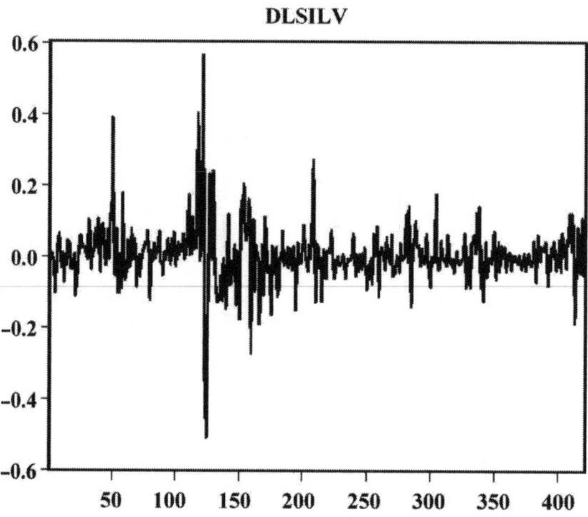

FIGURE 3.12 Commodity Price Returns Series, Silver

displays mostly small deviations from zero during the 34 years (408 months) for which data were obtained.

Table 3.1 shows the results of the Hristu-Varsakelis and Kyrtsou test, as well as the respective lags for the bivariate M-G model.

The results in Table 3.1 show the impact of the individual commodity series on inflation. Probabilities are generally close to zero with a few exceptions, for example: copper (prob=0.0824), nickel (prob=0.0881), and tin (prob=0.0917). Nevertheless, bidirectional causality or otherwise nonlinear feedback is achieved only for lead and crude oil, with crude oil (prob=0.0149) the dominant influence. Compared to the empirical findings of Kyrtsou and Labys (2006), the test for nonlinear causality brings new insights about the determination of the relationship between U.S. inflation

TABLE 3.1 Test for Nonlinear Causality*

X,Y	Relation	F statistic	Probability**	Lags for M-G
DLCPI, DLALUM	dlcpi→dlalum	2.3105	0.1293	$T_1=4$, $T_2=1$,
	dlalum→dlcpi	*4.0832*	*0.044*	$c_1=c_2=2$
DLCPI, DLCOP	dlcpi→dlcop	2.4196	0.1206	$T_1=T_2=1$,
	dlcop→dlcpi	*3.0322*	*0.0824*	$c_1=c_2=2$
DLCPI, DLGOLD	dlcpi→dlgold	0.2014	0.6538	$T_1=5$, $T_2=4$,
	dlgold→dlcpi	*5.5578*	*0.0189*	$c_1=c_2=2$
DLCPI, DLLEAD	dlcpi→dllead	*3.1487*	*0.0767*	$T_1=T_2=3$,
	dllead→dlcpi	*6.1904*	*0.0132*	$c_1=c_2=2$
DLCPI, DLNIC	dlcpi→dlnic	1.1729	0.2794	$T_1=T_2=4$,
	dlnic→dlcpi	*2.9228*	*0.0881*	$c_1=c_2=2$
DLCPI, DLPETR	dlcpi→dlpetr	*4.8246*	*0.0286*	$T_1=5$, $T_2=2$,
	dlpetr→dlcpi	*5.9844*	*0.0149*	$c_1=c_2=2$
DLCPI, DLPLAT	dlcpi→dlplat	0.3798	0.5381	$T_1=T_2=4$,
	dlplat→dlcpi	*5.7661*	*0.0168*	$c_1=c_2=2$
DLCPI, DLSILV	dlcpi→dlsilv	1.7160	0.1909	$T_1=4$, $T_2=3$,
	dlcop→dlcpi	*5.3213*	*0.0216*	$c_1=c_2=2$
DLCPI, DLTIN	dlcpi→dltin	0.9756	0.3239	$T_1=2$, $T_2=8$,
	dltin→dlcpi	*2.6912*	*0.0917*	$c_1=c_2=2$
DLCPI, DLTUN	dlcpi→dltun	0.4161	0.5193	$T_1=T_2=7$,
	dltun→dlcpi	*3.7991*	*0.0520*	$c_1=c_2=2$
DLCPI, DLZIN	dlcpi→dlzin	0.0013	0.9712	$T_1=4$, $T_2=3$,
	dlzin→dlcpi	*5.6552*	*0.0179*	$c_1=c_2=2$

*In model (1) for X we use the dlcpi series while for Y the primary commodity returns series is considered each time.
**If prob<0.05 (0.10), then at 5% (10%) we accept the H_α that A causes B. Values in italics indicate statistical significance.

and commodity price series. It comes out that the major part of the bidirectional comovement is largely driven by crude oil. Hence our analysis seems to confirm that among the selected commodity prices, crude oil prices appear to be a very important determining factor of fluctuations in U.S. inflation. Our work also confirms what was discovered in the works of Darby (1982), Ferderer (1996), Labys (2000), and Mork et al. (1994).

CONCLUSIONS

In this chapter we disaggregated the bidirectional causal relationship between U.S. inflation and the primary commodity price index based on the approach of Kyrtsou and Labys (2006), to analyze a number of individual commodity price series, in this case metals and energy prices. The application of a recent test developed by Hristu-Varsakelis and Kyrtsou (2006) reveals interdependence between the various price series. Unidirectional nonlinear causality is detected for all series except lead and crude oil. For these two commodities, an additional bidirectional nonlinear structure is identified. The results concerning crude oil are particularly interesting. They confirm the more general findings from studies of commodity prices and inflation, and particularly of the influence of crude oil prices–for example studies by Darby (1982), Ferderer (1996), and Mork et al. (1994). The results also confirm the lack of a relation between gold prices and inflation, which was discovered by Mahdevi and Zhou (1997).

These results have four implications:

1. In the United States, policy makers have neglected the impact of crude oil prices on inflation and have relied excessively on monetary policy to combat inflation.
2. The extremely high oil prices that we are currently experiencing should be considered with caution.
3. The asymmetry of the impact of U.S. inflation on commodity prices (in the sense that it affects only a few of them) could elucidate phases of economic process that aid commodity price stabilization.
4. Employing asymmetric versions of nonlinear causality tests could help policy makers better understand how commodity price fluctuations differ in upturns from downturns.

APPENDIX: PRICE SERIES USED

A list of price series that are used is presented next.

- **Aluminum.** London Metal Exchange, high grade, cash. From February 1970 to December 1978: virgin ingot, 99.5% purity, cif Europe. Prior to January 1970: virgin ingot, spot London (*Metal Bulletin,* London).
- **Copper.** London Metal Exchange, electrolytic wire bars, high grade, cash (*Metal Bulletin,* London).
- **Gold.** United Kingdom, 99.5% fine, London afternoon fixing, average of daily prices (*Metal Bulletin,* London).
- **Lead.** London Metal Exchange settlement and cash seller's price in warehouse excluding duty, range main United Kingdom ports, purity 99.97% Pb (*Lead and Zinc Statistics,* International Lead and Zinc Study Group, London).
- **Crude Oil.** Average of Dubai, United Kingdom Brent, and Alaska N. Slope crude prices, reflecting relatively equal consumption of medium, light, and heavy crude worldwide. Dubai Fateh 32 API, spot, fob Dubai; United Kingdom, Brent Bland 38 API, spot f.o.b. United Kingdom ports; United States, Alaskan N. Slope 27 API, spot, fob US Gulf of Mexico ports.
- **Platinum.** Monthly average of the London Fix PM, London Platinum and Palladium Market, $US/troy ounce. (Kitco.com).
- **Silver.** Handy & Harman, 99.5% grade refined, average daily quotations, New York (*Metal Bulletin,* London).
- **Tin.** Ex-works price Kuala Lumpur market (ITC reference price since July 4, 1972). Tin trade was suspended from October 24, 1985, to end of January 1986 (*Metal Week,* New York).
- **Tungsten.** Wolfram, cif European ports concentrates, basis minimum 65% WO3 (*Metal Bulletin,* London).

- **Zinc.** London Metal Exchange, settlement and cash seller's price in warehouses excluding duty, range main United Kingdom ports. Virgin zinc, high grade (*Lead and Zinc Statistics,* International Lead and Zinc Study Group, London).

REFERENCES

Beckerman, W., and T. Jenkinson. (1986). "What Stopped Inflation: Unemployment or Commodity Prices," *Economic Journal* 96: 39–54.

Borensztein, E., and C. Reinhart. (1994). "The Macroeconomic Determinants of Commodity Prices," Working Paper 94/9, International Monetary Fund, Washington, DC.

Bosworth, B., and R.Z. Lawrence. (1982). *Commodity Prices and the New Inflation.* Washington, DC: Brookings Institution.

Boughton, J.M., and W. Branson. (1988). "Commodity Prices as Leading Indicators of Inflation," Working Paper 88/87, Research Department, International Monetary Fund, Washington, DC.

Chu, K.-Y., and T.K. Morrison. (1984). "The 1981–82 Recession and Non-Oil Primary Commodity Prices," *Staff Papers* (International Monetary Fund) 31.1: 93–140.

Cooper, R.M., and R.Z. Lawrence. (1975). "The 1972–75 Commodity Price Boom," *Brookings Papers on Economic Activity* 3: 671–723.

Cristini, A. (1999). *Unemployment and Primary Commodity Prices.* London: Macmillan.

Darby, R. (1982). "The Price of Oil and World Inflation and Recession," *American Economic Review* 72: 738–751.

Durand, M., and S. Blondal. (1988). "Are Commodity Prices Leading Indicators of OECD Prices?"In O. Guvenen, W.C. Labys, and J.B. Lesourd, eds., *International Commodity Market Models.* London: Chapman and Hall.

Fama, E., and K.R. French. (1988). "Business Cycles and the Behavior of Metals Prices," *Journal of Finance* 43. 5: 1075–1093.

Ferderer, J.P. (1996). "Oil Price Volatility and the Macroeconomy," *Journal of Macroeconomics* 18.1: 1–26.

Fleisig, H., and S. van Wijnbergen. (1985). "Primary Commodity Prices, the Business Cycle and the Real Exchange Rate of the Dollar," Discussion Paper Series No. 90, Centre for Economic Policy Research.

Fraser, P., and C. Rogers. (1992). "Some Evidence on the Potential Role of Commodity Prices in the Formulation of Monetary Policy," *Manchester School* 60.4: 377–389.

Grilli, E., and M.C. Yang. (1988). "Primary Commodity Prices, Manufactured Goods Prices, and the Terms of Trade of Developing Countries: What the Long Run Shows," *World Bank Economic Review* 2: 11–47.

Hua, P. (1998). "On Primary Commodity Prices: The Impact of Macroeconomic/Monetary Shocks," *Journal of Policy Modeling* 20: 767–790.

Hristu-Varsakelis, D., and C. Kyrtsou. (2006). "Testing for Granger Causality in the Presence of Chaotic Dynamics," Working Paper, Working Group on Economic and Social Systems, University of Macedonia, Thessaloniki, Greece.

———. (2007). "Evidence for Nonlinear Asymmetric Causality in US Inflation, Metal and Stock Prices," Working Paper, Working Group on Economic and Social Systems, University of Macedonia, Thessaloniki, Greece.

Kyrtsou, C. (2005). "Evidence for Neglected Linearity in Noisy Chaotic Models," *International Journal of Bifurcation and Chaos* 15.10: 3391–3394.

Kyrtsou, C., and W. Labys. (2006). "Evidence for Chaotic Dependence between US Inflation and Commodity Prices," *Journal of Macroeconomics* 28.1: 256–266.

———. (2007). "Detecting Positive Feedback in Multivariate Time Series: The Case of Metal Prices and US Inflation," *Physica A*, 377.1: 227–229.

Kyrtsou, C., W. Labys, M. Terraza. (2004). "Noisy Chaotic Dynamics in Commodity Markets," *Empirical Economics* 29.3: 489–502.

Kyrtsou C., and A. Malliaris. (2007). "The Impact of Information Signals on Market Prices, When Agents Have Non-linear Trading Rules," *Economic Modelling*, accepted subject to revisions.

Kyrtsou, C., and M. Terraza. (2003). "Is It Possible to Study Chaotic and ARCH Behaviour Jointly? Application of a Noisy Mackey-Glass Equation with Heteroskedastic Errors to the Paris Stock Exchange Returns Series," *Computational Economics* 21: 257–276.

Kyrtsou, C., and A. Serletis. (2006). "Univariate Tests for Nonlinear Structure," *Journal of Macroeconomics* 28.1: 154–168.

Kyrtsou, C., and C. Vorlow. (2007). "Nonlinear Interest Rate Dynamics," *Journal of Macroeconomics*, forthcoming.

Labys, W. (2000). "Can World Market Volatility Upset the US Economy?" *Economic Directions*, St. Vincent College, Latrobe, PA.

Labys, W.C., and A. Maizels. (1993). "Commodity Price Fluctuations and Macroeconomic Adjustments in the Developed Economies," *Journal of Policy Modeling* 15.3: 335–352.

Mahdavi, S., and S. Zhou. (1997). "Gold and Commodity Prices as Leading Indicators of Inflation: Tests of Long-Run Relations and Predictive Performance," *Journal of Economics and Business* 49: 475–489.

Malliaris, A.G. (2005). "US Inflation and Commodity Prices: Analytical and Empirical Issues," *Journal of Macroeconomics* 28: 267–271.

Moore, G.H. (1988). "Inflation Cycles and Metals Prices," *Mineral Processing and Extracting Metallurgy Review* 3: 95–104.

Mork, K.A., T.H. Mysen, and O. Olsen. (1994). "Macroeconomic Responses to Oil Price Increases and Decreases in Seven OECD Countries." *Energy Journal* 15.4: 19–35.

UNCTAD. (Various issues). *Commodity Price Bulletin*. United Nations, Geneva.

CHAPTER 4

The Oil Price and the Dollar Reconsidered

Sadek Melhem and Michel Terraza

INTRODUCTION

Oil prices have historically been denominated in U.S. dollars. Therefore, the domestic price of oil in the currency of different countries may be quite different, depending on the exchange rate regime. For instance, in the euro zone increases in oil prices were cushioned from January 2002 to November 2006 by the sharp appreciation of the euro. The oil price rose by 211% in U.S. dollars. However, since the dollar depreciated by 44% against the euro, the jump in the oil price was only 115% in terms of euros. Figure 4.1 shows the evolution of the real price of oil in the U.S. dollar zone and in the euro zone, respectively. The dollar devaluation has been a relatively new pressure on the real oil price of crude oil (Amuzegar 1986).

The depreciation of the dollar, particularly against the euro, constitutes a key element in decisions to increase or decrease Organization of Petroleum Exporting Countries (OPEC) production quotas. The fact that the exports of the OPEC countries are denominated in dollars, but their imports come mainly from the euro zone and from Japan (yen), influences the decisions. The devaluation of the dollar against the euro and yen therefore directly affects OPEC members' economies (Alhajii, 2004; Mazraati, 2005). To maintain their purchasing power, they increase the price of oil. The fact that oil imports are denominated in U.S. dollars raises the question to what extent co.-movements occur between exchange rates and oil prices. This is even a more crucial question for those countries that not running fixed exchange rate pegs against the U.S. dollar.

PREVIOUS RESEARCH

Over the past 20 years, empirical research on the link between oil prices and the dollar found a positive relationship; that is, a rise in the oil price coincides with an appreciation of the dollar. Those investigations began with Golub (1983), continued and extended with Amano and Van Norden (1993, 1995, 1998), Lafrance and Van Norden (1995), Zhou (1995), and Chaudhuri and Betty (1998). More recently,

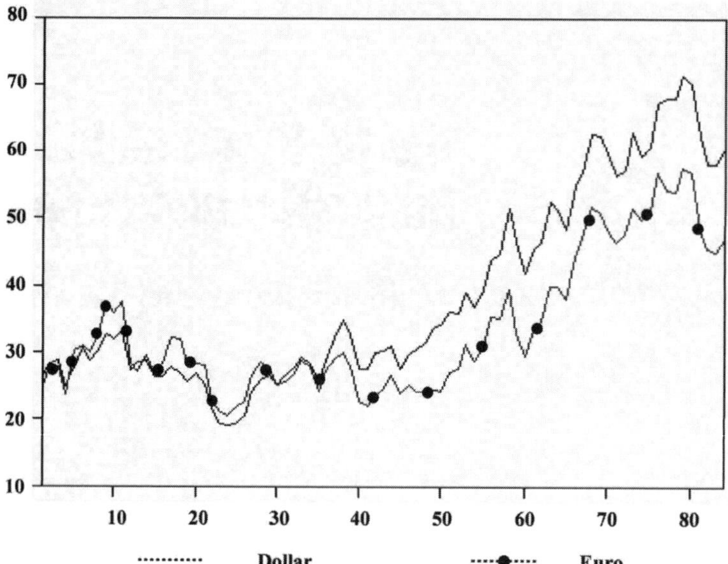

FIGURE 4.1 Oil Price in the Euro Zone and in the U.S. Dollar Zone
Source: International Energy Agency.

Mignon, Penot and Benassy (2005a, b) determined that the depreciation of the dollar between 2002 and 2004 was not primarily influenced by the evolution of oil prices but was caused by gaps in interest rates and external imbalances. The depreciation of the dollar also resulted from changes in U.S. monetary policy and to interest rates that were lower between mid-2001 and mid-2004 in the U.S. zone compared to the eurozone, as well as the deepening of the U.S. external deficit, which reached 6% of gross domestic product in 2005. These conditions seem to have dominated the link between oil prices and the dollar. The adopted point of view was that the oil price leads the exchange rate and the effect of the positive oil price shock was to increase the demand for the U.S. dollar, causing the dollar to appreciate (Clostermann and Schnatz 2000). However, Issa, Lafrance, and Murray (2006) found that the relationship between the two variables has changed: a rise in the oil price now coincides with a depreciation of the dollar in long run, in contrast to the earlier findings just mentioned.

We assert that the international demand for the U.S. dollar has increased since 2002, while the U.S. dollar has depreciated. In addition, during the period February 2005 to October 2007, U.S. interest rates rose higher than rates in the eurozone, although the gaps are now diminishing (Figure 4.2). Because of declining interest rates, the dollar continued to depreciate, reaching a record low of USD1.43 to euro1.00, while the oil price continued to increase, reaching USD100 per barrel in January 2008 and since then rising even higher.

Since 2000, changes in the price of oil have been an important source of macroeconomic fluctuations. Blanchard and Gali (2008) showed that the effects of oil price shocks have changed over time, with lesser effects on prices, wages, output, and employment; decreases in wage rigidities; increases in the influence of monetary

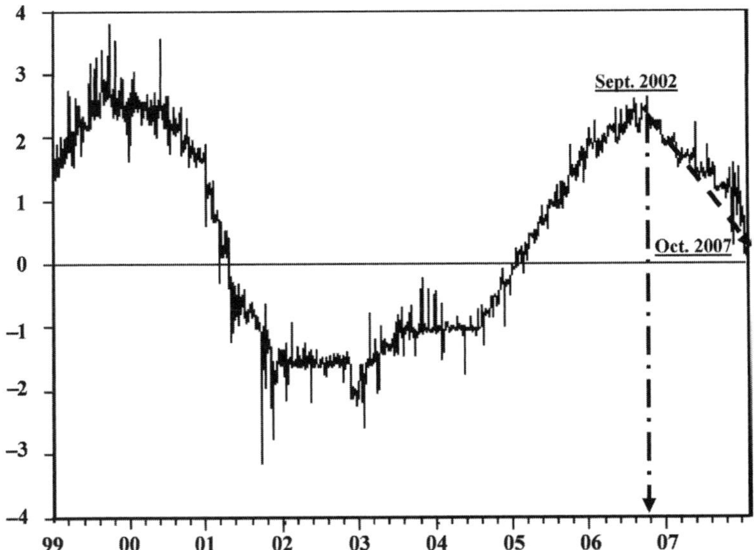

FIGURE 4.2 Gap between Interest Rates in the U.S. Dollar Zone and the Eurozone
Sources: U.S. Federal Reserve Bank and European Central Bank.

policy; and last decreases in the share of oil in consumption and in production. These various issues raise the question of whether changes in the impacts of oil prices are the reason or the result of the changes in the nature of relationship between oil prices and the exchange rate. One would also like to know the nature of the influence of monetary policy on this relationship and the predominance of exchange rate policies relative to that of oil price behavior.

To answer such questions, we study the sources of the relationship between the oil price and the USD exchange rate from 1999 to 2007 and the behavior of the dollar bilateral real exchange rate against a basket of five currencies.

Empirical Evidence

We begin by examining daily observations of real oil prices (West Texas Intermediate [WTI]) on the New York Mercantile Exchange (NYMEX), and USD real bilateral exchange rates from January 1, 1999, to May 31, 2007, some 2,163 observations. Sources include the U.S. Federal Reserve Bank, European Central Bank, International Energy Agency, and OANDA (international exchange rates). The oil price series is the U.S. dollar spot price of oil deflated by the U.S. consumer price index. We define the real U.S. dollar's bilateral exchange rate against a basket of five currencies: euro (LDER), British pound (LPER), Canadian dollar (LCER), Swiss franc (LFER), and Japanese yen (LYER). The variables are in logarithmic form.

Table 4.1 refers to the OPEC price band. OPEC established a basket price based on the average prices of seven different crude oil streams. It uses the basket price to monitor conditions in the world oil market. One of the measures based on the basket price is the basket price band. If the basket price stays above the upper limit of the

TABLE 4.1 Real Value of OPEC Oil Price Band, Corrected by Dollar-Euro Exchange Rate

	1999	2000	2001	2002	2003	2004	2005	2006
Average Exchange rate \$/£	1.066	0.923	0.896	0.945	1.132	1.243	1.244	1.256
OPEC Price Band (USD22–28)	23.45–29.84	20.30–5.90	19.70–25.10	20.80–26.50	24.90–31.70	27.40–34.80	27.40–34.90	27.70–35.20

Sources: OPEC, U.S. Federal Reserve Bank, and European Central Bank.

band for 20 consecutive trading days or below the lower limit for 10 consecutive trading days, then OPEC will consider making production adjustments (Kreil 2004).

Table 4.1 compares the evolution of the upper and lower limit of the band of OPEC basket prices (USD22.00–28.00), corrected by the real exchange rate of dollar against the euro (LDER). During 1999–2001, we observe that when the dollar appreciates, the width of OPEC's price band decreases and that since 2002, the oil price increases when the dollar depreciates. Figure 4.1shows that a depreciation of the US dollar results in a decrease in oil prices outside the United States.

In Figure 4.3, we compare the evolution of the dollar real exchange rates against the basket currencies mentioned earlier, with the real oil price (LOIL) between January 1999 and May 2007, expressed in logarithms. We note that the oil price is more volatile than the exchange rates, and the two variables have an opposite trend for four of the five currencies.

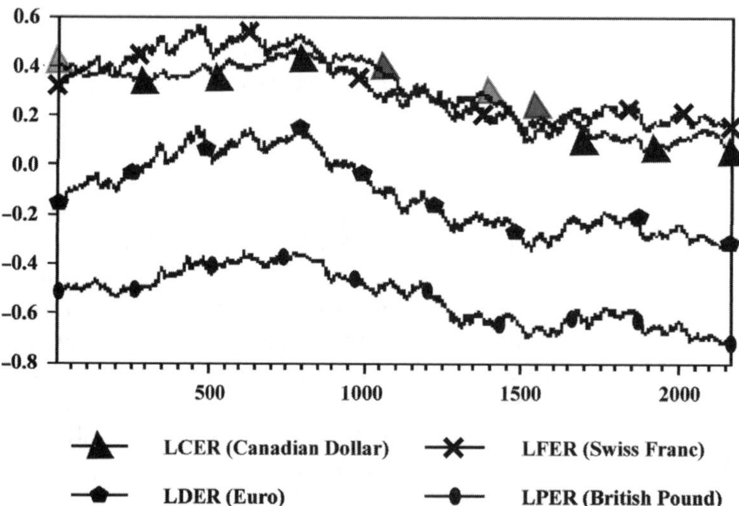

FIGURE 4.3 Dollar Real Exchange Rate against the Euro, British Pound, Canadian Dollar, and Swiss Franc
Sources: International Energy Agency, U.S. Federal Reserve Bank, European Central Bank, and OANDA.

As shown in Figure 4.4, the Japanese yen is the exception. These observations were confirmed by the linear correlation coefficients calculated from January 1999 to May 2007 between the oil price and the real exchange rates of the dollar against the basket of five currencies: −0.70 with the LDER; −0.71 with the LFER; −0.76 with the LPER; and −0.89 with the LCER; but only −0.28 with the LYER.

On average, the oil price increased when the dollar depreciated (scissor movement; see Figure 4.5). An appreciation of the dollar leads to a lower oil price denominated in dollar (Austvik 1987).

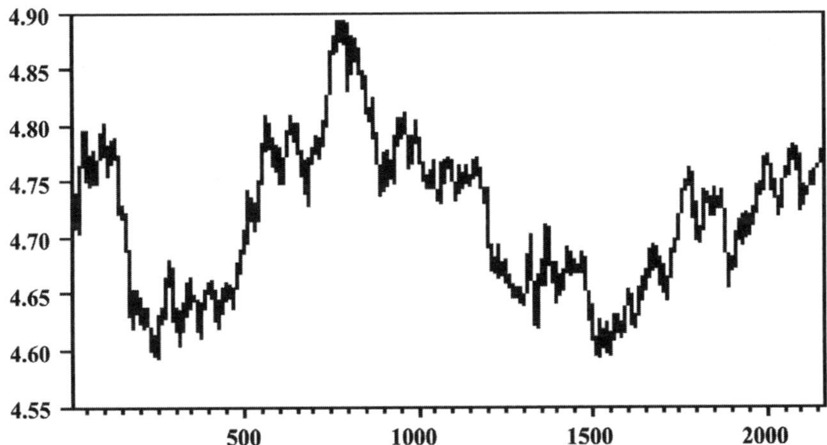

FIGURE 4.4 Dollar Real Exchange Rate against the Japanese Yen
Sources: International Energy Agency, U.S. Federal Reserve Bank, European Central Bank and OANDA.

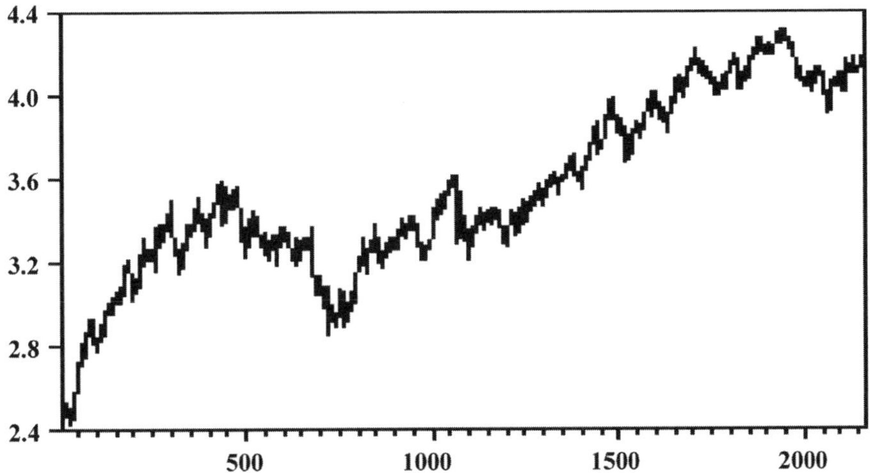

FIGURE 4.5 Evolution of Real Dollar Oil Price
Sources: International Energy Agency, U.S. Federal Reserve Bank, European Central Bank and OANDA.

EVALUATING THE COINTEGRATING RELATIONSHIP

To evaluate the existence a stable long-term relation between the exchange rate and the oil price, cointegration analyses between the two variables demands that we first perform tests of their individual stationarity (Burbidge and Harrison 1984). The econometric model is based on Bourbonnais and Terraza (2008). We employ Augmented Dickey-Fuller (ADF) (Dickey and Fuller 1979, 1981) and Phillips-Perron (1988) (PP) and Perron (1989) unit root tests, the latter including an exogenous structural break. The test results are in Tables 4.2 and 4.3. The results confirm that both series are integrated of order 1.

We next study the cointegration between the exchange rate and the oil price, employing the trace test proposed by Johansen (1991) and by Johansen and Juselius (1992, 1994). According to the trace test results in Table 4.4, we reject the null

TABLE 4.2 Unit Root Test of ADF and PP

	LDER	LPER	LFER	LCER
ADF	0.15	0.68	−0.70	−1.62
ADF(-1)	−42.44*	−44.74*	−47.22*	−47.03*
PP	0.15	0.69	−1.231	−1.16
PP(-1)	−42.44*	−41.50*	−44.07*	−43.61*

*Rejection of the null hypothesis of a unit root at the 5% significance level.
Model without intercept and without trend.

TABLE 4.3 Unit Root Test with Exogenous Structural Break

	Min T-statistic	Critical Value (5%)	Break Point
LOIL	−2,89*	−3,87	Dec-2001
LYER	3.10*	3.80	Jan-2001

*Rejection of the null hypothesis of a unit root at the 5% significance level.
Model with intercept and trend for LOIL and without trend for LYER. Test procedure based on Perron (1989).

TABLE 4.4 Cointegration Test

Series	Null Hypothesis	Trace Stat	P-value
LOIL-LDER	No relation	16.46*	0.050
LOIL-LPER	No relation	15.51*	0.007
LOIL-LFER	No relation	18.27*	0.004
LOIL-LCER	No relation	17.74*	0.008
LOIL-LYER	No relation	9.25 **	0.72

*Reject the null hypothesis at 5% significance level.
**Accept the null hypothesis at 5% significance level.
Model with intercept and without trend.

hypothesis of no cointegration between oil prices and the exchange rate of basket currencies at the 5% significance level, with the exception of the Japanese yen. Therefore, there exists a long-term equilibrium relationship between the oil price and the real bilateral exchange rate of the U.S. dollar, except in the case of the yen. The lag order *k* of the model has been determined by estimating an unrestricted vector autoregression (VAR) VAR also has a very specific and well-established meaning in time-series analysis (Vector Autoregression) model in levels and using the information criteria proposed by AIC (Akaike's information criterion) and BIC (Bayesian information criterion).

The results of the VAR estimation (Table 4.5) show that a depreciation of the U.S dollar coincides with a rise in oil prices on average. The sensitivity of the relationship is stronger for the pound sterling and Canadian dollar (3.05) than for the euro, Swiss franc (2.2), and the Japanese yen (1.85). These sensitivity differences likely result from the nature of the exchange rate regime for each of these currencies relative to the dollar, which is fixed for the yen but floating for the other currencies. In addition, distance and national borders can explain part of the elasticity and real exchange rate volatility. For example, Engel and Rogers (1996) suggest that the variation of the price is much higher for two cities located in different countries than for two equidistant cities in the same country.

We conclude that the residuals of the VAR regressions follow an innovation process, but the ADF unit root tests indicate that all of the residual series are stationary, meaning that oil prices and exchange rates series are cointegrated. The trace test confirmed this finding. In addition, the explained covariance between the oil price and exchange rates is significant, except for the yen (LYER). We can explain the case of the yen by the break observed in the time-series trend of this currency. The break seems to be the result of the direct control asserted by the Japanese central bank over the exchange rate (the other central banks let their currencies float); the fact that many Japanese invest in Australia and other markets, where interest rates are higher; and the immense U.S. dollar reserves held by the Japanese central bank.

The cointegration between the oil price and the exchange rates allows us to estimate an error correction model (ECM) to describe the dynamic adjustment of the variable to the equilibrium given by the long-term relationship. The model takes the

TABLE 4.5 Results of VAR Estimation

Estimated Equation	R^2	ADF Unit Root Test
$\widehat{LOIL_t} = 3.29 - 2.05LDER_t$	0.50	−3.90*
$\widehat{LOIL_t} = 1.89 - 3.06LPER_t$	0.51	−3.77*
$\widehat{LOIL_t} = 4.26 - 2.29LFER_t$	0.57	−3.69*
$\widehat{LOIL_t} = 4.40 - 3.05LCER_t$	0.79	−4.18*
$\widehat{LOIL_t} = 12.26 - 1.85LYER_t$	0.08	−2.10 **

*Reject the null hypothesis at 5% significance level.

**Reject the null hypothesis at 10% significance level.

Estimated model: $\widehat{LOIL_t} = \hat{\alpha} + \hat{\beta}\hat{X}_{t,i}$, LOIL is the real oil price (log).

form shown next. We only present the model formulation for $LOIL_t$ and $LDER_t$ as an example.

$$\Delta LOIL_t = \delta_1 z_{t-1} + \sum_{i=1}^{k} \theta_i \Delta LOIL_{t-i} + \sum_{j=1}^{q} \phi_j \Delta LDER_{t-j} + \mu_1 + \varepsilon_{1,t} \tag{4.1a}$$

$$\Delta LDER_t = \delta_2 z_{t-1} + \sum_{i} \theta'_i \Delta LDER_{t-i} + \sum_{j} \phi'_j \Delta LOIL_{t-j} + \mu_2 + \varepsilon_{2,t} \tag{4.1b}$$

where $z_t = LOIL_t - \hat{\beta} LDER_t$ are the residuals of the long-term relationship between the exchange rate and the oil price at time t

k and d = lag lengths μ_1, μ_2 = constants

$\varepsilon_{1,t}, \varepsilon_{2,t}$ = white-noise error terms

δ_i $(i = 1,2) < 0$ and $|\delta_1| + |\delta_2| \neq 0$ = equilibrium return conditions

The results reported in Table 4.6 show that the error correction term has a negative impact on the exchange rate series (LDER, LPER, and LFER) transformed to log variations, and a negative and significant impact on the other exchange rates series in log variations (LCER and LYER). The adjustment to equilibrium is very low, and so is the adjustment speed (between −0.001 and −0.0004). The adjustment speed (−0.001 and 0.0004) holds for the daily frequency of our data and corresponds to approximately 1% on an annual basis. Therefore, there is a no mean-reverting process of the exchange rates (LDER, LPER, and LFER) to their long-term target; that is, there is no long-run mean-reverting process of European currencies. We also note that the error correction term is negative in the oil price equation in all series, meaning that there is no mean-reverting process for the oil price toward its long-term equilibrium value.

EVALUATING THE CAUSAL RELATIONSHIP

The existence of a cointegration relationship between oil prices and the exchange rate, with the noted exception of the yen, means that at least one of them Granger-causes the other. The direction of causality and the nature (endogenous or exogenous) of the included variables is therefore our next interest. We test the existence of long-term causality between the variables using endogenous tests using two-stage least square regression (2SLS) to determine whether the exchange rate and/or oil prices are endogenous. This means that we need to test whether the long-term relationship, captured by the residuals, is significant in the equation of exchange rates and oil prices, transformed to log variations.

The results of the 2SLS test are in Table 4.7. They show that the oil price is endogenous in its relation to the three series LDER, LPER, and LFER, while both series are endogenous in the relation between LCER and oil prices. The oil price is the endogenous variable in the relationship with LYER. That means that the disturbance term of the exchange rates LDER, LPER, and LFER is correlated with, and cause, the oil price. In other words, the deviation from the long-term target significantly influences oil prices but does not affect the exchange rate of the euro (LDER), Swiss franc (LFER), and British pound (LPER), respectively.

TABLE 4.6 Error Correction Model

	ΔLOIL	ΔLDER		ΔLOIL	ΔLFER		ΔLOIL	ΔLPER
Z_{t-1}	−0.005 [−3.35]	−0.000 [−2.13]	Z_{t-1}	−0.005 [−3.02]	−0.001 [−2.3]	Z_{t-1}	−0.007 [−3.49]	−0.006 [−1.76]
ΔLOIL(-1)	−0.038 [−1.78]	−0.005 [−1.28]	**ΔLOIL(-1)**	−0.039 [−1.81]	−0.011 [−2.00]	**ΔLOIL(-1)**	−0.038 [−1.89]	−0.005 [−1.27]
ΔLOIL(-2)	−0.039 [−1.82]	−0.003 [−0.05]	**ΔLOIL(-2)**	−0.036 [−1.71]	−0.002 [−0.41]	**ΔLOIL(-2)**	−0.038 [−1.79]	−0.003 [−0.95]
ΔLDER(-1)	0.023 [0.27]	−0.007 [−0.33]	**ΔLDER(-1)**	0.086 [1.08]	−0.015 [−0.71]	**ΔLDER(-1)**	0.185 [1.78]	−0.038 [−1.77]
ΔLDER(-2)	0.015 [−1.18]	−0.011 [−0.55]	**ΔLDER(-2)**	0.010 [1.12]	−0.003 [−0.14]	**ΔLDER(-2)**	0.034 [0.33]	−0.024 [−1.12]
C	0.009 [1.79]	−0.001 [−0.59]	C	0.002 [1.77]	−0.001 [−0.29]	C	0.0009 [1.79]	−9.45E [−0.68]
	ΔLOIL	ΔLCER		ΔLOIL	ΔLYER			
Z_{t-1}	−0.009 [−3.52]	−0.001 [−1.87]	Z_{t-1}	−0.001 [−1.21]	−0.0004 [−1.76]			
ΔLOIL(-5)	−0.021 [−0.97]	0.001 [0.38]	**ΔLOIL(-1)**	−0.073 [−1.71]	−0.013 [−2.55]			
ΔLOIL(-7)	−0.022 [−1.03]	−0.007 [−0.09]	**ΔLOIL(-2)**	−0.038 [−1.78]	−0.011 [−2.24]			
ΔLCER(-5)	0.164 [1.35]	−0.039 [−1.82]	**ΔLYER(-1)**	0.124 [1.42]	0.008 [0.39]			
ΔLCER(-7)	0.148 [−1.23]	0.040 [1.90]	**ΔLYER(-2)**	−0.080 [−0.91]	−0.004 [−0.28]			
C	0.0008 [1.70]	−0.0001 [−1.56]	C	0.0008 [1.69]	8.95E [0.56]			

[] contains the t-statistics and Δ is the first-difference operator.
Model is with intercept and without trend.

TABLE 4.7 Results of Causal Endogeneity Tests (P-value)

Variable	P-Value	Variable	P-Value	Variable	P-Value
LDER	0.0136*	LFER	0.0295*	LYER	0.9146
Oil Prices	0.2019	Oil Prices	0.5321	Oil Prices	0.5055*
LPER	0.0067*	LCER	0.0025*		
Oil Prices	0.0858	Oil Prices	0.0265*		

*Accept the null hypothesis of endogeneity test, where the disturbance term of relationship $LOIL_t = \alpha + \beta \hat{X}_{t,i} + \varepsilon_t$ correlated with the endogenous variable.

Concerning the direction of causality between the two variables (oil prices and exchange rates, respectively), we estimate a VAR model in levels and we apply Granger causality tests. The null hypothesis is one of no causality. Table 4.8 shows that in the first four series (LDER, LFER, LPER, and LCER), we do not reject the hypothesis that oil prices do not Granger-cause exchange rates, but we reject the hypothesis that exchange rates do not Granger-cause oil prices, except the for Canadian dollar. In the last series (LYER), however, we do not reject the hypothesis that exchange rates do not Granger-cause oil prices, but we reject the hypothesis that oil prices do not Granger-cause exchange rates. Thus, the results show that the causality runs from exchange rates to oil prices.

CONCLUSIONS

The relationship between oil prices and the real bilateral dollar exchange rates has complex features because its nature and its direction have changed over time. During our study period, cointegration results show that there exists a long-term

TABLE 4.8 Causality Tests (P-value)

	VAR(1)	VAR(2)	VAR(4)	VAR(6)	VAR(10)	VAR(50)	VAR(100)
OIL→LDER	0.237	0.055	0.139	0.372	0.558	0.181	0.231
LDER→OIL	0.014*	0.038*	0.234	0.140	0.148	0.093	0.011*
OIL→LPER	0.097	0.144	0.346	0.481	0.696	0.121	0.391
LPER→OIL	0.007*	0.004*	0.035*	0.061	0.069	0.480	0.429
OIL→LFER	0.283	0.225	0.118	0.261	0.178	0.183	0.230
LFER→OIL	0.032*	0.047*	0.270	0.077	0.100	0.109	0.051*
OIL→LCER	0.032*	0.006*	0.007*	0.047*	0.0005*	0.002*	0.049*
LCER→OIL	0.002*	0.008*	0.089	0.119	0.249	0.755	0.800
OIL→LYER	0.520	0.040*	0.008*	0.009*	0.020*	0.087	0.013*
LYER→OIL	0.948	0.434	0.382	0.361	0.136	0.623	0.855

Exchange rate→OIL is for the null hypothesis of no causality from exchange rate to oil prices. *OIL→Exchange rate* is for the null hypothesis of no causality from oil prices to exchange rate.

**Reject null hypothesis at the 5% significance level.*

relationship between the exchange rates and oil price, except for the Japanese yen. The depreciation of the dollar during the years 2002 to 2007 could be caused by some shifting of official dollar reserves previously into euros—for example, in China, Japan, Russia, and Iran—the evolution of monetary policy in the United States, and current account deficits of the United States. This disequilibrium led to a sharp depreciation of the dollar (Cooper 2006). Increases in the oil price resulted from an increase in global oil demand caused by economic growth of, for example, 4.4% in the United States (2004), 3.0% in Japan (2004), more than 11% in China (2007), and 8% in India (2007). The depreciation of the dollar and speculation on oil futures also contributed.

These strong forces dominated the relationship between oil prices and exchange rates. The results of the causality tests made it clear that the direction of causality was from exchange rates to oil prices, and not vice versa, except in the case of the Japanese yen. The period studied is that between January 1999 and May 2007. The results suggest that a depreciation of the dollar could lead to a long-run rise in oil prices. However, there are differences in sensitivity in the relationship between exchange rates and oil prices. We can explain this phenomenon by the nature of the different exchange rate regimes in each of these currencies and by geographic distances and national borders with the United States.

In conclusion, the relation between the price of oil and the exchange rate, especially the dollar-euro exchange rate, has a significant impact because the depreciation of the dollar against the euro constitutes a key element in decisions to change OPEC production quotas. Exports of OPEC countries are denominated in dollars, but their imports come mainly from the euro- and yen zones. The devaluation of the dollar, therefore, adversely affects their economies' purchasing power. The desire to counteract this effect is what is currently driving oil prices upward.

REFERENCES

Alhajji, A.F. (2004). "The Impact of Dollar Devaluation on the World Oil Industry: Do Exchange Rates Matter? *Middle East Economic Survey* 47: 33.

Amano, R.A., and S. Van Norden. (1993). "Oil Prices and the Rise and Fall of the US Real Exchange Rate," Working Paper 93-15, Bank of Canada, Ottawa, ON.

———. (1995). "Exchange Rates and Oil Price," Working Paper, Bank of Canada.

———. (1998). "Oil Prices and the Rise and Fall of the US Real Exchange Rate," *Journal of International Money and Finance* 17: 299–316.

Amezegar, J. (1986). "OPEC and the Dollar Dilemma," *Foreign Affairs* 56: 740.

Austvik, O.G. (1987). "Oil Prices and the Dollar Dilemma," *OPEC Review* 4, www.kaldor.no/energy/OPEC8712.pdf.

Blanchard, O., and J. Gali. (2008). "The Macroeconomic Effects of Oil Shocks: Why Are the 2000s So Different from the 1970s?" Centre for Economic Policy Research, Discussion Paper Series, No. 6631, London.

Bourbonnais R., and M. Terraza. (2008). *Analyse des séries temporelles: Applications à l'économie et à la gestion*, 2nd ed. Paris: Dunod.

Burbidge, J., and A. Harrison. (1984). "Testing for the Effects of the Oil Price Rises Using Vector Auto Regressions," *International Economic Review* 25: 459–484.

Chaudhuri, K., and B.C. Daniel. (1998). "Long-Run Equilibrium Real Exchange Rates and Oil Prices," *Economics Letters* 58.2: 231–238.

Clostermann J., and B. Schnatz. (2000). "The Determinants of the Euro-Dollar Exchange Rates," Discussion Paper 2/00, Economic Research Group of the Deutsche Bundesbank, http://papers.ssrn.com/sol3/papers.cfm?abstract_id=229472#PaperDownload.

Cooper, R. (2006). "Almost a Century of Central Bank Cooperation," Bank for International Settlements Working Paper 198. Basel, Switzerland, www.bis.org/publ/work198.pdf.

Dickey, D.A., and W.A. Fuller. (1979). "Distribution of the Estimators for Autoregressive Time Series with Unit Root," *Journal of the American Statistical Association* 74: 427–481.

———. (1981). "Likelihood Ratio Statistics for Autoregressive Time Series with Unit Root," *Econometrica* 49: 1057–1072.

Engel, R.F., and C.W.J. Granger. (1987). "Co-Integration and Error Correction: Representation, Estimation and Testing," *Econometrica* 55: 251–276.

Engel, C., and J. Rogers. (1996). "How Wide Is the Border?" *American Economic Review* 86.5: 1112–1125.

Golub, S.S. (1983). "Oil Prices and Exchange Rates," *Economic Journal* 93: 576–593.

Issa, R., R. Lafrance, and J. Murray. (2006). "The Turning Black Tide: Energy Prices and the Canadian Dollar" Bank of Canada Working Paper 2006, 29. Ottawa, Ontario: International Department, Bank of Canada. www.bankofcanada.ca/en/res/wp/2006/wp06-29.pdf.

Johanson, S. (1988). "Statistical Analysis of Cointegration Vectors," *Journal of Economics Dynamics and Control* 12: 231–254.

———. (1991). Cointegration in Partial Systems and the Efficiency of Single-Equation Analysis," *Journal of Econometrics* 52: 389–402.

Johanson, S., and K. Juselius. (1990). "Maximum Likelihood Estimation and Inference on Cointegration with Application to the Demand for Money," *Oxford Bulletin of Economics and Statistics* 52: 169–210.

———. (1992). "Testing Structural Hypotheses in a Multivariate Cointegration Analysis of the PPP and the UIP for UK," *Journal of Econometrics* 53: 211–244.

———. (1994). "Identification of the Long Run and the Short Run Structure, An Application to the ISLM-Model," *Journal of Econometrics* 63.1: 7–36.

Kreil, E. (2004). "OPEC." *EIA Country Analysis Briefs*, U.S. Energy Information Administration, www.eia.doe.gov/emeu/cabs/opec.pdf.

Lafrance, R., and S. Van Norden. (1995). "Exchange rate fundamentals and the Canadian dollar," *Bank of Canada Review*, Spring: —17–31.

Mazraati, M. (2005). "Real Purchasing Power of Oil Revenues for OPEC Member Countries: A Broad Currency Basket and Dynamic Trade Pattern Approach," OPEC Review 29.3: 153–175.

Mignon, V., A. Benassy, and A. Penot. (2005a). "China and the Relationship between the Oil Price and the Dollar," Centre d'études prospectives et d'information internationale (CEPII), Working Paper 2005-16, www.cepii.fr/anglaisgraph/workpap/pdf/2005/wp05-16.pdf.

———. (2005b), "Oil and the Dollar: A Two-Way Game," *La Lettre du CEPII* 250, www.cepii.fr/anglaisgraph/publications/lettre/pdf/2005/let250ang.pdf.

Perron, P. (1989). "The Great Crash, the Oil Price Shock, and the Unit Root Hypothesis," *Econometrica* 57: 1316–1401.

Phillips, P., and P. Perron. (1988). "Testing for Unit Root in Time Series Regression," *Biometrika* 75: 347–353.

Zhou, S. (1995). "The Response of Real Exchange Rates to Various Economic Shocks," *Southern Economic Journal* 61: 936–954.

PART Two

Inventory Dynamics and Price Behavior

Inventories are the key to understanding the dynamic behavior of the economy. One of my teachers once said that without the possibility of keeping an inventory, the economy is like a fish market before the invention of refrigeration. Markets must clear at the end of every day, and what cannot be sold is given or thrown away. Day-to-day price and quantity changes may be more volatile, since market participants cannot rely on inventories to satisfy demand that exceeds production or to smooth production, that is, keep production going in the short run, and produce to inventory, in the knowledge that the time will soon come when demand exceed production. Thus, inventory allows a steadier rate of production, as long as the cost of carrying an inventory does not outweigh the benefits of not having to adjust production.

However, with the accumulation of inventory, the maximum difference between the high of the market and the low of the market is much greater, because without inventory, there is no stock accumulated over time, only what is produced on any given day. This becomes important in a downturn. Nobody worries a great deal about carrying a little extra inventory when demand pressures cause rising prices that increase the value of inventories. However, the same is not true in a market downturn. At first, when most firms still carry sizable inventories, none of them will be eager to cut prices and thereby lower the book value of their inventory. Thus, in the initial phase of the downturn, prices may be sticky. However, once a sufficient number of firms have reduced their stocks, prices will begin to adjust. Firms that are still carrying large inventories when market prices start dropping will experience asset value losses. Depending on the size of their remaining inventory, that loss could become a threat to their survival. In summary, inventories drive the dynamics of individual firms, markets, and whole economies.

The four chapters in Part Two make important contributions to our understanding of inventories. The authors use the latest time-series techniques to study the relationships between prices and inventories. Three chapters look at metals markets, and the fourth chapter studies the wine market. The methodological issues are interesting, but there are also challenging definitional questions to be resolved. In a theoretical account, such as the one just provided, we take the meaning of the word *inventory* as given. In empirical applications, however, it is not always clear what should or should not count. For example, are private wine collections inventories?

In Chapter 5, the author studies the relationship between metal prices and inventories and between primary metal and scrap metal prices. Scrap metal also is an inventory of sorts, albeit of a lesser quality. Chapter 6 looks at the supply of storage, and Chapter 7 tests the existence of asymmetric causality between commodity prices and inventories in the case of metals. We have already explained why this is important. Chapter 8 looks at the growing international wine market. Chapters 5 through 7 use data collected by the authors and that have not yet been widely analyzed. Thus the results of their analyses are new and should be of interest to many who study commodity markets. The scale of all four chapters is at the industry level.

Together the four chapters form an informative and innovative contribution to the inventory dynamics literature. Along with the chapters in Part One, they provide methodologies and techniques, as well as applications and illustrations, to analyze and better understand commodity markets in a very dynamic economic environment.

CHAPTER 5

Time-Varying Ratios of Primary and Scrap Metal Prices

Importance of Inventories

Irene M. Xiarchos

INTRODUCTION

Recycled materials act both as inputs into the production of and as substitutes for refined primary materials. As a consequence, fluctuations in demand and supply in the recycled material markets both influence and are influenced by the primary material markets. These links are evident in terms of prices, which express the market information available at every point in time.

In the 1970s and 1980s, many studies examined links between primary and scrap metal fundamentals, including prices, through structural modeling. Fisher and Owen (1981) expressed explicit structural relationships for scrap and primary aluminum and indicated a connection between primary and scrap prices. Employing a traditional structural analysis, Hashimoto (1983) argued that steel price fluctuations and comovements of primary and scrap steel prices are due to the industry's inherent inelasticities and its sensitivity to the business cycle. Stollery (1983) modeled the demand and supply relationships among scrap, primary input, and primary output for copper and steel. His empirical model of copper showed that the scrap price varies in direct proportion to the primary London Metal Exchange (LME) price.

Although some studies found intertemporal linkages between primary and scrap prices, they assumed that the relationship was stable. Additionally, even though metal markets are known to be inelastic in the short run and to follow flow and stock adjustment processes toward equilibrium, the majority of studies examining primary and scrap price links have been based on the concept of rapid market clearing. As a result, the literature has neglected disequilibrium between primary and scrap prices. Only Stollery's (1983) and Taylor's (1979) acknowledged the difference between primary and scrap copper prices, mostly as an investigation of the refiner's margin, and the annual studies of copper recycling from the U.S. Geological Survey (USGS), which include an examination of the difference between primary and scrap copper prices.

Understanding the changing character of primary and scrap price links is important, not only for those involved in the recycling sector, but also for those involved with the primary metal market, since greater than 50% of the industry's supply comes from recycling (USGS 2000). This study revives the interest in the primary and scrap market links and shows, through time-series methods, that the relationship between primary and scrap prices is not constant over time but dependent on market forces.

More specifically, this study shows that primary and scrap prices have a long-run equilibrium relationship but that their short-run interaction is unstable. This is important since metal products manufacturers and dealers in scrap metal markets may have to make different choices in the short run than in the long run. The changing relationship of the spread between primary and scrap prices is described in terms of their price ratios. Price ratios reflect both equilibrium and disequilibrium adjustments and are closely related to price differences. For example, $PS - aPP = 0$ is the same as $PS/PP = a$. In past studies, price differences have provided the only reference to short-run disequilibrium between primary and scrap metal markets. Price ratios vary over time, but price ratio series are mean-reverting in many cases. The mean reversion of primary-to-scrap price ratios is important for scrap metal markets, since it implies that policies that try to promote recycling through price manipulations may be able to decrease the spread between primary and scrap prices in the short term but may not lead to sustainable results.

The analysis also demonstrates that price ratio fluctuations are related to market conditions and to the physical availability of metal in the market, as reflected in inventory levels. Thus, increasing the role of scrap in metal markets through technological improvements and higher market integration could have a stronger impact on scrap demand and supply than price-based policies. The theoretical explanation for the relationship between price ratios and inventories is that production-smoothing incentives in metal production lead to tighter connections between primary and scrap prices when inventories are lower than when inventories are higher. In a tight market, the spread between primary and scrap prices becomes smaller. When supply is ample, as indicated by high inventory accumulation, the spread between primary and scrap prices becomes wider. Establishment of this relationship provides market participants with valuable insight into the relative behavior of the primary and scrap metal sectors by allowing them to anticipate and forecast primary-to-scrap price spreads.

PRIMARY AND SCRAP PRICE BEHAVIOR

The four metal markets—aluminum, copper, lead, and zinc—are analyzed, utilizing U.S. average monthly prices for the period 1984 to 2000, except aluminum, which is studied for the period 1985 to 2000, and zinc, which is studied for the period 1984 to 1996. Primary prices represent values for refined metal, which can be produced either from primary ore/concentrate or from scrap metal. The primary prices used are the producer price of primary aluminum (PPA), the producer price of delivered copper cathode (PPC), the New York delivery prices of the primary producers' pig lead (PPL), and the domestic and foreign producer prices for primary zinc slab delivered in the

United States (PPZ). PPA and PPC were obtained from USGS specialists P. Plunkert and D.L. Edelstein, respectively. PPL is published in the *Commodity Research Bureau Commodity Yearbook*, and PPZ is available in the *Metal Statistics* publication of the American Metal Market. The length of each time series is determined by data availability and compatibility. Commercial scrap metal can be divided into new and old scrap. New scrap, such as cuttings and turnings, is generated during processing and fabrication of metal products and is usually denoted as No.1 scrap. It is desirable for its higher quality and for its consistency in terms of content and supply. New scrap prices included in the study are for aluminum clippings (PS1A), for brass mills No. 1 copper scrap (PS1C), and for new zinc clippings (PSZ). Old scrap, usually labeled No. 2 scrap, is metal incorporated in postconsumer products, obsolete manufactured products, or spent materials. Old scrap prices in the study are for old sheet and cast aluminum (PS2A), the producer price for aluminum used beverage can scrap (PS3A), the price for refiners' No.2 copper scrap (PS2C), and the smelters' buying price for heavy soft scrap lead (PSL). The *Metal Statistics* publication of the American Metal Market is the source for PS1A, PS2A, PSL, and PSZ. We obtained PS1C and PS2C from USGS specialist D.L. Edelstein and PS3A from the *Commodity Research Bureau Commodity Yearbook*. The length of each time series is determined by data availability and compatibility.

Primary and Scrap Prices

Figures 5.1a–d show primary and scrap prices in each market, while Table 5.1 shows their time-series characteristics, including Phillips and Perron (P-P) (1988) unit root tests that indicate that the price series are integrated of order 1, that is, I(1). Table 5.2 provides a description of the relationship between primary and scrap prices by averaging their mean and volatility over three-year periods. Primary and scrap prices move in the same direction but are not always in correspondence. The degree of variation is higher for scrap prices in terms of coefficients of variation with the exception of aluminum cans and new scrap copper.

As Figures 5.1a–d demonstrate, primary and scrap prices are interrelated. However, in contrast to past studies, which assume instantaneous and simultaneous reactions, this description suggests that the links between primary and secondary prices are not constant over time. The differing degree of price variation for primary and scrap metals is an indication that the short-term primary and secondary price changes are not always synchronous. Both primary and secondary markets adjust to exogenous and endogenous changes with time lags and can be subject to disequilibrium conditions in their own market or in relation to each other, at least in the short term. The price ratio of primary and secondary metals in Figures 5.2a–d shows that the relationships between primary and scrap prices are not constant over time. (See also Table 5.3.)

Primary and Secondary Price Relationships

On average, one would expect the spread between the primary price and the scrap price to simply reflect the refinery margin. In the short run, however, changes in

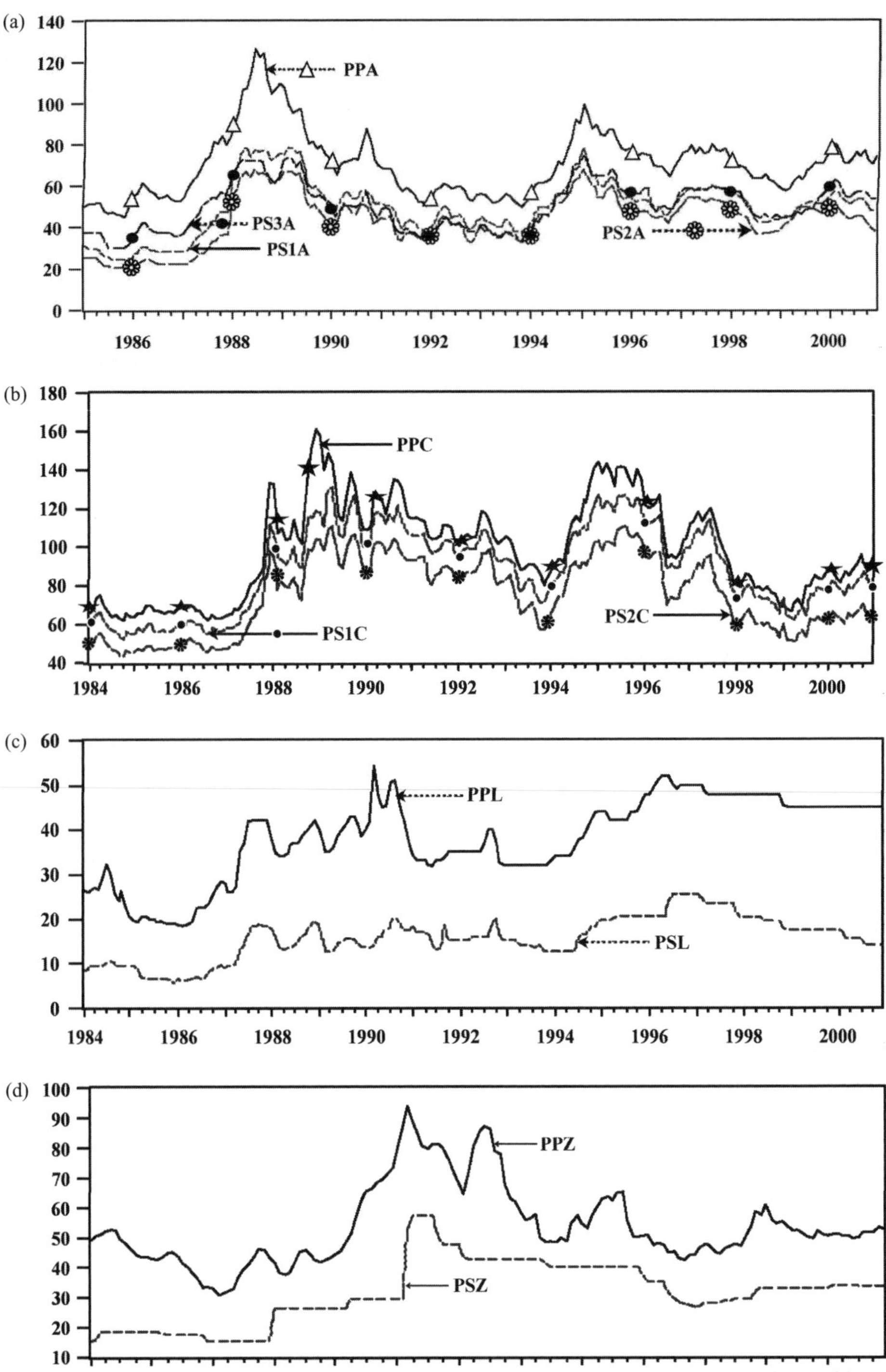

FIGURE 5.1 (a) Primary and Scrap Price of Aluminum, 1985–2000. (b) Primary and Scrap Price of Copper, 1984–2000. (c) Primary and Scrap Price of Lead, 1984–2000. (d) Primary and Scrap Price of Zinc, 1984–2000

TABLE 5.1 Characteristics of Primary and Scrap Prices by Metal

	Price Series										
	Aluminum				Copper			Lead		Zinc	
Characteristic	PPA	PS1A	PS2A	PS3A	PPC	PS1C	PS2C	PPL	PSL	PPZ	PSZ
Mean	70.66	49.74	43.45	50.30	98.43	88.80	75.02	37.96	15.61	53.58	31.30
Standard Deviation	16.16	13.29	12.36	11.38	24.86	22.00	19.73	9.24	4.86	13.45	10.44
Coeff. of Variation	0.229	0.267	0.284	0.226	0.253	0.248	0.263	0.243	0.312	0.251	0.334
Skewness	1.005	0.161	−0.056	0.260	0.284	0.003	0.019	−0.519	−0.159	0.997	0.277
Kurtosis	4.116	2.759	2.456	2.196	2.089	1.783	1.665	2.306	2.534	3.477	2.680
Jarque-Bera (J-B)	42.26	1.29	2.47	7.34	9.80	12.60	15.16	13.24	2.70	27.32	2.66
Probability (J-B)	0.000	0.524	0.291	0.025	0.007	0.002	0.001	0.001	0.259	0.000	0.264
P-P Unit Root Test											
Levels	−2.262	−2.220	−2.244	−2.244	−2.251	−2.063	−2.081	−1.614	−2.017	−1.888	−1.939
Probability*	0.186	0.200	0.192	0.192	0.189	0.260	0.253	0.474	0.280	0.337	0.314
First Differences	−10.55	−10.17	−9.84	−9.21	−10.56	−12.08	−11.90	−10.86	−11.60	−7.50	−10.07
Probability*	0.000	0.000	0.000	0.000	0.000	0.000	0.000	0.000	0.000	0.000	0.000
1% Critical Value	−3.465	−3.465	−3.465	−3.465	−3.462	−3.462	−3.462	−3.462	−3.462	−3.473	−3.473
5% Critical Value	−2.877	−2.877	−2.877	−2.877	−2.876	−2.876	−2.876	−2.876	−2.876	−2.880	−2.880

*MacKinnon (1996) one-sided p-values for rejection of hypothesis of a unit root.

TABLE 5.2 Primary and Scrap Prices and Volatility by Metal, 1985–1999

	Prices									
	Mean					Standard Deviation				
Series	1985–87	1988–90	1991–93	1994–96	1997–99	1985–87	1988–90	1991–93	1994–96	1997–99
Aluminum										
PPA	58.99	90.67	56.77	76.14	69.45	11.67	17.76	4.86	10.62	6.72
PS1A	31.47	65.21	43.05	56.16	51.87	6.79	10.53	4.10	8.15	5.95
PS2A	24.98	55.80	37.87	51.25	46.82	4.68	9.39	3.88	7.33	5.92
PS3A	40.52	60.57	39.08	57.00	52.17	8.24	10.00	4.07	9.14	5.91
Copper										
PPC	71.81	124.88	102.77	119.47	87.16	13.87	15.74	10.09	18.38	16.30
PS1C	63.08	109.85	94.17	108.56	81.19	12.10	11.03	11.04	14.63	15.30
PS2C	53.00	94.41	82.09	91.36	66.50	11.18	9.70	11.25	13.19	13.09
Lead										
PPL	25.92	40.65	33.74	43.86	46.98	8.49	5.14	2.13	5.86	1.64
PSL	9.62	15.67	15.32	19.51	20.11	4.33	2.22	1.82	4.07	2.62
Zinc										
PPZ	40.10	72.27	52.44	51.21	—	4.63	12.57	6.61	3.60	—
PSZ	19.84	40.33	37.45	32.01	—	4.87	10.46	5.07	2.09	—

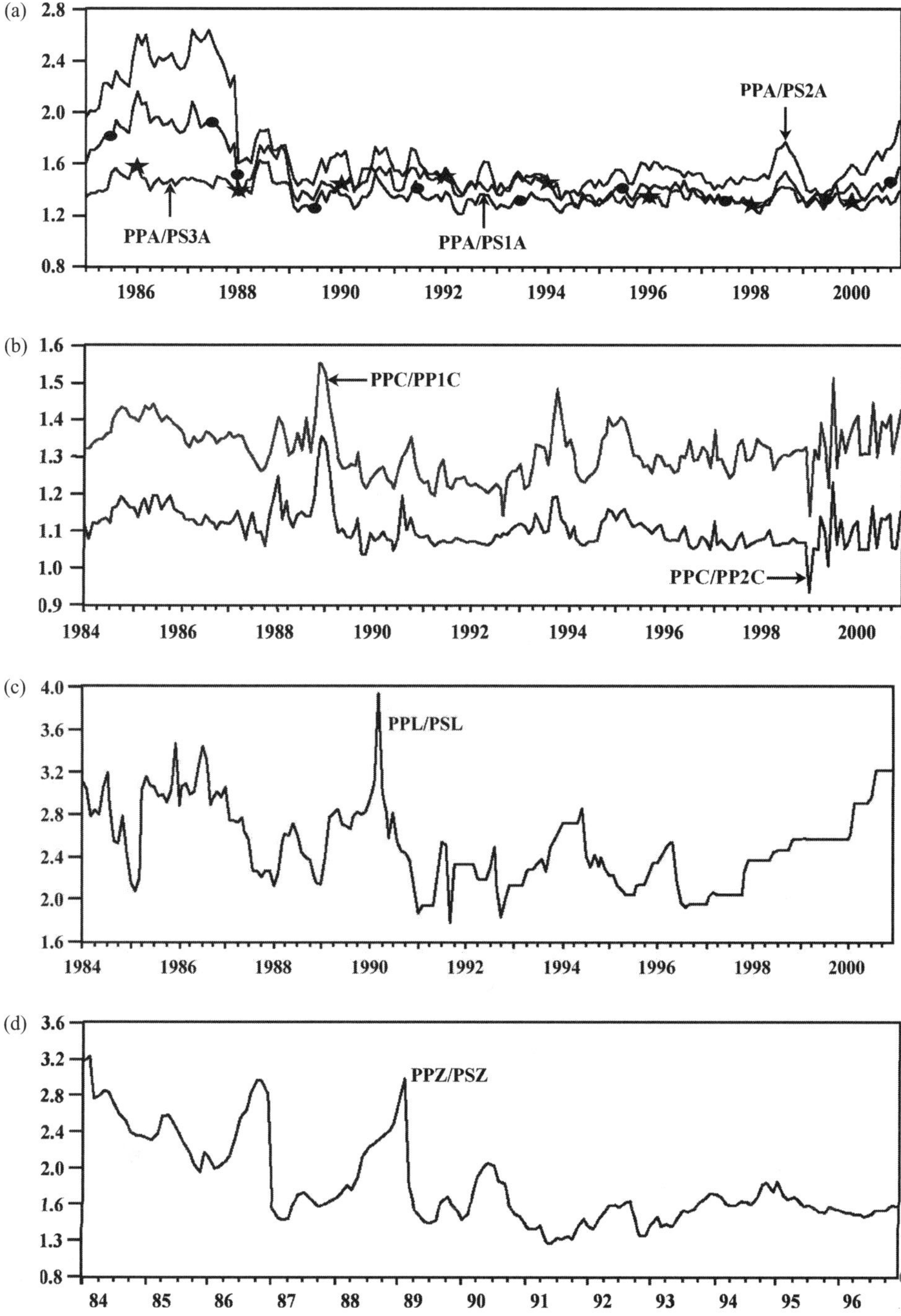

FIGURE 5.2 (a) Primary and Scrap Price Ratios of Aluminum, 1985–2000. (b) Primary and Scrap Price Ratios of Copper, 1984–2000. (c) Primary and Scrap Price Ratios of Lead, 1984–2000. (d) Primary and Scrap Price Ratios of Zinc, 1984–2000

TABLE 5.3 Price Ratios by Metal for Selected Time Periods

	Price Ratios				
Series	1985–87	1988–90	1991–93	1994–96	1997–99
Aluminum					
PPA/PS1A	1.883	1.387	1.321	1.358	1.343
PPA/PS2A	2.363	1.623	1.504	1.488	1.493
PPA/PS3A	1.459	1.495	1.456	1.341	1.335
Copper					
PPC/PS1C	1.139	1.137	1.094	1.098	1.074
PPC/PS2C	1.360	1.323	1.260	1.307	1.314
Lead					
PPL/PSL	2.820	2.621	2.224	2.296	2.365
Zinc					
PPZ/PSZ	2.112	1.861	1.412	1.602	—

primary prices may not completely explain changes in scrap prices because constraints do not always allow market clearing (Taylor, 1979). Cointegration analysis has established that variables may have an equilibrium relationship in the long run, even though disequilibria in the short term are possible. Engle and Granger (1987) point out that a linear combination of two or more nonstationary series may be stationary. If such a stationary linear combination exists, the nonstationary time series are said to be cointegrated. The stationary linear combination is called the cointegrating equation and is interpreted as a long-run equilibrium relationship between the variables. If two variables are cointegrated, they cannot move too far away from each other. In contrast, a lack of cointegration suggests that such variables have no long-run link and can wander arbitrarily far away from each other.

Since the primary and scrap prices in each market are nonstationary of order one [I(1)] (Table 5.1), cointegration testing allows for the establishment of a long-run equilibrium relationship between primary and scrap prices, even though short-run price dynamics may reflect disequilibrium. The Johansen (1991, 1995) cointegration tests reveal not only the long-run relationship but also short-run dynamic information based on the vector error correction (VECM) models that are produced. The results of the VECM models are presented next. In Model 1–Model 6, t-statistics are in parentheses below the coefficient and stars (*) indicate significance levels. One star indicates significance at the 0.10 level, two stars at the 0.05 level, and three stars at the 0.01 level.

Model 1

$$\Delta(PPA/PS1A)_t = \underset{(-2.682)^{***}}{-0.065}\left[PPA/PS1A_{t-1} - \underset{(-2.235)^{**}}{0.580}\ln USAS_{t-1} + 2.622\right] \underset{(-0.159)}{-0.0007} + \varepsilon_t \tag{5.1}$$

$\overline{R}^2 = 0.032, \quad AIC = -2.67$

Model 2

$$\Delta\left(\ln USAS\right)_t = \underset{(-3.029)^{***}}{-0.022}\left[PPA/PS1A_{t-1} - \underset{(-2.235)^{**}}{0.533}\ln USAS_{t-1} + 2.622\right] \underset{(-3.232)^{***}}{-0.004} + \varepsilon_t \qquad (5.2)$$

$\overline{R}^2 = 0.041, \quad AIC = -5.07$

Model 3

$$\Delta\left(PPA/PS2A\right)_t = \underset{(-2.216)^{**}}{-0.046}\left[PPA/PS1A_{t-1} - \underset{(-1.730)^{***}}{0.580}\ln USAS_{t-1} + 2.622\right]_t \underset{(-0.059)}{-0.0007} + \varepsilon \qquad (5.3)$$

$\overline{R}^2 = 0.020, \quad AIC = -2.03$

Model 4

$$\Delta\left(\ln USAS\right)_t = \underset{(-2.714)^{***}}{-0.012}\left[PPA/PS2A_{t-1} - \underset{(-1.730)^{*}}{0.809}\ln USAS_{t-1} + 2.622\right] \underset{(-3,217)^{***}}{-0.0007} + \varepsilon_t \qquad (5.4)$$

$\overline{R}^2 = 0.033, \quad AIC = -2.06$

Model 5

$$\begin{aligned}\Delta\left(PPZ/PSZ\right)_t = {} & \underset{(-3.503)^{***}}{-0.135}\left[PPZ/PSZ_{t-1} - \underset{(-2.235)^{***}}{0.554}\ln USZS_{t-1} + \underset{(3.352)^{***}}{3.255}\right] \\ & \underset{(2.8293)^{***}}{+0.277}\Delta\left(PPZ/PSZ\right)_{t-1} + \underset{(0.242)}{0.020}\Delta\left(PPZ/PSZ\right)_{t-2} \\ & \underset{(0.428)}{+0.036}\Delta\left(PPZ/PSZ\right)_{t-3} - \underset{(-0.624)}{0.048}\Delta\left(\ln USZS\right)_{t-1} \\ & \underset{(-1.558)}{-0.121}\Delta\left(\ln USZS\right)_{t-2} - \underset{(-1.640)}{0.126}\Delta\left(\ln USZS\right)_{t-3} + \varepsilon_t\end{aligned} \qquad (5.5)$$

$\overline{R}^2 = 0.105, \quad AIC = -0.76$

Model 6

$$\begin{aligned}\Delta\left(\ln USZS\right)_t = {} & \underset{(-3.326)^{***}}{0.126}\left[PPZ/PSZ_{t-1} - \underset{(-5.250)^{***}}{0.554}\ln USZS_{t-1} + \underset{(3.352)^{***}}{3.255}\right] \\ & \underset{(-3.217)^{***}}{-0.254}\Delta\left(PPZ/PSZ\right)_{t-1} - \underset{(-0.616)}{0.051}\Delta\left(PPZ/PSZ\right)_{t-2} \\ & \underset{(0.565)}{+0.047}\Delta\left(PPZ/PSZ\right)_{t-3} + \underset{(0.406)}{0.031}\Delta\left(\ln USZS\right)_{t-1} \\ & \underset{(1.934)^{*}}{+0.148}\Delta\left(\ln USZS\right)_{t-2} - \underset{(-2.698)^{***}}{0.203}\Delta\left(\ln USZS\right)_{t-3} + \varepsilon_t\end{aligned} \qquad (5.6)$$

$\overline{R}^2 = 0.150, \quad AIC = -0.79$

Johansen's method tests the restrictions imposed by cointegration on the unrestricted vector autoregression (VAR) model involving k series. For primary and scrap prices, the unrestricted VAR is

$$P_t = A_1 P_{t-1} + \cdots + A_p P_{t-p} + \varepsilon_t \tag{5.7}$$

where P_t = vector including one primary and one scrap price series (both nonstationary I(1) variables)
ε_t = vector of innovations

The VAR is transformed in this VECM:

$$\Delta P_t = \Pi P_{t-1} + \sum_{i=1}^{p-1} \Gamma_i \Delta P_{t-i} + \varepsilon_t \tag{5.8}$$

where

$$\Pi = \sum_{i=1}^{p} A_i - I_i, \Gamma_i = - \sum_{j=i+1}^{p} A_j \tag{5.9}$$

Granger's representation theorem (Engle and Granger 1987; Johansen 1991) asserts that if the coefficient matrix Π has reduced rank $r < 2$ for the bivariate case, then there exist $2 \times r$ matrices α and β, each with rank r, such that $\Pi = \alpha\beta'$ and $\beta' P_{t1}$ is stationary. In the bivariate case, there can be at most one independent combination of the variables in P_t $(\beta' P_{t-1})$ that is stationary. The variable r is the number of cointegrating relations. In the bivariate case, the cointegrating rank cannot be larger than 1. Each column of β is the cointegrating vector (characterizing the long-run relationship between the primary and scrap price) and the elements of α are known as the adjustment parameters of primary and scrap prices to their cointegrating (long-run) relationship.

The cointegrating term is also known as the error correction term since the deviation from long-run equilibrium between primary and scrap prices is corrected gradually through a series of short-run price adjustments toward this equilibrium. The adjustment rates measure the speed of adjustment of the short-run changes of prices to their long-run relationship and show the persistence of short-run disequilibrium conditions.

The first five columns in Table 5.4 show the cointegration test results. The sixth column shows the long-run relationship between the primary and scrap price for each pair. The last two columns show the adjustment rates of the price changes to their cointegrating relationship. Primary prices are found to hold a long-run relationship to scrap prices with the exception of old and new aluminum prices. The primary products of old and new scrap aluminum, cast aluminum products, are sold in markets that are separate from those of primary aluminum. As a consequence, it is consistent that these scrap prices are not found to have a long-run relationship to primary aluminum prices.

Table 5.5 shows tests of cointegration between price ratios and inventories.

TABLE 5.4 Evidence of Cointegration between Primary and Scrap Prices by Metal

		Max. Eigenvalue Test		Trace Test		Cointegrating	Adjustment Rates (α)	
Prices	H_o: r = p	Statistic	Prob[2]	Statistic	Prob.[2]	Relationship ($\beta' P_{t-1}$)	Primary Price	Scrap Price
Aluminum								
PPA,PS1A	$p = 0$	10.28	0.310	16.99	0.133			
	$p \leq 1$	6.71	0.142	6.71	0.142			
PPA,PS2A	$p = 0$	6.66	0.711	11.47	0.498			
	$p \leq 1$	4.81	0.305	4.81	0.305			
PPA,PS3A	$p = 0$	15.35[1]	0.009	15.38[1]	0.015	$PPA_{t-1} - 1.41PS3A_{t-1}$	−0.06	0.06
	$p \leq 1$	0.03	0.892	0.03	0.892	(−51.43)***	(−1.39)	(1.89)*
Copper								
PPC,PS1C	$p = 0$	28.33[1]	0.000	28.36[1]	0.000	$PS1C_{t-1} - 0.9PPC_{t-1}$	0.16	−0.16
	$p \leq 1$	0.04	0.871	0.04	0.871	(−124.18)***	(1.49)	(−1.84)*
PPC,PS2C		26.63[1]	0.001	30.73[1]	0.001	$PS2C_{t-1} - 0.82PPC_{t-1} + 5.66$	0.15	−0.14
		4.1	0.398	4.1	0.398	(−26.77)*** (1.83)*	(1.37)	(−1.76)*
Lead								
PPL,PSL	$p = 0$	26.13[1]	0.005	32.10[1]	0.007	$PSL_{t-1} - 0.65*PPL_{t-1} + 0.03t + 5.4$	−0.01	−0.14
	$p \leq 1$	5.96	0.465	5.96	0.465	(−7.99)*** (2.23)**	(−0.11)	(−5.02)***
Zinc								
PPZ,PSZ	$p = 0$	18.09[1]	0.022	20.87[1]	0.041	$PPZ_{t-1} - 1.24*PSZ_{t-1} - 13.86$	−0.02	0.08
	$p \leq 1$	2.78	0.622	2.78	0.622	(−6.28)*** (−2.14)**	(−0.87)	(4.15)***

[1]denotes rejection of the hypothesis at the 0.05 level.
[2]MacKinnon-Haug-Michelis (1999) p-values.
t-statistics in parentheses. Asterisks indicate significance at *−0.10, **−0.05, ***−0.01 level.

TABLE 5.5 Tests for Cointegration between Price Ratios and Inventories

		Maximum Eigenvalue Test			Trace Test		
Prices	Ho: r = p	Statistic	5% Crit.Val.	Prob.[2]	Statistic	5% Crit.Val.	Prob.[2]
Aluminum							
PPA/PS1A	$p = 0$	19.108[1]	14.265	0.008	19.843[1]	15.495	0.010
USAS	$p \leq 1$	0.735	3.841	0.391	0.735	3.841	0.391
PPA/PS2A	$p = 0$	15.234[1]	14.265	0.035	15.925[1]	15.495	0.043
USAS	$p \leq 1$	0.692	3.841	0.406	0.692	3.841	0.406
Zinc		22.500[1]	15.892	0.004	26.475[1]	20.262	0.006
PPZ/PSZ,	$p = 0$	3.975	9.165	0.416	3.975	9.165	0.416
USZS	$p \leq 1$						

[1]denotes rejection of the hypothesis at the 0.05 level.
[2]MacKinnon-Haug-Michelis (1999) p-values.

In relation to the short-run disequilibrium between primary and scrap prices, the results show that the adjustment rates of primary and scrap prices to their cointegrating relationship are not high, suggesting that short-run disequilibrium movements can be persistent. This also points to the importance of understanding the short-term relationships between primary and scrap prices. In addition, adjustment rates are statistically significant only for scrap prices. This means that most of the adjustment toward the long-run relationship between primary and scrap prices is borne by adjustments in the scrap market.

PRIMARY-TO-SCRAP PRICE RATIOS

The examination of the time-varying spread between primary and secondary prices relies on price ratios. Cointegration analysis separates the disequilibrium dynamics from the equilibrium adjustments of the primary and scrap prices. By using price ratios, it is possible to include both disequilibrium and equilibrium adjustments that occur between primary and scrap prices in the short run. The close relationship between price ratios and price differentials provides the connection of the VEC models of the primary and scrap prices analyzed earlier to their price ratios. As Granger indicated in his Nobel lecture, "a potentially useful property of forecasts based on cointegration is that when extended some way ahead, the forecasts of the two series will form a constant ratio" (Granger 2004: 362).

The secondary/primary price ratio indicates the relative attractiveness of choosing secondary versus primary inputs in the production process and can be used as an explanatory factor for recycling rates (Van Beukering and Bouman 2001). Price ratios are also important for secondary smelters and refineries that produce primary metal mainly from scrap since their profitability and survival depend on the price margin between scrap and the refined primary output. In this context, Taylor (1979) used the relative scrap to primary price ratio in explaining primary prices. More than 70 years ago, Fowler (1937) took an interest in iron ore and steel scrap price ratios relative to their consumption ratios for producing steel to examine the time-varying relationship between primary and scrap metals. He found that there were differences in the elasticity of substitution between different periods.

The primary-to-scrap price ratios are presented in Figures 5.2a–d. Tables 5.2 and 5.3 include a summary of the price ratio data averaged over three-year periods. Table 5.6 shows their time-series characteristics, including Phillips and Perron (1988) unit root tests. Three conclusions can be drawn for primary-to-scrap price ratios:

1. The means of the price ratios are not consistent over the 20-year period. In some periods, scrap prices are closer, indicating a stronger relationship to the primary metal prices relative to other periods.
2. The price ratios are stationary in many cases, and the evidence favors a constant mean. This supports the finding already indicated through cointegration analysis that the primary and scrap prices tend to revert to a long-run relationship.
3. The temporal patterns of price ratio means and volatility differ between markets. In addition, the temporal patterns of the price ratios within each market are similar for different types of scrap. This would suggest that a market specific explanation of the price ratio behavior is indicated.

Inventory Influences

In search of a market-specific explanation of the price ratio behaviour, inventories are examined for the same time period. From a historic perspective, it seems that

TABLE 5.6 Characteristics of Primary-to-Scrap Price Ratios by Metal

	Price Ratio Series						
	Aluminum			Copper		Lead	Zinc
Characteristic	$\frac{PPA}{PS1A}$	$\frac{PPA}{PS2A}$	$\frac{PPA}{PS3A}$	$\frac{PPC}{PS1C}$	$\frac{PPC}{PS2C}$	$\frac{PPL}{PSL}$	$\frac{PPZ}{PSZ}$
Mean	1.456	1.692	1.411	1.110	1.319	2.517	1.821
Standard Deviation	0.223	0.350	0.100	0.053	0.071	0.381	0.477
Coef. of Variation	0.153	0.207	0.071	0.048	0.054	0.151	0.262
Skewness	1.460	1.431	0.824	1.313	0.463	0.487	1.046
Kurtosis	3.905	3.770	4.013	7.304	3.523	2.965	3.154
Jarque-Bera (J-B)	74.743	70.283	29.919	216.126	9.603	8.069	28.626
Probability (J-B)	0.000	0.000	0.000	0.000	0.008	0.018	0.000
P-P Unit Root Test							
Levels	−1.853	−1.783	−4.086	−6.623	−5.839	−3.410	−1.468
Probability*	0.354	0.388	0.001	0.000	0.000	0.012	0.133
First Differences	−14.750	−13.500	–	–	–	–	−10.170
Probability*	0.000	0.000	–	–	–	–	0.000
1% Critical Value	−3.465	−3.465	−3.465	−3.462	−3.462	−3.462	−2.580
5% Critical Value	−2.877	−2.877	−2.877	−2.876	−2.876	−2.876	−1.943

*MacKinnon (1996) one-sided p-values for rejection of hypothesis of a unit root.

market fundamentals allow an understanding of the behavior of primary-to-scrap price ratios. Low price ratios seeming to reflect tight supply/demand balances (low stock levels) suggest that market fundamentals do influence the spread between primary and scrap prices. The graphs and time-series characteristics of the inventory series (in logarithmic form) for the period 1984 to 2000 are presented in Figure 5.3a–d and Table 5.7, respectively. The inventories used are U.S. stocks at the end of each month. Aluminum stock data was available only for North America.

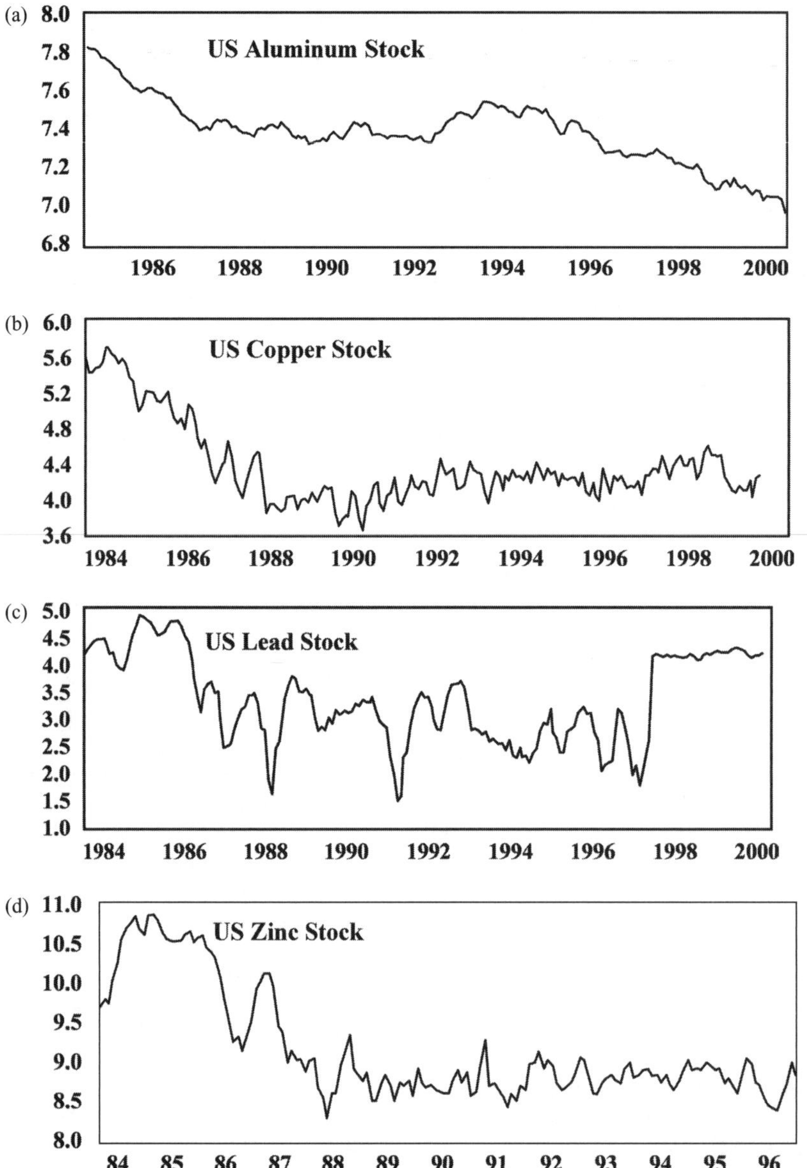

FIGURE 5.3 (a) Metal Stocks (in logarithmic form) of Aluminum (1985–2000). (b) Metal Stocks (in logarithmic form) of Copper (1984–2000). (c) Metal Stocks (in logarithmic form) of Lead (1984–2000). (d) Metal Stocks (in logarithmic form) of Zinc (1984–1996)

TABLE 5.7 Characteristics of U.S. Metal Stocks

	Inventory Series			
Characteristic	lnUSAS	lnUSCS	lnUSLS	lnUSZS
Mean	7.390	4.377	3.360	9.165
Standard Deviation	0.167	0.449	0.795	0.693
Coef. of Variation	0.023	0.102	0.237	0.076
Skewness	0.059	1.391	−0.017	1.250
Kurtosis	3.356	4.211	2.035	3.168
Jarque-Bera (J-B)	1.117	75.151	7.929	40.782
Probability (J-B)	0.572	0.000	0.019	0.000
Phillips-Perron Unit Root Test				
Levels	−1.666	−2.916	−2.641	−1.828
Probability*	0.763	0.045	0.087	0.366
First Differences	−11.19	–	–	−11.98
Probability*	0.000	–	–	0.000
1% Critical Value	−4.007	−3.464	−3.462	−3.473
5% Critical Value	−3.434	−2.876	−2.876	−2.880

*MacKinnon (1996) one-sided p-values for rejection of hypothesis of a unit root.

The source for the North American Aluminum stocks, denoted as USAS, is the International Aluminum Institute. The copper stocks (USCS) were estimated from segregated U.S. copper stocks compiled by the USGS specialist D.L. Edelstein. The *Metal Statistics* publication of the American Metal Markets provided the source for lead (USLS) and zinc (USZS) stocks. The length of each time series is determined by data availability and compatibility. Periods of low price ratios coincided with periods of low market inventories. For aluminum, the price ratio was low during 1988, 1990, 1993, 1996–1997, and 1999–2000, all periods of low inventories. For lead, low price ratios were experienced in the low inventory periods of 1984–1985, 1988, and 1991. In contrast, the periods of 1985–1986, 1986–1987, and 1995–1996 had high inventory accumulation with high lead price ratios. Independent demand and supply influences do not capture the dynamics between primary and scrap metal prices. A zinc supply shortage in 1987 to 1989 resulted in low price ratios, while worldwide supply shortages of aluminum in 1986 to 1988 coincided with high price ratios. The reason for this inconsistency in the relation of price ratios to supply is that supply shortages for aluminum during 1986 to 1988 were buffered by drawing from the industry's high inventories. Shortages for zinc in 1987 to 1989, however, coincided with low zinc inventories. Furthermore, reduced demand in 2000 coincided by increased ratios, except in the case of aluminum, where the period was characterized by a reduction in inventories and the price ratios were low.

It appears that the major determinant of price ratios is the tightness in the market, represented by inventory availability. Scatter plots of price ratios to U.S. inventories presented in Figures 5.4 to 5.7 attest to a positive relationship between price ratios and inventories. The plots also include a line of fit to improve interpretation of the relationship that connects them.

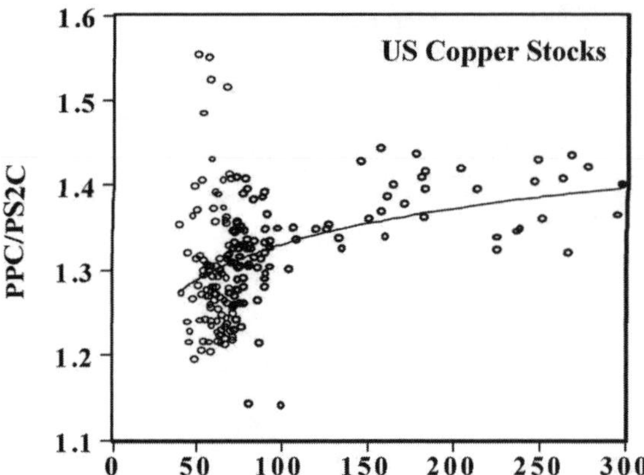

FIGURE 5.4 Scatter Plot of the Price Ratio of Primary to Old Scrap Copper to Copper Inventories

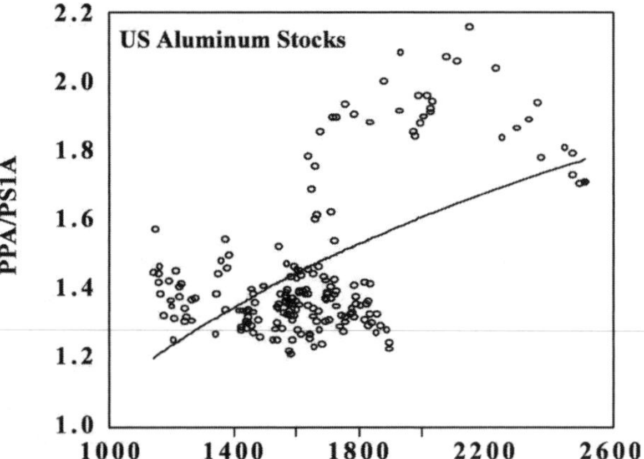

FIGURE 5.5 Scatter Plot of the Price Ratio of Primary to New Scrap Aluminum to Aluminum Inventories Lagged by One Month

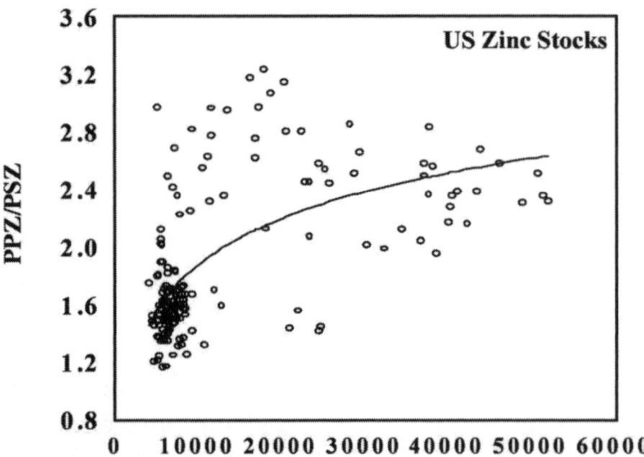

FIGURE 5.6 Scatter Plot of the Price Ratio of Primary to New Scrap Zinc to Zinc Inventories

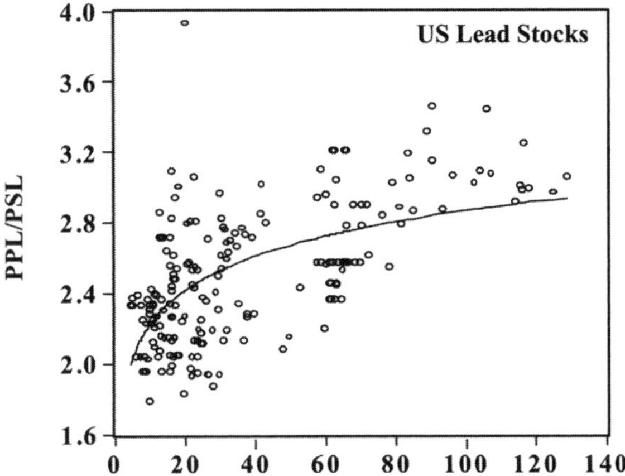

FIGURE 5.7 Scatter Plot of the Price Ratio of Primary to Old Scrap Lead to Lead Inventories Lagged by One Month

MODELING PRICE RATIOS

Stocks are a major factor in metal markets. They provide the intertemporal link in dynamic commodity systems and form the basis of price adjustment since demand and supply are inelastic (Labys and Kaboudan 1980). Primary and scrap metal demand and supply do not always clear in the short term because of technological, institutional, and psychological constraints. The discrepancy between supply and demand is then carried over to subsequent periods through inventory changes. When metal production exceeds demand, the excess is added to accumulated stocks. When demand exceeds supply, inventories are used to cover the excess demand. Current inventories are defined as the summation of supply and demand changes as well as inventory accumulation carried over from the past periods:

$$I_{p,t} = I_{p,t-1} + S_{p,t} - D_{p,t} \tag{5.10}$$

Thus, inventories express market conditions, both as current flow changes and as past accumulation of stocks. Consequently, they can allow inferences about how market conditions influence primary and secondary prices.

The role of inventories emphasizes the dynamic character of metal markets and indicates the disequilibrium forces that are embodied in the market. We expect the disequilibrium between primary and scrap prices to be related to a variable (such as inventories) that embodies disequilibrium conditions. In addition, stocks are a determinant of both primary and scrap prices.

When demand and supply are inelastic, as is the case in metal markets, a stock adjustment process determines primary metal price behavior. Taylor (1979) introduced the influence of stocks on scrap prices as well in his short-run model of the copper industry. Since both primary and scrap prices are functions of inventories, the ratio of primary-to-scrap prices should also be influenced by inventories. This is especially obvious if it is taken into account that the reactions of primary and scrap prices to market forces will be different and come with different adjustment rates.

Production Smoothing Model

Production smoothing is an explanation for the use of stocks in inelastic markets. Quickly changing production to demand fluctuations would be accompanied by high adjustment costs, because of high investment cost in production expansion and the rigidity of electricity, primary input, and labor contracts. In addition, firms face convex production cost curves and fluctuating market demand. Under such conditions, firms have incentives to use inventories to buffer demand shocks and smooth production (Holt et al. 1960) or production costs (Eichenbaum 1984, 1989).

In the presence of low demand, excess supply is stored as inventory to avoid production cuts and consequent adjustment costs; in periods of high demand, difficulties and increased costs resulting from higher production can be avoided by drawing from accumulated inventory. Capacity is unlikely to be expanded or contracted in the short run; expansion (contraction) would occur only when clear signals of long-term increasing (decreasing) demand and prices are present. Based on the incentives for production smoothing, low stocks, indicating high demand and short supply in the market, would also lead to the utilization of relatively more scrap than usual as a metal input or substitute. The cost of disrupting the flow of operations is linked to the use of primary ore and concentrate: Scrap, which is a more flexible input than primary ore, can be used to smooth production and production costs.

In periods of excess demand, increased supply orders can be covered by scrap, and higher marginal costs from the use of primary ore can be avoided. The relative use of scrap directly from metal consumers, as a substitute for primary metal, also increases as the market tightens and the primary metal industry is not able to respond swiftly to demand. Therefore, when inventories are low, the ratio of primary to secondary demand decreases, leading subsequently to a smaller primary-to-scrap price ratio. In contrast, during low demand, when stocks are high, production and production cost-smoothing implies that relatively less scrap is used as input into primary production. Ore and concentrate are preferred to scrap to avoid the idling of production capacity. Although both primary and scrap demand are low when inventories are high, their demand ratio widens and so does the primary-to-scrap price ratio. The first hypothesis that arises from this analysis is that the ratio of primary-to-scrap metal prices is positively linked to inventories. However, technological, psychological, and institutional constraints in the market, as well as the influence of expectations, could mean that the ratio of primary-to-scrap prices adjusts to inventories over time. Therefore, it is expected that the positive relationship between the ratios of primary to secondary metal prices and inventories occurs with time lags.

Time-Series Models

Since metal markets are characterized by stock adjustments and expectation functions, the hypotheses are tested under a dynamic framework with autoregressive (ARMAX) models as described in equation 5.2. Current and past inventories as well as lagged price ratios incorporate information about the fundamentals of the market. The scatter plots in Figures 5.4 to 5.7 indicate that the relationship between price ratios and inventories is asymmetric. Higher stocks lead to higher ratios at a decreasing rate since the difference between the primary and scrap prices is constrained by their technological and market relations. To express this asymmetry, inventories are transformed into logarithms.

$$(Pp/Ps)_t = c + \phi_k \sum_{1}^{k} (Pp/Ps)_{t-k} + \gamma \ln I_t + \delta \ln I_{t-1} + \varepsilon_t \tag{5.11}$$

The ARMAX models explain the movement of a variable through time in terms of its own past values as well as current and past values of other explanatory variables. Time and relationships through time are an explicit part of the formulation. The lagged values of the price ratios and inventories appear as a consequence of the theoretical basis of the model, which takes into account past market information and allows economic agents to respond not only to current values but to past values as well.

When price ratios and inventories are stationary, the number of lags is chosen based only on the goodness of fit. When the price ratios are stationary but inventories contain a unit root [I(1)], as in the case of modeling the ratio of aluminum primary to used aluminum can prices, regression equations including only current inventories or only inventories lagged by one period are meaningless because the error term contains a trend component. Including current and past values allows the individual coefficients of $\log I_t, \log I_{t-1}$ to be written as coefficients of stationary variables ,which imply that a t-statistic is appropriate for testing the influence of $\log I_t, \log I_{t-1}$individually on the price ratios (Sims, Stock, and Watson 1990). Specifically, the distributions of the estimated coefficients γ and δ each converge at a rate corresponding to $\sqrt{T}$ to a Gaussian distribution. An F test of the joint hypothesis that γ and δ are both zero has a nonstationary limiting distribution and cannot be conducted, but it is possible to test the hypothesis of $\gamma = 0$ and $\delta = 0$ being asymptotically N(0,1) separately for each variable (Hamilton 1994) .

When both price ratios and inventories are nonstationary [I(1)], it is necessary to check whether a long-run relationship exists between them. If cointegration is present, a VEC model is produced. This approach is followed for the primary-to-scrap zinc price ratio as well as the ratios of primary to new and old aluminum scrap prices. The model of the price ratios under this formulation is described by:

$$\begin{aligned} \Delta\left(Pp/Ps\right)_t = c + a\left[(Pp/Ps)_{t-1} + \beta \ln I_{t-1}\right] \\ + \sum_{1}^{k} \phi_k \Delta (Pp/Ps)_{t-k} + \sum_{1}^{k} \gamma_k \Delta \ln I_{t-1} + \varepsilon_t \end{aligned} \tag{5.12}$$

In this model, the relationship of inventories to price ratios is examined both in the long term and in the short term.

EMPIRICAL RESULTS

The empirical results for the price ratio models are presented next. The coefficients differ considerably between metal markets. The functions of all the price ratios have significant autoregressive coefficients. For price ratios that are nonstationary, the autoregressive coefficient is 1. The significance of the autoregressive coefficients testifies to the dynamic adjustment behavior of the metal markets. As in the case of the VECM model, t-statistics are in parentheses below the coefficient, and stars (*) indicate significance levels. One star indicates significance at the 0.10 level, two stars significance at the 0.05 level, and three stars significance at the 0.01 level.

Model 1

$$\begin{aligned}\Delta\,(PPA/PS1A)_t = {} & \underset{(-2.682)^{***}}{-0.065}\left[PPA/PS1A_{t-1} - \underset{(-2.235)^{**}}{0.58}\ln USAS_{t-1} + 2.622\right] \\ & \underset{(-0.159)}{-0.0007} + \varepsilon_t \end{aligned} \tag{5.13}$$

$\overline{R}^2 = 0.032, \quad AIC = -2.67$

Model 2

$$\begin{aligned}\Delta\,(PPA/PS2A)_t = {} & \underset{(-2.216)^{**}}{-0.046}\left[PPA/PS2A_{t-1} - \underset{(-1.730)^{*}}{0.809}\ln USAS_{t-1} + 4.295\right] \\ & \underset{(-0.059)}{-0.0003} + \varepsilon_t \end{aligned} \tag{5.14}$$

$\overline{R}^2 = 0.020, \quad AIC = -2.03$

Model 3

$$\begin{aligned}\Delta\,(PPA/PS3A)_t = {} & \underset{(0.339)^{***}}{0.316} + \underset{(19.369)^{**}}{0.819}PPA/PS3A_{t-1} - \underset{(-1.682)^{*}}{0.307}\ln USAS_{t-1} \\ & \underset{(2.443)}{+0.455}\ln USAS_{t-1} + \varepsilon_t \end{aligned} \tag{5.15}$$

$\overline{R}^2 = 0.710, \quad AIC = -2.97$

Model 4

$$\begin{aligned}PPC/PS1C_t = {} & \underset{(12.508)^{***}}{1.052} + \underset{(7.500)^{***}}{0.541}PPC/PS1C_{t-1} + \underset{(2.469)^{**}}{0.179}PPC/PS1C_{t-2} \\ & \underset{(-0.635)}{-0.013}\ln USCS_{t-1} + \underset{(1.274)}{0.027}\ln USCS_{t-2} + \varepsilon_t \end{aligned} \tag{5.16}$$

$\overline{R}^2 = 0.466, \quad AIC = -3.63$

Model 5

$$\begin{aligned}PPC/PS1C_t = {} & \underset{(11.977)^{***}}{1.109} + \underset{(7.718)^{***}}{0.497}PPC/PS1C_{t-1} + \underset{(2.935)^{**}}{0.234}PPC/PS1C_{t-2} \\ & \underset{2.286)^{**}}{+0.048}\ln USCS_{t-3} + \varepsilon_t \end{aligned} \tag{5.17}$$

$\overline{R}^2 = 0.533, \quad AIC = -3.20$

Model 6

$$PPL/PSL_t = \underset{(11.044)^{***}}{2.049} + \underset{(21.569)^{***}}{0.841}\,(PPC/PC1C)_{t-1} + \underset{(2.286)^{**}}{0.141}\left(\ln USLS\right)_{t-1} + \varepsilon_t$$

$$\overline{R}^2 = 0.77,\ AIC = -0.58 \tag{5.18}$$

Model 7

$$\begin{aligned}\Delta\,(PPZ/PSZ)_t = {} & \underset{(-3.503)^{***}}{-0.135}\left[PPZ/PSZ_{t-1} - \underset{(-5.250)^{***}}{0.554}\ln USZS_{t-1} + \underset{(2.829)^{***}}{3.255}\right] \\ & \underset{(2.829)^{***}}{+0.227}\Delta\,(PPZ/PSZ)_{t-1} + \underset{(0.242)}{0.020}\Delta\,(PPZ/PSZ)_{t-2} \\ & \underset{(0.428)}{+0.036}\Delta\,(PPZ/PSZ)_{t-3} - \underset{(-0.624)}{0.048}\Delta\left(\ln USZS\right)_{t-1} \\ & \underset{(-1.558)}{-0.121}\Delta\left(\ln USZS\right)_{t-2} - \underset{(-1.640)}{0.126}\Delta\left(\ln USZS\right)_{t-3} + \varepsilon_t\end{aligned} \tag{5.19}$$

$$\overline{R}^2 = 0.105,\ AIC = -0.76$$

The effect of inventories on primary/secondary price ratios is positive. Even though present inventory levels have a negative effect on the ratio of primary-to-used aluminum can prices, the positive effect of past inventory values surpasses the effect exerted by current inventories. The influence of stocks to price ratios is weakest in the copper market and is significant only for the ratio of primary-to-old scrap prices. Considerable inventory influence on the price ratios comes from past lags. Thus, the ratio of primary-to-secondary data adjusts to changing market conditions with time lags.

In the cases of zinc price ratios and aluminum primary-to-old and new scrap price ratios, inventories hold a positive long-run relationship to price ratios. Short-run changes in price ratios also hold a positive relationship to inventories for aluminum. In the case of zinc, price ratios are influenced positively by the lagged inventory levels but are negatively affected by short-run inventory changes. The short-run influence is not statistically significant, however. Finally, short-run dynamics in these markets can be persistent, since the adjustment rates to the long-run relationship between the price ratios and inventories are not high.

The ratio of primary-to-scrap metal prices is not constant, since market conditions influence primary and secondary metal prices to differing degrees. Price ratios increase as inventories grow and decrease when they decline. The positive relationship between the primary/scrap price ratio and metal market inventories suggests that scrap prices react more violently to market changes than primary prices. In times of ample supply, both primary and scrap prices decrease, but the fall in scrap prices is greater. In periods of excess demand and tight supply, both primary and scrap prices increase, with scrap price increases being relatively higher.

Secondary smelters and refineries depend on scrap for metal production and are therefore greatly affected by this phenomenon. They may find themselves at a disadvantage relative to primary smelters and refineries because their input costs are more volatile than their revenues and they have to engage in market speculation.

This may be the reason for suggestions in the copper industry to link scrap prices to LME copper prices (Blomberg and Hellmer 2000; Labys et al. 1971).

Finally, to the extent that price reactions to surface stocks could represent price adjustments to reduced underground stocks, long-term downward-sloping trends of the primary and scrap price ratio would indicate resource exhaustion. This is a possible direction for future research that may produce more conclusive results about resource exhaustion than the study of primary resource prices alone. The positive long-run relationship found between price ratios and inventories for zinc and aluminum validates this approach.

CONCLUSIONS

This study describes relationships between primary and scrap metal markets in terms of price ratios. Understanding the relative behaviors of primary and scrap prices is valuable, particularly in the decision-making process of managers of secondary smelters and refineries. In examining the dynamic relationship of primary and scrap metal prices through time-series methods, the results show that a long-run equilibrium ties primary-to-scrap prices but that short-run dynamics include movements away and adjustments toward equilibrium. The unstable short-run relationship between primary and scrap prices is supported by the time-varying ratios of primary-to-scrap prices. The long-run relationship of primary and scrap prices in most metal markets suggests that policies aimed at increasing recycling rates by decreasing the primary-to-scrap price ratio will not be able to sustain long-term results. Such policies could have a more significant effect in the old and new aluminum scrap markets, where a long-run relationship between primary and scrap prices is not present. In addition, knowledge of the existence of a long-term equilibrium between primary and scrap prices should make scrap market participants cautious about how to react to short-run fluctuations of scrap prices.

This study shows that price ratios are related to market fundamentals. Inventory levels and price ratios share a positive relationship. In the cases of zinc and new and old aluminum, this relationship is more pronounced in the long run than the short run. Moreover, considerable inventory influence on price ratios comes from past lags, since the ratio of primary to secondary prices adjusts to changing market conditions. The dynamic adjustment of price ratios to market information is indicated by the significant autoregressive coefficients of price ratios. These results can help metal market participants anticipate or forecast relative changes in primary and scrap prices.

Production smoothing incentives of metal producers provide a theoretical explanation for the positive relationship between primary and scrap price ratios to inventories. Such smoothing behavior leads to tighter connections between primary and scrap prices when inventories are low than when inventories are high. In a tight market, the spread between primary and scrap prices becomes smaller, whereas ample supply means wider spreads between primary and scrap prices. The empirical results indicate such a structure for aluminum, zinc, and lead, but the evidence is weaker for copper. Understanding the reasons why this relationship is not as pronounced in the case of copper could provide additional insights into the structural relationship between primary and scrap prices. Since production-smoothing incentives are a short-run phenomenon, the long-run equilibria between inventories and price ratios that we found in the case of zinc and new and old aluminum scrap suggest that additional factors may lead to this relationship.

Finally, the positive relationship between price ratios and metal inventories indicates that as inventories increase (decrease), both primary and secondary prices increase (decrease), but scrap price reactions to market conditions are more pronounced. The flexibility of scrap as an input to primary metal production is the reason that the ratio of primary to secondary prices is expected to be positive in relationship to inventory levels. The estimated vector error correction models of primary and scrap prices show that the partial adjustment toward the long-run relationship between primary and scrap prices comes about through scrap price movements. This indicates both the higher flexibility of scrap prices and the stabilizing force of the scrap sector for the metal markets.

REFERENCES

American Metal Market. (1984–2003). *Metal Statistics*. New York: American Metal Market.

Blomberg, J., and S. Hellmer. (2000). "Short-Run Demand and Supply Elasticities in the West European Market for Secondary Aluminium," *Resources Policy* 26: 39–50.

Commodity Research Bureau. (1984–2003). *The CRB Commodity Yearbook*. Chicago: Commodity Research Bureau.

Eichenbaum, M. (1984). "Rational Expectations and the Smoothing Properties of Inventories of Finished Goods." *Journal of Monetary Economics* 14: 71–96.

———. (1989). "Some Empirical Evidence on the Production Level and Production Smoothing Models of Inventory Investment." *American Economic Review* 79.4: 853–864.

Engle, R.F., and C.W.J. Granger. (1987). "Co-integration and Error Correction: Representation, Estimation, and Testing," *Econometrica* 55: 251–276.

EVIEWS (5.1). (2005). Irvine, CA: Quantitative Micro Software.

Fisher, L.A., and A.D. Owen. (1981). "An Econometric Model of the US Aluminum Market," *Resources Policy* 7.3: 150–160.

Fowler, R.F. (1937). "The Substitution of Scrap for Pig-Iron in the Manufacture of Steel," *Quarterly Journal of Economics* 52.1: 129–154.

Granger, C.W.J. (2004). "Time Series Analysis, Cointegration, and Applications." Nobel Lecture, December 8, 2003. http://nobelprize.org/nobel-prizes/economics/laureates/2003/granger-lecture.pdf.

Hamilton, J. D. (1994). *Time Series Analysis*. Princeton, NJ: Princeton University Press.

Hashimoto, H. (1983). "Modeling Price Fluctuations of Ferrous Scrap," *Resources Policy* June: 122–139.

Holt, C. C., F. Modigliani, J.F. Muth, and H.A. Simon. (1960). *Planning Production, Inventories, and Work Force*. Englewood Cliffs, NJ: Prentice-Hall.

International Aluminum Institute. (2003). "Statistics," www.world-aluminium.org, accessed March 24, 2004.

Johansen, S. (1991). "Estimation and Hypothesis Testing of Cointegration Vectors in Gaussian Vector Autoregressive Models," Econometrica 59: 1551–1580.

———. (1995). *Likelihood-Based Inference in Cointegrated Vector Autoregressive Models*. Oxford: Oxford University Press.

Labys, W.C., and M. Kaboudan. (1980). " A Short-Run Disequilibrium Model of the Copper Market," Working Paper 16, Morgantown: Department of Mineral and Energy Economics, West Virginia University.

Labys, W.C., H.B. Rees, and C.M. Elliott. (1971). "Copper Price Behavior and the London Metal Exchange" *Applied Economics* 3: 99–113.

MacKinnon, J.G. (1996). "Numerical Distribution Functions for Unit Root and Cointegration Tests," *Journal of Applied Econometrics* 11: 601–618.

MacKinnon, J.G., A.A. Haug, and L. Michelis. (1999). "Numerical Distribution Functions of Likelihood Ratio Tests for Cointegration," *Journal of Applied Econometrics* 14: 563–577.

Phillips, P.C.B., and P. Perron. (1988). "Testing for a Unit Root in Time Series Regression," *Biometrika* 75: 335–346.

Sims, C.A., H.S. James, and M.W. Watson. (1990). "Inference in Linear Time Series Models with Some Unit Roots," *Econometrica* 58.1: 161–182.

Stollery, K.R. (1983). " Secondary Supply of Copper and Ferrous Metals and Canadian Metal Markets," Center for Resource Policies, Technical Paper 3. Kingston, Ontario: Queens University.

Taylor, C. A. (1979). "A Quarterly Domestic Copper Industry Model," *Review of Economics and Statistics* 61.3: 410–422.

USGS. 1955–. "Copper," *Minerals Yearbook*. Washington DC: U.S. Geological Survey, U.S. Department of the Interior.

USGS. (2000). " Recycling—Metals," *Minerals Yearbook*. Washington DC: U.S. Geological Survey, U.S. Department of the Interior.

Van Beukering, P., and M.N. Bouman. (2001). "Empirical Evidence on Recycling and Trade of Paper and Lead in Developed and Developing Countries," *World Development* 29.10: 1717–1737.

CHAPTER 6

Metal Prices and the Supply of Storage

Paul Crompton and Irene M. Xiarchos

INTRODUCTION

Inventory behavior provides a key to understanding price and equilibrium adjustment processes in international metals markets, yet it has received only minimal attention in the economic and econometric analyses of these markets. One reason for this has been the lack of suitable inventory or stock data. Another has been the lack of any uniform theory of inventory behavior or inventory-price relationship to serve as a basis for research. Among the diverse theories that have appeared, the supply of storage was one of the first. Attempts have been made to apply this theory to metal markets but with only mixed results. One problem with such studies has been the lack of useful inventory data. This chapter reexamines this theory by employing time-series tests based on now-existing stock data for aluminum, copper, lead, and zinc. We question the rigor of this theory and show that most of its explanatory power rests between stock, cash, and futures prices, not the basis. Employing unit root tests for preliminary integration analysis, we then test for cointegration among stocks, cash, and futures prices employing the Johansen test procedure. Confirmation of cointegration dictates that causality be tested using the corresponding Granger error correction model. Results of this analysis suggest that inventories drive prices rather than the reverse causality.

INVENTORY BEHAVIOR AND PRICES

Not many studies that have attempted to analyze the inventory and price relationship exist. The principal effort has been to determine why commodity producers, consumers, and dealers hold stocks and in what quantities. Among early efforts, Brennan (1958) employed agricultural commodity data to evaluate the supply of storage theory developed by Working (1949), Kaldor (1939), and Keynes (1930). Other theories that have been proposed to explain inventory behavior are the accelerator, asset returns, buffer stocks, quadratic or S, production smoothing, and optimization, as discussed, for example, by Williams and Wright (1991). Supply of storage implies that firms will adjust their stock levels until the marginal revenue of holding stocks equals their marginal cost, the latter being determined by coverage and stockout yields as well as cost of storage. Tests of this theory have followed, for example, in studies by Brennan (1958, 1991) on precious metals, lumber, butter, eggs, wheat, oats, and wheat; Telser (1958) on cotton and wheat; Weymar (1966) on cocoa; and Considine and Heo (2000) on crude oil and its products.

Among more recent applications of supply of storage, Bresnahan and Suslow (1985) investigated copper market dynamics in the context of the London Metal Exchange (LME) by concentrating on the asset character of stocks. They examine the rate of return of holding copper and the implications of inventory stockouts on this rate of return. Thurman (1988) interpreted the supply of storage by estimating a structural model of stock equilibrium that utilizes in addition direct measurements of stocks. Pindyck (1994) concentrated on the cost aspect by studying how consumers and producers balance cost-adjusting consumption and production with the costs of decreasing inventory holdings as a reaction to metal price fluctuations. As the spread between spot and futures prices varies, the costs of drawing down inventories determine just what quantity of inventories will be held. His conclusions confirm production cost-smoothing behavior, in which inventories are used to shift production to periods in which costs are low and in which inventories are used to avoid stockouts and to reduce scheduling costs. Labys and Lord (1991) attempted to explain fluctuations in inventories as a response to how markets move in and out of equilibrium. Emphasis is placed more on production and consumption than price adjustments using the Granger and Lee (1988) multicointegration approach to equilibrium relationships.

Fama and French (1988) employed spot and futures prices to examine whether the convenience yield on inventory falls at a decreasing rate as inventory increases for aluminum, copper, gold, lead, platinum, silver, tin, and zinc. The implication of the theory examined is that futures prices are less variable than spot prices with inventory is low. But when inventories are high, spot and futures prices should have roughly the same variability. Fama and French explain price variability according to whether inventories are low or high and relate inventory levels to positive demand shocks induced by business cycle activity. While they focused on the variance of the basis, Ng and Pirrong (1994) estimated the effect of the basis on spot and futures return variances and on the correlation between spot and futures returns also for the nonferrous metals. The authors examined volatility at each point in the sample to test the related Samuelson (1965) hypothesis that spot prices should vary more than futures prices. Heaney (2001) investigated how estimates of convenience yield can be used to explain differences between imputed and actual futures prices for copper, lead, and zinc.

Most such studies have not employed actual metals inventory data in reaching any conclusions about the metals inventory and price relationship, with the exception of Pindyck (1994) and Thurman (1988). In fact, inferences about the nature of inventory levels and behavior have been made only in terms of the basis or the intertemporal price spread and related cost and financial factors. However, we know that the behavior of a variety of different forms of inventories is important for understanding metal industry price movements. Consumers acting as manufacturers or processors carry operational stocks to smooth activity of their production and distribution systems to serve as a buffer against interruptions, such as for maintenance, and to facilitate transactions accounting for periodic or cyclical variations. The convenience for manufacturers comes from avoiding plant closings and maintaining reasonable cost coverage against finished product price quotations. These activities require low stock holdings; additional stocks will be held only with the expectation of a return or risk premium for doing so.

Producers maintain stocks to facilitate sales and deliveries but sometimes are forced to carry inventories from periods of seasonally high production to periods of low production because of cyclical turndowns in sales. Dealers or merchants carry stocks just to facilitate their everyday business of buying and selling metals, some of which call for forward delivery. Finally the commodity exchanges themselves hold inventories not only to accommodate speculative transactions but also to better deal with market physical surpluses and deficits.

THEORY OF STORAGE

The theory of the supply of storage has expanded in its interpretation, since its appearance as Keynes's (1930) theory of normal backwardation. Working (1949) criticized this approach, stating that it simply implies the transfer of risk from speculator to hedger, and instead hypothesized that the intertemporal relationship between spot and futures prices was determined by the net cost of carrying stocks. The soon-to-be-found advantage of this theory was that it is relatively easy to test. Because of the difficulties in obtaining meaningful inventory data, however, only the agricultural and petroleum studies have been able to employ stock data. Here we take advantage of the metal inventory time series that have been compiled in recent years to evaluate the inventory and price relationship in physical terms.

Brennan (1958) provided the first testable version of the theory by solving the supply of storage function from the equilibrium conditions between the demand for storage and the supply of storage. Here the term *storage* refers to commodities as inventories or physical stocks and not to storage space. The demand for storage stems from consumers who want storage such that the flow of commodities for sale will be made relatively stable. The term *supply of storage* refers to the task of carrying stocks of a commodity from one period into the next and implies that that firms will adjust their stock levels until the marginal revenue of holding stocks or marginal convenience yield equals their marginal cost, the latter determined by coverage and stockout yields as well as the cost of storage. In a competitive market, firms will hold stocks from one period to the next if the net marginal cost of storage equals the expected price. Equilibrium requires that the net marginal cost of storage (positive or negative) must equal the price of storage. Brennan defined the total net cost of storage as a function of three components: physical costs of storage (o_t), risk aversion factors (r_t), and convenience yield (c_t). Physical costs of storage include interest expense, rent, insurance, handling, and other direct costs associated with storing a product. Interest costs, in particular, provide a transparent view of how storage costs are moving and can reflect the influence of changing business cycles. These costs are assumed to increase at constant rates except at high levels of inventory. At higher inventory levels physical storage costs rise quickly because of capacity limits.

The term *net cost* results from subtracting the convenience yield from the other two components. The total net cost of storage (m_t) can then be defined in terms of ending stocks (I_t) in this way:

$$m_t(I_t) = o_t(I_t) + r_t(I_t) - c_t(I_t) \tag{6.1}$$

The marginal values of these terms can be obtained by differentiating with respect to I_t.

$m'_t > 0$ or < 0 (marginal net total cost of storage)
$o'_t > 0$ and $o''_t \geq 0$ (marginal physical costs)
$r''_t > 0$ and $r''_t \geq 0$ (marginal risk aversion)
$c'_t \geq 0$ and $c''_t \leq 0$ (marginal convenience yield)

The marginal costs and marginal risk aversion are either constant or are increasing functions of stocks. The higher the level of stocks, the greater will be the loss to the firm from an unexpected price fall. The marginal convenience yield declines and reaches zero at a given level of stocks. At low levels of inventories, manufacturers and processors could possibly reach stockouts that could reduce orders fulfilments or limit capacity utilization. Since the costs of obtaining additional inventories may become high, the convenience yield becomes high with low stock levels, since pipeline stocks are necessary.

These marginal values can help to interpret the stock supply curve, since supply curves are marginal cost curves above minimum average variable costs. Differentiating the total net cost of storage (equation 6.1) thus gives the supply of storage.

$$m'_t(I_t) = o'_t(I_t) + r'_t(I_t) - C'_t(I_t) \tag{6.2}$$

The net marginal cost (m'_t) equals the marginal storage cost (o'_t) plus the marginal risk aversion factor (r'_t) minus the marginal convenience yield on stocks (c'_t). The net marginal cost of storage need not be positive. When stocks are small, c'_t will be large. If c'_t is large enough relative to o'_t plus r'_t, the net marginal cost of storage will be negative.

To derive the industry supply of storage curve (Figure 6.1), market equilibrium conditions must be satisfied. The total expected net revenue from holding stocks (u_t) is a function of the expected change in price from period t to some future period t+1. This should equal expected net total costs of storage.

$$u_t(I_t) = m_t(I_t) \tag{6.3}$$

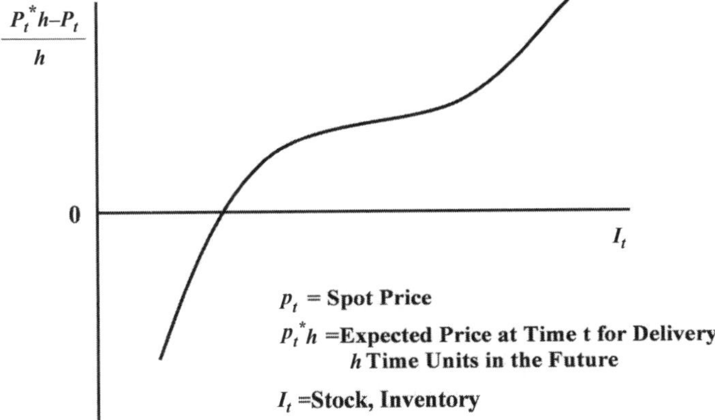

FIGURE 6.1 Supply of Storage Curve

Differentiating this equation gives the quantity of stocks that maximize expected net revenue.

$$u_t'(I_t) = m_t'(I_t) \tag{6.4}$$

This follows from condition 6.4 that expected marginal revenue equals net marginal cost. The conditions on the second derivatives of o_t, r_t and c_t insure that the solution is a maximum.

Assuming pure competition and no externalities, the supply of storage curve is the horizontal sum of all individual net marginal cost functions. The equilibrium level of stocks results from the demand for stocks and supply of stocks according to

$$u_t'(I_t) = EP_{t+1} - P_t \tag{6.5}$$

where EP_{t+1} = price expected in period $t + 1$
P_t is assumed to be known.

For stocks that are hedged on active futures markets, the price spread relevant to a decision about storage levels is the difference between a futures price and a spot price.

$$(P_t^* h - P_t)/h = f_h(I_t) \tag{6.6}$$

where $P_t^* h$ = futures or expected spot price h months in the future
h = horizon time of initial expectations

EMPIRICAL STORAGE CURVE

This section investigates the existence of supply of storage curves for aluminum, copper, lead, and zinc using a cubic polynomial function to reflect the basic structure of the theoretical supply of storage curve in Figure 6.1. These curves have rarely been observed, with the exception of the seminal Brennan (1958) paper. As indicated, the unavailability of reliable stock data for most commodities has resulted in supply of storage analysis being performed only with surrogate variables, usually the marginal net holding cost, marginal convenience yield, or marginal physical costs. We justify the current approach because of the need to provide basic stylized facts on how inventories and spot and futures prices relate to each other in the metals industry.

Concerning recent experience, the London Metal Exchange (LME 2004: 10) reports "to the extent that changes in LME inventories reflect the global pressures of demand for each metal there will be an inverse relationship between prices and stocks." While stock changes may be only one of several influences, such as business cycles on prices, stocks represent the basic forces that link metal supply and demand and that move markets in and out of equilibrium. What causes metal stocks to move into storage? When markets are tight, sharply rising prices can restore market balance, but they do not necessarily cause an increase or a decrease of the quantities of stocks being held. It would appear that the latter depend more on the basis or term structure of prices. Recall that *contango* represents the situation where the futures price for some horizon exceeds the spot price; in contrast, *backwardation* exists when the spot price exceeds the futures price. Over most periods, the LME (2004) reports that the persistence of backwardation encouraged metal to flow into LME warehouses, symptomatic of the supply of storage.

This study concentrates on inventory and price linkages in relation to the LME for aluminum, copper, lead, and zinc. Exchange transactions are recorded in the form of spot or cash (settlement) prices and near and more distant futures prices. The price basis selected represents the difference between the 30-day LME futures contract price and the LME spot price. Pindyck (1994) has expressed concern over the choice of the exact spot price to be used for the basis and prefers the spread between two successive futures contracts. The spot price might reflect discounts and premiums between buyers and sellers or open interest in spot contracts may decline as the end of the month nears. However, the use of LME spot prices possesses the advantage that there are simultaneous spot and forward prices designated for fixed maturities and transacted every business day.

A related consideration is the selection of the stock or inventory variables to be used. Stock data are normally available on a country-by-country case, but the evaluation of the storage curves for individual countries may not be fruitful. Instead a global analysis is performed based on the availability of such data from the World Bureau of Metal Statistics. These data measure total world stockholding and are also disaggregated into their components: LME warehouse stocks, world consumer stocks, world producer stocks, and world merchant stocks. Brennan (1958) makes no such distinction in his analysis of agricultural commodities and relies on data from obvious storage, such as grain elevators. In the current case, we initially examine the relation of the basis to each of the available categories and find that LME stocks provide the best evidence of a supply of storage relationship. As with other attempts to analyze commodity stocks, reported or measured stocks are not always synonymous with actual or total stocks. The LME (2004) has compared reported stocks with official market balances for these metals and has found reasonable correlations between the two to make the present use of the reported or measured stocks credible.

TABLE 6.1 Supply of Storage $(PF1_t - PC_t) = C + bI_t$[c]

Metals	Aluminum	Copper	Lead	Zinc
World Stocks	0.0074 (1.580) $R^2 = 0.172$	0.0408 (9.952) $R^2 = 0.409$	0.0034 (0.647) $R^2 = 0.003$	0.0146 (0.693) $R^2 = 0.003$
LME Stocks	0.0028 (1.662) $R^2 = 0.019$	0.0272 (12.804) $R^2 = 0.497$	0.213 (7.102) $R^2 = 0.262$	0.0136 (4.171) $R^2 = 0.109$
Consumer Stocks	−0.0006 (0.089) $R^2 = 0.000$	0.0911 (9.603) $R^2 = 0.388$	−0.0171 (1.270) $R^2 = 0.011$	−0.0107 (1.165) $R^2 = 0.010$
Producer Stocks	0.0110 (1.225) $R^2 = 0.104$	0.0230 (4.498) $R^2 = 0.116$	0.0248 (3.323) $R^2 = 0.072$	0.0092 (0.722) $R^2 = 0.003$
Merchant Stocks	−0.0063 (1.790) $R^2 = 0.022$	−0.0140 (3.307) $R^2 = 0.070$	0.0009 (0.616) $R^2 = 0.003$	0.0020 (0.690) $R^2 = 0.003$
U.S. Stocks	0.0242 (4.444) $R^2 = 0.122$	0.0348 (9.762) $R^2 = 0.384$	−0.0075 (1.665) $R^2 = 0.177$	−0.0227 (2.548) $R^2 = 0.052$
Sample	1992.01–1993.12	1990.01–1993.12	1992.01–1993.12	1992.01–1993.12

[c]PF1 = near futures price, PC = spot price, I = inventories, C = constant.

The data used in this study are monthly and cover the period 1990 to 2003 and have also been used by Xiarchos (2006).* Preliminary regression estimates provided in Table 6.1 suggest that the goodness of fit is strongest for copper, a market that experiences much greater trading interest than the others. Consumer stocks are likely to provide the strongest confirmation since the stock-holding behavior of consumers is closest to that specified in the supply of storage theory itself. The nonlinearities of the estimated curve are dealt with in the estimation process by using logarithms of both variables. The basis is formed as the difference between log futures prices and log spot prices. The stock variables also are in logs. The time span of estimation is from January 1992 to December 2003. The regression results show higher significance for the stock coefficients and adjusted correlation for world stocks, LME stocks, and consumer stocks than for producers or merchants stocks. The availability of U.S. refinery stocks also provides evidence for storage in that country. For aluminum, lead, and zinc the strongest storage curves are found for LME stocks.

Because of the relatively weak explanatory power of the estimated regressions, polynomial specification has been applied to the equations based on the use of LME stocks. The regression results are provided in Table 6.2. Empirical illustrations of the estimated storage curves are then presented for each of the metals in Figure 6.2. Copper and lead provide the most impressive confirmations of the theoretical storage curve. In the case of copper, in particular, the regression explains half of the observed variation (Figure 6.2), and in the case of lead, one-fourth (Figure 6.3).

* The inventory data were compiled by I.M. Xiarchos with the assistance of W.C. Labys. The most current version of the data is available on request from Labys.

TABLE 6.2 Cubic Supply of Storage Regressions $(PF1_t - PC_t) = C + bI_t$

Stock Variable*	Aluminum	Copper	Lead	Zinc
Constant	−0.803	−247.14	−30.96	−16.85
	(−0.03)	(−8.21)	(−1.67)	(−0.62)
LME	0.05	1.35	0.49	0.09
	(0.83)	(6.09)	(1.73)	(0.57)
LME^2	−0.01	−0.01	−0.01	−0.01
	(−0.97)	(−4.60)	(−1.50)	(−0.25)
LME^3	0.01	0.01	0.01	0.01
	(1.10)	(3.76)	(1.45)	(0.11)
R^2	0.03	0.50	0.25	0.08
Durbin-Watson	0.95	1.04	1.01	0.71

*Squared is 2; cubed is 3.

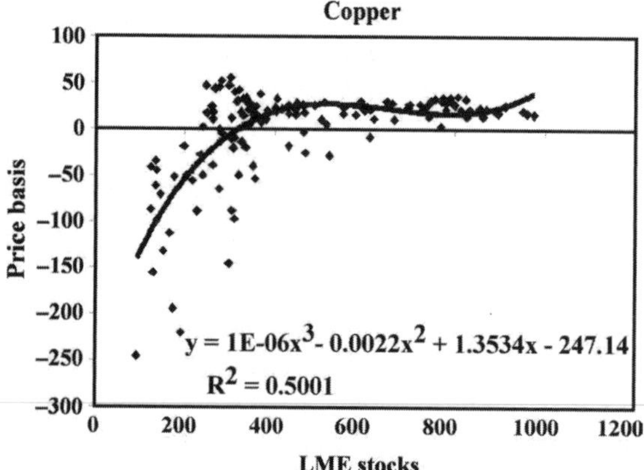

FIGURE 6.2 Monthly Empirical Supply of Storage Curve for Copper, 1992.01–2003.12

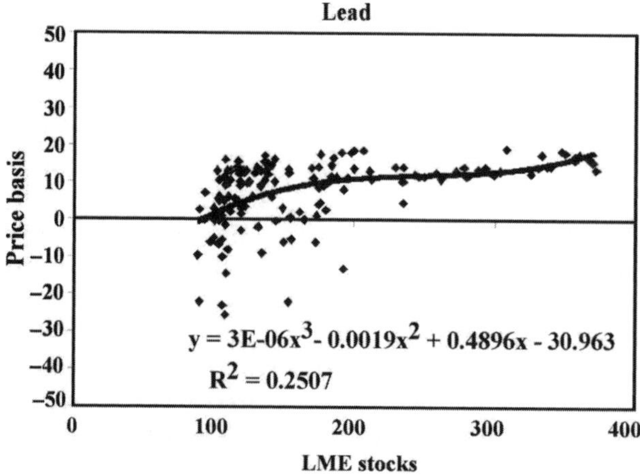

FIGURE 6.3 Monthly Empirical Supply of Storage Curve for Lead, 1992.01–2003.12

Aluminum and zinc, however, are less supportive (Figures 6.4 and 6.5), with R^2 values of less than 0.1 in both cases. The surprisingly weak confirmation of supply of storage for these latter two metals is an important result. It implies that the attempts to confirm this relationship without verifying the price basis to stock correlation can be called into question.

COINTEGRATION AND CAUSALITY

Given the discovered weak relationship between the price basis and inventories, it was not possible to test for the existence of causality between these two variables. Hence our quest to examine the price basis and inventory connection became one of testing

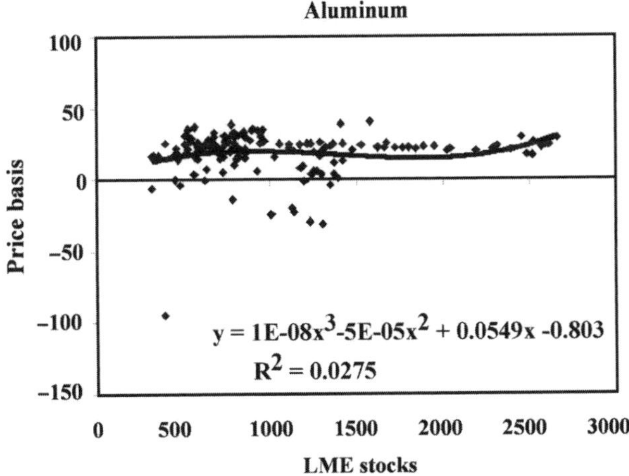

FIGURE 6.4 Monthly Empirical Supply of Storage Curve for Aluminum, 1992.01–2003.12

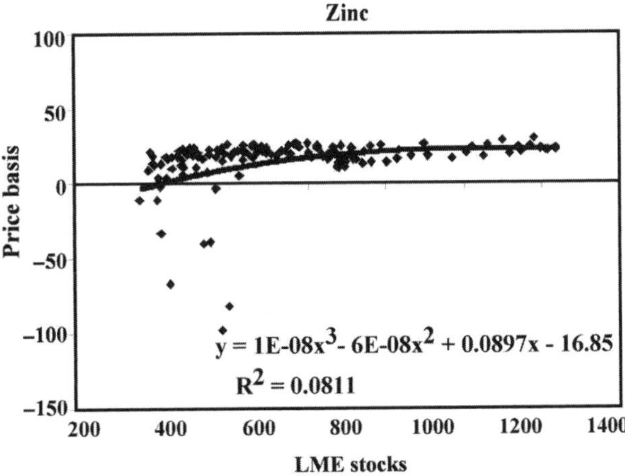

FIGURE 6.5 Monthly Empirical Supply of Storage Curve for Zinc, 1992.01–2003.12

the relationship between the separate cash and futures price series and inventories. To our knowledge, this analysis has not been performed using cointegration and causality tests in previous studies. While Pindyck (1994) and Thurman (1988) did use data for both variables, they did not move in this direction. Only Balabanoff (1995) performed such tests employing crude oil data for the U.S. market.

Our empirical tests begin with the Augmented Dickey-Fuller (ADF) method to test for the existence of unit roots and to identify the order of integration for each variable. This test has the advantage that it takes into account possible nonstationarity in the error process found in the ADF equation. The unit root tests are done allowing for a constant or drift in the test specification but no time trend. Results for the tests are reported in Table 6.3 for the stock variables that demonstrated the best possible fit from the empirical storage analysis: total, LME, and consumer stocks. As shown in the table, a unit root can be found for the price and stock variables but not for the basis for most of the metals. The results for aluminum are particularly poor and suggest that this metal be dropped from further analysis. Unit root tests for the residual in the corresponding cointegration equation (Engle and Granger 1987) confirm the lack of integration and thus the possibility of cointegration exists for each of the metal equations.

The simple cointegration results presented in Table 6.3 need to be elaborated further in order to provide a suitable test to determine whether any causality exists between the metal stock and price variables. We have chosen the Johansen (1995) method that implements vector autoregression (VAR)-based cointegration tests when a group of nonstationary series are under examination. Johansen's method tests the restrictions imposed by cointegration on the unrestricted VAR involving the series with p terms.

$$y_t = A_1 y_{t-1} + \cdots + A_p y_{t-p} + Bx_t + \varepsilon_t \tag{6.7}$$

where y_t = k-vector of nonstationary I(1) variables
x_t = d vector of deterministic variables
ε_t = vector of innovations

We can rewrite the VAR as:

$$\Delta y_t = \Pi y_{t-1} + \sum_{i=1}^{p-1} \Gamma_i \Delta y_{t-i} + Bx_t + \varepsilon_t \tag{6.8}$$

where

$$\Pi = \sum_{i=1}^{p} A_i - I_i, \Gamma_i = -\sum_{j=i+1}^{p} A_j \tag{6.9}$$

Granger's representation theorem asserts that if the coefficient matrix Π has reduced rank $r < k$, then there exist k $\times$ r matrices α and β each with rank r such that $\Pi = \alpha\beta'$ and $\beta' y_t$ is stationary. r is the number of cointegrating relations (the cointegrating rank), and each column of β is the cointegrating vector. The elements of α are known as the adjustment parameters in the vector error correction model. Johansen's method is to estimate the Π matrix in an unrestricted form, then test whether we can reject the restrictions implied by the reduced rank of Π.

By examining the Π matrix, we can detect the existence of cointegrating relations among the Y variables. The most interesting case is $0 <$ rank(Π) r $<$ p. This implies

TABLE 6.3 Unit Root Tests of Inventory and Price, January 1992 to December 2003

	ADF[1]		PP[2]		KPSS[3]	
	Levels[4]	Diffs	Levels	Diffs	Levels	Diffs
Aluminum						
Total stocks	−1.29	−8.35	−1.40	−8.48	0.58	0.15
LME stocks	−1.81	−5.74	−1.70	−5.96	0.47	0.11
Consumer stocks	−2.08	−10.13	−2.39	−14.52	0.54	0.19
Spot price	−2.26	−12.25	−2.31	−12.25	0.16*	0.06
Futures price	−2.10	−11.78	−2.24	−11.78	0.15*	0.08
Price basis	−6.51		−6.61		0.81*	0.11
Copper						
Total stocks	−3.19*	−11.91	−2.78	−17.63	0.62	0.07
LME stocks	−1.93	−8.09	−1.91	−7.24	0.71	0.07
Consumer stocks	−2.50	−12.58	−3.73*	−20.12	0.29*	0.09
Spot price	−1.69	−12.01	−1.79	−12.02	0.79	0.12
Futures price	−1.64	−11.52	−1.81	−11.55	0.82	0.12
Price basis	−3.41		−4.51		0.26	
Lead						
Total stocks	−1.41	−14.56	−1.56	−14.61	0.29*	0.28
LME stocks	−1.55	−7.56	−1.76	−8.01	0.40*	0.11
Consumer stocks	−2.44	−13.00	−2.38	−13.36	0.24*	0.10
Spot price	−1.47	−10.44	−1.68	−10.45	0.29*	0.16
Futures price	−1.38	−10.02	−1.66	−10.06	0.32*	0.15
Price basis	−5.68		−5.68		0.20	
Zinc						
Total stocks	−1.29	−10.29	−1.51	−10.32	0.29*	0.31
LME stocks	−2.86	−4.30	−2.26	−7.42	0.30*	0.29
Consumer stocks	−1.72	−14.40	−1.48	−14.63	0.43*	0.18
Spot price	−2.09	−11.82	−2.27	−11.84	0.55	0.06
Futures price	−1.94	−12.74	−2.17	−12.75	0.57	0.06
Price basis	−4.69		−5.26		0.14	
1% critical value	−3.47	−3.47	−3.47	−3.47	0.74	0.74
5% critical value	−2.88	−2.88	−2.88	−2.88	0.46	0.46

[1]ADF is the Augmented Dickey-Fuller (Dickey and Fuller 1981) unit root test. The ADF regression includes an intercept term, and the lag length of the ADF test is determined by minimizing the SBIC.
[2]PP is the Phillips and Perron (1988) unit root test.
[3]KPSS is the Kwiatkowski et al. (1992) unit root test.
[4]Levels and Diffs denote that the statistics are based on logarithmic levels and first differences respectively. Price basis is the futures price mines the spot price, where both variables are measured in levels.

that there are r cointegrating relations among the elements of Y_t, and there are $p \times r$ matrices α and β such that $\Pi = \alpha\beta'$. Hence α is a matrix of error correction parameters and β is interpreted as a matrix of cointegrating vectors, with the property that $\beta' Y_t$ is stationary even though Y_t itself is not stationary.

The results of the cointegration tests are reported in Table 6.4. T* and C* are test statistics and critical values for the null H_r^*, with at most r cointegrating vectors but no linear trend. T and C are test statistics and critical values for the null H_r, with at most r cointegration vectors and a linear trend. We conclude that there is one cointegration vector because the trace test rejects both the null hypothesis of zero cointegration rank and the null of at most one cointegration rank with no linear trend, but it does not reject the null of at most one cointegration rank with a linear trend.

The presence of cointegration dictates that one should not employ the standard Granger causality test (Granger 1988). Instead, we employ a vector error correction model (VECM) that also permits an interpretation of the short-run and long-run equilibrium dynamics. In essence, we take the VAR model into a VECM model, where the cointegrating errors from the Johansen model become the error correction variables for the Engle and Granger VECM given in equation 6.10.

$$\Delta Y_{it} = \mu_{it} + \beta' ECT_{t-1} + \sum_{i=1}^{m} a_i \Delta Y_{1,t-i} + \sum_{i=1}^{m} b_i \Delta Y_{2,t-i} + \sum_{i=1}^{m} c_i \Delta Y_{3,t-i} + \sum_{i=1}^{m} d_i \Delta Y_{4,t-i} + \varepsilon_i \tag{6.10}$$

TABLE 6.4 Johansen Cointegration Tests Results for Cash Prices and Stocks

	Trace Test[1]			Max-eigenvalue Test[2]		
Null Hypothesis	LME	Consumer	World	LME	Consumer	World
Aluminum						
$r = 0$	42.26	39.42	48.78	18.15	28.45	20.97
$r = 1$	24.11	10.96	20.84	12.86	6.61	14.07
$r = 2$	11.25	4.34	6.95	11.25	4.34	3.76
Copper						
$r = 0$	37.32	53.08	39.69	20.22	41.17	25.49
$r = 1$	17.10	11.91	14.20	13.38	8.77	11.07
$r = 2$	3.72	3.14	3.14	3.72	3.14	3.14
Lead						
$r = 0$	54.37	37.07	47.55	44.10	29.22	31.92
$r = 1$	10.26	7.84	15.63	6.63	4.93	10.59
$r = 2$	3.63	2.91	5.03	3.63	2.91	5.03
Zinc						
$r = 0$	51.16	67.01	61.06	39.54	56.03	52.50
$r = 1$	11.61	10.98	8.56	6.46	8.15	5.45
$r = 2$	5.14	2.83	3.11	5.14	2.83	3.11

[1]Trace test, 5% critical values: $r = 0$, 29.68; $r = 1$, 15.41; $r = 2$, 3.76.
[2]Max-eigenvalue test, 5% critical values: $r = 0$, 20.97; $r = 1$, 14.07; $r = 2$, 3.76.

where Y_{it} = inventories, cash prices, or futures prices

$\beta' ECT_{t-1}$ contains r cointegrating terms, reflecting the long-run equilibrium relationship among variables.

From the system, the Granger-causality tests are examined by testing whether all the coefficients of $\Delta Y_{2,t-i}$, $\Delta Y_{3,t-i}$, or $\Delta Y_{4,t-i}$ are statistically different from zero as a group based on a standard F-test and/or whether the β' coefficient of the error-correction term is also significant. Standard lag length of 2 is employed.

The results reported in Table 6.5 uncover bidirectional causality for LME and world aluminum and copper stocks and prices. Consumer stocks seem to cause prices for aluminum, copper, and zinc. Also for zinc the LME, consumer, and world stock

TABLE 6.5 Granger Causality Test Results for Cash Prices and Stocks

	Source of Causation				
	Short Run		Long Run		
	ΔStocks	ΔCash Price	ECT	ECT/ΔStocks	ECT/ΔCash Price
Aluminum					
ΔLME		5.07*	4.19*		5.79*
ΔCash price	4.19*		14.35*	7.53*	
ΔConsumer		0.20	0.69		0.42
ΔCash price	5.54*		12.92*	7.32*	
ΔWorld		6.30*	8.14*		8.53*
ΔCash price	5.28*		13.71*	7.58*	
Copper					
ΔLME		0.16	6.28*		2.38**
ΔCash price	5.98*		6.30*	6.42*	
ΔConsumer		1.25	7.95*		3.63*
ΔCash price	2.44**		1.58*	2.02	
ΔWorld		0.32	0.48		0.35
ΔCash price	2.22		2.50	2.40**	
Lead					
ΔLME		0.21	2.38		0.84
ΔCash price	1.51		22.36*	10.25*	
ΔConsumer		1.69	1.42		1.80
ΔCash price	0.07		15.03*	5.11*	
ΔWorld		1.16	0.23		0.79
ΔCash price	0.15		21.46*	7.17*	
Zinc					
ΔLME		0.67	12.52*		4.44*
ΔCash price	6.32*		10.58*	9.39*	
ΔConsumer		0.04	1.16		0.42
ΔCash price	2.25*		1.71	2.10*	
ΔWorld		0.02	2.05		0.81
ΔCash price	3.56*		5.42*	3.68*	

*Significant at the 5% level.
**Significant at the 10% level.

variables seem to cause cash prices. The error correction term is significant in most regressions.

CONCLUSIONS

Only weak empirical evidence has been found to confirm the existence of the theoretical supply of storage curve. Copper and lead provide the most impressive confirmations while aluminum and zinc are less supportive. This fact led to the search for possible relations between the price and stock variables, now omitting the basis. We then performed unit root tests to provide evidence for integration. We subsequently tested for cointegration among stocks, cash, and futures prices employing the Johansen test procedure. Confirmation of cointegration dictated that causality be tested using the corresponding Granger error correction model. The strongest results of this analysis suggest that consumer inventories drive price movements, with the absence of bidirectional causality, for aluminum, copper, and zinc.

REFERENCES

Balabanoff, S. (1995). "Oil Futures Prices and Stock Management: A Cointegration Analysis," *Energy Economics* 17.4: 205–210.

Brennan, M.J. (1958). "The Supply of Storage," *American Economic Review* 48: 50–72.

———. "The Price of Convenience and the Pricing of Commodity Contingent Claims." In D. Lund and B. Oskendal (eds.), *Stochastic Models and Options Values*. New York: Elsevier.

Bresnahan, T.F., and V.Y. Suslow. (1985). "Inventories as an Asset: The Volatility of Copper Prices," *International Economic Review* 26: 409–424.

Considine, T.J. and E. Heo. (2000). "Price and Inventory Dynamics in Petroleum Product Markets," *Energy Economics* 22: 527–547.

Dickey, D., and W. Fuller. (1981). "Likelihood Ratio Statistics for Autoregressive Time Series with a Unit Root," *Econometrica* 49: 1057–1072.

Engle, R., and C.W.J. Franger. (1987). "Cointegration and Error Correction: Representation, Estimation and Testing," *Econometrica* 55: 251–276.

Fama, E.F., and K.R. French. (1988). "Business Cycles and the Behavior of Metals Prices," *Journal of Finance* 43.5: 1075–1093.

Heaney, R. (2001). "Commodity Futures Pricing: A Simple Model of Convenience Yields," Working Paper, Department of Commerce, Australian National University, Canberra.

Kaldor. N. (1939). "Speculation and Economic Stability," *Review of Economic Studies* 7: 1–27.

Keynes, J.M. (1930). *A Treatise on Money*, New York: Harcourt Brace.

Kwiatkowski, D.P., C.B. Phillips, P. Schmidt, and Y. Shin. (1992). "Testing the Null Hypothesis of Stationarity Against the Alternative of a Unit Root: How Sure Are We That Economic Series Have a Unit Root?" *Journal of Econometrics* 54: 159–178.

Labys, W.C., and M.L. Lord. (1992). "Inventory and Equilibrium Adjustments in International Commodity Markets: A Multi-Cointegration Approach," *Applied Economics* 24: 77–84.

London Metal Exchange. (2004). *LME Stocks and Market Balances*. London: London Metal Exchange.

———. (various years). *Metal Price Data*. London: London Metal Exchange.

Ng, V.G., and C. Pirrong. (1994). "Fundamentals and Volatility: Storage, Spreads and the Dynamics of Metals Prices," *Journal of Business* 67: 203–230.

Phillips, P., and P. Perron. (1988). "Testing for a Unit Root in Time Series Regressions," *Biometrica* 75: 335–346.

Pindyck, R. (2002). "Volatility and Commodity Price Dynamics," Working Paper, Massachusetts Institute of Technology, Cambridge, MA.

———. (1994). "Inventories and the Short-Run Dynamics of Commodity Prices," *Rand Journal of Economics* 25.1: 41–59.

Samuelson, P.A. (1965). "Proof that Properly Anticipated Prices Fluctuate Randomly," *Industrial Management Review* 6: 41–49.

Telser, L. (1958). "Futures Trading and the Storage of Cotton and Wheat," *Journal of Political Economy* 66: 233–255.

Thurman, W.N. (1988). "Speculative Carryover: An Empirical Example of the US Refined Copper Market," *Rand Journal of Economics* 19: 420–437.

Weymar, H.F. (1966). "The Supply of Storage Revisited," *American Economic Review* 56: 1226–1234.

Williams, J.C., and B.D. Wright. (1991). *Storage and Commodity Markets.* Cambridge: Cambridge University Press.

Working, H. (1949). "The Theory of the Price of Storage," *American Economic Review* 39: 1254–1262.

World Bureau of Metal Statistics. (various issues). *Metal Statistics*, London.

Xiarchos, I.M. (2006). *Three Essays on Environmental Markets: Dynamic Behavior, Market Interactions, and Policy Implications.* Ph.D. dissertation. West Virginia University, Morgantown.

CHAPTER 7

Testing for Temporal Asymmetry in the Metal Price-Stock Relationship

Eugene Kouassi

INTRODUCTION

Many consumers complain that metal prices at the retail level respond faster to international metal market price increases (stock decreases) than to decreases (to an increase in stock). The perceived asymmetry, often construed as an abuse of market power, points to a potential gap in price and/or stock theory (Peltzman 2000). Despite this perception, the economic and econometric analyzes of international metal stock adjustments have received only minimal attention. One reason for this has been the lack of suitable inventory or stock data. Another has been the lack of any uniform theory of inventory behavior or inventory-price relationship to serve as a basis for research. Attempts to study this relationship in metal markets have only had mixed results.

This study uses recent advances in asymmetric time-series analysis (e.g., Enders 2001; Enders and Granger 1998; and Enders and Siklos 2001), and applies them to analyze price and/or stock transmission at various stages in the production and distribution chain in international metal markets. We depart from previous research in identifying the potential role metal future markets may play in asymmetric price or stock transmission. Our analysis takes advantage of newly available inventory data for aluminum, copper, lead, and zinc.

STOCKS AND MARKET EQUILIBRIUM

Not many studies that have attempted to analyze the inventory and price relationship exist. The principal past effort has been to determine why commodity producers, consumers, and dealers hold stocks and in what quantities. Among early efforts, Brennan (1958) employed agricultural commodity data to evaluate the supply of storage theory developed by Keynes (1930), Kaldor (1939), and Working (1949). Other theories to explain inventory behavior are the accelerator, asset returns, buffer stocks, quadratic or S, production smoothing, and optimization. For literature reviews, see Chikan (1984), Wright and Williams (1982), and Williams and Wright

(1991). Supply of storage implies that firms will adjust their stock levels until the marginal revenue of holding stocks equals their marginal cost; the latter depends on coverage and stockout yields as well as the cost of storage. Tests of this theory have been performed, for example, by Brennan (1958, 1991) on precious metals, lumber, butter, eggs, wheat, oats and wheat; Telser (1958) on cotton and wheat; Weymar (1966) on cocoa; and Considine and Heo (2000) on crude oil and its products.

Earlier studies dealing with supply of storage that focus particularly on metals inventory behavior include the work of Burrows (1971). Although published significantly later, Ghosh et al.'s study (1987) also fits in this earlier tradition. Among the more recent applications, Bresnahan and Suslow (1985) investigated copper market dynamics in the context of the London Metal Exchange (LME) by concentrating on the asset character of stocks. They examined the rate of return of holding copper and the implications of inventory stockouts on the rate of return. Thurman (1988) interprets the supply of storage by estimating a structural model of stock equilibrium that utilizes, in addition, direct measurements of stocks. Pindyck (1994) concentrates on the cost aspect by studying how consumers and producers balance the costs of adjusting consumption and production with the costs of decreasing inventory holdings as a reaction to metal price fluctuations. As the spread between spot and futures prices varies, the costs of drawing down inventories determine the quantity of inventories held. Pindyck's conclusions confirm production cost smoothing behavior, in which inventories are used to shift production to periods in which costs are low, to avoid stockouts, and to reduce scheduling costs. Taking a different direction, Labys and Lord (1991) sought to explain fluctuations in inventories as a response to how markets move in and out of equilibrium. They employed Granger's and Lee's (1989) multicointegration approach and focused more on production and consumption adjustments than on price adjustments.

Fama and French (1988) employed spot and futures prices to examine whether the convenience yield of inventory for aluminum, copper, lead, and zinc falls at a decreasing rate as inventory increases. The implication of the theory is that futures prices exhibit less variation than spot prices when inventories are low. However, when inventories are high, spot and futures prices should have roughly the same variability. The authors further test this theory by relating inventory levels to positive demand shocks induced by business cycle activity.

Except for Pindyck (1994) and Thurman (1988), most studies do not employ metals inventory data in reaching conclusions about the metals inventory and price relationship. Inferences about the nature of inventory levels and behavior have mostly been made based on the intertemporal price spread and related cost and financial factors. We know, however, that the behaviors of a variety of different forms of inventories are important for understanding metal industry price movements. Consumers acting as manufacturers or processors carry operational stocks to smooth activity of their production and distribution systems to serve as a buffer against interruptions, such as for maintenance, and to facilitate transactions accounting for periodic or cyclical variations. The convenience for manufacturers comes from avoiding plant closings and maintaining reasonable cost coverage against finished product price quotations. These activities require only low stock holdings; additional stocks will be held only with the expectation of a return or risk premium for doing so.

Producers maintain stocks to facilitate sales and deliveries, but sometimes they are forced to carry inventories from periods of seasonally high production to periods of low production because of cyclical turndowns in sales. Dealers or merchants carry stocks just to facilitate their everyday business of buying and selling metals, some of which call for forward delivery. Finally, the commodity exchanges themselves hold inventories not only to accommodate speculative transactions, but also to better deal with market physical surpluses and deficits.

Even though the literature on international metal markets seems abundant, most of these studies are based only on the description, behavior, and interaction between price and stocks variables in these markets. Four questions arise:

1. How do variables in international metal markets react when these markets are in equilibrium or disequilibrium?
2. How do variables in international metal markets react when these markets are below or above a threshold equilibrium value?
3. Do price levels respond faster to international metal market disequilibrium than stocks?
4. Do negative changes for both prices and stocks have stronger effects than positive changes in these international metal markets?

ECONOMETRIC METHODOLOGY

Our research approach depends on tests of cointegration and causality. Testing for cointegration and temporal causality between price and stock is based on a bivariate vector autoregression (VAR) representation involving two series, price and stock. The bivariate VAR representation in the presence of cointegration is written as,

$$\Delta x_t = \omega + \sum_{i=1}^{p} \beta_i \Delta x_{t-i} + \sum_{j=1}^{q} \gamma_j \Delta y_{t-j} + \theta_1 \mu_{t-1} + \zeta_{x,t} \tag{7.1}$$

$$\Delta y_t = \delta + \sum_{i=1}^{p} \varphi_i \Delta x_{t-i} + \sum_{j=1}^{q} \phi_j \Delta y_{t-j} + \theta_2 \mu_{t-1} + \zeta_{y,t}, \tag{7.2}$$

where x = price variable
y = stock variable
μ_{t-1} = error correction term
Δ = lag operator
p = lag length for price
q = lag length for stock

A crucial limitation of equations 7.1 and 7.2 is that they do not capture the asymmetric nature of the responses of x and y to each other; nor they capture the asymmetry, if any, of the responses in the presence of asymmetric cointegration. These equations are not valid if the responses of prices to stocks depend on whether stocks are increasing or decreasing and vice versa. In addition, they are not valid in the presence of asymmetric cointegration. In order to capture these asymmetric effects, we decompose y and x and account for asymmetric cointegration as follows, and incorporate these decompositions into equations 7.1 and 7.2.

$$y_t^+ = \begin{cases} y_t & \textit{if } y_t \geq 0 \\ 0 & \textit{otherwise} \end{cases} \tag{7.3}$$

$$y_t^- = \begin{cases} y_t & \textit{if } y_t \leq 0 \\ 0 & \textit{otherwise} \end{cases} \tag{7.4}$$

$$x_t^+ = \begin{cases} x_t & \textit{if } x_t \geq 0 \\ 0 & \textit{otherwise} \end{cases} \tag{7.5}$$

$$x_t^- = \begin{cases} x_t & \textit{if } x_t \leq 0 \\ 0 & \textit{otherwise} \end{cases} \tag{7.6}$$

In addition, as in Enders and Granger (1998) and Enders and Siklos (2001), we introduce asymmetric adjustments in the model by letting the deviation from the long-run equilibrium ($\hat{\mu}_t$) behave as a threshold autoregressive (TAR) process. Thus, we have,

$$\Delta\hat{\mu}_t = I_t\rho_1\hat{\mu}_{t-1} + (1 - I_t)\,\rho_2\hat{\mu}_{t-1} + \varepsilon_t, \tag{7.7}$$

where $I_t =$ Heaviside indicator such that

$$I_t = \begin{cases} 1 & \textit{if } \hat{\mu}_{t-1} \geq \tau \\ 0 & \textit{if } \hat{\mu}_{t-1} < \tau \end{cases}. \tag{7.8}$$

where $\tau =$ value of the threshold
ρ_1 and $\rho_2 =$ parameters to be estimated

Petrucelli and Wooldford (1984) show that the necessary and sufficient conditions for stationarity of μ_t are $\rho_1 < 0$, $\rho_2 < 0$, and $(1 + \rho_1)(1 + \rho_2) < 1$. As the threshold value τ in equation 7.8 is unknown (and there is no a priori reason to expect that it should be zero), the procedure suggested in Chang (1993) and Enders and Siklos (2001) was used to perform a grid search. Specifically, the estimated residuals from the long-run equation were sorted in ascending order and called $\hat{\mu}_1^\tau < \hat{\mu}_2^\tau < \cdots < \hat{\mu}_T^\tau$, where T is the number of usable observations. The largest and smallest 15 percent of the $\{\hat{\mu}_t^\tau\}$ values were discarded and the remainder considered as possible thresholds. Then, for each possible threshold, the underlying model is estimated, and the preferred threshold value is selected as the one that minimizes the sum of squared residuals. In our study, we consider a consistent estimation of the threshold (Enders and Siklos, 2001). In addition, since the exact nature of the nonlinearity may not be known, it is possible to allow the adjustment to depend on the change in $\hat{\mu}_{t-1}$ (*i.e.*, $\Delta\hat{\mu}_{t-1}$)

instead of the level of $\hat{\mu}_{t-1}$. In this case, the Heaviside indicator in equation 7.8 becomes

$$I_t = \begin{cases} 1 & if\ \Delta\hat{\mu}_{t-1} \geq \tau \\ 0 & if\ \Delta\hat{\mu}_{t-1} < \tau \end{cases} \tag{7.9}$$

Enders and Granger (1998) and Enders and Siklos (2001) show that this specification is especially relevant when the adjustment is such that the series exhibit more "momentum" in one direction than the other; the resulting model is called a momentum-threshold autoregressive (M-TAR) model. Caner and Hansen (2001) present a statistical argument for M-TAR adjustment. If μ_{t-1} is a near-unit root process, setting the Heaviside indicator using $\Delta\mu_{t-1}$ can perform better than the specification using a pure TAR adjustment.

By allowing ρ_1 and ρ_2 in equation 7.7 take different values, the model recognizes that positive and negative deviations from equilibrium can be corrected for at different speeds. In other words, different values of ρ_1 and ρ_2 imply asymmetric adjustment (Enders and Siklos 2001; Chen et al. 2005). If cointegration exists, $\rho_1 < 0$ and $\rho_2 < 0$. Testing for cointegration is performed based on the t_{Max} and Φ tests proposed by Enders and Siklos (2001). The t_{Max} statistic is given by the larger t-statistic of ρ_1 and ρ_2. A significantly negative t_{Max} statistic would imply that ρ_1 and ρ_2 are both negative (see Enders 2001 for improved critical values). The Φ test is an F-test examining the joint hypothesis of $\rho_1 = 0$ and $\rho_2 = 0$ (see Enders 2001 for improved critical values).

If the errors in equation 7.7 are serially correlated, it is possible to use a TAR or an M-TAR model augmented with lagged values of $\Delta\mu_t$ for the residuals. Thus, equation 7.7 could be replaced by

$$\Delta\hat{\mu}_t = I_t\rho_1\hat{\mu}_{t-1} + (1 - I_t)\,\rho_2\hat{\mu}_{t-1} + \sum_{i=1}^{k}\gamma_i\Delta\hat{\mu}_{t-i} + \varepsilon_t \tag{7.10}$$

Assuming a classic TAR or M-TAR model holds, equations 7.1 and 7.2 can be rewritten as

$$\Delta x_t = \omega + \sum_{i=1}^{p}\beta_i\Delta x_{t-i} + \sum_{j=1}^{q}a_j\Delta y_{t-j}^{+} + \sum_{j=1}^{q}b_j\Delta y_{t-j}^{-} - \alpha_1^{+}I_t\hat{\mu}_{t-1} - \alpha_1^{-}(1 - I_t)\,\hat{\mu}_{t-1} + \zeta_{x,t} \tag{7.11}$$

$$\Delta y_t = \delta + \sum_{i=1}^{p}c_i\Delta x_{t-i}^{+} + \sum_{i=1}^{p}d_i\Delta x_{t-i}^{-} + \sum_{j=1}^{q}\phi_j\Delta y_{t-j} - \alpha_2^{+}I_t\hat{\mu}_{t-1} - \alpha_2^{-}(1 - I_t)\,\hat{\mu}_{t-1} + \zeta_{y,t} \tag{7.12}$$

In equation 7.1, the null hypothesis in the Granger causality test is that y does not cause x, which is represented by

$$\mathrm{H}_0 : \gamma_1 = \gamma_2 = \cdots = \gamma_q = 0 \quad \text{and} \quad \theta_1 = 0, \tag{7.13}$$

while the alternative hypothesis is given by

$$\mathrm{H}_1 : \gamma_j \neq 0 \quad \text{for at least one } j \text{ or } \theta_1 \neq 0 \tag{7.14}$$

Similar hypotheses can be formulated for equation 7.2 to test for causality in the reverse direction. Obviously, the value of the test statistic depends on p and q, which makes it necessary to use various information criteria to choose the optimal lag length.

If equation 7.11 is adopted, then to find out whether or not y_t^+ has any effect on x, the null may be written as,

$$\mathrm{H}_0^+ : a_1 = a_2 = \cdots = a_q = 0 \quad \text{and} \quad \alpha_1^+ = 0 \tag{7.15}$$

while the alternative hypothesis is given by

$$\mathrm{H}_1^+ : a_j \neq 0 \quad \text{for at least one } j \text{ or } \alpha_1^+ \neq 0 \tag{7.16}$$

To find out whether y_t^- has any effect on x, the null hypotheses may be written as

$$\mathrm{H}_0^- : b_1 = b_2 = \cdots = b_q = 0 \quad \text{and} \quad \alpha_1^- = 0, \tag{7.17}$$

and the alternative hypothesis as

$$\mathrm{H}_1^- : b_j \neq 0 \quad \text{for at least one } j \text{ or } \alpha_1^- \neq 0 \tag{7.18}$$

Similar hypotheses can be formulated for testing the effects of $x^+$and x^-on y, based on equation 7.12.

To find out whether y^- has a stronger effect on x than y^+, these null and alternative hypotheses are used in conjunction with equation 7.11:

$$\mathrm{H}_{\alpha 0} : b_j \geq a_j \quad \text{for } j = 1, 2, \ldots, q \quad \text{and} \quad \alpha_1^- \geq \alpha_1^+ \tag{7.19}$$

and

$$\mathrm{H}_{\alpha 1} : b_j \ngeq a_j \quad \text{for } j = 1, 2, \ldots, q \quad \text{or} \quad \alpha_1^- \ngeq \alpha_1^+ \tag{7.20}$$

To examine these restrictions, three different but asymptotically equivalent Granger-causality tests are considered. More specifically, we use the Wald (W), likelihood ratio (LR), and the Lagrange multiplier (LM) tests based on constrained and unconstrained estimates. The main reason for the simultaneous use of all three tests is that, even though they are asymptotically equivalent, they may yield different results, especially in finite samples, such as ours. Although the inequality $W > LR > LM$ holds theoretically and is widely cited, particularly in the case of linear regressions, in individual cases it is possible that the three statistics could lead to different inferences. Unfortunately, this is a frequent problem in finite samples and is difficult to resolve because there is no theoretical justification for the superiority of one technique over the others. The appendix provides a description of the three causality-testing procedures.

EMPIRICAL TESTS FOR THRESHOLD COINTEGRATION

The data used in this study are monthly and cover the period 1990 to 2003. They have been collected, with the assistance of Labys, and used by Xiarchos (2006).* Table 7.1 provides a summary of the variables and their sources.

This study concentrates on inventory and price linkages in relation to the London Metal Exchange (LME) for aluminum, copper, lead, and zinc. Exchange transactions are recorded in the form of spot or cash (settlement) prices and near and more distant futures prices. The use of LME spot prices possesses the advantage that there are simultaneous spot and forward prices designated for fixed maturities and transacted every business day.

A related consideration is the selection of the stock or inventory variables to be used. Stock data are normally available on a country-by-country case, but the evaluation of the storage curves for individual countries may not be fruitful. Instead a global analysis is performed based on the availability of such data from the World Bureau of Metal Statistics. These data measure total world stockholding and are also disaggregated by its components: LME warehouse stocks, world consumer stocks, world producer stocks, and world merchant stocks. Brennan (1958) makes no such distinction in his analysis of agricultural commodities and relies on data from obvious storage such as grain elevators. In the current case, we initially examine the relation of the basis to each of the given categories and report those results in Table 7.2. As with other attempts to analyze commodity stocks, reported or measured stocks are not always synonymous with actual or total stocks. The LME (2004) has compared reported stocks with official market balances for these metals and has found sufficient

*The inventory data were compiled by I.M. Xiarchos with the assistance of W.C. Labys. The most current version of the data is available on request from Labys.

TABLE 7.1 Variable Names and Data Sources

STOCK VARIABLES

Metal	Variable	Explanation	Sources
Aluminum	awtots	World total stocks	World Bureau of Metal Statistics
Copper	cwtots	World total commercial stocks	Various issues. *Metal Statistics.*
Lead	lwtots	World total commercial stocks	London
Zinc	zwtots	Total country stocks	London Metal Exchange (2004) *LME Stocks and Market Balances*

PRICE VARIABLES

Metal	Variable	Explanation	Sources
Aluminum	alcp	LME cash price for aluminum	London Metal Exchange, various
Copper	cucp	LME cash price for copper	years; *Metal Price Data*
Lead	lecp	LME cash price for lead	
Zinc	zncp	LME cash price for zinc	

TABLE 7.2 Unit Root Tests

	KPSS (Level)				ERS (Level)		DF-GLS (First Diference)		KPSS (First Difference)		ERS (First Difference)	
	W/o trend	With trend	W/o trend	With trend	W/o trend	With trend	W/o trend	With trend	W/o trend	With trend	W/o trend	With trend
(i) **Aluminum**												
lalcp	−2.38[b]	−2.48	0.10[a]	0.09[a]	2.62	7.77	−1.29	−2.21	0.04[a]	0.04[a]	0.66[a]	1.54[a]
lawlots	−1.12	−1.27	0.56[c]	0.18[c]	8.39	26.64	−1.75[c]	−2.55	0.16[a]	0.16[a]	0.67[a]	1.61[a]
(ii) **Copper**												
lcucp	−1.75	−2.02	0.92	0.09	4.12[c]	10.97	−1.15	−1.18	0.10[a]	0.08[a]	1.06[a]	2.27[a]
lcwtots	−0.55	−1.21	0.61[b]	0.20	17.97	33.06	−1.84[c]	−1.68	0.06[a]	0.06[a]	0.41[a]	1.38[a]
(iii) **Lead**												
llecp	−1.42	−1.57	0.36[b]	0.11[a]	6.77	14.75	−0.90	−2.20	0.15[a]	0.08[a]	3.71[c]	5.51[b]
llwtots	−0.13	−1.00	0.23[a]	0.16[c]	33.00	51.94	−14.58[a]	−14.31[a]	0.31[a]	0.30[a]	0.40[a]	1.37[a]
(iv) **Zinc**												
lzncp	−1.56	−2.59	0.73[c]	0.12[b]	5.72	7.21	−1.16	−2.01	0.06[a]	0.03[a]	2.57[b]	4.11[a]
lzwtots	0.14	−0.82	0.23[a]	0.16[c]	48.58	76.97	−1.82[c]	−1.95[c]	0.30[a]	0.30[a]	17.14	55.81

Data are in logs. Superscripts a, b, and c indicate statistical significance at 1%, 5%, and 10% levels, respectively.
Lag length is selected based on AIC and BIC,

correlations between the two to make the use of the reported or measured stocks credible.

Before performing the cointegration analysis, we used the efficient Dickey-Fuller generalized least squares (DF-GLS) and the Elliot et al. (ERS) unit root tests (Elliot et al. 1996; Cheung and Lai 1995), together with the Kwiatowski et al. (1992) (KPSS) unit root test, which relies on the hypothesis that a series is a strong mixing variable, to check for nonstationarity in individual price and stock series for aluminum, copper, lead, and zinc. In both unit root tests, the lag length determined using the Akaike Information Criterion (AIC) and the Bayesian Information Criterion (BIC) approach with a maximum lag order of 8 allowed. Although the unit root hypothesis could not be rejected for all level series, the first differenced price and stock series were always found to be stationary. The test results support the hypothesis that metal prices and stocks for aluminum, copper, lead, and zinc are each integrated of order 1, or I(1). This integration property readily lends itself to cointegration analysis.

Next in our analysis of price and stock asymmetric relationship, we employ Enders and Siklo's (2001) test for threshold cointegration, which extends Engle and Granger's (1987) procedure to encompass possible asymmetric adjustments to disequilibrium. Table 7.3 reports cointegration test results on bilateral price-stock relationships for aluminum, copper, lead, and zinc assuming threshold and momentum adjustment. The table reports value of the adjustment coefficients ρ_1 and ρ_2, their t-values, and the Φ_μ and Φ_μ^* statistics for the null hypothesis of a unit root in μ_t (no cointegration) against the alternative of cointegration with asymmetric adjustment. The lag length is selected such that the AIC and the BIC are minimized. The F-test for symmetric adjustment $\rho_1 = \rho_2$, the underlying long-run relations, the consistent estimate of the threshold as well as the value of AIC and BIC are also presented in the table.

The estimated Φ_μ and Φ_μ^* statistics for the relationship between prices and stocks are 3.97 and 7.17 for aluminum, 5.51 and 8.64 for copper, 2.00 and 2.89 for lead, and 3.03 and 13.95 for zinc. We compare those values with the critical values reported in Enders and Siklos (2001). We conclude that there is strong evidence in favor of cointegration with asymmetric adjustment between prices and stocks for aluminum, copper, lead, and zinc. Even though there is evidence of cointegration with both TAR adjustment and M-TAR adjustment, clearly the AIC and BIC favor the M-TAR specification over that of TAR.

Notice that the F-statistics for the null hypothesis of symmetric adjustment ($\rho_1 = \rho_2$) reject symmetric adjustment for both TAR and M-TAR specifications at conventional significance levels in all models (aluminum, copper, lead, and zinc). Also, since the AIC and BIC selects the M-TAR specification for all models, in what follows we emphasize the M-TAR models.

The point estimates for ρ_1 and ρ_2 suggest substantially faster convergence for negative (below threshold) deviations from long-run equilibrium than positive (above threshold) deviations for copper and zinc while the reverse is true for aluminum and lead. For example, in the zinc price-stock model, the point estimates of ρ_1 and ρ_2 suggest that negative deviations from long-run equilibrium resulting from decreases in copper stocks or increases in copper prices (such that $\Delta\hat{\mu}_{t-1} < -0.001$) are eliminated at a rate of 18% per month while positive deviations are eliminated at only 0.6% per month. Of the four models considered, the largest discrepancy between the elimination of below- and above-threshold deviations occurs for the

TABLE 7.3 Asymmetric Cointegration Tests

	lalcp to lawtots		lcucp to lcwtots		llelcp to lwtots		lzncp to lzwtots	
	TAR	M-TAR	TAR	M-TAR	TAR	M-TAR	TAR	M-TAR
ρ_1	−0.12	−0.28	−0.04	−0.06	−0.08	−0.05	−0.04	−0.02
	(−2.46)	(−3.52)	(−1.46)	(2.42)	(−1.92)	(−1.80)	(−1.01)	(−0.64)
ρ_2	−0.07	−0.06	−0.26	−0.18	−0.02	−0.08	−0.12	−0.46
	(−1.50)	(−1.75)	(−3.30)	(−3.79)	(−0.69)	(1.57)	(−2.37)	(−5.27)
$\rho_1=\rho_2=0$ Φ_u or Φ_u^*)	3.97[b]	7.17[a]	5.51[a]	8.64[a]	2.00	2.89[b]	3.03[b]	13.95[a]
$\rho_1=\rho_2$ (F − Test)	0.68	6.71[a]	4.96[b]	10.97[a]	0.85	2.60[c]	1.45	22.50[a]
Estimated threshold	0.06	−0.10	−0.14	−0.001	−0.16	−0.07	−0.05	−0.009
				Cointegrating Relationship				
Constant	8.51[a]		10.48[a]		5.75[b]		8.35[a]	
Upstream or downstream stock	−0.15[b]		−0.42[a]		0.06[b]		−0.20[a]	
Number of lags	7	7	6	6	6	6	6	6
AIC	−145.74	−145.78	27.62	27.63	−95.05	−96.28	−125.15	−127.10
BIC	−118.80	−125.10	52.49	41.47	−71.08	−72.92	−101.81	−122.27

Lag length is determined based on the AIC and BIC. The t-statistics are in parentheses. Superscripts a, b, and c indicate significance at 1%, 5%, and 10% respectively.

zinc model, where negative deviations are eliminated at the rate of 46% per month, while positive deviations are eliminated at 2% per month. These results are mostly consistent with asymmetric adjustment on metal markets and supportive of the so-called rockets and feathers story. However, the asymmetry here is not defined in terms of positive versus negative deviations from a long-run equilibrium, as in the rockets and feathers literature; rather it is defined in terms of the rate of change of the deviations from long-run equilibrium that are below or above a certain threshold.

EMPIRICAL TESTS FOR CAUSALITY AND IMPLICATIONS

Next, for the purpose of testing for causality on the basis of equations 7.11 and 7.12, we need to ensure that p and q in those equations are adequate and close to the lags of the true models and therefore that lags are not included unnecessarily. For this purpose, we use the AIC and BIC defined earlier. After trying many combinations of the values of p and q between 1 and 8, we decided that the optimal values $p = q = 1$ for aluminum and lead, $p = q = 2$ for copper, and $p = q = 3$ for zinc.

The results of causality testing under the assumption of asymmetry, based on Wald, LR, and LM tests, are reported in Table 7.4. The superscripts + and – indicate positive and negative changes respectively. These results show that causality runs from positive and negative price changes to stock and vice versa only for aluminum. For copper, causality runs from positive and negative price changes to stocks and from negative stock changes to prices. For lead, causality runs from positive and negative stock changes to prices only. For zinc, it is only negative volume changes that cause prices.

TABLE 7.4 Causality Testing under Asymmetry

	Price $\nRightarrow$ Stock				Stock $\nRightarrow$ Price		
	W	LR	LM		W	LR	LM
(i) Aluminum							
Price$^+$ $\nRightarrow$ Stock	9.14[b]	9.04[b]	8.66[b]	Stock$^+$ $\nRightarrow$ Price	14.02[a]	13.92[b]	12.83[a]
Price$^-$ $\nRightarrow$ Stock	14.36[a]	14.25[a]	13.11[a]	Stock$^-$ $\nRightarrow$ Price	5.87[c]	5.77[c]	5.70[c]
(ii) Copper							
Price$^+$ $\nRightarrow$ Stock	5.21[c]	5.13[c]	5.08[c]	Stock$^+$ $\nRightarrow$ Price	3.48	3.41	3.34
Price$^-$ $\nRightarrow$ Stock	9.45[a]	9.34[a]	8.93[b]	Stock$^-$ $\nRightarrow$ Price	7.80[b]	7.72[b]	7.47[b]
(iii) Lead							
Price$^+$ $\nRightarrow$ Stock	4.09	4.05	4.02	Stock$^+$ $\nRightarrow$ Price	8.29[b]	8.03[b]	7.91[b]
Price$^-$ $\nRightarrow$ Stock	0.67	0.65	0.63	Stock$^-$ $\nRightarrow$ Price	7.98[b]	7.77[b]	7.62[b]
(iv) Zinc							
Price$^+$ $\nRightarrow$ Stock	0.99	0.97	0.95	Stock$^+$ $\nRightarrow$ Price	1.33	1.28	1.23
Price$^-$ $\nRightarrow$ Stock	0.25	0.22	0.21	Stock$^-$ $\nRightarrow$ Price	27.07[a]	25.71[a]	22.69[a]

Superscripts a, b, and c indicate statistical significance at 1% 5% and 10% level respectively. $\nRightarrow$denotes "does not cause"

Finally, Table 7.5 reports results that reinforce the results reported in Table 7.4. These results show that negative price and stock changes have stronger effects than positive changes.

Before we present the economic interpretation of the results, and in order to place them into perspective, we need to highlight some features of metals markets, based on previous research. These features pertain to the behavior and roles of various market participants. First, Labys and Granger (1971) and Labys (1980) demonstrate that the behavior of hedgers in metal markets resembles the behavior of speculators in the sense that they act on the same decision variables. The models presented in these papers do not make a distinction between hedgers and speculators acting in both markets because they have similar demand for and supply of contracts functions.

The second feature is that the market is dominated by speculators, who cause the prices to deviate from the level determined by the cost-of-carry relationship. Labys and Granger (1971) argue that one important difference between speculators and hedgers is that the latter are more likely to be the market participants, who actually require the physical commodity (e.g., industrial companies), whereas speculators are the participants who are not interested in the physical commodity per se but rather in generating profit from holding ownership in that commodity (e.g., financial institutions). They further argue that since financial activity dominates real activity, it is plausible to conclude that the bulk of commodity trading can be traced back

TABLE 7.5 Testing for Asymmetric Relationship

	Price $\nRightarrow$ Stock ($H_{\alpha 0}: a_j \geq b_j$) and $\alpha_1^- \geq \alpha_1^+$	Stock $\nRightarrow$ Price ($H_{\alpha 0}: c_i \geq d_i$) and $\alpha_2^- \geq \alpha_2^+$
(i) Aluminum		
W	4.01	0.26
LR	3.95	0.25
LM	3.89	0.23
(ii) Copper		
W	3.49	2.78
LR	3.43	2.75
LM	3.39	2.73
(iii) Lead		
W	0.33	3.54
LR	0.31	3.48
LM	0.28	3.44
(iv) Zinc		
W	0.66	0.88
LR	0.64	0.87
LM	0.59	0.85

The W, LR and LM tests are tests for the composite null. Superscripts a, b, and c indicate statistical significance at the 1%, 5%, and 10% level, respectively.

to speculators and not as much to those who actually need the physical commodity. Furthermore, Labys and Granger (1970) present several intuitive explanations as to why speculators react to the arrival of new information by buying and selling in the futures market rather than the spot market. The conclusion that we want to arrive at based on this discussion is that the price-inventory relationship in the metal markets depends largely on the behavior of speculators, since they are the dominant players in this market. Hence, whether the relationship is symmetric or not depends on the behavior of speculators.

So, what is the economic interpretation of our results? The finding of bidirectional causality for aluminum and to some extend for copper markets and causality from stocks to prices for lead and zinc seems to be consistent with the noise trading model of De Long et al. (1990).

This model postulates that the activity of noise speculators is not based on economic fundamentals, and hence it results in a temporary mispricing. The price, however, moves toward its mean value in the long run in the absence of transitory component. Hence, the model predicts that a positive causal relationship running from prices to inventories is consistent with a feedback trading strategy of noise speculators who base their decisions on past price movements. Moreover, the model predicts that a positive causal relationship from inventories to prices is consistent with the hypothesis that price changes are caused by the actions of noise speculators.

The finding of asymmetry may sound strange, given that there is a nice intuitive explanation as to why the price-inventory relationship should be symmetric in metal market. In fact, following Karpoff (1988), we may argue that the constraints on short selling (which may take the form of either a prohibition or differential costs of short and long positions) make the relationship asymmetric, as indicated by high positive correlation between inventory and prices. In the absence of these constraints, which is the case in the futures markets, there should be a symmetric relationship, as indicated by zero correlations between the two variables. This intuitive explanation is, however, not inconsistent with our findings for a number of reasons. First, this explanation pertains to the first definition of symmetry given in Enders and Granger (1998) and Enders and Siklos (2001). According to this definition, symmetry implies that inventories in a declining market tend to be different from that associated with a bear market, and so the ratio of inventories to (absolute) price change tends to vary between bull and bear markets. Although this definition of symmetry is about temporal asymmetry, which is defined to exclude contemporaneous behavior, our evidence pertains to a different concept of symmetry. Second, using another definition of asymmetry, for instance, contemporaneous asymmetry in metal markets and applying these tests directly to the inventory-price ratio could have changed our results.

But even if we accept this relationship, for the sake of argument, and even if we assume that the short-selling constraints explanation is valid for temporal asymmetry, there is no reason to assume that this factor plays an exclusive role in determining the nature of the price-inventory relationship. Surely there are other explanations and factors that play a role. It is these explanations and factors that validate our finding of asymmetry. Although temporal symmetry is indicative of a market where trades have a linear unbiased response to information, asymmetry is based on trader or speculator heterogeneity and hence on the distinction between bulls and bears, between optimists and pessimists, and between informed and uninformed traders or speculators. These distinctions are the basis of the theories proposed by Epps (1975), Copeland (1976), Jennings et al. (1981), and Wang (1994).

The results obtained in this study show that negative changes have stronger effects than positive changes. Unlike the prediction of the Epps model, this result implies that the demand function of the bears is steeper than that of bulls, and hence a greater level of inventory will be associated with a negative price change than with a positive price change. This proposition makes a lot of sense if we put forward the proposition that bears are quick in reacting to negative price changes, motivated by the desire to cut losses, while bulls are "greedy," preferring to wait for further price rises before they sell (Moosa et al. 2003). The same proposition appears to be valid if we base the reasoning on the distinction between informed and uninformed traders or speculators.

The results can also be explained by putting forward the proposition that expectations are stabilizing in a bull market and destabilizing in a bear market (see Moosa et al. 2003). Hence, when the price rises in a bull market, traders or speculators believe that it will not rise any further, and so they sell and dampen the price rise and the subsequent trading inventories. When the price falls in a bear market, however, traders or speculators believe that it will fall further and so they sell, leading to further price falls and rising trading inventories.

CONCLUSIONS

This chapter investigated international metals markets and presented some evidence for the presence of temporal asymmetry in the price-inventory relationship. Using a sample of monthly observations over the period 1990 to 2003, these two results were found:

1. Results of threshold cointegration clearly indicate cointegration with asymmetric adjustment between price and stock for aluminum, copper, lead and zinc.
2. In most metals market, causality with asymmetry is present.

These results provide evidence in support of several hypotheses, but they appear to be in contrast with the Epps (1975) hypothesis. Specifically, the results imply that the bears' demand function is steeper than the bulls' demand function. The results also indicate that expectations are stabilizing in a bull market and destabilizing in a bear market.

APPENDIX: THREE ASYMPTOTICALLY EQUIVALENT TESTS FOR GRANGER-CAUSALITY

This appendix presents three asymptotically equivalent tests (Wald, Lagrange multiplier, and likelihood ratio) for examining Granger-causality in vector autoregressive (VAR) processes.

Wald Tests

Let $\theta = vec\left[\Pi_{ij}\right]_{i,j=1,2}$ be the vector of all VAR coefficients. Noncausality restrictions can be formulated as $R\theta = 0$ with suitably chosen restrictions matrix R having full row rank. Thus, testing for Granger-causality means testing the null hypothesis $H_0 : R\theta = 0$ against $H_1 : R\theta \neq 0$.

Suppose an asymptotically normally distributed estimator $\hat{\theta}$ of θ is available, that is, $\sqrt{T}(\hat{\theta} - \theta) \xrightarrow{d} N\left(0, \Sigma_{\hat{\theta}}\right)$, where T is the sample size, $\xrightarrow{d}$ denotes convergence in distribution, and $\Sigma_{\hat{\theta}}$ is the covariance matrix of the asymptotic distribution. Then $\sqrt{T}(R\hat{\theta} - R\theta) \xrightarrow{d} N\left(0, \Sigma_{\hat{\theta}} R'\right)$. Thus, the standard Wald statistic for testing H_0 is

$$\lambda_W = T\hat{\theta}' R' \left(R\hat{\Sigma}_{\hat{\theta}} R'\right)^{-1} R\hat{\theta} \tag{7A.1}$$

where $\hat{\Sigma}_{\hat{\theta}}$ = consistent estimator of $\Sigma_{\hat{\theta}}$

If H_0 is true, it then follows that

$$\lambda_W = T\hat{\theta}' R' \left(R\hat{\Sigma}_{\hat{\theta}} R'\right)^{-1} R\hat{\theta} \xrightarrow{d} \chi^2_{[J]}, \tag{7A.2}$$

where J = number of restrictions

Lagrange Multiplier Tests

Again, let $\theta = vec\left[\Pi_{i,j}\right]_{i,j=1,2}$ be the vector of all VAR coefficients. Noncausality restrictions can be formulated as $R\theta = 0$ with suitably chosen restrictions matrix R having full row rank. Thus, testing for Granger-causality means testing the null hypothesis $H_0 : R\theta = 0$ against $H_1 : R\theta \neq 0$.

To conduct the LM test for Granger-causality, we need the restricted maximum likelihood estimator, θ_R, which can be obtained by maximizing the constrained likelihood or by solving the first-order conditions from the Lagrangian function

$$\phi(\theta, \eta) = L(\theta) + \eta' R\theta, \tag{7A.3}$$

where $L(\theta)$ = log-likelihood function
η = a J-dimensional vector of Lagrange multipliers

The first-order conditions are given by

$$d_R + F_R \eta_R = 0, \tag{7A.4}$$

where

$$d_R = \left.\frac{\partial L}{\partial \theta}\right|_{\theta=\theta_R}$$

$$F_R = \frac{\partial (R\theta)'}{\partial \theta}|_{\theta=\theta_R}$$

$$\eta_R = \text{optimal solution for } \eta$$

Furthermore, if H_0 is true, then we would expect θ_R to be close to θ^2 and d_R to be close to 0. Under suitable regularity conditions

$$\frac{d}{\sqrt{T}} = \frac{1}{\sqrt{T}}\frac{\partial L}{\partial \theta} \xrightarrow{d} N\left(0, \lim\left(\frac{I(\theta)}{T}\right)\right). \tag{7A.4}$$

If H_0 is true, it then follows that

$$\lambda_{LM} = d'_R I(\theta_R)^{-1} d_R \xrightarrow{d} \chi^2_{[J]}, \tag{7A.5}$$

where $I(\theta_R)$ = a consistent estimator of the information matrix based on the restricted estimator θ_R

Another formulation of the LM test is that

$$\lambda_{Lm} = \eta'_R F'_R I(\theta_R)^{-1} F_R \eta_R \xrightarrow{d} \chi^2_{[J]} \tag{7A.6}$$

From $\lambda_{Lm} = \eta'_R F'_R I(\theta_R)^{-1} F_R \eta_R \xrightarrow{d} \chi^2_{[J]}$ and from $\lambda_W = T\hat{\theta}' R' \left(R\hat{\Sigma}_{\hat{\theta}} R'\right)^{-1} R\hat{\theta} \xrightarrow{d} \chi^2_{[J]}$, it is clear that the LM test is based only on the restricted ML estimator, while the Wald test is based only on the unrestricted ML estimator.

Likelihood Ratio Tests

The LR tests for Granger-causality uses both the restricted and unrestricted estimators. Thus, testing for Granger-causality means testing the null hypothesis $H_0 : R\theta = 0$ against $H_1 : R\theta \neq 0$. The testing procedure is based on this statistic:.

$$\lambda_{LR} = 2\left[L\left(\tilde{\theta}\right) - L(\theta_R)\right] \xrightarrow{d} \chi^2_{[J]} \tag{7A.7}$$

REFERENCES

Burrows, J. (1971). *Tungsten: An Industry Analysis.* Lexington, MA: DC Heath.

Brennan, M.J. (1958). "The Supply of Storage," *American Economic Review* 48: 50–72.

———. (1991). "The Price of Convenience and the Pricing of Commodity Contingent Claims."In D. Lund and B. Øksendal (eds.), *Stochastic Models and Option Values—with Applications to Resources, Environment, and Investment Problems.* Amsterdam: Elsevier North-Holland: 33–71.

Bresnahan, T.F., and V.Y. Suslow. (1985). "Inventories as an Asset: The Volatility of Copper Prices," *International Economic Review* 26: 409–424.

Caner, M., and B.E. Hansen. (2001). "Threshold Autoregression with a Unit Root," *Econometrica* 69: 1555–1596.

Chang, K.S. (1993). "Consistency and Limiting Distribution of the Least Squares Estimator of a Threshold Autoregressive Model," *Annals of Statistics* 21: 520–533.

Chen, L.H.C., M. Finney, and K.S. Lai. (2005). "A Threshold Cointegration Analysis of Asymmetric Price Transmission from Crude Oil to Gasoline Prices," *Economics Letters* 89: 233–239.

Cheung, Y.W., and K.S. Lai. (1995). "Lag Order and Critical Values of a Modified Dickey-Fuller Test," *Oxford Bulletin of Economics and Statistics* 57: 411–419.

Chikan, A. (1984). *New Results in Inventory Research*. Amsterdam: Elsevier Science.

Copeland, T.E. (1976). "A Model of Asset Trading Under the Assumption of Sequential Information Arrival," *Journal of Finance* 31: 1149–1168.

Considine, T.J., and E. Heo. (2000). "Price and Inventory Dynamics in Petroleum Product Markets," *Energy Economics* 22: 527–547.

De Long, J., A. Shleifer, L. Summers, and B. Waldman. (1990). "Positive Feedback, Investment Strategies and Destabilising Rational Speculation," *Journal of Finance* 45: 379–395.

Elliott, G., T.J. Rothenberg, and J.H. Stock. (1996). "Efficient Tests for an Autoregressive Unit Root," *Econometrica* 64: 813–836.

Enders, W. (2001). "Improved Critical Values for the Ender-Granger Unit Root Test," *Applied Economic Letters* 8: 257–261.

Enders, W., and C.W.J. Granger. (1998). "Unit-Root Tests and Asymmetric Adjustment with an Example Using the Term Structure of Interest Rates," *Journal of Business and Economic Statistics* 16: 304–311.

Enders, W., and P. Siklos. (2001). "Cointegration and Threshold Adjustment," *Journal of Business and Economic Statistics* 19: 166–176.

Engle, R.F., and C.W.J. Granger. (1987). "Cointegration and Error Correction: Representation, Estimation and Testing," *Econometrica* 55: 251–276.

Epps, T.W. (1975). "Security Price Changes and Transaction Volumes: Theory and Evidence," *American Economic Review* 65: 586–597.

Fama, E.F., and K.R. French. (1988). "Business Cycles and the Behavior of Metals Prices," *Journal of Finance* 43: 1075–1093.

Geweke, J. (2004). "Issues in the 'Rockets and Feathers' Gasoline Price Literature." Report, Federal Trade Commission, Washington, DC.

Ghosh, S., C.A. Gilbert, and A.J. Hughes. (1987). *Stabilizing Speculative Commodity Markets*. Oxford: Clarendon Press.

Granger, C.W.J., and T.H. Lee. (1989). "Investigation of Production, Sales and Inventory Relationships Using Multi-Cointegration and Non-Symmetric Error Correction Models," *Journal of Applied Econometrics* 4: 145–159.

———. (1989). "Multi-Cointegration." In F. Rhodes Jr. and T.B. Fomby (eds.), *Advances in Econometrics: Cointegration, Spurious Regressions, and Unit Roots*. New York: JAI Press: 71–84.

Jennings, R.H., L.T. Starks, and J.C. Fellingham. (1981). "An Equilibrium Model of Asset Trading with Sequential Information Arrival," *Journal of Finance* 36: 143–161.

Kaldor, N. (1939). "Speculation and Economic Stability," *Review of Economic Studies* 7: 1–27.

Karpoff, J.M. (1988). "Costly Short Sales and the Correlation of Returns with Volume," *Journal of Financial Research* 11: 173–188.

Keynes, J.M. (1930). *A Treatise on Money*. New York: Harcourt Brace.

Kwiatowski, D., P.C.B. Phillips, P.I. Schmidt, and Y. Shin. (1992). "Testing Null Hypothesis of Stationarity Against the Alternative of a Unit Root," *Journal of Econometrics* 54: 159–178.

Labys, W.C. (1980). "Commodity Price Stabilization Models: A Review and Appraisal," *Journal of Policy Modeling* 2: 121–136.

Labys, W.C., and C.W.J. Granger. (1970). *Speculation, Hedging and Commodity Price Forecasts*. Lexington, MA: Heath Lexington Books.

Labys, W.C., and M.L. Lord. (1992). "Inventory and Equilibrium Adjustments in International Commodity Markets: A Multi-Cointegration Approach," *Applied Economics* 24: 77–84.

London Metal Exchange. (2004). *LME Stocks and Market Balances*. London Metal Exchange, London.

———. (Various years). *Metal Price Data*. London: London Metal Exchange.

Moosa, I.A., P. Silvapulle, and M.J. Silvapulle. (2003). "Testing for Temporal Asymmetry in the Price-Volume Relationship," *Bulletin of Economic Research* 55: 373–389.

Peltzman, S. (2000). "Prices Rise Faster than They Fall," *Journal of Political Economy* 108: 466–502.

Petrucelli, J., and S. Woolford. (1984). "A Threshold AR(1) Model," *Journal of Applied Probability* 21: 270–286.

Pindyck, R. (1994). "Inventories and the Short-Run Dynamics of Commodity Prices," *RAND Journal of Economics* 25: 41–59.

Telser, L. (1958). "Futures Trading and the Storage of Cotton and Wheat," *Journal of Political Economy* 66: 233–255.

Thurman, W.N. (1988). "Speculative Carryover: An Empirical Example of the US Refined Copper Market," *RAND Journal of Economics* 19: 430–437.

Tong, H. (1983). *Threshold Models in Nonlinear Time Series Analysis*. New York: Springer Verlag.

———. (1990). *Non-linear Time Series: A Dynamical Approach*. Oxford: Oxford University Press.

Wang, J. (1994). "A Model of Competitive Stock Trading Volume," *Journal of Political Economy* 102: 127–168.

Weymar, H.F. (1966). "The Supply of Storage Revisited," *American Economic Review* 56: 1226–1234.

Williams, J.C., and B.D. Wright. (1991). *Storage and Commodity Markets*. Cambridge: Cambridge University Press.

Working, H. (1949). "The Theory of the Price of Storage," *American Economic Review* 39: 1254–1262.

World Bureau of Metal Statistics. (Various issues). *Metal Statistics*. London.

Wright, B.D., and J.C. Williams. (1982). "The Economic Role of Commodity Storage," *Economic Journal* 92: 596–614.

Xiarchos, I. (2006). *Three Essays on Environmental Markets: Dynamic Behavior, Market Interactions, and Policy Implications*. Ph.D. dissertation, West Virginia University, Morgantown.

CHAPTER 8

Do Fluctuations in Wine Stocks Affect Wine Prices?

James O. Bukenya

INTRODUCTION

Globalization and the expansion of the world wine trade, helped by agricultural subsidies, have caused a wine boom. This has made fluctuations in wine inventories a more critical issue than in the past. In the case of domestic and international wine markets, little is known about intertemporal inventory adjustments and how they relate to prices. Data on wine inventories and prices have been difficult to obtain; and this problem has been aggravated because wines are heterogeneous commodities. We know that wine inventories increase during times of abundant and decline during years of poor grape harvests. Inventories ultimately affect wine prices. There is a need to investigate possible dynamic relations between these variables in a time series context, to improve our understanding of how wine producers and traders can face price and financial volatility. In this chapter, we study countries for which meaningful data series could be constructed: Argentina, Australia, France, Germany, Italy, Spain, and the United States.

The study begins with an examination of the empirical evidence relating inventories in these markets to prices. Stationarity tests are first performed to assess likely trends in wine inventory and price variables. Cointegration analysis follows to analyze the stationary relationships between these variables. To explain the dynamics of the interrelationship between these variables, vector autoregressions have been estimated and impulse functions computed to measure possible delays between variable reactions.

BACKGROUND

The observation that the role of commodity stocks is little understood is surprising. In wine markets, this topic has hardly been researched at all. Most often commodity inventories and price behaviors have been considered as an intertemporal adjustment process, reflecting demand and supply disequilibrium in a closed market or economy. However, inventory adjustments as such can influence domestic and international price fluctuations, and their understanding is important for producers and consumers alike. Since demand (particularly for agricultural food and beverages) and supply (particularly for agricultural perennial crops) tend to be relatively price inelastic in the short run, inventory movements, which are more price elastic, provide the vehicle whereby markets achieve equilibrium. Nonetheless, stock behavior should not be explained only in terms of residual adjustments or unintended accumulations. Stock holding can also take place for precautionary, transactions, and speculative purposes. Other intervening influences also exist. Stock changes not only reflect agricultural surpluses and deficits due to climatic changes, but exogenous business cycle effects as well. For the case of wine, see Labys (2001). Also of concern are uncertain flows of information, income and financial fluctuations, market persistence to shocks, and sudden trade flow disruptions. Such factors, together with more complex behavioral motives, exist in the inventory-theoretic literature, as summarized later in the text.

The most basic aspect of commodity stockholding behavior is that it represents intertemporal arbitrage, initially in a closed system. Earlier studies of this behavior appear in Labys (1973); later reviews include Antonini (1988), Blinder and Maccini (1991), Chikan (1984), Labys (1989), Williams and Wright (1991), and Wright and Williams (1982). Among these studies, the popular supply of storage model is based on the premise that each firm will adjust its inventory level until the marginal revenue of holding stocks equals its marginal costs. As developed by Working (1949), Brennan (1958, 1959), and Weymar (1969a, b), the motives for inventory holding include convenience yield, stockout yield, and coverage yield. Intertwined in this process is the role of inventories as the allocating agent, particularly to avoid stockout and to facilitate the scheduling of production and sales.

Research in stockholding expanded in the 1980s with the consideration of disequilibrium adjustments and rational expectations in the work of Kawai (1983) and Otani (1983). Attention to problems of speculative demand and convenience yield appear in Newberry and Stiglitz (1982), Gilbert (1988), and Larson (1994). Of special interest in analyzing convenience yield is the test of speculative carryover. Also of significance are theories that consider inventories in the context of portfolio theory of asset holding suggested earlier by Yver (1971). While Yver applied that theory to cattle inventories, Orden (1982) later developed an asset theory relevant for agricultural commodities in general. The production cost-smoothing model, whereby inventories are used to shift output to periods in which production costs are low, also can be used to avoid stockouts and to reduce scheduling costs. Eichenbaum (1984, 1989) and Eckstein and Eichenbaum (1985) analyzed a target level of inventories and the linear-quadratic cost of deviating from that level. Further tests of this model were made by Labys and Lord (1992) using error-correction model (ECM) analysis for several of the major traded agricultural commodities.

Agricultural producers have long been searching for an inventory-holding model that would optimize the level of inventories, given other influencing factors. Gilbert (1991), Knapp (1982), Pindyck (1994), and others have suggested an inventory theory based on intertemporal optimization. The few studies that address inventory holdings in the case of wine employ inventory variables either as a measure of disequilibrium market adjustment present in the price equation (as is the present study) and/or as variables that define the market closing of a system. Further insights can be obtained from Amspacher (1988) and Gijsbers and Labys (1988). Wohlgenant (1978, 1982), in particular, developed a dynamic model of wine processor behavior in which price, production, and input demand functions are derived from an optimal control model that takes into account inventory growth from aging and the linkage between product inventories and input purchases.

INVENTORY AND PRICE BEHAVIOR

Wine research has neglected problems of wine market disequilibrium, although market instability problems have long been recognized by policy makers. This international problem has been exacerbated because of a growing trade in wines and excess world wine production relative to declining consumption (i.e., Labys and Cohen 2006). The greatest impact of the disequilibrium between production and consumption appears to be in the European Union (EU), where it has proven politically difficult to modify the Common Agricultural Policy. Rather large surpluses have created problems, such as the need to distill considerable volumes of wine every year or to export wines below cost. In other parts of the world, production and consumption imbalances appear to have declined and markets seem to be closer to stable equilibrium. Although vineyard and wine management programs have resulted in severe reduction in surfaces planted, restructuring and replanting activities have resulted in increased productivity. The general trend is in the direction of expanding the production of wines of higher quality, although table wine production remains relatively large.

To study the nature of stock and price movements and their interactions, we constructed national wine inventory and price series beginning in 1975 for France and the United States, and in 1986 for Argentina, Australia, Germany, Italy, and Spain. All series end in 2003. The series result from individual year-by-year compilation and estimation, based on inventory and price data reported to trade and governmental organizations. Sources of the data include historical documents from the Office of International Wines and Vines (OIV) in Paris, the Food and Agricultural Organization in Rome (FAO), along with the world wine data published by Wittwer and Rothfield (2006), Anderson and Norman (2003) and Berger, Anderson, and Stringer (1998). The price data have the same origins, but the longer French series come from INSEE (Institut national de la statistique et des études économiques) historical data and the longer U.S. series stem from U.S. Department of Labor data archives. Even with this care, the inventory data represent only bulk wine holdings by private and commercial holders, and in the case of France, wine producer and wholesaler stocks. The U.S. stocks for the most part are those held in California. No data are available by quality designation. Similarly, the price data are in the form of aggregate indexes and do not include individual wine types. A detailed list of sources appears at the end of the chapter as a list of references, separate from the traditional references, for the convenience of the interested reader.

Figure 8.1 demonstrates changes in the trends and fluctuations in inventory holdings for our sample group of countries. Beginning in 1975, French wine stocks have fluctuated about an average of 394 million liters (Ml) annually, with a sharp dip occurring between 1987 and 1991. U.S. wine stocks have fluctuated less, around an average of 182 Ml.

Beginning in 1986, Argentinean stocks have declined continuously at the rate of 246 Ml annually, while Australian wine stocks have risen on average 78 Ml annually.

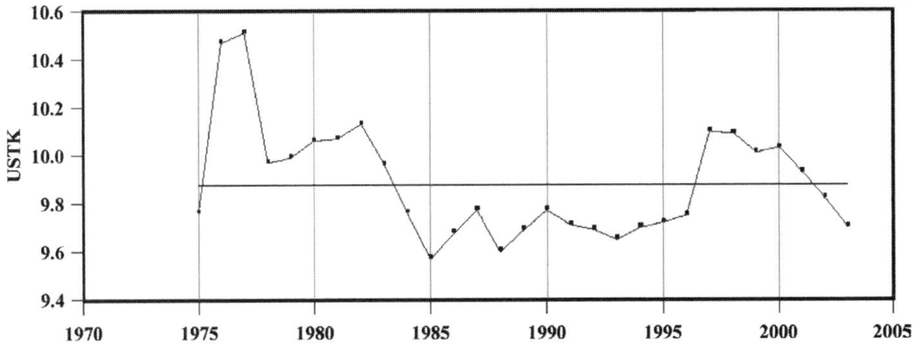

FIGURE 8.1a United States, Wine Inventory Fluctuations, 1975–2000

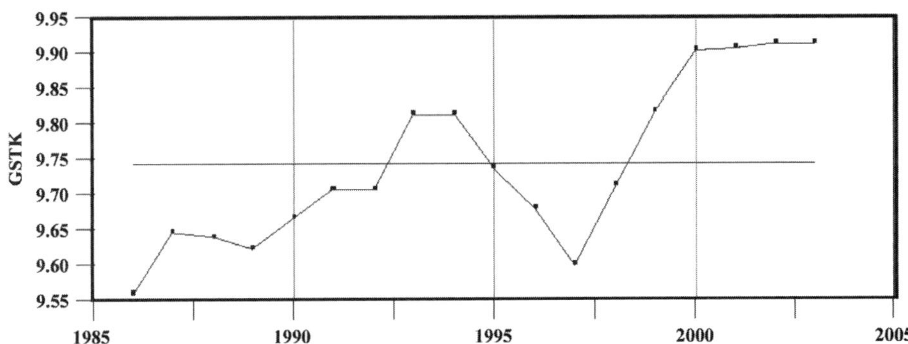

FIGURE 8.1b Germany, Wine Inventory Fluctuations, 1986–2000

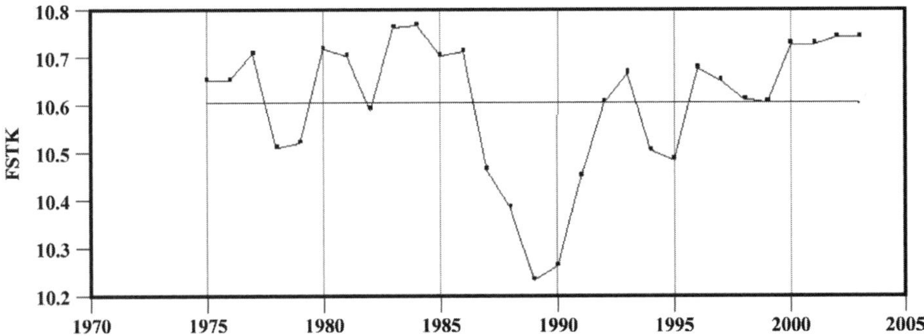

FIGURE 8.1c France, Wine Inventory Fluctuations, 1975–2003

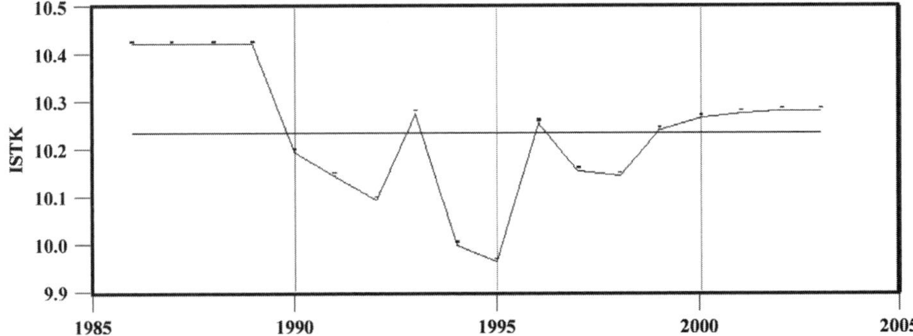

FIGURE 8.1d Italy, Wine Inventory Fluctuations, 1986–2003

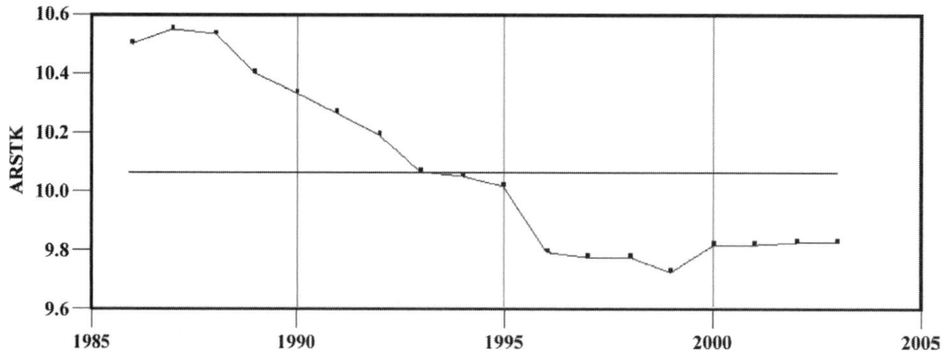

FIGURE 8.1e Argentina, Wine Inventory Fluctuations, 1986–2003

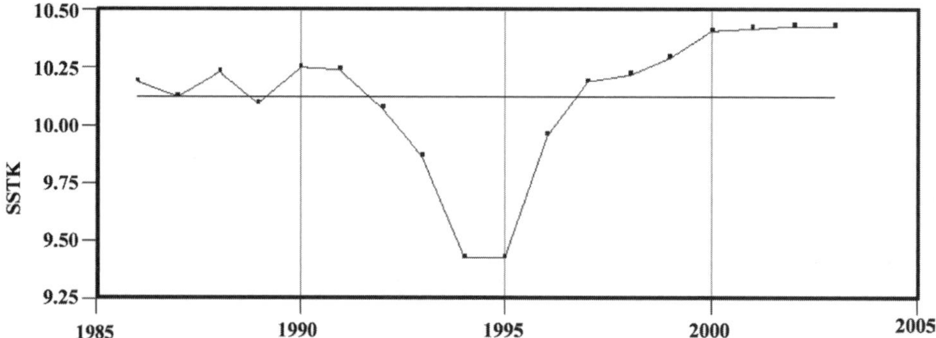

FIGURE 8.1f Spain, Wine Inventory Fluctuations, 1986–2003

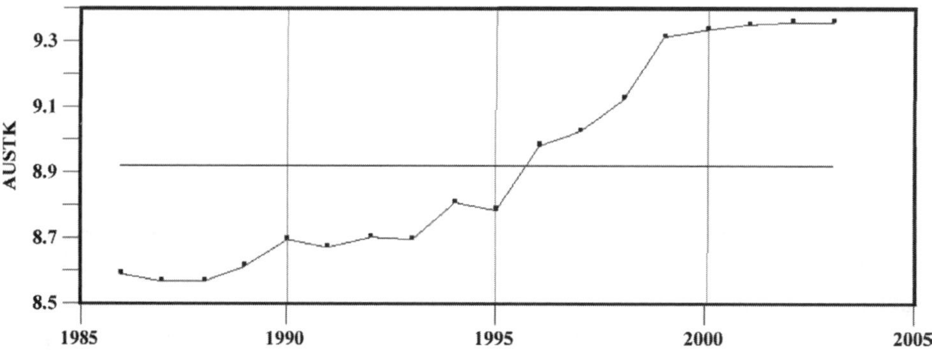

FIGURE 8.1g Australia, Wine Inventory Fluctuations, 1986–2003

German, Italian, and Spanish stocks fluctuated during these years at an annual average rate of 171 Ml, 281 Ml, and 26 Ml, respectively.

Table wine prices reflect changes in production, consumption, and stock changes. Stocks themselves embody the history of past market imbalances. When table wine demand is growing relative to production and stocks, prices will rise accordingly. When fluctuations in weather conditions cause wine production to decrease or increase, prices will adjust. Other factors, such as price supports (e.g., the Common Agricultural Policy), rates of inflation, or interest rates, also influence table wine prices. Quality wine prices, in contrast, are determined in other markets and reflect other price-making influences. Because the disparities between wine production and the actual grape varieties vary appreciably from country to country, it is difficult to determine how wine prices move in the face of wine market disequilibria.

Figure 8.2 shows the results of compiling wine price indexes. Since 1975, French wine prices have fluctuated considerably around a slightly falling trend, reflecting the impact of unstable wine production relative to a fairly constant, but steadily

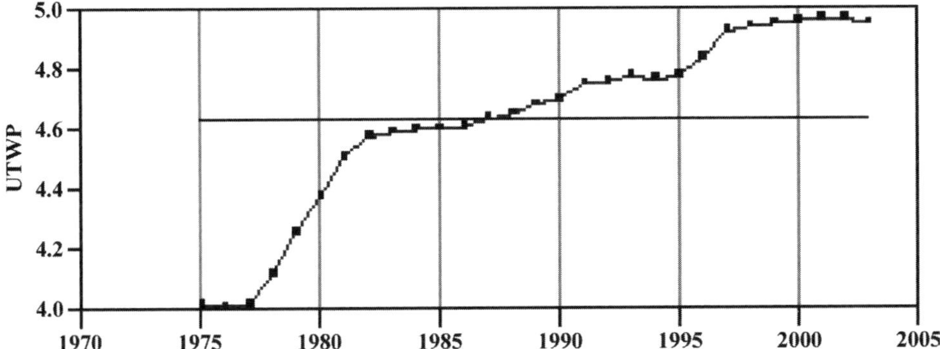

FIGURE 8.2a United States, Wine Price Fluctuations, 1975–2003

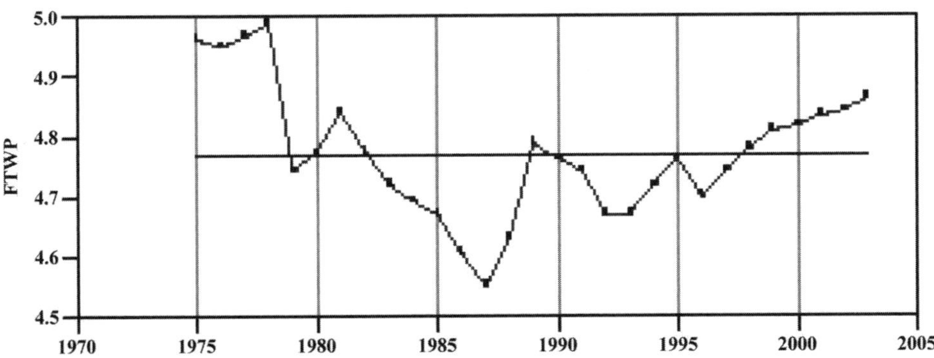

FIGURE 8.2b France, Wine Price Fluctuations, 1975–2003

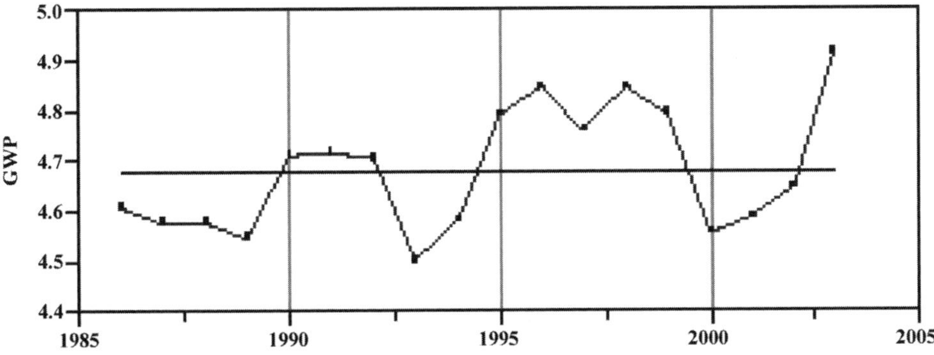

FIGURE 8.2c Germany, Wine Price Fluctuations, 1986–2003

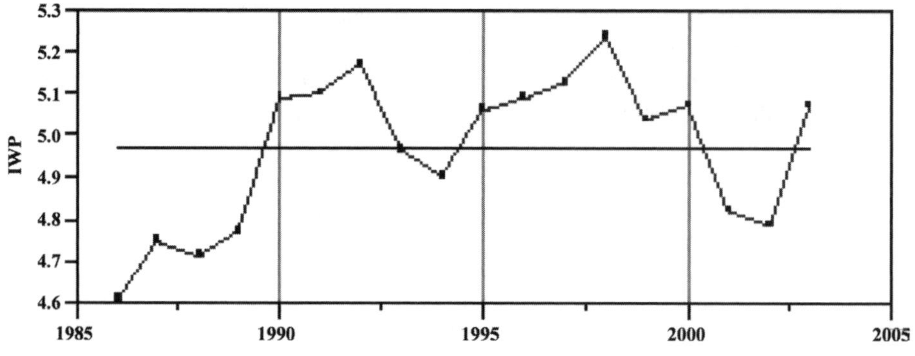

FIGURE 8.2d Italy, Wine Price Fluctuations, 1986–2003

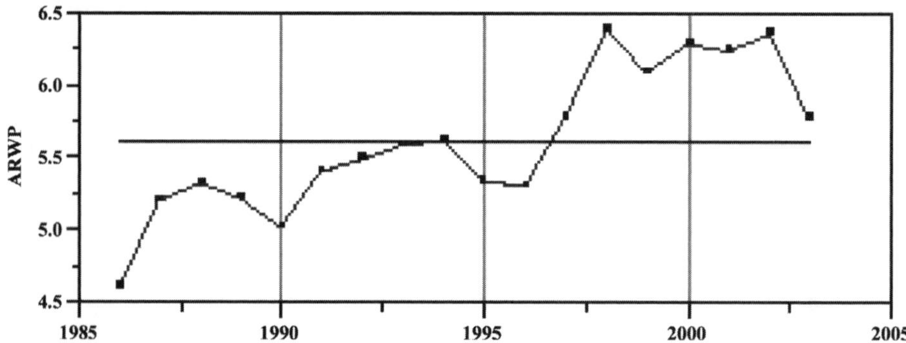

FIGURE 8.2e Argentina, Wine Price Fluctuations, 1986–2003

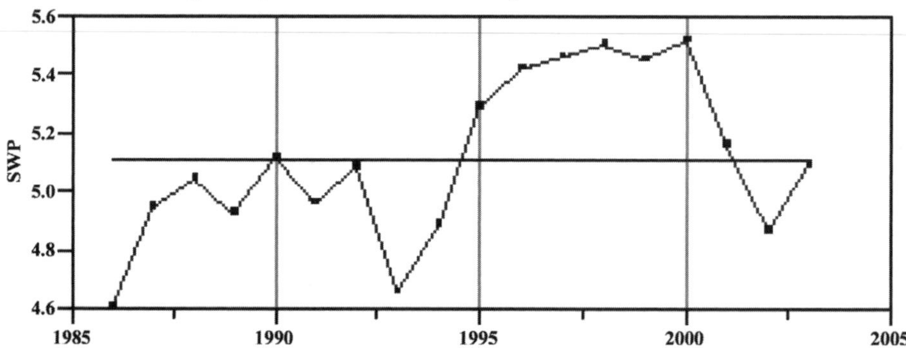

FIGURE 8.2f Spain, Wine Price Fluctuations, 1986–2003

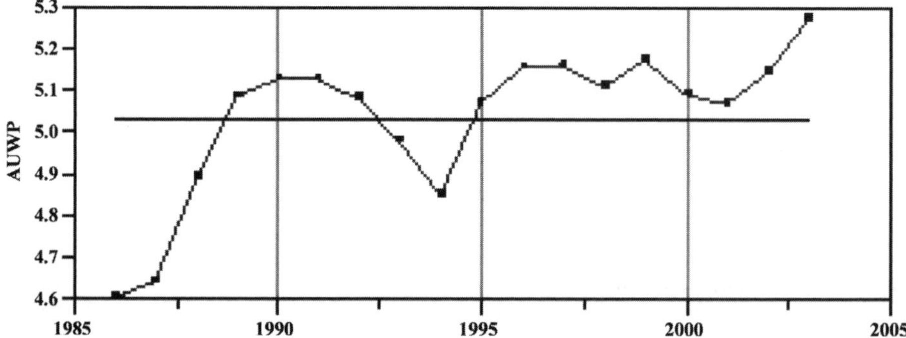

FIGURE 8.2g Australia, Wine Price Fluctuations, 1986–2003

declining, demand. Relative wine surpluses in the United States have been reduced, leading to increases in domestic table wine prices.

The prices in Germany, Italy, and Spain have fluctuated over the same period. The lower-quantity vintages in 1988–1989 in many major European countries, the strengthening of market interventions to remove surpluses from the market, and increases in EU allocations to structural programs to reduce wine acreage have caused wine prices to recover in Europe. Some of the price increases shown around 1995 are due to the relatively smaller harvests and vintages.

Since 1986, Australian wine prices also have continued to rise, reflecting the growing quality and popularity as well as successful marketing.

Figure 8.3 provides graphs of wine inventories related to prices over time. The individual country plots are not easily interpreted because of the previously mentioned intervening factors that confound the usual relationship between these variables. There is also lack of clarity what exactly the inventory data mean, for three reasons:

1. Producers hold stocks in the form of carryover.
2. Consumers, such as restaurants, hold stock, awaiting resale, and wine connoisseurs hold wine in storage.
3. Traders and/or speculators who are anticipating resale to others also hold stocks in wines.

Carryover stocks act similar to supply: Stocks accumulate (deplete) as prices rise (fall), in anticipation of further price increases (decreases). Alternatively,

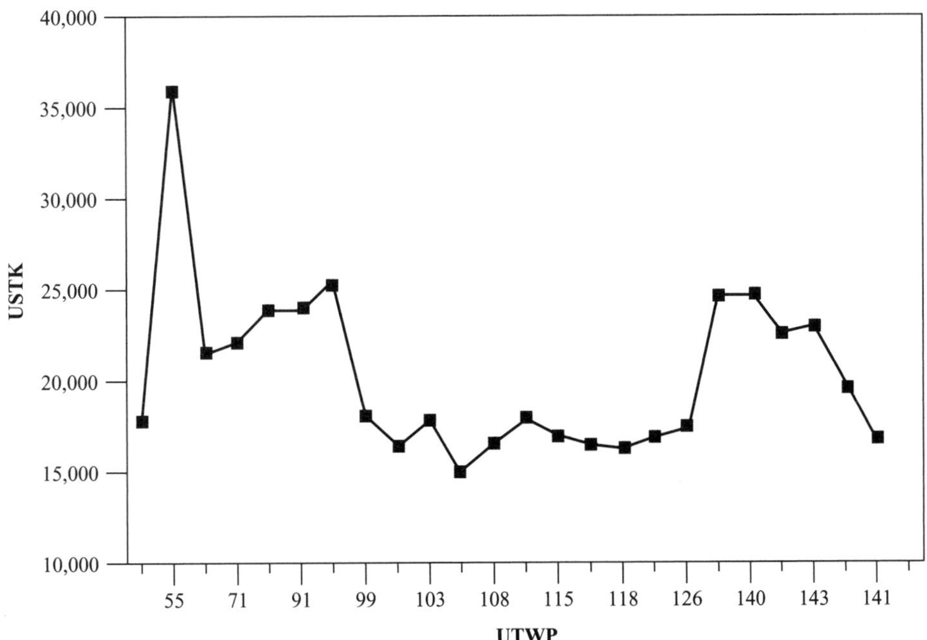

FIGURE 8.3a United States, Wine Inventory versus Price Fluctuations, 1975–2003

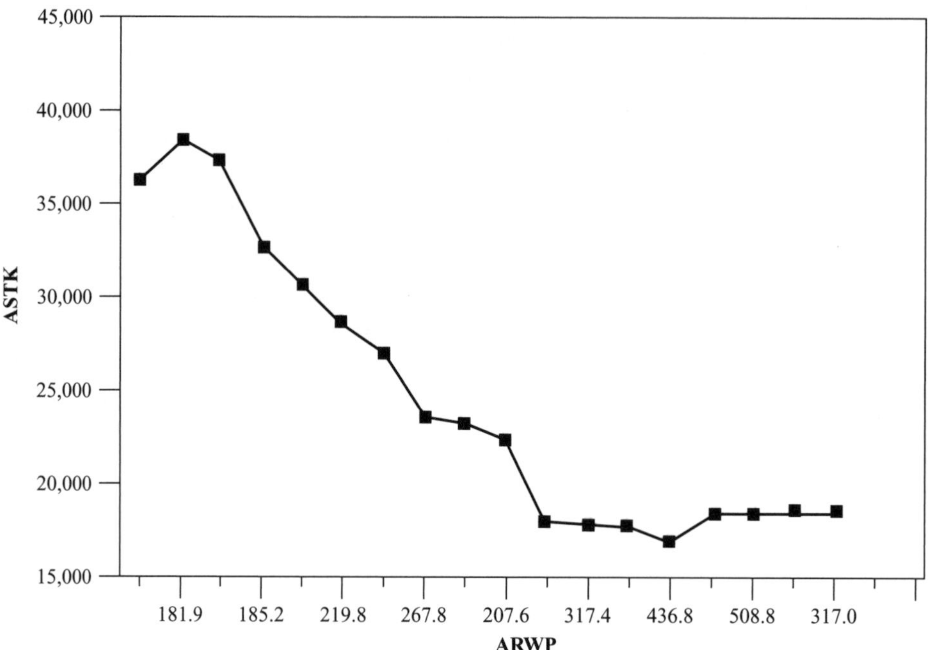

FIGURE 8.3b Argentina, Wine Inventory versus Price Fluctuations, 1986–2003

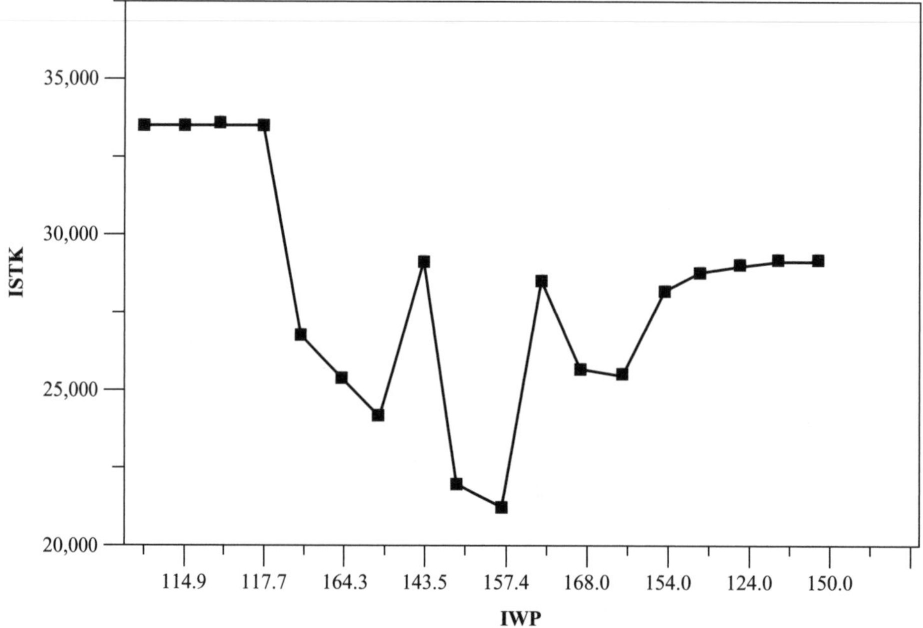

FIGURE 8.3c Italy, Wine Inventory versus Price Fluctuations, 1986–2003

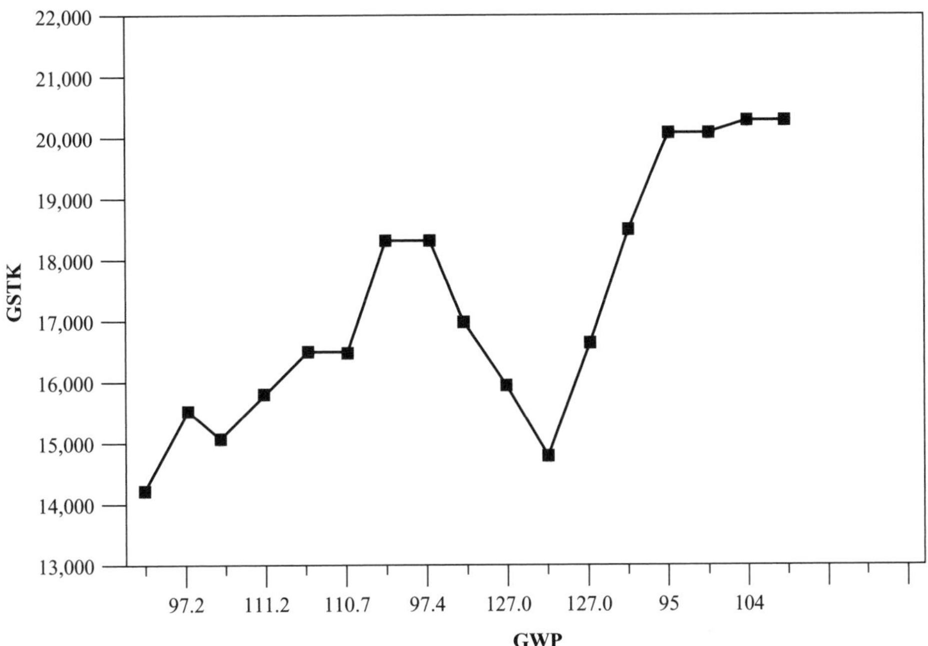

FIGURE 8.3d Germany, Wine Inventory versus Price Fluctuations, 1986–2003

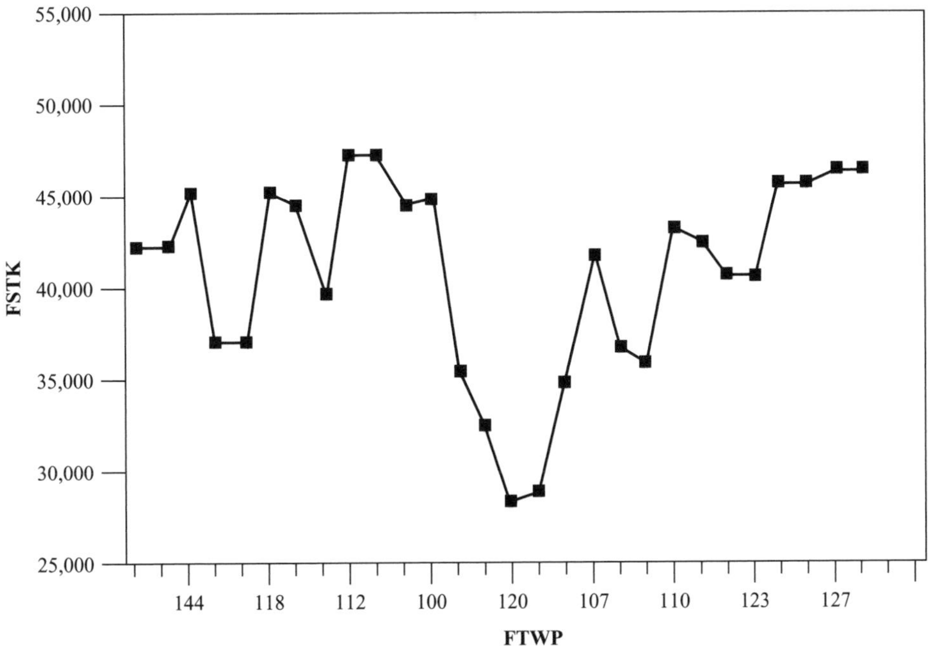

FIGURE 8.3e France, Wine Inventory versus Price Fluctuations, 1975–2003

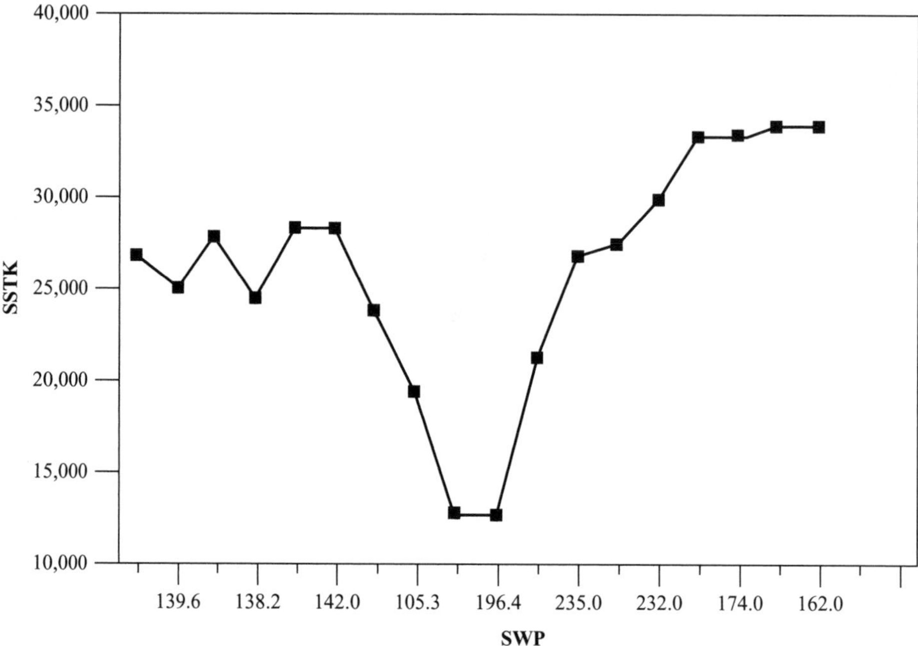

FIGURE 8.3f Spain, Wine Inventory versus Price Fluctuations, 1986–2003

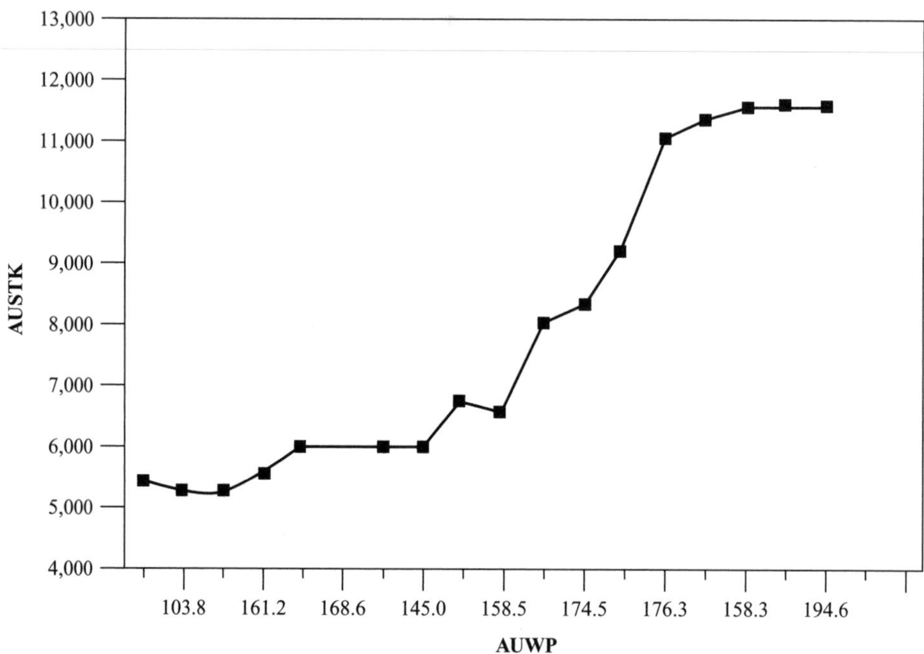

FIGURE 8.3g Australia, Wine Inventory versus Price Fluctuations, 1986–2003

stockholding acts like demand and more (fewer) stocks are purchased when prices are low (high). Where sufficient data exist, one can employ the more complex theories of stockholding mentioned earlier. Returning to Figure 8.3, only Argentina, Italy, and the United Sates appear to have a stock-price relationship roughly resembling a demand nature.

The curves of Germany, France, Australia, and Spain appear to reflect carryover or more of a supply nature.

TESTING FOR TRENDS

Examination of the autocorrelation and partial autocorrelation coefficients for the inventory and prices series has suggested that the series are dissimilar with respect to persistency and mostly have unstable trends. With the exception of the Australian, German, Italian, and Spanish series, the graphs of the autocorrelation functions decay very slowly. This suggests possible unit roots for the series. Therefore, trend tests follow.

Unit Root Tests

The results from the Augmented Dickey-Fuller (ADF) test in levels under the no-constant-no-trend specifications suggest that we cannot reject the null hypothesis of non-stationarity at the 5% significance level (Table 8.1). Therefore, we conclude that wine price levels and wine inventory levels are nonstationary at the 5% significance level. The series were differenced and the ADF tests run again. The results for the first differences suggest that the null hypothesis of a unit root can be rejected at the 5% significance level for all series. Thus, the ADF tests indicate that wine prices and wine inventory series in their first differences are stationary at the 5% significance level for all countries.

TABLE 8.1 Augmented Dickey-Fuller Tests

	Wine Prices		Wine Inventory	
Country	Levels	First Differences	Levels	First Differences
Germany	0.41	−2.92*	0.45	−3.10*
Argentina	0.03	−2.57*	−1.50	−2.01*
Spain	−0.25	−2.81*	−0.09	−2.88*
Italy	0.18	−2.70*	0.28	−4.47*
Australia	0.68	−2.87*	1.93	−1.65*
France	0.54	−5.38*	−0.11	−4.81*
United States	0.78	−2.37*	−1.73	−7.47*

No intercept and no trend.
*Significant at 5% critical value.
Note: Critical values = −1.95 for 29 observations and −1.96 for 16 observations. With the exception of the United States and France, all countries have 16 observations.

When a constant and trend are included (Table 8.2), the ADF test results for the levels series suggest that in all series except one (Australia), the null hypothesis of a unit root cannot be rejected at the 5% level, implying that the series are non-stationary in their levels. In their first differences, the null hypothesis of a unit root is rejected for wine inventories in France, Italy, and the United States. In France, the null hypothesis is also rejected for wine prices. For wine prices in the United States, Argentina, Australia, Germany, Italy, and Spain; and for wine inventories in Germany, Argentina, Spain, and Australia, the null hypothesis of a unit root cannot be rejected at the 5% significance level. Overall, the unit root tests suggest that under the no-constant-no-trend specification, all series are I(1), but when a constant and trend are introduced, only the wine price series for France and the wine inventory series for Italy, France, and the United States are I(1).

Since the results of conventional tests can change with sample size, we conducted periodiogram-based unit root tests, which are not influenced by sample size, to check the stability of our results.

Periodiogram-Based Unit Root Test

Akdi's and Dickey's (1998) periodiogram-based unit root test method has three advantages over conventional tests:

1. Conventional tests require the estimation of too many AR parameters to account for the dynamics of the series.
2. Test results change with the sample size in conventional tests, while the periodogram based method requires no parameter estimation except for variance.
3. The critical values of the test statistics are free of sample size constraints. Thus, these might have considerable advantages, especially for the small-sample wine data.

TABLE 8.2 Augmented Dickey-Fuller Tests

	Wine Prices		Wine Inventory	
Country	Levels	First Differences	Levels	First Differences
Germany	−3.38	−2.64	3.08	−3.25
Argentina	−2.09	−2.30	−1.80	−2.23
Spain	−1.82	−2.65	−2.03	−2.86
Italy	−2.19	−2.74	−1.82	−4.40*
Australia	−4.51*	−2.56	−1.99	−2.23
France	−1.56	−6.19*	−2.38	−4.78*
United States	−2.62	−3.54	−3.63	−8.04*

With intercept and trend.
*Significant at 5% critical value.
Note: Critical values = −3.57 for 29 observations and −3.74 for 16 observations. Except for the United States and France, all countries have 16 observations.

As described in Akdi, Berument and Cilasun (2007), one may use the trigonometric transformation of the series for this test. Given a time series$\{Y_1, Y_2, \ldots, Y_n\}$, the periodiogram ordinate (without any model specification) is

$$I_n(w_k) = \frac{n}{2}\left(a_k^2 + b_k^2\right) \tag{8.1}$$

where a_k, b_k are the Fourier coefficients and defined as

$$a_k = \frac{2}{n}\sum_{t=1}^{n}(Y_t - \bar{Y})\cos(w_k t) \quad \text{and} \quad b_k = \frac{2}{n}\sum_{t=1}^{n}(Y_t - \bar{Y})\sin(w_k t). \tag{8.2}$$

Note that when $w_k = 2\pi k/n$, this following equality holds:

$$\sum_{t=1}^{n}\cos(w_k t) = \sum_{t=1}^{n}\sin(w_k t) = 0.$$

This causes the Fourier coefficients to be invariant to the mean and, therefore, the periodiogram ordinate to be invariant to the mean (Akdi, Berument, and Cilasun 2007). Moreover, periodiogram-based unit root/cointegration tests have the advantage of being seasonality robust and model free from the selection of the lag lengths (see Akdi 1995; and Akdi and Dickey 1998).

In order to reject the null hypothesis of a unit root, one needs to observe small values of the periodiogram ordinates. Therefore, the values of the test statistics, $T(w_k)$, can be used to test for a unit root where

$$T(w_k) = \frac{2\,(1 - \cos(w_k))}{\hat{\sigma}^2} I_n(w_k) \tag{8.3}$$

The test statistics are distributed as a mixture of Chi-squares exactly for AR(1) series under the assumption of stationarity (Akdi, Berument, and Cilasun 2007). In this case, the normalized periodiogram will be distributed asymptotically Chi-squared with two degrees of freedom. In conventional applications, the power of the test is not exact. However, the power can be calculated analytically for the periodiogram method to test for a unit root (Akdi 1995). For higher-order series, the same distribution is obtained asymptotically:

$$T(w_k) = \frac{2\,(1 - \cos(w_k))}{\hat{\sigma}^2} I_n(w_k) \xrightarrow{D} Z_1^2 + 3Z_2^2 \tag{8.4}$$

where Z_1 and Z_2 = independent standard normal random variables
σ^2 = variance of the error term
$\xrightarrow{D}$ = convergence in distribution

The critical values of this distribution are provided by Akdi and Dickey (1998). Table 8.3 presents the results and critical values. As shown in the table, the periodiogram results support the conclusion derived from the conventional tests that

TABLE 8.3 Periodiogram-Based Unit Root Test

	$I_n(w_1)$	$\hat{\sigma}^2$	$T_n(w_1)$	$I_n(w_1)$	$\hat{\sigma}^2$	$T_n(w_1)$	Critical Values
	Wine Prices			Wine Inventory			
Levels							
Germany	554.95	0.0192	49605	16647.43	0.0038	13359228	0.178
Argentina	2393.95	0.0081	3063.6	746583.3	0.0044	6487305.3	0.178
Spain	21779.64	0.0508	105621	432053.8	0.0371	24125950	0.178
Italy	4722.25	0.0263	707118	150380.8	0.0168	1460875.5	0.178
Australia	1636.31	0.0127	433656	6250.414	0.0053	4508908.3	0.178
France	2989.43	0.0049	148776	243767.1	0.0126	62384683	0.178
United States	11105.26	0.0013	571908	316242.3	0.0312	38028975	0.178
First Difference							
Germany	0.00434	0.02006	0.000062	0.0035	0.0043	0.000225	0.178
Argentina	0.01991	0.11683	0.000343	0.0304	0.0060	0.006389	0.178
Spain	0.01906	0.06249	0.000349	0.1045	0.0454	0.001044	0.178
Italy	0.03476	0.02903	0.002112	0.0251	0.0178	0.000422	0.178
Australia	0.01910	0.00639	0.005258	0.0278	0.0139	0.006379	0.178
France	0.01057	0.00526	0.000244	0.0096	0.0149	0.000046	0.178
US	0.00712	0.00161	0.000691	0.0378	0.0473	0.000012	0.178

all series are I(1) and, hence, that we can conduct cointegration tests under the no-constant-no-trend specification.

COINTEGRATION BETWEEN STOCKS AND PRICES

In this section, we conduct cointegration analyses, using three alternative techniques: the Engle-Granger (1987) two-step test, the maximum likelihood method developed by Johansen (1988) and Johansen and Juselius (1990), and the periodiogram method proposed by Akdi (1995). The Johansen method is preferred when more than two time-series variables are involved, because it can determine the number of cointegrating vectors. Furthermore, there is less error propagation in the Johansen technique because only one step is involved rather than the two steps required in the Engle-Granger technique. As noted earlier, the periodiogram-based method also has certain advantages over conventional tests, especially for small samples.

Beginning with the Engle-Granger cointegration test, if a series Y_t is nonstationary and there is a β vector (or matrix) such that $W_t = \beta' Y_t$ becomes stationary, then Y_t is considered cointegrated and the vector β is called the cointegrating vector. In Table 8.1, it was shown that under the no-constant-no-trend specification, both wine price series (WP) and wine inventory series (WI) are I(1). Thus, these nonstationary series can be written as a linear combination of stationary and nonstationary series as

$$\begin{aligned} WP_t &= a_{11}\phi_t + a_{12}\varpi_t \\ WI_t &= a_{21}\phi_t + a_{22}\varpi_t \end{aligned} \tag{8.5}$$

where ϕ_t = unit root of these series
ϖ_t = stationary component of these series

Since each component of the bivariate series includes the nonstationary component ϕ_t, both components of Y_t are nonstationary. However, if the coefficients $(a_{ij}, i, j = 1, 2)$ are known, then

$$WP_t - \frac{a_{21}}{a_{11}} WI_t = \left(a_{22} - \frac{a_{21}a_{12}}{a_{11}} \right) \varpi_t = c\varpi_t \qquad (8.6)$$

is stationary, and the system is cointegrated with the cointegrating vector $\beta = (-a_{21}/a_{11}, 1)'$. Since we do not know the coefficients, we normally need to estimate all coefficients in equation 8.5. But now it is sufficient only to estimate the ratio a_{21}/a_{11}, using ordinary least squares (OLS). The differenced series in equation 8.6 look like the residuals from the regression of WP on WI. Hence, if the residual series is stationary, then the bivariate series is cointegrated. Moreover, the OLS estimator of the parameter WP obtained from that regression is a consistent estimator for the ratio a_{21}/a_{11} (Engle and Granger 1987). The results for the cointegration equations when wine prices (WP) are regressed on wine inventories (WI) and vice versa are reported in Tables 8.4 and 8.5, respectively.

TABLE 8.4 Cointegration Regression: Prices Regressed on Inventories

Country Name	Coefficients	t-Ratio	R^2	D-W Test
United States	−77.570*	−2.289	0.162	0.999
France	65.075	0.835	0.025	0.931
Germany	4.379	0.119	0.001	0.295
Italy	−103.65*	−3.893	0.487	1.403
Spain	22.677	0.684	0.028	0.352
Argentina	−35.355*	−4.147	0.518	0.768
Australia	59.901*	2.963	0.354	0.306

*Denotes significance at 5% level or higher.

TABLE 8.5 Cointegration Regression: Inventories Regressed on Prices

Country Name	Coefficients	t-Ratio	R^2	D-W Test
United States	−0.002*	−2.289	0.163	0.199
France	0.000	0.835	0.025	0.477
Germany	0.000	0.119	0.001	1.075
Italy	−0.005*	−3.893	0.487	1.418
Spain	0.001	0.684	0.028	0.556
Argentina	−0.015*	−4.147	0.518	1.218
Australia	0.006*	2.963	0.354	0.672

*Denotes significance at 5% level or higher.

To check for cointegration, the errors from the cointegration equations are recovered to perform nonstationarity tests using equation 8.7 since cointegration requires stationary residuals:

$$\Delta\varepsilon_t = \varpi\varepsilon_{t-1} + \sum_{i=1}^{p} \psi_i \Delta\varepsilon_{t-i} + \eta_t \tag{8.7}$$

where ε_t = error from the cointegration equation
η_t = stationary random error

Here the nullhypothesis of nonstationarity is rejected when ϖ is significantly negative. The summation runs to 'p' where p is 2. Tables 8.6 and 8.7 report the ADF test statistics and the critical values. As shown in Table 8.6, nonstationary of the residuals cannot be rejected at the 5%significance level for all series. In Table 8.7, nonstationary of the residuals can be rejected only at the 5% level for Italy and Australia series. For France, Germany, Spain, Argentina, and the United States, the hypothesis cannot be rejected at the 5% level.

Johansen's Cointegration Test

Next, we perform the Johansen cointegration test using the described procedure. The test results appear in Table 8.8. Although the residual-based test rejected the null hypothesis of no cointegration for the U.S., France, Italy, and Argentina series, the Johansen's cointegration test results suggest that the null hypothesis of no

TABLE 8.6 ADF Tests for Errors when Prices Are Regressed on Inventories

Country Name	ADF Test (Levels Series)	5% Critical value
United States	−2.082	−3.37
France	−2.117	−3.37
Germany	−1.767	−3.37
Italy	−2.244	−3.37
Spain	−1.793	−3.37
Argentina	−2.941	−3.37
Australia	−1.436	−3.37

TABLE 8.7 ADF Tests for Errors when Inventories Are Regressed on Prices

Country Name	ADF Test (Levels Series)	5% Critical value
United States	−0.994	−3.37
France	−2.571	−3.37
Germany	−2.909	−3.37
Italy	−9.573*	−3.37
Spain	−1.764	−3.37
Argentina	−2.065	−3.37
Australia	−6.003*	−3.37

*Denotes significance at 5% level or higher.

TABLE 8.8 Johansen's Cointegration Test Results

Test Specifications: No-intercept-no-trend

Series: USTK versus UTWP
Lags interval: 1 to 2

Eigenvalue	Likelihood Ratio	5% Critical Value	1% Critical Value	Hypothesized No. of CE(s)
0.850186	59.10055	25.32	30.45	None**
0.312529	9.743133	12.25	16.26	At most 1

Series: FSTK versus FTWP
Lags interval: 1 to 2

Eigenvalue	Likelihood Ratio	5% Critical Value	1% Critical Value	Hypothesized No. of CE(s)
0.434781	22.13221	25.32	30.45	None
0.244742	7.298108	12.25	16.26	At most 1

Series: GSTK versus GWP
Lags interval: 1 to 2

Eigenvalue	Likelihood Ratio	5% Critical Value	1% Critical Value	Hypothesized No. of CE(s)
0.708330	25.22351	25.32	30.45	None
0.362012	6.741530	12.25	16.26	At most 1

Series: ISTK vs. IWP
Lags interval: 1 to 2

Eigenvalue	Likelihood Ratio	5% Critical Value	1% Critical Value	Hypothesized No. of CE(s)
0.610421	21.29830	25.32	30.45	None
0.379480	7.157956	12.25	16.26	At most 1

Series: SSTK versus SWP
Lags interval: 1 to 2

Eigenvalue	Likelihood Ratio	5% Critical Value	1% Critical Value	Hypothesized No. of CE(s)
0.618633	20.14434	25.32	30.45	None
0.315428	5.684425	12.25	16.26	At most 1

(Continued)

TABLE 8.8 *(Continued)*

Series: ARSTK versus ARWP
Lags interval: 1 to 2

Eigenvalue	Likelihood Ratio	5% Critical Value	1% Critical Value	Hypothesized No. of CE(s)
0.861254	34.15469	25.32	30.45	None**
0.260565	4.528031	12.25	16.26	At most 1

Series: AUSTK vs. AUWP
Lags interval: 1 to 2

Eigenvalue	Likelihood Ratio	5% Critical Value	1% Critical Value	Hypothesized No. of CE(s)
0.610966	19.03397	25.32	30.45	None
0.277359	4.872631	12.25	16.26	At most 1

**Denotes rejection of the hypothesis at the 1% significance level. In all but two instances, hypothesis is rejected at a confidence level of less than 5%.

cointegration can be rejected only for the U.S. and Argentina series. The observed inconsistencies in the cointegration results might be due to problems associated with sample size. Therefore, we examine cointegration using the periodiogram test, which is not influenced by sample size.

Periodiogram Cointegration Tests

We now apply Akdi's (1995) periodiogram method to determine if there is a cointegrating relationship between the series. When the real part of the cross periodiogram ordinate of WI and WP series (say, y_k) is regressed on the periodiogram of WI (or WP) series (say,x_k), the coefficient of x_k is also a consistent estimator for the ratio a_{21}/a_{11} (Akdi 1995). That is, when we consider the model

$$y_k = \alpha + \beta x_k + \eta_k, \;\; k = 1, 2, 3, \ldots, [n/2], \tag{8.8}$$

the OLS estimator of β is a consistent estimator for the ratio a_{21}/a_{11}. The calculated values of $\hat{\beta}$ from equation (8) are reported in Table 8.9.

If the series $Z_t = Y_{2,t} - \hat{\beta} Y_{1,t}$ is stationary, then these two series are cointegrated. If Z_t is stationary, we will conclude that the WI and WP series are cointegrated. In order to perform this test, we regressΔZ_t on Z_{t-1} and calculate the value of the t−statistics. The critical values are –3.43564 at the 5% level and –3.12867 at the 10% level. The estimated results of this regression ($Z_t = Y_{2,t} - \hat{\beta} Y_{1,t}$) are reported in Table 8.10.

Based on the periodiogram results in Table 8.8, we fail to reject the null hypothesis of no cointegration for all series at the 5% significance level. Thus, while the evidence from the conventional tests was mixed, the periodiogram-based analysis suggests that wine inventories and wine prices are not cointegrated. There could be

TABLE 8.9 OLS Regression Results for Periodiogram-Based Tests

Country	Constant	$\hat{\beta}$	P-value	R^2
United States	1.337	75.3	0.000	0.96
France	−2.386	159.2	0.004	0.52
Argentina	9.096	40.3	0.000	0.89
Australia	7.288	43.3	0.000	0.86
Germany	0.998	83.3	0.005	0.71
Italy	1.758	40.3	0.004	0.71
Spain	4.383	105.6	0.000	0.84

various reasons for the discrepancy of the test results. One possible reason is that the conventional tests require estimation of too many parameters to address the dynamics of the series with AR parameters. The periodiogram-based method is seasonally robust and requires no parameter estimation except the variance (any consistent estimator of the variance can be used in the test statistics). These may account for the differences in the test results (see Akdi 1995 for details).

VECTOR AUTOREGRESSION AND IMPULSE RESULTS

The interrelationship between wine inventories and prices can be more directly examined using causality and vector autoregression analysis (VAR) (Cromwell et al. 1994). By incorporating time lags between the inventory and price variables, VAR approaches are particularly relevant because changes in inventories typically do not cause price changes at once, but over several periods, and vice versa. Producers and consumers must first realize stock changes in order to form price expectations. Wine inventories in bottles are not perishable in the short to medium run. Some storage can even increase wine quality. Wine consumers may therefore not feel the need to purchase quickly but may wait in anticipation of more favorable price developments. In the case of high-quality wines such as Bordeaux or Burgundy, life expectancy may last beyond 20 years and can go as high as 50 years.

The results of the Granger (1969) causality test between the inventory-price pairs revealed no strong forms of causality. We therefore move directly to the VAR approach, which provides a useful means of analyzing the broad correlation in the variables of a system. This approach sidesteps the need for structural modeling

TABLE 8.10 Estimated Values of the Periodiogram-Based Tests

Country	t-Statistics	R^2	5% Critical Value
United States	1.78541	0.11	−3.43564
France	2.19396	0.16	−3.43564
Argentina	−0.51608	0.02	−3.43564
Australia	−0.48016	0.02	−3.43564
Germany	−3.03394	0.38	−3.43564
Italy	−1.33291	0.11	−3.43564
Spain	−1.29607	0.10	−3.43564

by modeling every endogenous variable in the system as a function of the lagged values of all of the endogenous variables in the system. Although the approach does not confirm causality, it at least evaluates the intertemporal influences between the variables. Estimated VARs are used to calculate the percentages of each endogenous variable that are explained by innovations in each of the other endogenous as well as explanatory variables and to provide information about the relative importance of each random innovation to the variable in the VAR.

The mathematical form of a VAR is

$$Y_t = A_1 Y_{t-1} + \cdots + A_p Y_{t-p} + \beta X_t + \varepsilon_t \tag{8.9}$$

where $Y_t = k$ vector of endogenous variables
$X_t = d$ vector of exogenous variables
$A_1, \ldots, A_p$ and $\beta =$ matrices of coefficients to be estimated
$\varepsilon_t =$ vector of innovations that may vary contemporaneously

The VAR model highlights the impact of changes in wine stocks on wine prices in two ways: It decomposes the variance into forecast errors and analyses the impulse shocks.

Our interest is in discovering the lags and the signs of the lags, because they measure the impacts of wine stock changes on prices. Wohlgenant (1982) found that lags in inventory and shipment variables play an important role in explaining wine prices. This is best accomplished through impulse response functions that simulate the impacts of a shock of a given variable (leaving all variables endogenous) and then compute the predicted dynamic responses of each of the included variables. By treating the residuals of each variable/equation as unexplained innovations, the impacts of innovations are traced through the system by shocking the error terms. To employ the impulse functions, the VAR equations must first be estimated and the impulse response computed. The lack of strong cointegration between the endogenous wine variables permits us to proceed in this direction. Because some nonstationarity was found in the time series of these variables, it is best to ensure stationarity by using some transform, in this case percentage changes. This transformation also conforms to the tenets of price theory. It is really changes in stocks that induce changes in prices in the short term (rather than the relationship in levels).

The method of estimating the VAR's is normally of an unrestricted nature. All endogenous variables are thus of the same lag length in the estimation process. These forms of regressions were first performed for both variables. An attempt also was made to divide the later data span into 1986 to 1994 and 1995 to 2003 periods and to reestimate the equations to investigate whether the inventory-price relation varied between the earlier and the later parts of the total time span. No clear evidence of a difference was found here. However, we discovered that the regression results could be improved by estimating restricted VARs in which only first-order price lags and country-specific inventory lags were used. The method employed was to estimate the cross-correlograms between the variable pairs and to discover which variable lags (i.e., 1, 2, 3 or higher) had the highest statistical significance. The estimation results from the restricted VARs are summarized in Table 8.11. The equation t-statistics and R-squared values are normally low because of the use of first differences. Only first or second inventory lags are significant for all countries, except for Spain, where a third-order lag proved significant.

TABLE 8.11 Summary of VAR Regression Results by Country

United States			Germany		
Vector Autoregression Estimates Standard errors in () t-statistics in [ ]			Vector Autoregression Estimates Standard errors in () t-statistics in [ ]		
	DUTWP	DUSTK		DGWP	DGSTK
DUTWP(-1)	0.704785	$-3.35E-16$	DGWP(-1)	−0.061869	−0.088249
	(0.15431)	(1.5E−16)		(0.35410)	(0.16115)
	[4.56728]	[−2.18636]		[−0.17472]	[−0.54761]
DUSTK(-1)	−0.027712	$-1.97E-17$	DGSTK(-1)	−0.579763	0.192011
	(0.03174)	(3.2E−17)		(0.63496)	(0.28897)
	[−0.87301]	[−0.62408]		[−0.91307]	[0.66446]
C	0.009630	$2.07E-17$	C	0.034944	0.013663
	(0.00873)	(8.7E−18)		(0.03930)	(0.01789)
	[1.10358]	[2.38768]		[0.88916]	[0.76392]
DUSTK	−0.016292	1.000000	DGSTK(-2)	−0.082583	−0.093852
	(0.04417)	(4.4E−17)		(0.47880)	(0.21791)
	[−0.36882]	[$2.3e+16$]		[−0.17248]	[−0.43070]
R^2	0.500410	1.000000	R^2	0.070643	0.099725
$\overline{R}^2$	0.435246	1.000000	$\overline{R}^2$	−0.161697	−0.125344
Sum sq. resids	0.025700	2.54E−32	Sum sq. resids	0.249360	0.051647
S.E. equation	0.033427	3.32E−17	S.E. equation	0.144153	0.065604
F-statistic	7.679247	$1.86E+32$			
Log likelihood	55.60964		Log likelihood	10.58856	23.18423
Akaike AIC	−3.822937		Akaike AIC	−0.823570	−2.398029
Schwarz SC	−3.630961		Schwarz SC	−0.630423	−2.204881
Mean dependent	0.034878	−0.028445	Mean dependent	0.020993	0.016617
S.D. dependent	0.044481	0.153987	S.D. dependent	0.133745	0.061843
Determinant resid covariance (dof adj.)		$1.22E-36$	Determinant resid covariance (dof adj.)		7.79E−05
Determinant resid covariance		8.88E−37	Determinant resid covariance		4.38E−05
Log likelihood		1044.035	Log likelihood		34.87741
Akaike information criterion		−76.74332	Akaike information criterion		−3.359677
Schwarz criterion		−76.35937	Schwarz criterion		−2.973382

France			Italy		
Vector Autoregression Estimates Standard errors in () & t-statistics in [ ]			Vector Autoregression Estimates Standard errors in () & t-statistics in [ ]		
	DFCWP	DFSTK		DIWP	DISTK
DFCWP(-1)	0.099775	0.346445	DIWP(-1)	−0.103283	−9.71E−17
	(0.25174)	(0.68953)		(0.33450)	(1.3E−16)
	[0.39633]	[0.50243]		[−0.30877]	[−0.74631]
	−0.141769	0.251110		−0.409931	2.03E−16

(Continued)

TABLE 8.11 *(Continued)*

France			Italy		
Vector Autoregression Estimates Standard errors in () & t-statistics in [ ]			Vector Autoregression Estimates Standard errors in () & t-statistics in [ ]		
	DFCWP	DFSTK		DIWP	DISTK
DFSTK(-1)	(0.09795)	(0.26829)	DISTK(-1)	(0.38959)	(1.5*E*–16)
	[−1.44737]	[0.93598]		[−1.05220]	[1.34171]
	0.026975	−0.008802		0.012991	3.48*E*–18
C	(0.01305)	(0.03574)	C	(0.04201)	(1.6*E*–17)
	[2.06731]	[−0.24628]		[0.30920]	[0.21314]
DFSTK(-2)	−0.141692	−0.133356	DISTK	−0.537577	1.000000
	(0.10599)	(0.29032)		(0.36356)	(1.4*E*–16)
	[−1.33679]	[−0.45934]		[−1.47864]	[7.1*e* + 15]
DISTK(-2)				−0.115273	1.36*E*–16
				(0.36694)	(1.4*E*–16)
				[−0.31414]	[0.95195]
R^2	0.319468	0.114097	R^2	0.210925	1.000000
$\overline{R}^2$	0.173639	−0.075740	$\overline{R}^2$	−0.076012	1.000000
Sum sq. resids	0.026753	0.200707	Sum sq. resids	0.302567	4.58*E*–32
S.E. equation	0.043714	0.119734	S.E. equation	0.165850	6.45*E*–17
F-statistic	2.190711	0.601027	F–statistic	0.735092	1.62E+31
Log likelihood	33.06250	14.92562	Log likelihood	9.041316	
Akaike AIC	−3.229167	−1.213958	Akaike AIC	−0.505165	
Schwarz SC	−3.031307	−1.016098	Schwarz SC	−0.263731	
Mean dependent	0.030638	0.002213	Mean dependent	0.020694	−0.008708
S.D. dependent	0.048088	0.115442	S.D. dependent	0.159884	0.134249
Determinant Residual Covariance		2.59*E*–05	Determinant resid covariance (dof adj.)		1.14*E*–34
Log Likelihood		43.97841	Determinant resid covariance		5.40*E*–35
Akaike Information Criteria		−3.997601	Log likelihood		585.8201
Schwarz Criteria		−3.601880	Akaike information criterion		−71.97751
			Schwarz criterion	−71.49464	

Argentina			Spain		
Vector Autoregression Estimates Standard errors in () & t-statistics in [ ]			Vector Autoregression Estimates Standard errors in () & t-statistics in [ ]		
	DARWP	DARSTK		DSWP	DSSTK
DARWP(-1)	0.015152	0.022086	DSWP(-1)	−0.153130	0.439610
	(0.30269)	(0.07880)		(0.30194)	(0.25293)
	[0.05006]	[0.28030]		[−0.50715]	[1.73804]
	−1.073901	0.071431		−0.383418	0.301977

TABLE 8.11 (*Continued*)

Argentina			Spain		
Vector Autoregression Estimates Standard errors in () & t-statistics in [ ]			Vector Autoregression Estimates Standard errors in () & t-statistics in [ ]		
	DARWP	DARSTK		DSWP	DSSTK
DARSTK(-1)	(1.16381)	(0.30297)	DSSTK(-1)	(0.33448)	(0.28019)
	[−0.92274]	[0.23577]		[−1.14631]	[1.07775]
	−0.060259	−0.045857		0.019372	0.012158
C	(0.10456)	(0.02722)	C	(0.06174)	(0.05172)
	[−0.57634]	[−1.68479]		[0.31376]	[0.23507]
	−1.228213	−0.023028		−0.477549	−0.062099
DARSTK(-2)	(1.03307)	(0.26893)	DSSTK(-3)	(0.32098)	(0.26888)
	[−1.18890]	[−0.08563]		[−1.48778]	[−0.23095]
DSSTK(-2)				−0.002601	−0.117863
				(0.35667)	(0.29878)
				[−0.00729]	[−0.39448]
R^2	0.198556	0.018653	R^2	0.278636	0.402614
$\overline{R}^2$	−0.001805	−0.226684	$\overline{R}^2$	−0.009909	0.163659
Sum sq. resids	1.110202	0.075235	Sum sq. resids	0.559834	0.392854
S.E. equation	0.304166	0.079181	S.E. equation	0.236608	0.198205
F-statistic	0.990993	0.076030	F-statistic	0.965658	1.684896
Log likelihood	−1.358643	20.17478	Log likelihood	3.377164	6.033685
Akaike AIC	0.669830	−2.021848	Akaike AIC	0.216378	−0.137825
Schwarz SC	0.862978	−1.828701	Schwarz SC	0.452395	0.098192
Mean dependent	0.034715	−0.045552	Mean dependent	0.003160	0.013110
S.D. dependent	0.303892	0.071491	S.D. dependent	0.235444	0.216732
Determinant Residual Covariance		0.000565	Determinant resid covariance (dof adj.)		0.001961
Log Likelihood		14.42798	Determinant resid covariance		0.000872
Akaike Information Criteria		−0.803498	Log likelihood		10.26973
Schwarz Criteria		−0.417203	Akaike information criterion		−0.035964
			Schwarz criterion		0.436070

Australia			Australia		
Vector Autoregression Estimates Standard errors in () & t-statistics in [ ]			Vector Autoregression Estimates Standard errors in () & t-statistics in [ ]		
	DAUWP	DAUSTK		DAUWP	DAUSTK
DAUWP(-1)	0.210177	0.176227	Sum sq. resids	0.138980	0.058151
	(0.25283)	(0.16354)	S.E. equation	0.107618	0.069612
	[0.83130]	[1.07756]	F-statistic	1.620091	0.833025
	−0.301299	−0.065912	Log likelihood	15.26511	22.23543
	(0.40022)	(0.25888)	Akaike AIC	−1.408139	−2.279428

(*Continued*)

TABLE 8.11 (*Continued*)

Australia			Australia		
Vector Autoregression Estimates Standard errors in () & t-statistics in [ ]			Vector Autoregression Estimates Standard errors in () & t-statistics in [ ]		
	DAUWP	DAUSTK		DAUWP	DAUSTK
DAUWP(-1)	[−0.75283]	[−0.25460]	Schwarz SC	−1.214992	−2.086281
	0.078423	0.032394	Mean dependent	0.039280	0.049392
	(0.04034)	(0.02609)	S.D. dependent	0.114096	0.068440
C	[1.94427]	[1.24159]	Determinant resid covariance (dof adj.)		5.55*E*–05
	−0.694038	0.309379			
	(0.39344)	(0.25449)	Determinant resid covariance		3.12*E*–05
DAUSTK(-2)	[−1.76404]	[1.21567]	Log likelihood		37.59268
R^2	0.288268	0.172361	Akaike information criterion		−3.699085
$\bar{R}^2$	0.110335	−0.034549	Schwarz criterion		−3.312791

In order to use the estimated VAR to analyze the interaction among wine prices and stocks in the structural models, impulse-response functions were computed by recovering structural innovations from the estimated residuals (linear combinations of uncorrelated structural shocks) from the VAR. The computed impulse function gives the difference between the expected value of the variable at time $t + i$ after a hypothetical shock at time t, and the expected value of the same variable at time $t + i$, given the observed history of the system. The impulse functions for each equation are shown in Figure 8.4.

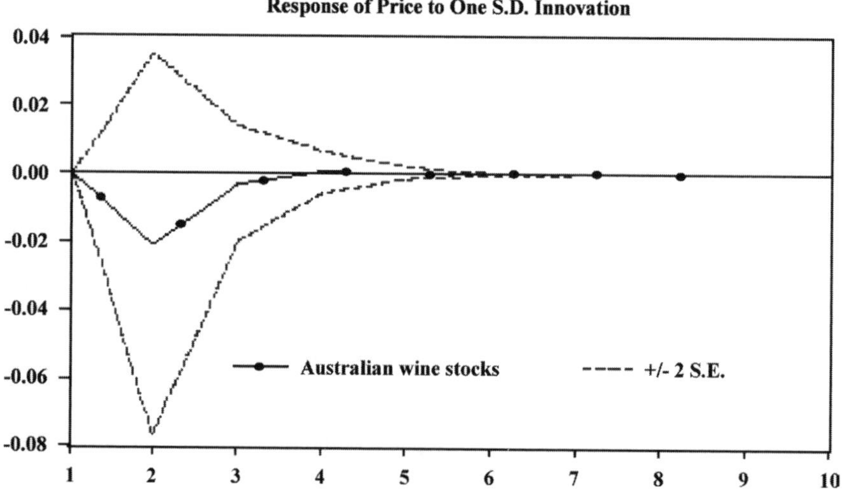

FIGURE 8.4a Australia, Impulse Response Functions

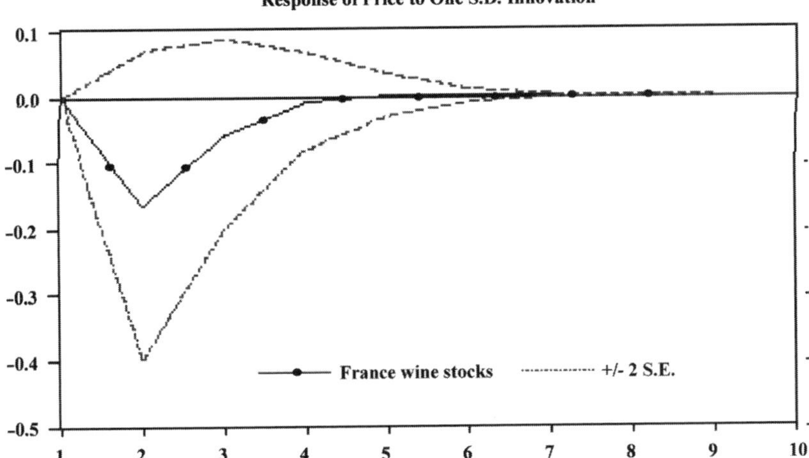

FIGURE 8.4b France, Impulse Response Functions

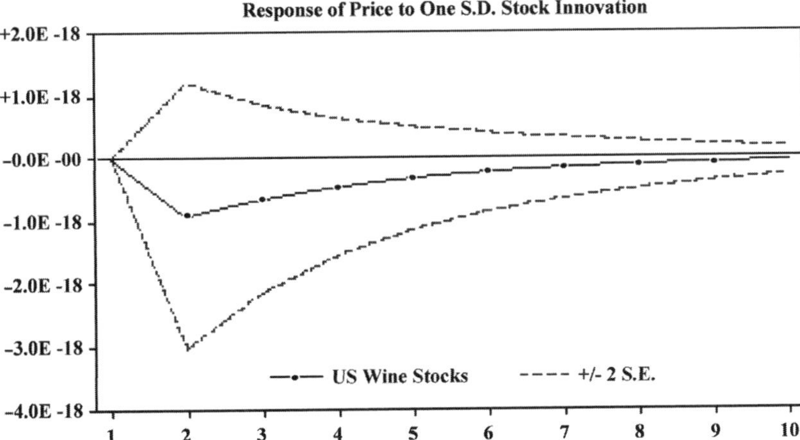

FIGURE 8.4c United States, Impulse Response Functions

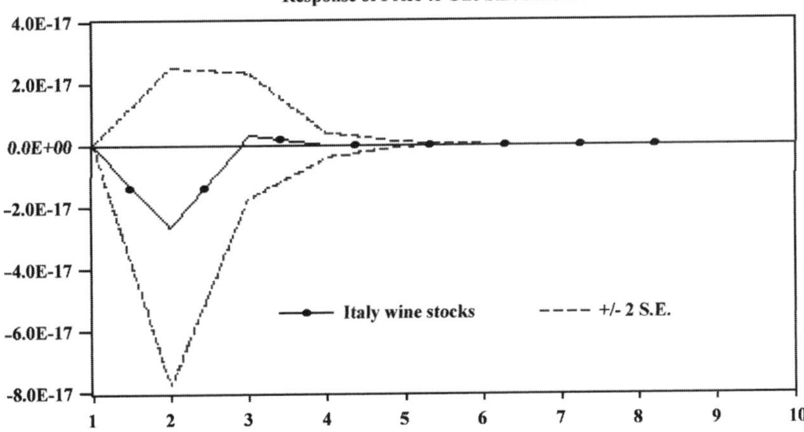

FIGURE 8.4d Italy, Impulse Response Functions

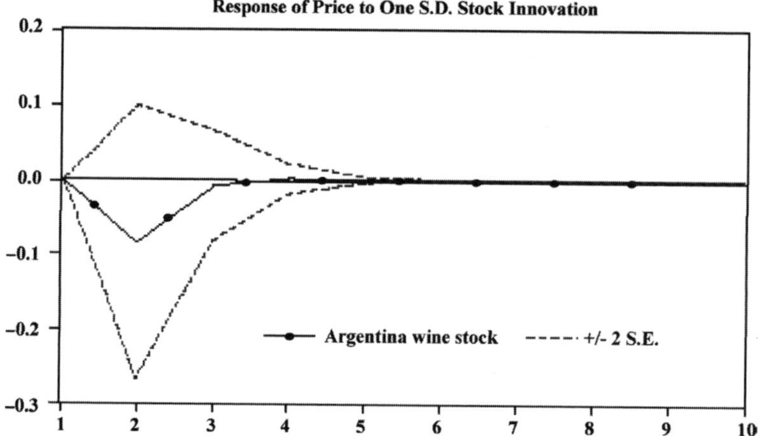

FIGURE 8.4e Argentina, Impulse Response Functions

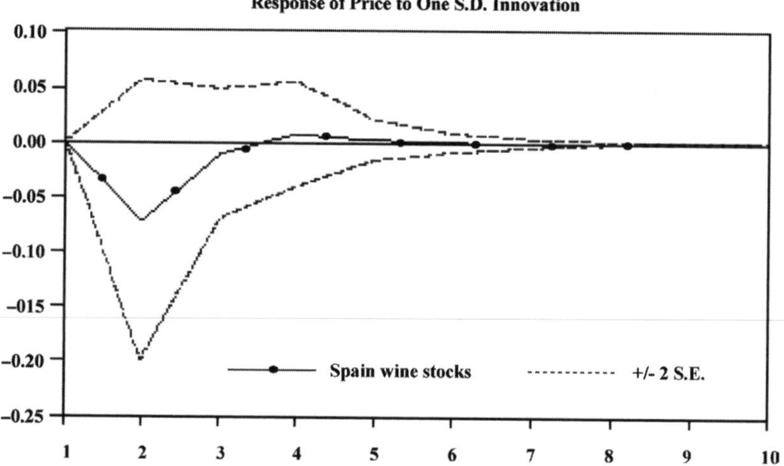

FIGURE 8.4f Spain, Impulse Response Functions

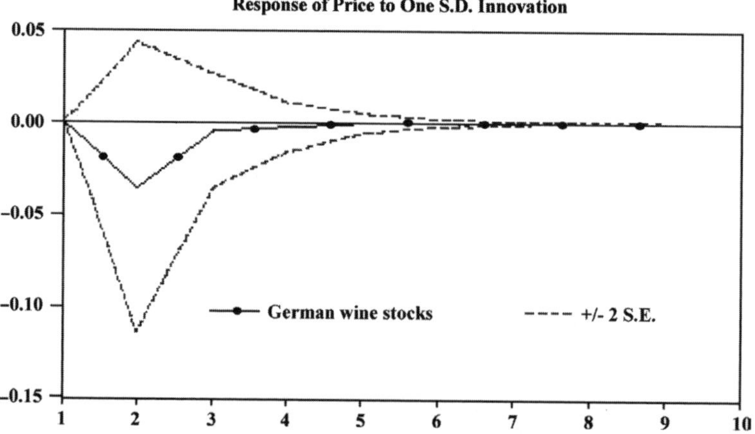

FIGURE 8.4g Germany, Impulse Response Functions

The equation results and impulses provide the strongest evidence for France and Australia of interaction between wine prices and wine inventories. The impulse-response functions indicate that French inventories are affecting wine prices and that positive changes in French inventories are decreasing prices for up to four periods. At two periods, lag dependency is strongest for Australia, but it declines by the third period.

The explanation for the United States is the "next best" and shows the longest lag dependency, extending to seven periods.

The results for Argentina, Italy, and Spain indicate weaker dependence. In these three cases, the strongest inventory lag is at two periods and finishes at three lags.

For Germany, the inventory influence is weakest, most important at two lags but quitting at three.

CONCLUSIONS

This study has employed carefully constructed national wine inventory and price series to determine what kind of relationships, if any, might exist between these variables. The underlying data, however, have been generated by national statistical agencies that have not compiled all the data most useful for this type of economic analysis.

Microeconomic theory provides possible theories of how inventory and price variables might be interlinked. Previous studies examined only elementary aspects of the relationship between wine inventory and wine price behavior.

The empirical results of univariate and multivariate time series analysis provide support for the existence of only a weak relationship. The results of the VAR analysis are correspondingly limited. However, the shapes of the impulse functions confirm the expected negative relationship between positive stock changes and falling prices and negative stock changes and rising prices. The impulse function results are strongest for the wine markets of Argentina, Australia, France, Italy, and Spain and weakest for Germany.

We hope that the results of this study motivate further research in this area. To do so successfully, more detailed inventory and price data are necessary. Particularly useful additional insights could be obtained from data for specific wines and quality levels. This would permit not only improved price explanations but also the evaluation of some of the more complex inventory behavioral theories mentioned earlier.

REFERENCES

Akdi, Y. (1995). *Periodiogram Analysis for Unit Roots*. Ph.D. dissertation, North Carolina State University, Raleigh, NC.

Akdi, Y., and D.A. Dickey. (1998). "Periodiogram for Unit Root Time Series: Distributions and Tests." *Communications in Statistics* 27. 1: 69–87.

Akdi, Y., H. Berument, and S. M. Cilasun. (2007). "The Relationship between Different Price Indices: Evidence from Turkey." Paper presented at the Sixth International Conference of the MEEA, Zayed University, Dubai, UAE, March 14–16.

Amspacher, W.H. (1988). *An Econometric Analysis of the California Wine/Grape Industry*. Ph.D. dissertation, University of California, Davis.

Anderson, K., and D. Norman. (2003). *Global Wine Production, Consumption and Trade, 1961–2001*. CIES Monograph, Centre for International Economic Studies, University of Adelaide.

Antonini, A. (1988). *Price and Inventory Dynamics of Primary Commodities*. Ph.D. dissertation, Columbia University, New York.

Berger, N., K. Anderson, and R. Stringer. (1998). *Trends in the World Wine Market: A Statistical Compendium, 1961 to 1996*. CIES Monograph, Centre for International Economic Studies, University of Adelaide.

Blinder, A.S., and S.J. Maccini. (1991). "Taking Stock: A Critical Assessment of Recent Research on Inventories," *Journal of Economic Perspectives* 5: 73–96.

Brennan, M.J. (1958). "The Supply of Storage," *American Economic Review*, 43: 50–72.

———. (1959). "A Model of Seasonal Inventories," *Econometrica* 27: 228–244.

Chikan, A. (1984). *New Results in Inventory Research*. Amsterdam: Elsevier Science.

Cromwell, J., M. Hannan, W.C. Labys, and M. Terraza. (1994). *Multivariate Tests of Time Series Models*. Thousand Oaks, CA: Sage.

Dickey, D.A., and W.A. Fuller. (1979). "Distribution of Estimates for Autoregressive Time Series with Unit Root," *Journal of the American Statistical Association* 74: 427–431.

Eckstein, Z., and M. Eichenbaum. (1985). "Inventories and Quantity Constrained Equilibria: The U.S. Petroleum Industry 1947–1972." In T.J. Sargent, ed., *Energy, Foresight and Strategy, Resources for the Future*, 70–100. Baltimore: Johns Hopkins University Press.

Eichenbaum, M. (1989). "Some Empirical Evidence on the Production Level and Production Cost Smoothing Models of Inventories," *American Economic Review* 79. 4: 853–864.

———. (1984). "Rational Expectations and the Smoothing Properties of Inventories of Finished Goods," *Journal of Monetary Economics* 14. 1: 71–96.

Engle, R.F., and C.W.J. Granger,(1987). "Cointegration and Error Correction: Representation, Estimation and Testing," *Econometrica* 55: 251–271.

Engle, R.F., and B.S. Yoo. (1987). "Forecasting and Testing in Cointegrated Systems," *Journal of Econometrics* 35: 143–159.

FAO (2000). *Production, Trade and Food Balance Sheet Database*. Rome: United Nations.

Gijsbers, D., and W.C. Labys (1988). "Modeling the California Wine Market." AEA-World Bank Conference on Advances in Commodity Modeling, Washington DC.

Gilbert, C.L. (1986). "Developments in the Study of Cointegrated Economic Variables. *Oxford Bulletin of Economics and Statistics* 48: 213–228.

———. (1988). "Optimal and Competitive Storage Rules: The Gustafson Problem Revisited." In O. Guvenen, W. Labys, and J.B. Lesourd (eds.): 27–52, *International Commodity Market Models*. London: Chapman-Hall.

Granger, C.W.J. (1969). "Investigating Causal Relations by Econometric Models and Cross-Spectral Methods," *Econometrica* 37: 424–438.

Johansen, S. (1988). "Statistical Analysis of Cointegrating Vectors," *Journal of Economic Dynamics and Control* 12: 231–254.

Johansen, S., and K. Juselius. (1990). "Maximum Likelihood Estimation and Inference in Cointegration," *Oxford Bulletin of Economics and Statistics* 52: 169–210.

Kawai, M. (1983). "Price Volatility of Storable Commodities under Rational Expectations in Futures Markets," *International Economic Review* 24: 435–459.

Knapp, K.C. (1982). "Optimal Grain Carryovers in Open Economies," *American Journal of Agricultural Economics* 55: 584–594.

Labys, W. C. (1973). *Dynamic Commodity Models: Specification, Estimation and Simulation* Lexington, MA: Heath Lexington Books.

———. (1989). *Primary Commodity Markets and Models*. London: Gower Publishers.

———. (1992). "The Wine Processing Industry, in Industry and Development," *UNIDO Global Report for 1991/92*. Vienna: United Nations Industrial Development.

———. (2001). "Business Cycles and Wine Market Impacts," CIES Working Paper 21, Institute for International Economic Studies, University of Adelaide.

Labys, W.C., and B.C. Cohen. (2006). "Trends versus Cycles in Global Wine Export Shares," *Australian Journal of Agricultural and Resource Economics* 50: 527–537.

Labys, W.C., and M. Lord. (1992). "Inventory and Equilibrium Adjustments in International Commodity Markets: A Multi-Cointegration Approach," *Applied Economics* 24: 77–84.

Larson, D.F. (1994). "Copper and the Negative Price of Storage," PR Working Paper 1282, International Economics Department, World Bank, Washington, DC.

Newbery, D.M.G., and J.E. Stiglitz. (1982). "Optimal Commodity Stock-Piling Rules," *Oxford Economic Papers* 34: 403–427.

Office International dela Vigne et du Vin. (2000). *Situation de la Viticulture dans le Monde*, Office International de la Vigne et du Vin, Paris.

Orden, D. (1982). "Preliminary Empirical Evidence Concerning an Asset Theory Model of Markets for Storable Agricultural Commodities," Staff Papers, Department of Agricultural and Applied Economics, University of Minnesota.

Otani, K. (1983). "The Price Determination in the Inventory Stock Market: A Disequilibrium Analysis," *International Economic Review* 24: 709–719.

Pindyck, R.S. (1994). "Inventories and the Short-Run Dynamics of Commodity Prices," *RAND Journal of Economics* 25: 141–159.

U.S. Department of Agriculture. (1976). "Analysis of Grain Reserves, A Proceedings." Economic Research Service No. 634, USDA, Washington, DC.

Weymar, H.F. (1969). *Dynamics of the World Cocoa Market*. Cambridge, MA: MIT Press.

———. (1969). "The Supply of Storage Revisited," *American Economic Review* 56: 1226–1234.

Williams, J.C., and B.D. Wright. (1991). *Storage and Commodity Markets*. Cambridge: Cambridge University Press.

Wittwer, G., and J. Rothfield. (2006). *The Global Wine Statistical Compendium, 1961–2004*. Australian Wine and Brandy Corporation and Grape and Wine Research and Development Corporation, Monash University (Clayton) Victoria.

Wohlgenant, M.K. (1978). "An Econometric Analysis of the Dynamics of Price Determination: Study of the Californian Grape/Wine Industry." Ph.D. Dissertation, University of California at Davis.

———. (1982). "Inventory Adjustment and Dynamic Winery Behavior," *American Journal of Agricultural Economics* 64. 2: 222–231.

Working, H. (1949). "The Theory of the Price of Storage," *American Economic Review* 31: 1254–1262.

Wright, B.D., and J.C. Williams. (1982). "The Economic Role of Commodity Storage," *Economic Journal* 92: 596–614.

Yver, R.E. (1971). "The Investment Behavior and the Supply Response of the Cattle Industry of Argentina," Ph.D. Dissertation, University of Chicago.

WINE DATA REFERENCES

Prices

Argentina, Australia, Germany, Italy, Spain:

"OIV Price Index," *Bulletin de L'OIV*, International Office for Wines and Vines, Paris.

Wittwer, G., and J. Rothfield. (2006). *The Global Wine Statistical Compendium, 1961–2004*. Australian Wine and Brandy Corporation and Grape and Wine Research and Development Corporation, Monash University (Clayton) Victoria. In addition:

Italy: Average price from the markets for table wine. Istituto Statistica Mercati Agro-Alimentari (ISMEA), Rome, Italy.

Spain: Average of daily quotations, *Semana Vitivinicola*, Spain.
France: Wines for current consumption, *vins de consommation courante*, Institut National de Statistiques et des Etudes Economiques, Paris.
United States: Grape table wines, Producer price index WPU02610431, US Department of Labor, Washington, DC.

Inventories

All Countries "OIV Price Index," *Bulletin de L'OIV*, International Office for Wines and Vines, Paris.
Reported private and commercial stocks.
Wittwer, G., and J. Rothfield. (2006). *The Global Wine Statistical Compendium, 1961–2004*. Australian Wine and Brandy Corporation and Grape and Wine Research and Development Corporation, Monash University (Clayton) Victoria.

PART Three

Dynamics of Resource Markets

The eight chapters in the first two parts studied the price behaviors of commodities from different perspectives and levels of aggregation. In Part Three, we are changing the focus, particularly methodologically. While the first eight chapters showed the power of time-series analyses, in this part of the book, the focus is on the process of production and the tools of analysis are various forms of mathematical programming.

Here, too, the chapters complement each other nicely. Chapter 9 provides an application at the firm level, and Chapters 10 to 12 deal with economy-wide industries or with the whole economy.

Chapter 9 provides an application in the energy sector, specifically, the quality of coal loaded on barges. The author had to solve this problem for his company by blending to obtain the desired quality.

Chapter 10 is a spatial model of the U.S. coal market. The authors use it for a policy exercise of imposing pollution taxes. Such taxes are popular among economists, but the authors are able to show that, because of the spatial structure of the U.S. coal market, they result in outcomes that may not be politically feasible. Because coal producers and coal consumers in the United States are spatially separated, policy analyses that neglect space miss a critical factor that determines the eventual outcome.

Chapter 11 looks at Indonesia's energy market, and particularly to role of coal. Indonesia is currently a net oil exporter. However, unless new large oil reserves are discovered there, in some 15 years, the country will turn from net exporter to net importer. Indonesia has another large energy source, coal. After Australia, China, and India, it has the fourth largest coal reserves in East Asia. At present, it uses only 27% of what it produces and exports the rest, making it the second largest coal exporter in the world. In 2005, Indonesia accounted for 21% of world coal exports. The Indonesian government has been preparing for the time when it no longer can meet its oil demand for a long time and has tested coal liquefaction processing, coal briquette, and other coal value-added products, as a means to use coal "as a bridge to the future," until such a time when a more sustainable energy source will become available. This chapter is of interest for several reasons. First, a successful change in how Indonesia uses coal in its domestic consumptions will likely impact its coal exports. Since the country is one of the world's largest coal exporters, effects on the world coal price are possible. Second, other countries are also working on coal liquefaction and other coal value-added products. In fact, many Indonesian products are joint ventures with foreign companies and governments. Thus, if the technology is commercially successful in Indonesia, it will spread quickly to other countries. Third, Indonesia is a large developing economy. It serves as an illustration for the many developing economies elsewhere that are changing the world economy. The author worked for the Ministry of Energy and Mineral Resources and has firsthand experience with the projects he explains and analyzes.

Chapter 14 applies structural decomposition analysis to take a close look at the U.S. economy between 1972 and 1982. During this period, technological change contributed to one of the most dramatic changes in material use in the United States. The authors are able to provide insights into how the change affected different sectors of the economy, and why. The methodology utilizes input-output analysis, but it overcomes shortcomings of that method to address how technological change affected different sectors of the U.S. economy. The strengths of input-output analysis, however, which show how different sector of the economy related to one another, are an important aspect of this study, because it allows the authors to trace the effects of change beyond their first impact only.

CHAPTER 9

Dynamic Quadratic Programming in Process Control

Bruce A. Bancroft

INTRODUCTION

In the coal industry, real-time blending is in many cases required to satisfy contractual requirements on coal quality, for example, ash. Continuous nuclear analyzers are used to obtain real-time feedback of the quality of the blended product and produce a quality generally at a rate of one per minute. The product typically consists of two sources of coal: one that has a quality higher than the target quality and one that is lower than the target quality. The object is to control the proportions of the two sources to achieve the target quality while maximizing the usage of the lower quality, which is typically a lower-cost source. This presents some problems because the two sources are each autocorrelated in time, the proportions of the sources are measured with error, and the blended product quality measured by the analyzer, although free of bias, is subject to significant measurement error. This chapter describes a methodology to blend coal to meet a barge specification.

PROCESS CONTROL MODELS COMPARED

In process control, the workhorse methodology for feedback control is the proportional-integral-derivative (PID) controller. Mathematically it is given by:

$$Output(t) = K_p e(t) + K_i \int_0^t e(t)dt + K_d \frac{de}{dx} \tag{9.1}$$

where $e(t) = SP - PV(t)$ (9.2)

SP = setpoint(desired quality)

$PV(t)$ = process variable (i.e., the value measured by the continuous analyzer)

In practice, generally only a P or a PI controller is implemented (i.e., just the first term or the first two terms in PID. The first term is proportional in that the control action is proportional to the deviation between the *SP* and the *PV*. Sometimes this is good enough even though it can be shown that it will result in a sustained bias; it never quite gets there, much like if you move from one side of a room to the other in increments of half the remaining distance. To correct for this bias, often the integral term is implemented, resulting in a control action proportional to the sum of the errors, which eliminates steady state errors. The bad news is it also guarantees overshoot since the integral value will continue to be added to the output value. Derivative control can be useful in many instances; however, in the presence of noise, one can end up chasing this noise and thus inducing unwanted oscillations in the process variable. Detailed descriptions of PID controllers can be found in most control engineering textbooks (e.g., de Vegte 1990; Nies 1992).

Implementation of a P controller was attempted in this application with mixed results. Its performance was satisfactory if the control period was long; what is desired is that the average quality over the time period hits the target. When the time period was short, the performance was not acceptable.

An alternative approach was investigated since sufficient information exists to optimally forecast the impact a control action will have on the process variable in real time. In the control literature, this approach is called model predictive control. It has become very popular over the last 20 years especially in the chemical processing industry (Camacho and Bordons 2007; Maciejowski 2002).

The first method attempted was to implement ordinary least squares (OLS) in order to disaggregate the product ash into the two sources. Given the quality of coal already loaded on the barge, the estimates could then be used to set blend proportions for the coal to be added, so that the final barge quality would meet specifications while at the same time maximizing the amount of raw coal loaded. Each signal from the analyzer can be written as:

$$y_t = \beta_1 x_{1t} + \beta_2 x_{2t} + \varepsilon_t \tag{9.3}$$

where y_t = the analyzer signal in tons of ash at time t
β_1 = clean ash fraction at time t
x_{1t} = tons of clean coal at time t
β_t = raw ash fraction at time t
x_{2t} = tons of raw coal at time t
ε_t = analytical error from analyzer at time t

A set of T signals can be represented by this system of equations:

$$\mathbf{y} = \mathbf{x}\beta + \varepsilon \tag{9.4}$$

where $\mathbf{y}$ = T×1 vector of the observed ash signals in tons of ash
$\mathbf{x}$ = T×2 matrix of source tons
β = 2×1 vector of the clean and raw coal ashes
ε = T×1 vector of errors

The sum of squared errors, viewed as a function of the regression coefficients, is given by:

$$\varepsilon'\varepsilon = (\mathbf{y} - \mathbf{x}\beta)'(\mathbf{y} - \mathbf{x}\beta) \tag{9.5}$$

$$= \mathbf{y}'\mathbf{y} - 2\mathbf{y}'\mathbf{x}\beta + \beta'\mathbf{x}'\mathbf{x}\beta = \sum_{t=1}^{T} [y_t - (\beta_1 x_{1t} + \beta_2 x_{2t})]^2 \tag{9.6}$$

The estimates of β will be obtained by finding $\beta \subset D \subset R^2$ such that β minimizes $\varepsilon'\varepsilon$. This is a standard OLS regression formulation of the problem and the objective function to be minimized is equation 9.5, which is a polynomial of order 2 in the coefficients of β. Since $\mathbf{y}'\mathbf{y}$ is a constant, then minimizing

$$k = -2y'x\beta + \beta'x'x\beta \tag{9.7}$$

is equivalent to minimizing equation 9.5.

The OLS formulation has some pitfalls and shortcomings. A major pitfall is that for many sets of T signals, the independent variables will not change significantly, and when they do change, total tonnage is kept constant. Thus the two independent variables will be almost linearly related (whether in tons or fraction of total), producing a large instability in the estimated regression coefficients. This instability is seen in the Figure 9.1, where OLS regression was performed on product ash for 16 hours in order to resolve the ash into its clean and raw component qualities. The regressions were of size N = 25 and updated every minute with the most recent 25

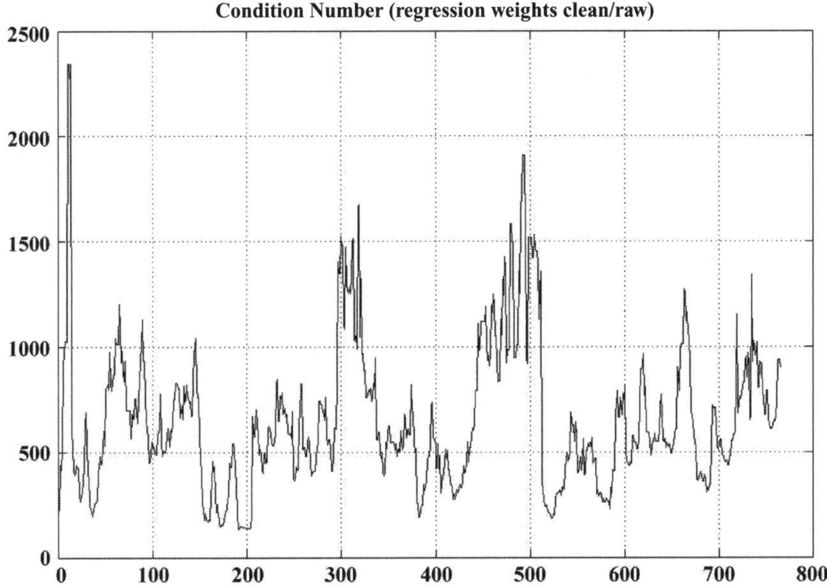

FIGURE 9.1 Condition Number (Regression Size = 25) for 16 Hours

observations. the figure displays is the condition number for each regression. The condition number is the ratio of the largest to the smallest calculated eigenvalue on $X'X$.

Certainly multicollinearity in the regressors is a problem. Estimates achieved from OLS correspondingly were highly variable and in many cases not sensible. Another shortfall of OLS is that it does not incorporate all of the information that is available for forecasting. First, it is known that raw ash is always greater than clean ash and that the clean ash can be bounded. Second, coal quality is spatially autocorrelated in situ. This spatial autocorrelation in the ground manifests itself in a temporal autocorrelation in both raw plant feed and clean plant product and thus in the raw/clean blend. It is known that the temporal correlation is nonstationary. This nonstationarity results from what mining faces are running at any point in time, where they are mining (and they move), and varying mining conditions on any one mining face (Bancroft and Hobbs 1986).

A way to incorporate a priori knowledge about the mix of raw and clean ashes is via the constraints methods of quadratic programming where the objective is to minimize the error sum of squares. This objective is a quadratic function of the regression coefficients, and the optimization can be performed subject to linear inequality constraints.

A way to explicitly accommodate autocorrelation is via generalized (weighted) least squares, where the weighting matrix contains the autocorrelation coefficients (Goldberger 1962). If the observations are weighted, then the objective function is the weighted sum of squared errors:

$$(\mathbf{W}\varepsilon)'(\mathbf{W}\varepsilon) = [\mathbf{W}(\mathbf{y} - \mathbf{x}\beta)]'[\mathbf{W}(\mathbf{y} - \mathbf{x}\beta] \tag{9.8}$$

where W = T×T diagonal matrix with the **1** on the diagonal and the off diagonals containing the autocorrelation coefficients:

$$\mathbf{W} = \begin{pmatrix} 1 & \rho_1 & \cdots & \rho_{T-1} \\ \rho_1 & 1 & \cdots & \rho_{T-2} \\ \vdots & \vdots & \ddots & \vdots \\ \rho_{T-1} & \rho_{T-2} & \cdots & 1 \end{pmatrix} \tag{9.9}$$

In this case the covariance matrix is $\sigma^2\mathbf{W}$. Unfortunately, the temporal correlation is nonstationary. This nonstationarity arises from nonstationarity in in-situ ash, variations in the percent contribution of the different mining sections to mine product, movement of mining sections over time, and varying mining conditions on any one mining face. To dynamically model and estimate the autocorrelational structure would add a layer of complexity to the real-time algorithm that it would be better to avoid.

If all we care about is a forecast and not standard errors of the regression estimates or prediction intervals, but we want somehow to accommodate autocorrelation, a simple weighting matrix can be used. Furthermore, while there is considerable variation in raw ash at a short scale about a mean level that may be drifting, there is a clear need for protection from gross changes in the raw ash level that does occur and can be traced to changes in how the coal is being mined and/or loaded. If data are autocorrelated and protection is desired from abrupt shifts in raw ash level, more recent information is more important for estimating purposes and should carry more weight than older data. If the weighting matrix takes the form

$$\mathbf{W} = \begin{pmatrix} w_1^{1/2} & \cdots & 0 \\ \vdots & \ddots & \vdots \\ 0 & \cdots & w_T^{1/2} \end{pmatrix} \tag{9.10}$$

then each error in the objective function is being weighted by wt, as shown next.

Expanding equation 9.8, the weighted objective function can be rewritten as

$$\varepsilon'\mathbf{W}^2\varepsilon = \mathbf{y}'\mathbf{W}^2\mathbf{y} - 2\mathbf{y}'\mathbf{W}^2\mathbf{x}\beta + \beta\mathbf{x}'\mathbf{W}^2\mathbf{x}\beta \tag{9.11}$$

$$= \sum_{t=1}^{T} w_t \left[y_t - (\beta_1 x_{1t} + \beta_2 x_{2t})\right]^2 \tag{9.12}$$

The weights are generated by the next function, where T is the regression size and the weight assigned to the oldest error is given by w_1 and the weight assigned to the most recent error by w_T:

$$w_t = \lambda\,(1-\lambda)^{T-t} \Big/ \sum_{t=1}^{T} \lambda\,(1-\lambda)^{T-t} \tag{9.13}$$

for $t = 1, \ldots,$ T and $0 \leq \lambda \leq 1$. Generally, from experience, optimal lambdas are in the interval [0.1,0.4]. The denominator in equation 9.13 normalizes the weights to sum to 1. Thus for a regression of size 25 the nonnormalized weight for the most recent observation is λ, since $T - t = 0$, and the nonnormalized weight assigned to the oldest observation is $\lambda\,(1-\lambda)^{25}$. Note that these are the same the weights used to generate an exponentially weighted moving average.

Since $\mathbf{y}'\mathbf{W}^2\mathbf{y}$ is constant, the QP problem is formulated as:

$$Minimize\, k = -2\mathbf{y}'\mathbf{W}^2\mathbf{x}\beta + \beta'\mathbf{x}'\mathbf{W}^2\mathbf{x}\beta \tag{9.14}$$

subject to:

$$A_C < A_C(\max) \tag{9.15}$$

$$A_C > A_C(\min) \tag{9.16}$$

$$A_R > A_C \tag{9.17}$$

where A_C = clean ash
A_R = raw ash

An example illustrating the advantage of weighting the observations is shown via simulation in Figures 9.2a and b. In this case a shift in raw ash from a mean level of 22% to an average of 30% was simulated. Figure 9.2a shows the estimated raw ash against the simulated actual using a QP where the observations are not weighted. Figure 9.2b shows the impact of weighting the observations. The illustration shows that the recovery from the shift occurred much more rapidly.

CONCLUSIONS

This dynamic QP method for blending barges was implemented at a coal mine for the purpose of blending raw and clean coal to a high ash specification on 1,000- to 1,500-ton barges, where the purpose was to maximize the amount of raw on each barge. The method worked extremely well for three years until the end of the mine's life.

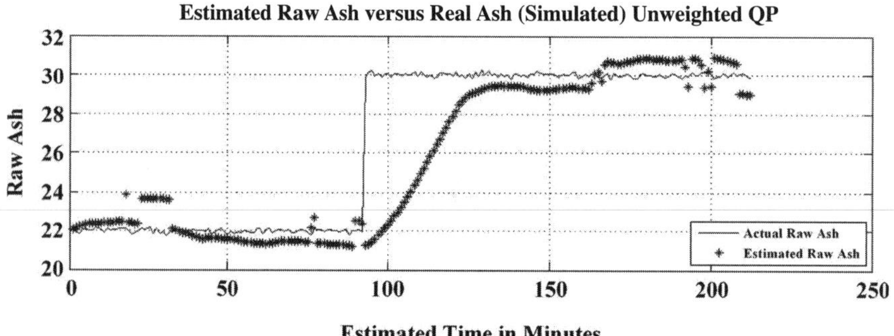

FIGURE 9.2a Unweighted QP.

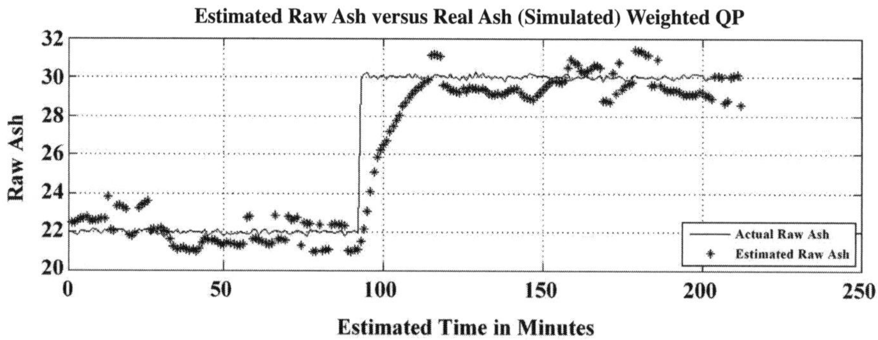

FIGURE 9.2b Weighted QP

REFERENCES

Bancroft, B.A., and G.R. Hobbs. (1986). "Distribution of the Kriging Error and Stationarity of the Variogram in a Coal Property," *Mathematical Geology* 18.7: 635–651.

Camacho, E.F., and C. Bordons. (2007). *Model Predictive Control*, 2nd ed. London, UK: Springer Verlag.

De Vegte, J.V. (1990). *Feedback Control Systems*, 2nd ed. Englewood Cliffs, NJ: Prentice-Hall.

Goldberger, A.S. (1962). "Best Linear Unbiased Prediction in the Generalized Linear Regression Model," *Journal of the American Statistical Association* 57: 369–375.

Maciejowski, J.M. (2002). *Predictive Control with Constraints*. Englewood Cliffs, NJ: Prentice-Hall.

Nies, N.S. (1992). *Control Systems Engineering*. San Francisco, CA: Benjamin/Cummings Publishing Co.

CHAPTER 10

Pollution Taxes and Price Control in the U.S. Coal Market

A Rent Minimization Model

Chin W. Yang and Ming-Jeng Hwang

INTRODUCTION

Coal plays an important role in the national U.S. energy household. However, one of the disadvantages of coal, as of all fossil fuels, is that it has a high social cost that is born in the form of pollution. Past studies have explored this issue, including how to alleviate the problem through pollution taxes. What we are contributing that is new is the spatial analysis of pollution taxes.

Spatial equilibrium models date back to the classical linear programming model pioneered by Hitchcock (1941), Kantorovich (1942), and Koopmans (1949). Enke (1951) extended the transportation model through appeal to analogies to Kirchhoff's law of electrical circuits, and introduced price and regional transportation demand and supply. The common origins of the market-oriented spatial equilibrium models are generally traced back to the influential work of Samuelson (1952), in which price differentials between demand and supply regions must be less than or equal to the corresponding transportation cost.

Takayama and Judge (1964) reformulated Samuelson's approach into a standard quadratic programming model and created an operationally efficient and conceptually convenient model that spawned numerous empirical applications and theoretical extensions. They include a new algorithm (Liew and Shim 1978), sensitivity analysis (Irwin and Yang 1981), and extensions of their original model (Florian and Los 1982; Takayama and Judge 1982 a, b). The inclusion of income (Thore 1982), an iterative algorithm (Irwin and Yang 1982), linear complementarily applications (Takayama and Uri 1983; Labys and Yang 1985), and a spatial equilibrium model with transshipment (Tobin and Friesz 1983; Chao and Friesz 1984) followed. Pang and Chang (1982), Deffermos (1983), Deffermos and Nagurney (1984), Pang (1984), Tobin (1986), and Nagurney (1987) added variational inequality. Harker's efforts (1987, 1988) yielded imperfect spatial competition and dispersed spatial equilibrium, and were followed by an entropy-maximization model (Yang 1990), and models of oligopolistic competition (Nelson and McCarl 1984; Yang 1985; Sheppard et al. 1992). Yang and Page (1993) explored spatial tax incidence, and Yang et al. (2002) studied spatial Cournot equilibrium model in terms of linear complementarity programming. In three publications, Labys and Yang (1991, 1996, 1997) wrote a detailed history of the many applications dating back to the work of Takayama and Judge.

Smith (1963) proposed an often-overlooked alternative to Takayama's and Judge's spatial equilibrium model. His rent minimization model is the dual to Takayama's and Judge's (1964) welfare maximization formulation. Three advantages of Smith's model over the latter stand out.

1. The objective function of the Takayama-Judge model is net social payoff, which does not have serious economic interpretations.
2. The rent minimization model is a natural formulation for ad valorem taxes, which are common in energy industries.
3. In most cases, we estimate the quantity of demand and supply and have price as one of the independent variables, not the other way around. This suggests that the rent minimization formulation is a natural and correct choice for modeling spatial equilibrium modes. Note that the mathematical inverse of a statistically estimated inverse demand function (quantity formulation) is not the same as the statistically estimated demand function, unless the coefficient of determination equals one, which is highly unusual. Unfortunately, most empirically estimated demand and supply functions are quantity formulations. As a result, they would be inappropriate from the viewpoint of statistics, especially when ad valorem taxes and price controls are simulated.

This chapter presents the results of the U.S. coal market, using a rent minimization spatial equilibrium model. Statistically estimated demand and supply functions are obtained from Hwang et al. (1994). Pollution taxes are simulated with and without price controls. The negative effects of pollution from burning coal are well known. Emissions of sulfur oxides in the air and water have adverse effects on human health and the environment. Taxes can reduce levels of pollution and bring them closer to the social optimum.

SMITH'S RENT-MINIMIZATION SPATIAL EQUILIBRIUM MODEL

Consider the case of n spatially separated markets. The concept of competitive markets implies the minimization of economic rent, which some have sought to tax and others sought to steal (Smith, 1963). Economic rent can be viewed as an opposite of economic welfare and, according to Henry George, needs to be minimized. Given a set of constant positive unit transportation costs, the objective is to minimize rent subject to constraints, which state that the price differentials between two markets cannot exceed the corresponding unit transportation cost or

$$\text{Minimize } R_{i\in I} = \sum \left[-\int_{P_i}^{\infty} y_i\,(p_i) + \int_{0}^{P_i} x_i\,(p_i) \right] dp_i \tag{10.1}$$

$$\text{subject to} \quad P_j - P^i \leq t_{ij}\ \forall i,\ j \in I \tag{10.2}$$

$$P^i \geq 0 \quad \text{and} \quad P_j \geq 0 \tag{10.3}$$

where $y_i(p_i)$ = statistically estimated demand function of the price in region i, or P_i
$x_i(p^i)$ = statistically estimated supply function of P_i
y_i and x_i = quantity demanded and supplied in region i
t_{ij} = unit transportation cost between regions i and j
I = set of positive integers

Smith (1961, 26) showed that the economic rent R can be decomposed into two parts: one incurred under autarky, R_i^0, and the other incurred under interregional trade. We can rewrite equation 10.1 as:

$$R = \sum R_i^0 + \sum \left[-\int_{P_i}^{P_i} y_i\,(p_i) + \int_{\hat{P}_i}^{P_i} x_i\,(p_i) \right] dp_i \tag{10.4}$$

where $\hat{P}_i$ = pretrade price in region i

The first term on the right-hand side of equation 10.4 measures the *degree of deviation from the competitive equilibrium under autarky* (Smith 1963; Takayama and Judge 1971). For a given set of linear demand and supply functions, and without loss of generality, the economic rent under autarky is constant. Equations 10.1 through 10.4 provide the framework of the rent-minimization spatial equilibrium model.

In order to tackle the pollution generated by burning sulfur-rich coals in the United States, Hwang et al. (1994) estimated a pollution tax, which equals a fraction of marginal damage (cost) incurred to society. Suboptimal use (overuse) of fossil fuels is a prime suspect of acid rain and growing global warming. Consequently, this study provides background information for policy implementation. Our study's simulation results indicate that a 100% pollution abatement tax would lead to the closure of half of all of the mines in the United States. This is politically infeasible. Therefore, in this chapter, we simulated the U.S. model based on the assumption that only 20% or 50%, respectively, of all potential damages are taxed. The tax takes the form shown in equation 10.5.

$$P_j - P_i \leq t_{ij} + \beta MSC_i \tag{10.5}$$

where β = 0.2 or 0.5
MSC_i = marginal social cost incurred by burning coal in region i
t_{ij} = unit cost of shipping coal from region i to region j

SIMULATED RESULTS OF THE U.S. COAL MARKET

Coal modeling is of primary importance because coal reserves are abundant in the United States, and oil prices are currently at record high levels. The coal industry in the United States has several important characteristics that make the spatial equilibrium model an excellent choice: numerous and spatially separated mines and consumers (e.g., utility companies). Although coal is not a homogenous commodity, we can express it as a homogenous commodity in terms of heat content (Btu [British thermal unit]). Several empirical spatial allocation models were implemented in the U.S. coal markets (e.g., Henderson 1958; Labys and Yang 1980; Hwang et al. 1994), but spatial analysis of the pollution tax is still lacking. In this chapter, we fill this void.

First, we report the demand and supply functions. Hwang et al. (1994) estimated them from time-series data from 1960 to 1985 (Table 10.1).

Based on optimum market area analysis, the U.S. coal market was segmented into five subregions (Campbell et al. 1982). Table 10.2 reports the 25 unit transportation costs, estimated by Hwang et al. (1994). We add the pollution tax, assessed at 20% of marginal social cost, to the transportation costs. Using the GINO nonlinear

TABLE 10.1 Statistically Estimated Demand and Supply Functions

Region	Intercept of Demand Function	Slope of Demand Function	Intercept of Supply Function	Slope of Supply Function
1	12.23	−0.0735	−3.754	0.1658
2	9.474	−0.066	−2.8485	0.0558
3	12.759	−0.0711	−12.546	0.1779
4	19.541	−0.137	−38.773	0.4202
5	23.793	−0.152	−12.535	0.1225

Source: Hwang et al. (1994).

TABLE 10.2 Calculated Unit Transportation Cost with Pollution Abatement Costs

	Region 1	Region 2	Region 3	Region 4	Region 5
Region 1	28.73	42.04	23.98	60.81	70.5
	(37.808)*	(54.628)	(48.172)	(67.126)	(77.476)
Region 2	39.31	31.1	33.22	60.32	59.62
	(48.388)	(43.688)	(57.412)	(66.636)	(63.884)
Region 3	32.24	39.98	18.61	50.83	56.05
	(41.318)	(52.568)	(42.802)	(57.146)	(63.014)
Region 4	62.55	63.41	54.25	34.0	42.29
	(71.628)	(75.998)	(78.442)	(40.316)	(49.254)
Region 5	68.56	59.28	61.56	43.42	19.82
	(77.638)	(71.868)	(85.752)	(49.736)	(26.784)

*Figures in parenthesis are the sum of the unit transportation cost and 20% of the marginal social cost caused by potential acid rain damage.
Source: Hwang et al. (1994).

programming software package (Liebman et al. 1986), the rent-minimization model yields eight optimal coal shipments for the U.S. steam coal market.

Table 10.3 reports optimum prices, quantities and coal shipments with a 20% and a 50% pollution tax, respectively. An examination of Table 10.3 shows that the optimal solution with a 20% pollution tax generates eight positive coal flows. Region 4 is isolated from the U.S. coal market, while the rest of the market is interrelated by the constraint expressed in equation 10.2. In spatial equilibrium models, trade isolation is called degeneracy (Samuelson 1952). The degenerated spatial equilibrium solution in the U.S. coal market results from the assumption common to such models, that there exists only one nodal point in each consumption region. The high share of transportation costs in the U.S. coal industry also limits positive flows (Labys and Yang 1991). We expect that the number of positive coal shipments will not exceed nine $(5 + 5 - 1)$. Any solution that produces fewer than nine positive flows is degenerate.

If we impose a 20% pollution tax, several interesting features emerge. There are only six positive coal flows: x_{11}, x_{13}, x_{22}, x_{33}, x_{44}, and x_{55} (see Table 10.3; the first five columns/rows entries show the flows between coal market regions). The highly

TABLE 10.3 Optimum Solutions of Rent-Minimization Models with 20 Percent and 50 Percent Pollution Tax, Respectively

From To	Region 1	Region 2	Region 3	Region 4	Region 5	Demand Price	Consumption
Region 1	4.797*					100.99	4.797
	(4.05)					(111.14)	(4.05)
	[3.466]					[119.24]	[3.466]
Region 2	0.853	1.257				111.57	2.11
		(1.475)				(121.2)	(1.475)
		[0.895]				[142.26]	[0.085]
Region 3	2.576		2.742			104.5	5.318
	(4.354)		(0.242)			(114.65)	(4.596)
	[4.028]		[0]			[127.8]	[4.028]
Region 4				1.784		130.56	1.784
				(1.135)		(135.34)	(1.135)
				[0.08]		[142.05]	[0.08]
Region 5		0.383			2.168	139.75	2.551
					(1.867)	(144.25)	(1.867)
					[1.156]	[148.93]	[1.156]
Supply	72.26**	80.47	85.89	96.56	119.93		
Price	(73.33)	(77.51)	(71.85)	(95.02)	(117.47)		
	[67.84]	[68.70]	[70.52]	[92.46]	[111.76]		
Production	8.226	1.64	2.742	1.784	2.168		16.56
	(8.404)	(1.475)	(0.242)	(1.135)	(1.867)		(13.123)
	[7.494]	[0.895	[0]	[0.08]	[1.156]		[9.625]

*Quantities are in 10^{15} Btu.
**Prices are in cents per million Btu.
Figures without parentheses are optimum solution without the tax.
Figures in parentheses () are the optimum solution with a 20% pollution tax.
Figures in brackets [] are the optimum solution with a 50% pollution tax.

degenerate spatial equilibrium solution implies a severe lack of spatial interaction in terms of interregional coal flows. Only region 1 has some spatial activity ($x_{13} = 4.354$). Although the degree of spatial interaction without a pollution tax was not very high, the imposition of a 20% pollution tax caused a noticeable decrease in the degree of spatial interaction.

This solution of the 20% pollution tax differs significantly from that using the quantity formulation (Hwang et al. 1994: 71). The price formulation of the rent-minimization model has a clear advantage over the quantity formulation. The added pollution abatement costs are equivalent to increased transportation costs. Consequently, the economic rent increased by $153.3 million, from $8,399.1 million (value of the objective function) to $8,552.4 million. *This increased yet unearned economic rent represents a loss in economic efficiency*. However, tax revenue collected from mines that produce sulfur-rich coal partially compensates for this loss. This tax revenue amounts to $24.3331 million. Hence, the net social loss is $128.9669 million. The incurred net loss implies that Smith's rent-minimization model with zero pollution tax offers the most efficient solution to the allocation problem, if we completely ignore the adverse effect of pollution externalities. Any deviation from this solution would be less efficient in terms of balancing tax revenues and economic rents.

We observe that the pollution tax *increased* production in region 1 from 8.226 to 8.404 units (10^{15} Btu). With the pollution tax, shipments from region 1 to region 3 (x_{13}) increased significantly and largely replaced production in region 3 (region 3 curtailed coal production from 2.742 units to 0.242 units). The region's consumption pattern (x_{33}) also changed. Region 1 almost entirely captured the coal market of region 3 ($x_{13} = 4.354$) because of the lower shipment cost from the Eastern U.S. market to the Midwest market, despite the fact that Eastern coal, on average, has higher sulfur content. Overall production in region 1 increased, while all other regions experienced a production loss. Finally, with the pollution tax in place, all coal demand prices (utility plant) increased and all supply or mouth-of-mine prices decreased, except for region 1.

The imposition of a pollution tax of 50% causes a reduction in the shipment of eastern coal to the Midwest of only 0.326 units (4.354 – 4.028), or −7.49%. Because of higher pollution cost, Midwest mines will shut down and x_3 will be zero. This is a politically unrealistic scenario.

All mouth-of-mine prices would have to decrease while all delivered prices in the U.S. coal markets increase. Total production drops from 16.56 units without pollution tax, to 9.625 units, a 41.87% decrease. Such a reduction is politically infeasible, but this simulation result gives some idea of the cost of internalizing pollution cost through Pigouvian taxes.

We know from the public finance literature that a pollution tax would cause higher delivered prices for consumers. A policy of spatial price control might therefore be politically popular. Similar to price controls on gasoline in the 1970s, we simulate this possibility by imposing the condition that all demand prices be less than or equal to 120 cents per million Btu. Table 10.4 shows that such a policy most likely will cause a reduction in the production in region 2 (Southwest U.S. coal market). The policy will leave the production, consumption, and coal shipment of regions 1 and 3 unchanged because their delivered prices were below 120 cents per million Btu before price control, but it will wipe out production and consumption in regions 4 and 5, because of the significant drop in delivered prices under price control. Price control will drive mines with high production costs out of business.

TABLE 10.4 Optimum Solution of Rent-Minimizing Models with Spatial Price Control

From To	Region 1	Region 2	Region 3	Region 4	Region 5	Demand Price	Consumption
Region 1	(4.05)					(111.14)	(4.05)
	[4.05]					[111.14]	[4.05]
Region 2		(1.475)				(121.2)	(1.475)
		[1.408]				[120.0]	[1.408]
Region 3	(4.354)		(0.242)			(114.65)	(4.596)
	[4.354]		[0.242			[114.65]	[4.596]
Region 4				(1.135)		(135.34)	(1.135)
						[120.00]	[0]
Region 5					(1.867)	(144.25)	(1.867)
						[120.00]	[0]
Supply	(73.33)	(77.51)	(71.85)	(95.02)	(117.47)		
Price	[73.33]	[76.31]	[71.85]	[92.32]	[102.24]		
	(8.404)	(1.475)	(0.242)	(1.135)	(1.867)		(13.123)
	[8.404]	[1.408]	[0.242]	[0]	[0]		[10.054]

Figures in parentheses () are the optimum solution with the 20% tax.
Figures in brackets [] are the optimum solution with the 20% tax and spatial price control.

Thus a policy of spatial price controls would have a significant impact on economic activities, especially of high cost mines that produce pollution-causing coal, and it would end the use of coal in regions 4 and 5. On the positive side, closing down high cost mines would reduce air and water pollution.

CONCLUSIONS

In this chapter, we implement a rent-minimization spatial equilibrium model of the U.S. coal market with an assessed 20% and 50% pollution tax, respectively, which applies in all coal-producing regions. It is equivalent to a tax on outgoing shipments. We find that the U.S. coal market is expected to disintegrate into four independent submarkets. The sizable decrease in interregional shipments would lead to an increased level of autarky in the U.S. coal market. In addition, pollution taxes would lead to lower efficiency levels because of increased economic rent. The Eastern Appalachian coal region, rather than the western mines, would largely take over the Midwest market, because of lower transportation costs. In general, coal production would be much lower, except for the Eastern Appalachian region. In addition, all consumption would be reduced.

A spatial price control regime would significantly curtail coal production and consumption. The net efficiency loss, after accounting for tax revenues, suggests that a suitable pollution tax policy based on the rent-minimizing spatial equilibrium model is politically infeasible without overall consideration of the impacts on the economic activities of all regions. Alleviating the environmental damage caused by burning fossil fuels cannot be evaluated without simulation of the impacts within a spatial equilibrium model.

Finally, reducing the production in or closing mines with the highest cost (supply price plus pollution tax) would be beneficial for the environment but would increase economic rent and, therefore, inefficiency.

REFERENCES

Campbell, T., M.J. Hwang, and S. Shahrookh. (1982). "Market Delineation in the Coal Industry," *Review of Regional Studies* 9: 6–17.

Chao, G.S., and T.L. Friesz. (1984). "Spatial Price Equilibrium Sensitivity Analysis," *Transportation Research* 18B: 423–440.

Daffermos, S. (1983). "An Iterative Scheme for Variational Inequalities," *Mathematical Programming* 26: 40–47.

Daffermos, S., and A. Nagurney. (1984). "Sensitivity Analysis for the General Spatial Economic Equilibrium Problem," *Operations Research* 32: 1069–1086.

Enke, S. (1951). "Equilibrium Among Spatially Separated Markets: Solution by Electric Analogue," *Econometrica* 19: 40–47.

Florian, M., and M. Los. (1982). "A New Look at Static Spatial Price Equilibrium Models," *Regional Science and Urban Economics* 12: 579–597.

Harker, P.T. (1986). "Alternative Models of Spatial Competition," *Operations Research* 34.3: 410–425.

———. (1988). "Dispersed Spatial Price Equilibrium," *Environment and Planning A* 20.3: 353–368.

———. (1987). "The Case of a Spatial Price Equilibrium Game," *Journal of Regional Science* 27.3: 369–389.

Henderson, J.M. (1958). *The Efficiency of the Coal Industry: An Application of Linear Programming*. Cambridge, MA: Harvard University Press.

Hitchcock, F.L. (1941). "Distribution of a Product from Several Sources to Numerous Localities," *Journal of Mathematics and Physics* 21: 224–230.

Hwang, M.J., C.W. Yang, J. Kim, and C.L. Irwin. (1994). "Environmental Regulations on the Optimal Allocation of Coal among Regions in the United States," *International Journal of Environment and Pollution* 4: 59–74.

Irwin, C.L., and C.W. Yang. (1982). "Iteration and Sensitivity for a Spatial Equilibrium Problem with Linear Supply and Demand Functions," *Operations Research* 30.2: 319–335.

———. (1983). "Iteration and Sensitivity for a Nonlinear Spatial Equilibrium Problem." In A. Fiacco, ed., *Lecture Notes in Pure and Applied Mathematics* 91–107, 85. New York: Marcel Dekker Inc.

Kantorovich, L.V. (1958). "On the Translocation of Masses," *Doklady Adad Nauk SSR* 37 (1942), trans. in *Management Science* 5.1.

Koopmans, T.C. (1949). "Optimum Utilization of the Transportation System," *Econometrica* 71: 136–146.

Labys, W.C., and C.W. Yang. (1980). "A Quadratic Programming Model of the Appalachian Steam Coal Market," *Energy Economics* 2: 86–95.

———. (1991). "Advances in the Spatial Equilibrium Modeling of Mineral and Energy Issues," *International Regional Science Review* 14: 61–94.

———. (1996). "Le Chatelier Principle and the Flow Sensitivity of Spatial Commodity Models." In J.C.J.M. van de Bergh and P. Nijkamp and P. Rietveld, eds., *Recent Advances in Spatial Equilibrium Modeling: Methodology and Applications* 96–110. Berlin: Springer.

———. (1997). "Spatial Price Equilibrium as a Foundation to Unified Spatial Commodity Modeling," *Papers in Regional Science* 76.2: 199–228.

Liebman, J., L. Lasdon, L. Schrage, and A. Waren (1986). *Modeling and Optimization with GINO*. Redwood City, CA: Scientific Press.

Liew, C.K., and J.K. Shim. (1978). "A Spatial Equilibrium Model: Another View," *Journal of Urban Economics* 5: 526–534.

Nelson, C.H., and B.A. McCarl. (1984). "Including Imperfect Competition in Spatial Equilibrium Models," *Canadian Journal of Agricultural Economics* 32 (March): 55–69.

Pang, J.S. (1984). "Solution of the General Multi-Commodity Spatial Equilibrium Problem by Variational and Complementarity Models," *Journal of Regional Science* 24.3: 403–414.

Samuelson, P.A. (1952). "Spatial Price Equilibrium and Linear Programming," *American Economic Review* 42: 283–303.

Sheppard, E., R.P. Haining, and P. Plummer. (1992). "Spatial Pricing in Interdependent Markets," *Journal of Regional Science* 32.1: 55–75.

Smith, T.E. (1984). "A Solution Condition for Complementarity Problems: With an Application to Spatial Price Equilibrium," *Applied Mathematics and Computation* 15: 61–69.

Smith, V.L. (1963). "Minimization of Economic Rent in Spatial Price Equilibrium," *The Review of Economic Studies* 30: 24–31.

Takayama, T., and G. Judge. (1964). "Equilibrium among Spatially Separated Markets: A Reformulation," *Econometrica* 32: 510–524.

———. (1971). *Spatial and Temporal Price and Allocation Model*. Amsterdam: North-Holland.

Takayama T., and N. Uri. (1983). "A Note on Spatial and Temporal Price and Allocation Modeling," *Regional Science and Urban Economics* 13: 455–470.

Thore, S. (1982). "The Takayama-Judge Model of Spatial Equilibrium Extended to Convex Production Set," *Journal of Regional Science* 22: 203–212.

———. (1982). "The Takayama-Judge Spatial Equilibrium Model with Endogenous Income," *Regional Science and Urban Economics* 12: 351–364.

Tobin, R.L. (1987). "Sensitivity Analysis for General Spatial Price Equilibrium," *Journal of Regional Science* 27: 77–102.

Tobin, R.L., and T.L. Friesz. (1983). "Formulating and Solving the Spatial Price Equilibrium Problem with Transshipment in Terms of Arc Variables," *Journal of Regional Science* 2.2: 187–198.

Tobin, R.L., and T.L. Friesz. (1986). "Sensitivity Analysis for Variational Inequalities," *Journal of Optimization Theory and Applications* January: 191–204.

Yang, C.W. (1990). "An Evaluation of the Maxwell-Boltzmann Entropy Model of the Appalachian Steam Coal Market," *Review of Regional Studies* 20.1: 21–29.

———. (1985). "Including Imperfect Competition in Spatial Equilibrium Models: A Comment," *Canadian Journal of Agricultural Economics*, 33 (March): 111–112.

Yang, C.W., M.J. Huang, and S.N. Sohng. (2002). "The Cournot Competition in the Spatial Equilibrium Model," *Energy Economics* 24: 139–154.

Yang, C.W., and W.C. Labys. (1981). "Stability of Appalachian Coal Shipments under Policy Variations," *Energy Journal* 2.3: 111–128.

———. (1982). "A Sensitivity Analysis of the Stability Property of the QP Commodity Model," *Journal of Empirical Economics* 7: 93–107.

———. (1985). "A Sensitivity Analysis of the Linear Complementarity Programming Model: Appalachian Steam Coal and Natural Gas Markets," *Energy Economics* 7.3: 145–152.

Yang, C.W., and W.P. Page. (1993). "Sensitivity Analysis of Tax Incidence in a Spatial Equilibrium Model," *Annals of Regional Science* 27: 241–257.

CHAPTER 11

A Forecasting Simulation of Coal in Indonesia's Energy Future

Ukar W. Soelistijo

INTRODUCTION

At current extraction rates, Indonesian oil reserves will remain productive for another 15 to 20 years. Without new oil field discoveries, by the end of that period, Indonesia will become a net oil importer. Because oil exports fund an oil subsidy provided to Indonesian consumers, this subsidy would disappear when oil reserves run out. There is only a short period remaining before Indonesia will revert from being a net oil exporter to becoming a net oil importer, and the Indonesian government has been planning for years to prepare for this time (Soelistijo 1984).

Indonesia's other major domestic source of energy is coal. It has the fourth largest coal reserve in the Asia-Pacific region, yet it only consumes some 27% of what it produces and exports the rest, making it the world's second largest exporter of coal after Australia. In 2005, its exports accounted for 21% of world coal trade (World Coal Institute, not dated, but most data are for 2004 or 2005). The estimated life of its coal reserves is 100 years and possibly longer. The government has carried out efforts to increase the value-added of Indonesian coal since the 1950s and 1960s, using various measures, including plant-scale tests for blast furnace coke using dry distillation. From the 1970s and 1980s to the present, efforts to achieve coal diversification advanced to include efforts to substitute coal briquettes for firewood and similar sources. Coal liquefaction became a focus by the end of the 1990s because of high prices of kerosene and diesel fuels, which resulted from increased demands, fueled by population increases and economic growth.

Indonesia has some 61 billion tons in coal reserves. At current production levels, and assuming future production of about 150 to 200 million tons per year, the coal reserves would last for 200 to 250 years. At a production level of 400 million tons per year, coal reserves could meet Indonesia's energy demand for only about 100 years (Badan Pusat Statistik 2000; Directorate of Mineral and Coal Enterprises 2003; Ministry of Energy and Mineral Resources 2000; Pusat Informasi Energy 2002a, b).

CHRONOLOGY OF COAL DEVELOPMENT

Coal Liquefaction Projects

From 1957 to 1963, the German company Wedexro manufactured coke by using a carbonization or dry distillation process at several locations to supply a sample of Indonesia's iron and steel industry. It also treated the tar product that resulted from the distillation process at a demonstration plant that had a capacity of 30 tons of coal per day, using the Lurgi process (a high-pressure coal gasification process). The plant, located at the Tajung Enim coal mines in South Sumatra, was demolished when the coal mine was expanded to supply the coal-fired power plant of Suralaya in West Java.

From 1980 to the present, the Coal and Mineral Technology Research and Development Center (CMTRDC, which is part of Indonesia's Ministry of Energy and Mineral Resources) carried out experiments with coal liquefaction at the laboratory scale, using autoclaving.

Starting in 1994, Indonesia's Agency for the Investigation and Application of Technology, in cooperation with Indonesia's Ministry of Energy and Mineral Resources and New Energy Development Organization Japan (NEDO), carried out a bench scale unit (BSU) with a capacity of 1 ton of coal per day, located at Takasoga Kobe Steel, Japan, using Indonesian Banko coal from South Sumatra. The agency also supported a pilot plant in Victoria, Australia. It used the data from the experience with this plant for simulations to study the feasibility of Indonesian Banko coal liquefaction at rates of 6,000 tons per day, 12,000 tons per day, and 30,000 tons per day, respectively (BPPT, NEDO, Kobe Steel, Ltd. 2002).

In May 2007, 13 private, mostly energy businesses and public organizations formed a consortium to construct a "semipermanent" brown coal liquefaction plant, as a stepping-stone toward a commercial plant with a planned capacity of 27,000 barrels per day. The anticipated completion date for the commercial plant is in 2013 (Berau Coal 2007).

Nonliquefaction Value-Added Projects

Although coal liquefaction received much attention, there were other efforts to increase the value of coal to Indonesia's economy. The production of coal briquettes and bio-coal was one of these other value-added activities. The production and distribution of coal briquettes were initiated by the state-owned coal company Bukit Asam (PTBA) in the early 1990s, when it created a pilot plant at Tanjung Enim in South Sumatra. This effort was expanded at Gresik, East Java, and continued with other types of coal briquettes, such as a bio-coal pilot plant at Palimanan, Cirebon, West Java (tekMIRA 2003). This latter plant, a cooperative project of the Indonesian and Japanese governments, opened in 2001.

The Palimanan, Cirebon, West Java, pilot plant has the capacity to produce 10,000 tons of bio-coal briquettes per year. The plant location is close to many small-scale industries, particularly brick/roof-tile/lime burning, food, poultry breeder, and rattans that could use the briquettes as substitutes for some of their current energy sources (tekMIRA 2003). Although the effort has been successful, initial production has been below capacity. The task now is to increase demand and production by making it attractive to small and medium scale industries in place of firewood and residual fuel oils (RFO), diesel, and other fuels. The briquettes are also suitable for household uses.

An upgraded brown coal (UBC) pilot plant was built at the Palimanan coal center at Cirebon in cooperation with Japan's Ministry of International Trade and Industry (MITI). The plant has a capacity of 1,500 tons per year. Most of Indonesia's coal is of low rank (below 5,000 kilocalorie per kilogram [kcal/kg]). UBC would better utilize brown coal, which is plentiful in Indonesia, by increasing its calorific content as a fuel supply for steam generating power plants or other boilers. Through a dewatering procedure, the UBC will approach high-rank quality of 6,000 to 6,800 kcal/kg (Ministry of Energy and Mineral Resources 2004).

Gas produced from coal has been used in Indonesia since the Dutch occupation era. Gasification plants use a coal carbonization technology that produces coke in addition to town gas. CMTRDC uses coal to produce gas for tealeaf drying at tea plantations at a plant located at Gembong Ciwide, West Java. Utilizing coal gasification is encouraged at a large scale because of the large brown coal reserves and for meeting the growing demand for fuel (e.g., by fertilizer plants). A material survey from 1997 to 2000 by the Coal Gasification Team of Indonesia's Ministry of Energy and Mineral Resources produced an inventory of the characteristics of Indonesian coal and of international technologies for coal gasification (Suseno et al. 2000; Tim Gasifkasi Batubara 2000). The effort was amended to include the possibility of utilizing methane gas, which is available in very large quantities within coal seam deposits.

TECHNO-ECONOMIC EVALUATION OF COAL'S POTENTIAL

Evaluation of Coal Liquefaction

We now evaluate the results of a feasibility study based on simulations of coal liquefaction and use by the Indonesian Agency for the Investigation and Application of Technology (BPPT, NEDO, Kobe Steel Ltd. 2002; Soelistijo et al. 2003). The study used data from these production units:

- Takasoga Kobe Steel Japan: bench scale unit (BSU) 0.1 dry ton of coal per day, Banko Coal of Indonesia.
- Brown Coal Liquefaction of Victoria (BCLV), Morwell, Victoria, Australia: Pilot plant at 150 tons of dry coal per day.
- Japanese experiences with coal liquefaction (BSU 0.1 ton of coal per day); a pilot plant at 10 tons of coal per day at Oga, Japan; a pilot coal liquefaction plant at 1 ton per day and with 150 tons per day Nedol process in Japan; Hycol 50 tons of coal per day at Sodegura Chiba (1986–1994); and a pilot plant EAGLE gasification plant for combined cycle power plant in Kiba Kyushiusita, Fukuoka, Japan (150 tons per day, 1998–2006).

The simulations resulted in these breakeven points: Given a production capacity of 6,000 dry tons of coal per day, the breakeven point is 4,432 tons per day. If the production capacity is 12,000 tons per day, the breakeven point is 8,042 tons per day. Finally, if the capacity is 30,000 tons per day, the breakeven point is 20,127 tons per day.

Based on information from NEDO, the average total cost (ATC) of synthetic crude oil (SCO) in 2001 was USD25.70/bbl for a plant with a production capacity of 6,000 tons of coal per day. The equivalent numbers are USD22.60/barrel (bbl) and USD20.30/bbl for plants with capacities of 12,000 and 30,000 tons of coal per day, respectively. The team from the Indonesia Ministry of Energy and Mineral Resources estimated the rates at USD25.63/bbl (6,000 tons/day capacity), USD22.34/bbl (12,000 tons/day capacity, and USD16.24/bbl (30,000 tons/day capacity), respectively. Related transportation costs assume the use of a pipeline and amount to USD1.1/bbl, or about 10% of ATC, constituting 4.87% of the SCO price free on board.

To provide comparisons of marketing possibilities, liquefaction feasibility simulations were conducted at several coal locations. Figure 11.1 provides an overview of the study simulation locations while Table 11.1 shows simulation results at different locations.

The results show that the price of Berau SCO (USD23–29.00/bbl) is lower than that of Mulia SCO (USD26–34.00/bbl). The Banko SCO (USD29–34.00/bbl) is the most expensive and is likely about the same as Mulia SCO. This is due to transportation costs because the Banko coal is located the farthest from the coast or port.

Evaluation of Briquettes, Bio-coals, and Coke

The subsidy allocated for fuel oil is such a burden that the government of Indonesia (GOI) should make a decision to reduce it, with the goal of gradually eliminating it (Cahyono 2000; Soelistijo 2000). This decision will remove a market distortion that keeps coal briquettes from entering the domestic market more strongly. The reduction and eventual elimination of the fuel oil subsidy could be accompanied by promotion and information about briquettes.

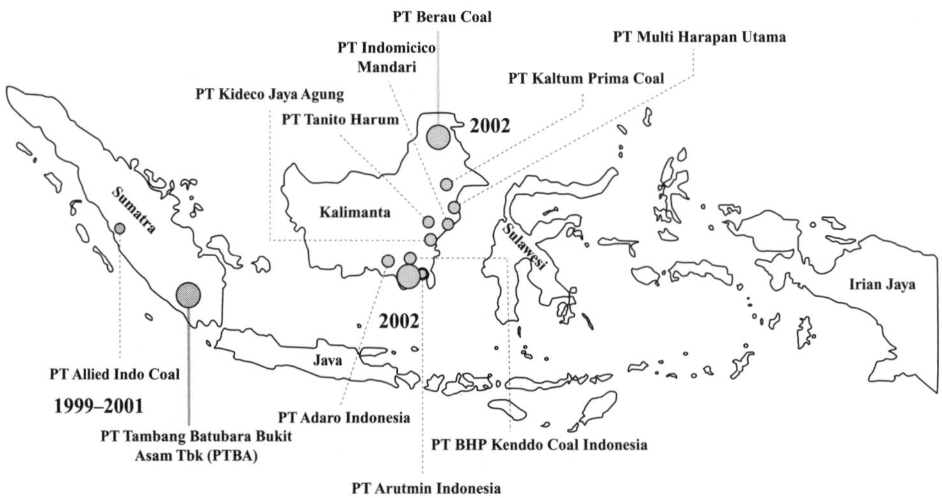

FIGURE 11.1 Feasibility Study Locations

TABLE 11.1 Input-Output Profile of Synthetic Crude Oil (SCO) Plants

Variables	Banko	Mulia PT[1] Arutmin Indonesia	Berau PT Berau Coal
Fuel Price (USD/ton)	13	13	13
Construction Cost at different Production Capacities (tons/day)			
3,000 tons/day	–	799.8	808.3
6,000 tons/day	1,502	1,342	1,358
12,000 tons/day	2,618	2,368	2,399
Price of Synoil[2] at Different Production Capacities (USD/barrel)			
3,000 tons/day	–	26.00	23.00
6,000 tons/day	29.00	29.00	26.00
12,000 tons/day	34.00	34.00	29.00
By-products	Sulfur \$45/ton Phenol \$750/ton Ammonia \$200/ton	Sulfur \$45/ton Phenol \$750/ton Ammonia \$200/ton	Sulfur \$45/ton Phenol \$750/ton Ammonia \$200/ton

[1]PT is the Indonesian equivalent of "Inc."
[2]Synthetic crude oil

The demand for coal briquettes on Java Island was studied for distribution to 32 types of small industries. Java Island has the densest population and the largest number of small industries in Indonesia. The demand for coal briquettes was estimated to be about 14.4 million tons of coal equivalent (TCE) per year. This amount of TCE corresponds to 13.09 million kiloliters of kerosene. Under current law, this much kerosene would cost the GOI an annual subsidy of IDR* 17.6 trillion. If the kerosene could be exported instead of consumed, it would generate about USD4.9 billion per year in foreign exchange (assuming a price of oil of USD 50–60/bbl, IDR9,500/USD). Since this calculation was made, oil prices have soared, so that the foreign exchange earning would be significantly higher.

If popularizing the use coal briquettes is successful and their utilization gradually increases, market demand would shift away from kerosene. If necessary, in the early stages of promotion, a subsidy could support coal briquettes as well.

The next comparison is that of the price of coal and the price of coal briquette to the price of fuel oil. We use calorific value as the basis for the comparison. Note that 1 TCE equals 4.8 BOE (barrels of oil equivalent). However, if the handling cost of coal is 30 to 35% less than that of oil, then 1 TCE effectively equals 3.2 BOE. By using USD22.00/bbl (year 2001) as the price of oil, and based on the above-mentioned parameters, then the economically feasible price of coal is about USD70.40 per TCE, or about IDR675,840 per TCE. If coal briquettes contain 5,500 kcal/kg, the price of coal could be as high as IDR531,017/ton or IDR531/kg. If the current price of coal briquettes were IDR575/kg, the switch from oil to briquettes

*The Indonesian rupiah, international currency symbol IDR, is the Indonesian currency. In March 2008, USD100.00 converted to approximately IDR920,800, and IDR100 converted to USD0.01086.

should be worthwhile from the calorific value point of view at 2001 oil prices. Today the price of crude oil is above $100/bbl.

Let us now extend the comparison with the price of coal briquettes to that of kerosene and of diesel fuel. Based on the comparison of fuel consumption, the usage of 1 liter of kerosene corresponds to the use of 1.4 kg of coal briquette.*

At the 2001 price of briquettes, coal briquettes are not yet cheaper than kerosene. If the price of kerosene were equal to its production cost of IDR1,746/liter, then consumers of coal briquettes would gain a surplus of 2.3 kg in terms of coal briquettes compared to the consumption of 1 liter of kerosene. The surplus would be 0.5 kg of coal briquettes relative to the consumption of 1 liter of diesel fuel.

The higher the price of fuel oil, the more competitive the price of coal briquette will be, particularly to small and medium-size industries. Currently the price of kerosene at the state-owned Oil Company or Pertamina terminal is IDR 2,000/liter and that of diesel fuel is IDR6,300/liter. Thus, at present market conditions, the future of coal briquette looks more and more promising.

Comparing coal briquettes, kerosene, and diesel fuel, coal briquettes can be assumed to be "normal goods" (neither inferior nor Giffen goods) and not inferior to kerosene and diesel fuels. Thus, the income effect of coal briquettes in the process of substitution is positive. This assumption is valid mainly for small and medium-scale industries. Small industry entrepreneurs (e.g., poultry, brick, and tile producers) state that they prefer coal briquettes because this fuel increases profitability compared with using fuel oil (Isdinarmiati 2000; Soelistijo, Suseno, and Sherman 2003)

We judge the emerging potential of producing coal briquettes, assuming that that the market will be competitive, even though in the early period it will be oligopolistic because of the limited number coal briquette producers (e.g., the state-owned Coal Company of Bukit Asam [PTBA] and a few private companies). In the case of coke, if the price of the imported coke is IDR4,500/kg or IDR6,300/1.4 kg, then it will not be competitive with kerosene, which has a price of IDR2,000/liter. Without a subsidy, the price of coal briquettes will be IDR575/kg or IDR885/1.4 kg. Thus, imported coke is more expensive than unsubsidized kerosene or domestic coal briquettes/coke. The capital investment of a coking plant with a capacity of production of 3,000 tons per day is about IDR10 billion (USD1.05 million).

Evaluation of the Development of Coal Gasification

During the pilot plant–scale investigation of tealeaf drying at tea plantations, it was determined that the production of 1 kg of dry tealeaf requires 0.3 to 1.5 liters of subsidized diesel fuel. Fuel costs account for 11 to 20% of total costs, depending on the type of tealeaf. The comparison of fuel utilization found that diesel fuel use is about 20 liters/hour, while using gasified coal requires approximately 40 kg/hour. Thus, using coal would reduce fuel requirement for drying by 40%. The price of diesel fuel is IDR513.37/liter and the price of coal is IDR500/kg. Based

*Based on CMTRDC investigation. Boiling 10 liters of water requires 0.3 liter of kerosene or 0.45 kg coal briquette (brown coal). One liter of kerosene corresponds to 1.4 kg of coal briquette. One liter of kerosene contains 9,220 calories. One kg of coal briquette contains 5,500 calories, thus 1.4 kg of coal briquette contain 7,700 calories. The efficiency of the stove also figures into the comparison.

on the price of diesel fuel of IDR5,400/liter and that coal of IDR500/kg, it is likely that gasification of coal would be competitive, and recent market development have made this even more likely. The capacity of a gasification unit of 50 kg of coal per hour would require a capital investment of IDT200 million. Other comparisons of gasification have been studied and compiled by the Team of Coal Gasification of the Indonesia Ministry of Energy and Mineral Resources (Heyadi 2003; Tim Gasifkasi Batubara 2000).

MACROECONOMIC IMPACTS OF FUEL DEVELOPMENT

Based on an estimated annual growth rate of 6.5% of fuel oil demand in the transportation sector, estimated consumption should increase to 354.69 million bbl by 2015, 485.95 million bbl by 2020, 1,249.79 million bbl by 2035, and 3,214.27 million bbl by 2050. The oil fuel consumption of the transportation sector in 2015 could be met by SCO produced by nine coal liquefaction plant units with a production capacity of 30,000 dry tons of coal per day, requiring a capital investment of USD69.22 billion. Fuel demand in 2035 could be met by 31 plant units, requiring a capital investment of USD178.81 billion. Finally, by 2050, 78 coal liquefaction plant units of would be necessary, with a capital investment of USD449.91 billion.

Developing coal liquefaction will affect regional development through multiplier effects by increasing employment and income. This can be seen through regional macroeconomic analysis using an input-output (I-O) model of Indonesia. Several economic multipliers can be computed by using provincial I-O tables. Based on multipliers and backward and forward linkages, using the I-O tables of 1994, 2001, and the projection of 2011 for South Sumatra Province, we are able to show that backward and forward linkages of the coal sector in 1994 were less than 1.0. This indicates that at that time, the coal sector did not significantly affect other economic sectors either through backward or forward linkage effects. However, by 2001, linkages of the coal to other sectors of the economy had strengthened, especially forward linkages, which had grown and be greater than 1.0.

Looking to the future, the 2011 I-O table was constructed, assuming economic growth at a rate of 3% per year. If a coal liquefaction plant were developed by 2011, the simulation revealed:

- The employment multipliers of the coal mining sector (CMS), oil and gas mining sector (OGMS), and oil refining sector (ORS) would be 1.08, 3.67, and 5.67, respectively.
- The investment multipliers of CMS, OGMS and ORS would be 1.11, 1.13, and 3.41, respectively.
- The value-added multipliers of CMS, OGMS, and ORS would be 1.16, 1.05 and 2.50, respectively.

Thus, by 2011, the processing industry of SCO is expected to significantly contribute value added to the regional economy, because ORS has greater economic multipliers than CMS and OGMS. It is likely that ORS will be replaced by the SCO sector, coming from CMS. The backward linkages of CMS, OGMS, and ORS are 0.84, 0,.75 and 1.20 and the forward linkages are 0.80, 1.4, and 1.36, respectively.

Thus, ORS has a stronger linkage (>1.0) than the other two sectors. Finally, the analysis shows that processing SCO domestically is important if it is to make a greater contribution than the export of coal. The utilization of SCO will contribute more to the economy than coal per se.

CONCLUSIONS

Indonesia will soon become a net oil importer, a situation for which it has been preparing for years. Coal plays a major role in the plan to adapt and continue to meet the country's energy needs. However, coal, too, is an exhaustible resource, and environmental considerations demand the search for alternative energy in the future. In an interim period, however, coal and fuels produced from coal will contribute a significant share of Indonesia's energy needs. Figure 11.2 provides an overview of coal's role in Indonesia's energy future.

Our study suggests that the future utilization of bio-coal, coal briquettes, and coke raises these important considerations:

- The equivalent price of interfuels as the downstream tip of intensification, diversification, and conservation should be considered as a "balanced energy price" between types of energy.
- Oil fuel price decisions should be made to push toward the utilization of energy alternatives. If possible, part of the fuel oil subsidy should be shifted to encourage energy alternatives.
- Marginal profits should be given to private companies to stimulate the production of coal briquette.
- Firms should produce high-quality coal briquette (i.e., odorless, clean, flammable, storable, and the heat should be adjustable according to needs).

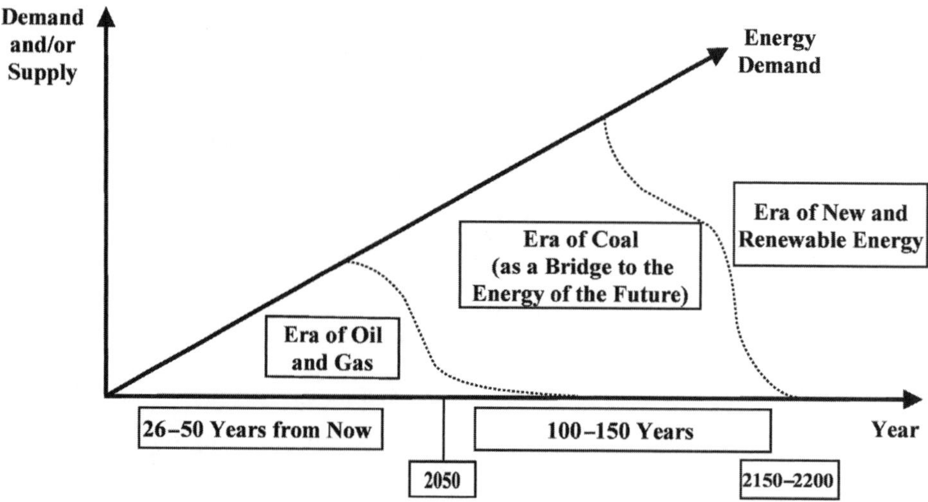

FIGURE 11.2 Coal's Role as a Bridge into Indonesia's Sustainable Energy Future

- Firms should formulate a marketing strategy to inform potential users about the availability of coal briquette.
- The utilization of the products of a coking pilot plant in iron casting has been very promising, and an initiative to find investors willing to develop it at an economic scale is very desirable.
- A major goal should be the development of the large-scale production of coal briquettes to guarantee a supply to consumers. Price levels should be as low as possible by using a subsidy.
- Low-income residents should be compensated for the loss of the oil fuel subsidy, and the program of developing new and renewable energy should be supported financially to encourage the transition from fossil fuels or coal and oil and gas.

In conclusion, if liquefaction of South Sumatra coal is canceled due to its noncompetitive price or if the prices of coal liquefaction of the coal from other areas (East Kalimantan and South Kalimantan) are more promising because of their closer location to a port or beach, then South Sumatra coal could be utilized through UBC or through gasification. Gasification of South Sumatra coal can be achieved by using internationally available conventional and commercial technology (e.g., such as technology used in the United States in steam power–generating plants, which produces by-products such as sulfur, ammonia, etc.), in addition to supplying gas for the fertilizer industry in Indonesia. Coal briquettes have been utilized in tea plantations for drying tealeaf and have proved to be technologically and economically very promising. To guarantee success, it is necessary, however, to work more intensively with entrepreneurs interested in developing a plant at a large scale of production, particularly by providing a sufficient supply of coal.

REFERENCES

Badan Pusat Statistik. (2000). *Statistik Pertambangan Non Minyak dan Gas Bumi*, Jakarta, Indonesia. [Statistics Indonesia. (2000). *Statistics for Mining Non-Oil and Natural Gas Production.*]

Berau Coal. (2007). " The MOU of Brown Coal Liquefaction (BCL)," *Berau Coal News*, June 13, www.beraucoal.co.id/newsdetail.php?idNews=13.

BPPT, NEDO, Kobe Steel Ltd. (2002). *Feasibility Study on Direct Liquefaction of Banko Coal in Indonesia.* [Badan Pengkajian dan Penerapan Teknologi (BPPT) is an Indonesian government research agency. New Energy and Industrial Development Organization (NEDO) is an agency within the Japanese Ministry of Economy, Trade, and Industry.]

Cahyono, Budi. (2000). "Subsidi BBM: Buah Simalakama yang Harus Ditelan," Trenddata (Jakarta, Indonesia). ["The Fuel Oil Subsidy: Bitter Realities Need to Be Faced."]

Directorate of Mineral and Coal Enterprises. (2003). *Coal.* Jakarta: Ministry of Energy and Mineral Resources.

Heryadi, D. (2003). "Pengembangan Gasifikasi Batubara," Litbang tekMIRA No. 36.2003. ["Development of Coal Gasification," tekMIRA Research and Development Paper 36.2003, Ministry of Energy and Mineral Resources, Jakarta, Indonesia.]

Isdinarmiati, T. (2000). *Mampukah Batubara Sebagai Alternatif Pengganti Minyak Bumi?* Trenddata: Jakarta, Indonesia. [*Would Coal Be an Alternative Fuel to Replace Oil?*]

Ministry of Energy and Mineral Resources. (2000). *Oil & Gas Statistik of Indonesia, 1996–2000.* Jakarta, Indonesia.

Ministry of Energy and Mineral Resources. (2004). "Development of Low Rank Coal Technology." Information on Energy and Mineral Resources of the Republic Indonesia, www.esdm.go.id/newsmining.php?news_id=376.

Pusat Informasi Energi. (2002a). *Buku Pegangan Statistik Ekonomi Energi Indonesia 2002*, Departemen Energi dan Sumber Daya Mineral, Jakarta, Indonesia, May. [Central Bureau for Energy Information. (2002a). *Statistical Handbook of Indonesian Energy Economics*, Ministry of Energy and Mineral Resources, Jakarta, Indonesia.]

Pusat Informasi Energi. (2002b). *Prakiraan Energi Indonesia 2010*. Departemen Energi dan Sumber Daya Mineral. [Central Bureau for Energy Information. (2002b). *Indonesian Energy Forecast 2010*, Ministry of Energy and Mineral Resources, Jakarta, Indonesia.]

Soelistijo, U.W. (1984). "Evaluation of the Potential Economic Benefit of Coal-Oil Substitution in the Indonesian Economy: An Interindustry Approach." West Virginia University, University Microfilms International, MI 48106.

Soelistijo, U.W. (2000). "Peninjauan Kembali Alokasi Subsidi Bahan Bakar Minyak Berdasarkan Keekonomian." tekMIRA, Ministry of Energy and Mineral Resources, Jakarta, Indonesia. ["Economic Re-Evaluation of the Fuel Oil Subsidy Allocation."]

Soelistijo, U.W., R. Saepudin, T. Suseno, and S. Palamba. (2003). "Economic Evaluation of the NEDO (Japan)-BPPT (Indonesia) Feasibility Study on the Indonesia Banko Coal Liquefaction, 2002," Proceedings of the 28th International Technical Conference on Coal Utilization & Fuel System, March 10–13, Clearwater, FL.

Soelistijo, U.W., T. Suseno, and I. Suherman. (2003). "Tinjauan Ekonomi Pengembangan Briket Batubara Sebagai Salah satu Sumber Energi Alternatif BBM," Prosiding Kolokium Pertambangan dan Energi 2001, Bandung. Dipublikasikan dalam Buku: Ekonomi Regional dan Model penerapannya: Pengembangan Sumber Daya Mineral dan Energi Dalam Rangka Otonomi Daerah di Indonesia, Puslitbang teknologi Mineral dan Batubara. ["Analysis of the Development and Economics of Coal Briquette as an Alternative to Fuel Oil." Proceedings of the Colloquium on Mining and Energy, 2001, Bandung, Indonesia. In: *Regional Economics and Applications: The Development of Mineral Resources and Indonesia's Energy Autonomy*, Puslitbang Mineral Technology and Coal.]

Suseno, T. Saleh, Ridwan. dan Mujib, (2000). Potensi Pasar Briket Batubara di Provinsi Jawa Tengah. Bandung: Makalah Teknik, tekMIRA. [*Potential Market for Coal Briquette in Central Java*, tekMira working paper. Ministry of Energy and Mineral Resources, Jakarta, Indonesia.]

tekMIRA. (2003). "A Pilot Project of Bio-Coal Briquette at Palimanan, Cirebon-West Java." Research and Development Center for Mineral and Coal Technology, www.tekmira.esdm.go.id/en/aset/briket/index.asp.

Tim Gasifikasi Batubara. (2000). *Laporan Gasifikasi Batubara Indonesia*. Volume I, *1997–1998*. Volume II, *1998–1999*. Volume III, *1999–2000*. Departemen Energi dan Sumber Daya Mineral. [Coal Gasification Team. (2000). *Report on Indonesian Coal Gasification*: Volume I, *1997–1998*. Volume II, *1998–1999*. Volume III, *1999–2000*. Jakarta, Indonesia: Ministry of Energy and Mineral Resources.]

World Coal Institute. (not dated). "Coal Info: Indonesia," www.worldcoal.org/pages/content/index.asp?PageID=458.

CHAPTER 12

Structural Decomposition Analysis of Changes in Material Demand in the U.S. Economy

Adam Rose and Chia-Yon Chen

INTRODUCTION

The "intensity of use" concept has frequently been applied to the study of mineral and material demand. One group of researchers has examined this ratio of minerals/materials to gross national product in terms of a single theme. These studies range from Malenbaum's (1978) simple correlation of intensity of use (IU) with the level of development to the sophisticated analysis of IU in relation to product life cycles by Labys and Waddell (1988) and Labys (2004). Another, larger group of researchers has analyzed mineral/material demand in terms of a "decomposition" of the IU ratio into two or more components, such as input substitution, technological change, and product mix. Advances in this approach have emanated from applications of growth accounting (productivity measurement), input-output analysis, and econometrics. Until the original research summarized in this chapter was begun, there was no comprehensive methodology capable of a consistent estimation of the role that the many hypothesized variables might play in the utilization of materials.

Input-output (I-O)–based structural decomposition analysis (SDA) represents a major advance in this direction. It is defined as a method of distinguishing major shifts within an economy over time by means of comparative static changes in key sets of parameters (Rose and Miernyk 1989). This methodology is able to overcome the major limitations of the basic, static I-O model, including the fixed coefficient requirement. In fact, work by the authors (Rose and Chen 1987, 1991) has presented the case that our version of SDA is capable of yielding results comparable to those derived from two-tier KLEM (capital, labor, energy, and materials) models based on flexible functional from neoclassical production functions yet with much less demanding data requirements (see also Rose and Casler 1996).

This chapter explains the usefulness of SDA in analyzing changes in materials demand and illustrates the workings of the methodology by analyzing the situation in the United States between 1972 and 1982. This was a dramatic period of rapidly changing technology, including major breakthroughs in the creation of advanced materials, escalating energy prices, and structural shifts in the economy. The results provide perspective on changes during other time periods and countries as well.

REVIEW OF THE LITERATURE

The intensity of use concept is usually ascribed to Schurr and Netschert (1960) in the context of their study of energy in the U.S. economy. The first formal decomposition of IU is due to Tilton (1985) and Roberts (1985) in the manner of splitting an identity:

$$\frac{X_i}{Y} = \sum_{j}^{n} \left[\frac{X_{ij}}{Q_j} \right] \frac{\sum Q_j}{Y} \qquad (12.1)$$

where X_i = the apparent use of material i
X_{ij} = the amount of material i used in the production of major material using industry j
Q_j = the output of material-using industry j, $j = 1, \ldots, n$
Y = gross national product

Following Tilton (1985), the first term on the right-hand side has come to be known as the material composition of product (MCP), and the second term as the product composition of income (PCI). The first term is intended to capture supply-side considerations while the second embodies demand-side effects.

Table 12.1 lists the methodological advances in decomposing IU. These contributions are distinguished according to studies expressly concerned with IU of minerals and materials and those in the domain of I-O structural decomposition analyses applied to materials/minerals or the closely related area of energy resources.

TABLE 12.1 Methodological Advances in Decomposing Changes in Materials Demand

Intensity of Use Approach	
Tilton (1985)	Material composition of product and product composition of income
Roberts (1985, 1986)	Production function formulation including productivity trend
Considine (1991)	Flexible functional form production function; divisia index for materials
Evans and Lewis (2005)	Dynamic times-series analysis
Structural Decomposition Approach	
Myers (1986)	Econometric estimation of I-O coefficient change and price linkage
Rose and Chen (1987, 1991)	Two-tier KLEM formulation equivalent to flexible functional form production functions
Devine (1988)	Decomposition of final demand expenditure categories
Hoekstra and van den Bergh (2002)	Mixed physical-value I-O table

For example, Roberts (1985) decomposed materials-using industries according to the useful distinction of durable and nondurable goods sectors. In addition, he incorporated a crude production function and its statistical estimation into the framework in order to better analyze the MCP term (see also Roberts 1986). Considine (1991) has analyzed the intensity of use concept using modern duality-based methods within a partial equilibrium framework. In the process, he resolved the problem of comparability of material substitutes by the use of the divisia index (see also Considine 1990).

Input-output structural decomposition analysis is attributable to Leontief (1951) and was first applied to an analysis of general structural change in eh economy. Although Leontief and his associates performed major studies of mineral demand, their focus in this area was forecasting, and, hence, they utilized a dynamic I-O formulation rather than the more historically oriented SDA (see Leontief et al. 1983).

The motivation of SDA is the same as the identity splitting of direct IU methodologies. The apparent advantages of the I-O approach are that the economy is disaggregated into the various materials-using sectors and that direct effects can be distinguished from indirect effects. Additional advantages will be explained in the next section. Note also that there are some minor terminological differences between the two approaches. MCP is referred to as technical coefficient change in SDA parlance, while PCI is often referred to as the (final demand) product mix effect. A (final demand) growth effect is also included, so that the results yield both intensities and levels of materials utilization.

Myers (1986) was the first to apply SDA directly to minerals use. After performing a critical review of the literature on IU, Auty (1985) concluded that an I-O approach was needed to analyze the influence of technological change on materials consumption. Devine (1988) demonstrated the insights that could be obtained via a decomposition of final demand according to its major categories (consumption, investment, inventories, imports, exports, federal defense expenditures, other federal expenditures, and state and local government). As will be explained in more detail later, Rose and Chen (1987, 1991) broadened and deepened the analysis to a two-tier KLEM production function level, thus creating distinctions between technological change and technical (input) substitution within the general category of coefficient change. Other major applications of this methodology to analyzing changes in material demand have been performed by Hoekstra and van den Bergh (2002). Duchin (1989) has modified the basic I-O framework to incorporate recycling, a feature that might be integrated into SDA versions of the I-O model. Casler and Rose (1998) have extended SDA to analyze changes in greenhouse gas emissions stemming from energy and material use.

Note that advances in theory and method sometimes are misconstrued as representing sophistication for its own sake. The advances listed in Table 12.1 serve the practical purpose of analyzing a broader set of determinants of intensity of use and in a more accurate fashion. The divisia index provides a means of adjusting for quality (of characteristics) differences between materials. Flexible functional forms allow for more realistic production functions and more meaningful analyses of substitution. Disaggregation of final demand is a major step toward analyzing behavioral differences among categories of decision makers. As noted, the two-tier KLEM formulation of SDA overcomes the vagueness of coefficient change results of the rudimentary SDA approach. Moreover, it does not require the extensive data or complex specification/estimation of, say, a translog cost function.

Not surprisingly, each major methodological advance has yielded important new insights into the intensity of use of materials. Tilton (1983, 1985) found a greater role for technological change than had previous researchers, while Considine (1990, 1991) identified a relatively more prominent role for material input substitution in response to relative price changes. Myers (1986), using an innovative combination of I-O and econometrics, also found price changes to be an important explanatory variable for material input coefficient change. Our methodology provides a means by which to analyze these and other sources of change in greater depth.

CONCEPTUAL FRAMEWORK

The economics of production typically is couched in terms of primary factors capital, labor, and sometimes land or other natural resources. A major departure from this tradition for over 50 years has been input-output analysis, which explicitly recognizes the role of intermediate inputs. As issues relating to energy and resources became more prominent in the 1970s, there was a shift toward complete input accounting. This approach has come to be known as KLEM modeling, where the acronym represents capital, labor, energy and materials (actually all nonenergy intermediate inputs). It is often further subdivided into two tiers, with the delineation of subaggregates within some of the KLEM components (e.g., coal, oil, gas, and nuclear components of the energy aggregate). This formulation typically has been estimated using a flexible functional form production functions (e.g., Hudson and Jorgenson 1974; Hazilla and Kopp 1984).

Overall, the neoclassical KLEM modeling approach has proven to be a powerful and versatile tool in analytical studies and forecasting models. Hudson and Jorgenson (1974), Berndt and Wood (1975), and others have used a time series of I-O data to estimate the parameters of the dual-price frontier of a translog specification of the KLEM model. The resulting parameters yield elasticity measures that are invaluable in policy simulation modeling. Later the approach was also been used for structural analysis, as in the case of Considine's (1991) investigation of intensity of use.

We choose as our model framework input-output analysis applied in the manner of what has come to be referred to as "structural decomposition analysis." This approach dates from the work of Leontief (1951), Chenery et al. (1962), and Carter (1970), and seeks to distinguish major sources of change in the structure of the economy by means of a set of comparative static changes in key parameters of an I-O table. Research in this area has reached a high level of sophistication both on theoretical and empirical levels (e.g., Skolka 1989; Kanemitsu and Ohnishi 1989; Hoekstra and van den Bergh 2002).

Rose and Chen (1987, 1991) first advanced this approach in two major directions. First, we expanded the framework to the level of a full two-tier KLEM model by distinguishing between four groups of aggregate inputs and various fuel and material subaggregates. Second, unlike the majority of I-O structural decomposition analyses, which have been specified in an ad hoc manner, the estimating equations are derived formally, thereby ensuring consistency. The authors were also able to show heuristically that the modified SDA approach is capable of yielding as much insight into structural questions as the neoclassical KLEM approach and with only slightly more restrictive assumptions. The advantage of the I-O formulation is that it makes use of more readily available data (tables for the initial and terminal year), as contrasted to the time series of tables needed for econometric estimation of KLEM parameters in aggregated models.

Equation 12.2 shows the basic two-tier KLEM function.

$$Q = F\left[K, L, E\left(E_1 \ldots E_g\right), M\left(M_1 \ldots M_h\right)\right] \tag{12.2}$$

In its typical neoclassical form, this model is assumed to be a positive, twice differentiable, strictly quasi-concave function. In addition, it is often assumed to be homothetically weakly separable, meaning that the optimal mix of components in each aggregate is independent of the optimal mix across aggregates.

This latter assumption makes the neoclassical production function more restrictive than usual. For example, it means that indirect (general equilibrium) changes in fuel use take place in fixed proportions, just as they would in an I-O model. At the same time, our I-O variant is modified to be less rigid than its basic counterpart. Our approach readily allows for changes in coefficients over time, due either to technological change or technical substitution.

Thus, in the typical neoclassical version of the KLEM model, material conservation in the aggregate does not alter the material mix (though changes in individual material prices bring about a substitution response within the aggregate as a separate response). The exact same results take place in our modified I-O model. In fact, the only adjustment within the context of a KLEM framework that differs between the two models corresponds to output effects associated with changes in input costs. Here the neoclassical model allows for nonlinear responses in the indirect effects for the aggregates, where the I-O model does not. However, in cases where the actual production functions are characterized by constant returns to scale, our model is no more restrictive than its neoclassical counterpart.

ESTIMATING EQUATIONS

Table 12.2 present the decomposition equations of our I-O approach. We refer the reader to Rose and Chen (1991) for the formal derivation. The equations reflect the comparative static computations, which differ from each other only in terms of altering one set of key I-O coefficients. However, the reader should note one initial modification of the KLEM formulation of equation 12.2, that of using M to distinguish "major materials" from "other materials" (general intermediate inputs), denoted by O.

The first two equations on the table decompose changes in final demand other than exports into "mix" and "level" components. For example, in equation (2), the effect of a change in the mix of final economic activity is modeled by utilizing the 1972 material and other technical coefficients throughout, but with the 1982 mix of final demands set at 1972 levels. This means subtracting actual material use in 1972 from the material use in the U.S. economy that would have been required if the total of the 1982 mix of final demand were the same as in 1972. In the term $Y^{82(72)}$, the first superscript refers to the year coefficient values (i.e., proportions, or the mix) are set, while the superscript in parentheses refers to the year that serves as the control total (level). The analysis is subject to an index number problem relating

TABLE 12.2 Decomposition of Change in Material Demand

Source	Estimating Equations
(1) Level of final demand	$M^{72}G^{72}Y^{82} - M^{72}G^{72}Y^{82(72)}$
(2) Mix of final demand	$M^{72}G^{72}Y^{82(72)} - M^{72}G^{72}Y^{72}$
(3) Technological change in capital	$M^{72}G^{72}_{K82(LEMO)82(72)}Y^{82} - M^{72}G^{72}_{K82(LEMO)82(72)}Y^{82}$
(4) Technological change in labor	$M^{72}G^{72}_{K82L82(EMO)82(72)}Y^{82} - M^{72}G^{72}_{K82(LEMO)82(72)}Y^{82}$
(5) Technological change in energy	$M^{72}G^{72}_{K82L82E82(MO)82(72)}Y^{82} - M^{72}G^{72}_{K82L82(EMO)82(72)}Y^{82}$
(6) Linkage technological change in major materials	$M^{72}G^{72}_{K82L82E82M82O82(72)}Y^{82} - M^{72}G^{72}_{K82L82E82(MO)82(72)}Y^{82}$
(7) Linkage technological change in major materials	$M^{82}G^{82}Y^{82} - M^{82(72)}G^{82}Y^{82}$
(8) Technological change in other materials	$M^{72}G^{82}Y^{82} - M^{72}G^{72}_{K82L82E82M82O82(72)}Y^{82}$
(9) Linkage major material substitution	$M^{72}G^{72}_{M82(72)}Y^{82} - M^{72}G^{72}Y^{82}$
(10) Direct major material substitution	$M^{82(72)}G^{82}Y^{82} - M^{72}G^{82}Y^{82}$
(11) Other material substitution	$M^{72}G^{72}_{M82(72)O82(72)}Y^{82} - M^{72}G^{72}_{M82(72)}Y^{82}$
(12) Interfuel substitution	$M^{72}G^{72}_{E82(72)M82(72)O82(72)}Y^{82} - M^{72}G^{72}_{M82(72)O82(72)}Y^{82}$
(13) KLEMO substitution	$M^{72}G^{72}_{(KLEMO)82(72)}Y^{82} - M^{72}G^{72}_{M82(72)O82(72)E82(72)}Y^{82}$

Variables:
M = Material input coefficients
G = Leontief inverse
Y = Final demand
See text for explanation of G matrix subscripts and time superscripts.

to whether the reference point is the base or the terminal year. This problem can also arise with respect to the sequencing of equations. However, sensitivity tests by the authors indicate that the problem is not a serious one (see also the discussion by Skolka 1989, pertaining to simple decomposition analyses).

Equations (3) through (8) on the table isolate productivity changes in each of the five KLEMO components, respectively. Here the subscript symbols of the G matrix (Leontief inverse) refer to individual elements that differ from the status of the generic input category G. The notation can be confusing. For example, in the left-hand term of equation 12.3, K^{82} means that capital is set at its 1982 level and $(LEMO)^{82(72)}$ means that the other three aggregate inputs are set at their 1982 mix but at their 1972 level. The right-hand term has all four aggregates set at their 1982 mix and their 1972 levels. Thus, the two sides differ simply with respect to the level of capital usage per unit of output (technological change in capital). The simplified expression $B^{72}G^{72}\ Y^{82}–B^{72}G^{72}Y^{82}$ conveys the same intent, but the K^{82} empirical estimate differs slightly. The more complex expressions in Table 12.2 are used to insure consistency of the equation set.

For technological change in capital and labor, in each case that is changed, there is only a single row of coefficients. In the case of energy and materials, both of which are aggregates of inputs, 1982 coefficients are used as relative proportions of these component inputs, adjusted to their overall 1972 levels. Due to a lack of data and time, we employed a simple aggregator operation for both materials and energy. This implies perfect substitutability across materials characteristics and the perfect substitutability of a British thermal unit (BTU) of each fuel type. No doubt, this has introduced bias into our analysis, but we cannot tell to what extent (cf. Considine 1990a; Tilton and Radetzki 1990). Note also that there is a pair of equations relating to technological change in materials. Equation (7) refers to direct productivity changes operating through the matrix of material input requirements, M. Equation (6) covers the indirect and induced (linkage) effects of technological change in materials via the total requirements (Leontief Inverse) matrix. That is, a reduction in materials use per unit of output will lead to a reduction in the demand for materials and their various direct and indirect inputs, which in turn sets off additional rounds of material production reductions.

Equations (9) through (12) in Table 12.2 refer to substitution within the bottom tier of the material and energy aggregates. In these four equations, we utilized 1982 coefficients of individual components of M, O, and E, respectively, as weights for the corresponding aggregates, set at 1972 levels to capture substitution effects. Again, we split the material-related estimation into two components. The first refers to the pure intermaterial substitution effect, which, in an ideal market where prices reflect material utilization characteristics, should sum to zero. The second refers to the indirect and induced repercussions of this substitution. Finally, equation (13) reflects substitution within the top tier of the production function. We maintain that our equation set is mutually exclusive and completely exhaustive of outcomes within the KLEM production function framework. The results, in which we account for 100 percent of the change in material demand, support both of these considerations. However, some researchers have suggested that various interaction effects need to be modeled (e.g., Campbell 1986; Casler et al. 1990).

APPLICATION

The decomposition equations, presented in Table 12.2, were applied to the analysis of the change in energy use in the intermediate sectors of the U.S. economy between 1972 and 1982. This period was chosen because the endpoints correspond to benchmark years for two U.S. I-O tables and because this period coincides with one of the major periods of change in materials use in the nation's history.

Empirical Model

The I-O tables in the analysis consist of a 1982 constant dollar version of the official benchmark 1972 U.S. Bureau of Economic Analysis (BEA) input-output table (Ritz 1979) and the update to 1982 of the BEA's 1977 I-O table (BEA 1991). Although a decomposition analysis is best performed at the finest level of detail possible, the nature of our inquiry lends itself to a more aggregated, and hence more manageable, two-digit BEA classification consisting of 83 industries. At this level there are five major materials sectors: plastics and synthetic materials (BEA industry 28), rubber and miscellaneous plastics (32), glass and glass products (35), primary iron and steel (37), and primary nonferrous metals manufacturing. In her study, Devine (1988) analyzes sectors 37 and 38 along with their corresponding mining operations (BEA two-digit industries 4 and 5). Thus, her analysis includes some double counting.

The advantage of using 500 sector (four-digit) I-O tables is that it would enable us to distinguish between individual plastics and metals and also enable us to consider some stone and clay products (BEA two-digit industry 36), such as ceramics. Table 12.3 presents material production by type for intermediate use in the U.S. economy as well as intensity of use measures. Utilization of metals has decreased during this period, while the utilization of nonmetals has generally increased. A higher level of disaggregation would reveal more information about this occurrence.

In order to determine induced effects as well as direct and indirect ones, a closed I-O inverse was used for equations (3) through (13) from Table 12.2. The employee compensation row of the tables was included in the inverse and also served as the basis for the labor input of the KLEMO formulation. The personal consumption column of the I-O table served as the spending counterpart of the income row. On the capital side, we used a gross measure of capital services, including depreciation and the cost of capital, though the total conformed to the depreciation estimates from the National Income and Product Accounts for 1972 and 1982. The capital cost estimates are based on fixed proportions of total capital-related income accruing to each sector. The counterpart columns represent purchases of replacement investment goods from individual supplying sectors. In the absence of explicit sectoral data for this variable, we used the sectoral proportions of the Total Capital Formation columns of the 1972 and 1982 tables. This will result in biased results to the extent that the sectoral composition of plant and equipment purchases for replacement purposes differs from the sectoral composition of total investment.

Results

Tables 12.4 and 12.5 show the results of the decomposition analysis of the structure of change in materials use. We summarize them in text in relation to the individual sources of change in energy use. Again, we remind the reader of several caveats we noted in the previous section.

1. The largest overall positive stimulus to material use in the U.S. economy over the course of our study period was the real change in the level of final demand of 18.2%. This amount, which corresponds to the real level of economic growth

TABLE 12.3 Material Use in the U.S. Economy

Year	(28) Plastics	(32) Rubber	(35) Glass	(37) Iron and Steel	(38) Nonferrous Metals	Total
1972						
level	22,167	35,761	11,329	101,653	56,193	227,103
intensity	0.00944	0.01523	0.00482	0.04329	0.02393	0.09671
1982						
level	25,682	44,727	10,681	71,386	52,330	204,806
intensity	0.00915	0.01593	0.00380	0.02542	01864	.07294
1982–1972						
level	3,514	8,965	−648	−30,267	−3,863	−22,297
intensity	−0.0003	0.0007	−0.0010	−0.0179	−0.0053	−0.0238

TABLE 12.4 Percentage Change in Material Demand in the United States, 1972–1983

	(28) Plastics	(32) Rubber	(35) Glass	(37) Iron and Steel	(38) Nonferrous Metals	Weighted Avg.
1. Level of final demand	19	20	19	17	19	18.2
2. Mix of final demand	−4	1	−4	−14	−1	−7.0
3. Tech. change in capital	9	9	8	8	9	8.3
4. Tech. change in labor	9	8	9	6	6	6.8
5. Tech. change in energy	2	2	2	2	2	2.0
6. L. tech. change in materials	−1	−0	−0	−0	1	*
7. D. techc Change in materials	0	−25	−14	−13	−15	−14.4
8. Tech. change in intermediates	0	1	3	2	0	1.4
9. L. material substitution	8	1	−0	−2	−1	−0.3
10. D. material substitution	4	29	−7	−11	1	−0.0
11. Intermediate substitution	−19	−16	−17	−23	−15	−19.1
12. Interfuel substitution	1	1	1	0	1	0.5
13. KLEMO substitution	−12	−6	−5	−1	−14	−6.3
Totals	16	25	−6	−30	−7	−9.8

*Less than 0.5%.

TABLE 12.5 Relative Contribution to Change in Material Demand in the United States, 1972–1982

	(28) Plastics	(32) Rubber	(35) Glass	(37) Iron and Steel	(38) Nonferrous Metals	Weighted Avg.
1. Level of final demand	119	78	330	57	281	185.3
2. Mix of final demand	−25	2	−64	−47	−18	−71.6
3. Tech. change in capital	54	36	145	26	124	84.2
4. Tech. change in labor	56	34	149	20	92	69.7
5. Tech. change in energy	15	10	39	6	29	20.7
6. L. tech change in materials	−6	−1	−1	−1	13	−0.1
7. D. tech. change in materials	2	−100	−249	−45	−220	−146.6
8. Tech. change in intermediates	2	6	48	7	3	14.6
9. L. material substitution	51	6	−2	−8	−13	−3.0
10. D. material substitution	26	115	−117	−36	15	−0.0
11. Intermediate substitution	−120	−66	−302	−76	−214	−194.7
12. Interfuel substitution	4	3	11	2	8	5.6
13. KLEMO substitution	−77	−23	−85	−4	−200	−64.1
Totals	100	100	−100	−100	−100	−100.0

The numbers in Table 12.5 are calculated by dividing each of the numbers in Table 12.4 by its respective column sum.

between 1972 and 1982, represents the change in overall material demand that would have taken place had there been no other parametric changes. The minor variation in materials use increases across sectors (17% to 20%) is due to rounding and to some problems associated with the computations we used to obtain constant dollar I-O tables.

2. Had there been only a change in the mix of final demand, materials use would have dropped overall by 7.0%. The results reflect a shift by consumers (along with investment and government) away from relatively more expensive, heavy and traditional items. Iron and steel were affected by this source of change by a far greater margin than any other material.
3. Technological change, or productivity improvement, in capital represents one of the more significant positive sources of change, accounting for an 8.3% overall increase in materials use, or a relative contribution of 84.2% of the total (Table 12.5). The increase stems from the fact that the production of the mix of capital goods became directly and indirectly more material intensive, thus offsetting any material decreases stemming from a decrease in capital per unit of output. Note that this is the pure productivity effect; the effect of increased capital intensity is included in estimating equation (13) from Table 12.2.
4. Technological change relating to labor represents another positive source of change in material demand. This could stem from the fact that wage increases out-paced labor productivity increases, with further increases in labor-output ratios, when expressed in wage-bill terms, reflecting this. The increase in wages per unit of output translates into higher income, then higher consumption, and eventually to a higher derived demand for materials.
5. Technological change in energy has a very minor effect on material use. This is not surprising since materials are not a significant input into energy production.
6. and 7. The indirect technological change in materials is the second largest negative influence. As such it represents "material conservation" and is prominently reflected in the outcome for four of the five material sectors. The results for plastics are not surprising, although they merit some further investigation. The reader may at first conclude that all sector changes should be equivalent because of the I-O model property analogous to the assumption of homothetic weak separability. However, because of differing overall and individual materials intensities across sectors, these changes need not be a constant proportion over 1972 base-year values for the economy as a whole. Finally, note that linkage effects are very insignificant.
8. Changes in materials use stemming from technological change (TC) in intermediates (other materials) is also very small. This is due either to a small level of TC or the possibility that the material composition of intermediates does not vary much by material type. As will be discussed later, the results for equation (11) indicate that the latter is not the case.
9. and 10. By definition, the overall effect of direct material substitution is zero. The important result here is the direction of the change for individual materials sectors. The substitution toward plastics, rubber, and even nonferrous metals and away from iron and steel and glass is not surprising, especially in relation to relative price changes between 1972 and 1982. The linkage effect is rather insignificant, however.

11. The major negative overall influence on materials use is intermediate substitution. The size of this result is especially surprising. Pending further study, our explanation is that costs and pushes for conservation in general caused a shift toward less material intensive intermediate products. Examples would be smaller component parts for items such as automobiles and computers.
12. Interfuel substitution has a trivial effect on materials use. Again, materials are not a significant input into energy production.
13. Overall substitution of KLEMO aggregates results in a significant negative impact. Again, the nonuniform effect on individual fuel demand is consistent with the assumption of weak homothetic separability, since it pertains only to direct effects in any given sector. Also, the mix of sectors can change significantly as a result of the second-order effects of KLEMO substitution.

Note that our analysis has been able to account for 100% of the change in demand for each of the major categories of materials. Of course, to a great degree, this is due to the inherent nature of the identity splitting involved even in the I-O version of the intensity of use measure. Still, it lends support to the correctness of our model specification.

CONCLUSIONS

The intensity of use of minerals and materials has been the subject of considerable study in recent years. We have summarized a major advance in the domain of structural decomposition analysis for this purpose. Prior work by the authors in deriving the methodology and indicating its near equivalence to flexible functional form versions of the KLEM production function provide a solid conceptual basis. We hope that these results illustrate its usefulness and shed light on factors that caused some of the most dramatic shifts in materials use in U.S. history.

REFERENCES

Auty, R. (1985). "Materials Intensity of GDP," *Resources Policy* 11: 275–283.

BEA. (1991). "Benchmark Input-Output Accounts for the U.S. Economy, 1982," *Survey of Current Business* 71.7: 30–71.

Berndt, E., and D. Wood. (1975). "Technology, Prices and the Derived Demand for Energy," *Review of Economics and Statistics* 57: 259–268.

Blair, P., and A. Wyckoff. (1989). "The Changing Structure of the U.S. Economy." In R. Miller, K. Polenske, and A. Rose, eds.: 293–307, *Frontiers of Input-Output Analysis*. New York: Oxford University Press.

Campbell, G. (1986). "Reflections on the Derived Demand for Metals," *Materials and Society* 10: 345–349.

Canavan, P.D. (1983). *The Determinants of Intensity-of-Use: A Case Study of Tin Solder End Uses*, Ph.D. Dissertation, Pennsylvania State University, University Park, PA.

Carter, A. (1970). *Structural Change in the American Economy*. Cambridge, MA: Harvard University Press.

Casler, S., A. Afrasiabi, and M. McCauley. (1991). "Decomposing Change in Energy Input-Output Coefficients," *Resources and Energy* 13: 95–109.

Casler, S., and A. Rose. (1998). "Structural Decomposition Analysis of Changes in Greenhouse Gas Emissions from the U.S.," *Environmental and Resource Economics* 11: 349–363.

Chenery, H., S. Shishido, and T. Watanabe. (1962). "The Pattern of Japanese Growth, 1914–1954," *Econometrica* 30: 98–139.

Considine, T. (1986). "Atrophy in Metal Demand: Truth or Consequences," *Materials and Society* 10: 529–538.

———. (1990). "Recent Trends in Material Consumption: The Role of Technology and Economics," *Materials and Society*, 14: 167-182.

———. (1991). "Economic and Technological Determinants of the Material Intensity of Use," *Land Economics* 67: 99–115.

Devine, P. (1988). "The Effects of Economic Growth, Technology Change, Consumption Pattern Change and Foreign Trade on Domestic Demand for Primary Metals, 1963–82," open file report, Division of Policy Analysis, U.S. Bureau of Mines, Washington, DC.

Evans, M., and A. Lewis. (2005). "Dynamic Metals Demand Model," *Resources Policy* 30: 55–59.

Feldman, S., D. McClain, and K. Palmer. (1985). "Sources of Structural Change in the United States, 1963–78: An Input-Output Perspective," *Review of Economics and Statistics* 69: 503–510.

Hawkins, T., C. Hendrickson, C. Higgins, and H. Suh. (2007). "A Mixed-Unit Input-Output Model for Environmental Life-Cycle Assessment and Material Flow Analysis" *Environmental Science & Technology* 41: 1024–1031.

Hazilla, M., and R. Kopp. (1984). "A Factor Demand Model for Strategic Nonfuel Minerals in the Primary Metals Sector," *Land Economics* 60: 328–339.

Hoekstra, R., and van den Bergh, J. (2002). "Structural Decomposition Analysis of Physical Flows in the Economy," *Environmental and Resource Economics* 23: 357–378.

Hudson, E., and D. Jorgenson. (1974). "U.S. Energy Policy and Economic Growth, 1975–2000," *Bell Journal of Economics* 5: 461–514.

Kanemitsu, H., and H. Ohnishi. (1989). "An Input-Output Analysis of Technological Change in the Japanese Economy: 1970–1980." In R. Miller, K. Polenske, and A. Rose, eds., *Frontiers of Input-Output Analysis*: 308–323. New York: Oxford University Press.

Labys, W. (2004). "Dematerialization and Transmaterialization: What Have We Learned?" Regional Research Institute Research Paper 2004-1, West Virginia University, Morgantown, WV.

Labys, W., and L. Waddell. (1988). "Commodity Life Cycles in U.S. Materials Demand," *Resources Policy* 15: 238–253.

Leontief, W. (1951). *Structure of the American Economy*, 2nd ed. New York: Oxford University Press.

Leontief, W., *et al.* (1983). *The Future of Nonfuel Minerals in the World Economy*. Lexington, MA: Lexington Books.

Malenbaum, W. (1978). *World Demand for Raw Materials in 1985 and 2000*. New York: McGraw-Hill.

Myers, J. (1986). "Testing for Structural Change in Metals Use," *Materials and Society* 10: 271–283.

Radetzki, M., and J. Tilton. (1990). "Conceptual and Methodological Issues." In J. Tilton (ed.), *World Metal Demand: Trends and Prospects*: 13–34. Washington, DC: Resources for the Future.

Ritz, P.M. (1979). "The Input-Output Structure of the U.S. Economy, 1972," *Survey of Current Business* 59.2: 34–72.

Roberts, M. (1985). *Theory and Practice of the Intensity of Use Method of Mineral Consumption Forecasting*. Ph.D. Dissertation, University of Arizona, Tucson, AZ.

———. (1986). "An Aggregate Model for Long Term Mineral Requirements," *Materials and Society* 10: 303–328.

Rose, A., and S. Casler. (1996). "Input-Output Structural Decomposition Analysis: A Critical Appraisal," *Economic Systems Research* 8: 33–62.

Rose, A., and C.Y. Chen. (1987). "Sources of Change in Energy Use in the U.S. Economy, 1972–1982." In J. Rowse (ed.), *World Energy Markets: Coping with Instability*. Calgary: Friesen.

———. (1991). "Sources of Change in Energy Use in the U.S. Economy, 1972–1982: A Structural Decomposition Analysis," *Resources and Energy* 13: 1–21.

Rose, A., C.Y. Chen, and S. Lin. (1987). "The Role of International Competition in Changing Energy Use Patterns in the U.S.," Paper presented at the American Economic Association Meetings, Chicago, IL.

Rose, A., and W. Miernyk. (1989). "Input-Output Analysis: The First Fifty Years," *Economic Systems Research* 1: 229–271.

Schurr, S.H., and B.C. Netschert. (1960). *Energy in the American Economy 1850–1975*. Baltimore: John Hopkins University Press.

Skolka, J. (1989). "Input-Output Structural Decomposition Analysis for Austria," *Journal of Policy Modeling* 11: 45–66.

Tilton, J. (1983). *Material Substitution: Lessons from Tin-Using Industries*, Washington, DC: Resources for the Future.

———. (1985). "Atrophy in Metal Demand," *Earth and Mineral Sciences* 54: 13, 16–18.

———. (1986). "Beyond Intensity of Use," *Materials and Society*, 10: 245–250.

PART Four

Environmental Resource Dynamics

The final part of this book deals with the trade and the environment, the linkage between the growing use of some commodities and the environment, and public policy. Ultimately, if policies and economic systems do not meet the fundamental needs of the members of our societies, they will fail. Therefore, these four chapters form a fitting conclusion to this volume.

Chapter 13 develops and simulates a trade-and-environment model for China. Given that country's large size, very impressive recent growth, and its impact on world markets on the demand and supply side, the results are relevant to a wide range of interests. They show that trade is essential to helping China simultaneously achieve economic growth and a reduction in environmental pollution.

Chapter 14 complements Chapter 13. It provides a detailed study of China's water crisis in terms of quantity and quality, and thus highlights the dilemma of environmental degradation that often accompanies rapid economic growth based on extractive and manufacturing industries. The author describes why the crisis developed to this point and the reasons behind its uneven geographic distribution. Its causation is also uneven among industries, with agriculture, not manufacturing, the biggest culprit. Although China has laws that potentially can deal effectively with water pollution, and technology to use water more efficiently is available in China, some administrative structures are not effective and prices do not always send the signal that water is a scarce commodity. The author explains how China intends to address these problems to alleviate its severe water crisis.

Those who work in natural and environmental resource policy are familiar with surveys among the public to obtain values of nonmarket goods or attitudes about proposed new policies that govern such goods. We are also familiar with the shortcomings of such methods. Chapter 15 presents a novel approach for analyzing answers to survey questions, when the respondent can state preferences on a Likert scale. This approach is based on the idea that, although the respondent is asked to make a "one-step" decision, individuals may in fact make two separate decisions. First, they decide to support or oppose a policy, and second, they decide on the strength of their support or opposition. If this were the case, then it is possible that we could find preference asymmetry. Dealing with preference asymmetry requires an approach different from the one traditionally used. The authors apply their method to land-use decisions, which provides an interesting illustration of this new approach.

Finally, Chapter 16 deals with an issue of great importance in many poor countries: the economic role of women. Africa is very rich in mineral deposits. However, for these resources to have a larger impact on everyday lives, they must include a meaningful economic role for women. Currently, most women in the mining sector are not working for mainstream operators. They are therefore less likely to be properly equipped, trained, and knowledgeable of safety issues. They earn less than those working for mainstream companies, and they are more likely to suffer work-related injuries. In today's economy, African families are increasingly relying on women's financial contributions to the household income. Therefore, enhancing women's earnings capacity in the promising mining sector would contribute significantly to the well-being of African households and families.

CHAPTER 13

Linking Trade and the Environment in China

Haixiao Huang

INTRODUCTION

This study simulates the empirical interactions between trade and the environment in China based on a trade and environment model (TEM). The simulation results show that increased trade can lead to increased gross domestic product (GDP), wastewater discharges, levy rates, and foreign direct investment (FDI). An increase in levy rates, a measure of the strictness of environmental policies, may have negative impacts on GDP, industrial wastewater discharges, trade values, and FDI inflows. If levy rates increase at the same rate as trade, wastewater pollution can be reduced and positive GDP growth achieved. However, an increase in levy rates and FDI alone may result in a reduction not only in wastewater pollution but also in GDP levels. Thus, the simulation results suggest that trade is essential to achieving development that balances economic and environmental concerns.

Econometric attempts to model relationships between trade and the environment have been limited, and their results show little evidence that freer trade will bring about significant changes in environmental quality (Antweiler et al. 2001). There is also little evidence that differences in the strictness of environmental policy represent a significant determinant of trade patterns and flows (Huang and Labys 2002; Tobey 1990). The empirical ambiguity is the result of at least two methodological pitfalls:

1. Most studies have tended to analyze cross-country or panel data, typically for a sample of both developing and developed countries. In a cross-country setting, positive and negative effects probably cancel each other out.
2. Most studies use single-equation models. Such models reveal only a one-directional relationship among trade, income, and the environment. However, trade, income, and the environment are interrelated with each other.

The purpose of this study is to develop, estimate, and simulate a simultaneous model of these interactions based on the work of Dean (1999) related to China.

Although interesting efforts have been made to analyze Chinese environmental problem (Dean 1999; Wu 2000), the environmental implications of the surge in foreign trade and investment in China are complex and largely contested, and to the best of our knowledge, they have not been empirically investigated.

TRADE AND THE ENVIRONMENT IN CHINA

Rapid economic growth and expansion is causing environmental problems in China (Fox 1999; World Bank 1997; Wu 2000), particularly increased volumes of wastewater, air pollutants, industrial solid wastes, and toxic hazards. These factors, together with widespread depletion of natural resources, have adversely affected human health, increased natural disasters, dampened gains from trade, and caused social instability and conflicts.

To mitigate the effects, the Chinese government has begun to treat environmental protection as an important national policy, and it has become to be widely accepted that the pace of environmental protection must be commensurate with economic growth in order for China to achieve sustainable development (Qu 1991). China first promulgated and implemented its Environmental Protection Law in 1979 and amended it in 1989. A number of other laws also related to environmental issue also exist, and China has established an extensive pollution charge system. From its inception in the early 1980s to 1996, about 30 billion RMB yuan (USD3.66 billion) have been collected from more than 500,000 major polluters. In 1996 alone, the system collected about 4 billion RMB yuan (USD0.49 billion). Charges are levied for effluents of wastewater, air pollutants, and solid waste discharge. According to the *China Environmental Yearbook* 1997 (NEPA 1998), about 63% of total environmental levies in 1996 were derived from water pollution sources.

Historically, China's trade policy regime was aimed at stimulating export growth to generate foreign exchange without regarding its costs, while its import policy has been hampered with controls to reduce import growth. This approach neglected relationships between trade and the environment. According to Jha et al. (1999), unchecked production from export-oriented rural small and medium-size enterprises led to the deterioration of China's environment. Although not intended by the central government, exporters encountered few domestic environmental controls due to provincial regional protectionism (Jha et al. 1999; Wu 2000).

The impacts of FDI on the environment have been mixed and controversial. In China's case, Jha et al. (1999) note that FDI enterprises have a higher investment share in pollution abatement (2.27%) than their local counterparts (0.94%). Moreover, the former tend to use more efficient technology and equipment. However, because rising costs of pollution abatement in their parent country or other developed countries, some foreign firms have diverted their pollution-intensive production sites to China. In 1991, for example, over 36% of all FDI was in highly polluting industries, such as printing, dyeing, and electroplating (Xia 1995). Research by Xia (1995) confirms that some parts of China may indeed be "pollution havens" for foreign investors.

MODEL SPECIFICATION AND ESTIMATION

Our analysis builds on Dean's (1999) simultaneous equations model that links the environment and economic growth and adds trade and FDI. The proposed model consists of six equations. In equation 13.1, which is similar to Dean's model, total output (Y) is a function of labor input (L), capital input (K), and emissions released to the environment in the course of production. Trade values (T) is modeled as an efficiency component leading to a shift in the production function.

$$Y = A(T)h\,(L, K, E) \tag{13.1}$$

We expect that $h_L > 0$, $h_K > 0$, and $h_E > 0$ (where the subscript refers to the derivative of the function with respect to L, K, and E, respectively). In addition, assume that $dA/dT > 0$: The more an economy is engaged in trade, the higher the total factor productivity.

In equation 13.2, the derived demand for emissions is expressed as a function of the levy rate (r), output (Y), and the share of pollution-intensive goods in output (S), where, $f_r < 0$ and $f_S > 0$ (Dean 1999). f_r, f_Y and f_S are derivatives of function f with respect to r, Y, and S respectively.

$$E = f\,(r, Y, S) \tag{13.2}$$

Assuming an inverted-U relationship exists between per capita emissions and per capita outputs, as reported in studies by Seldon and Song (1994) and Shafik (1994), the relationship between emissions and output is an inverted-U shape as well. We may then expect that $f_Y > 0$, given a position on the left side of the inverted U, and $f_Y < 0$ on the right side of the inverted U.

Equation 13.3 is the inverse supply curve for emissions (E), where we expect $g_E > 0$ and $g_Y > 0$, assuming that clean environment is a normal good and that the community will allow higher levels of emissions only if polluters pay a higher charge.

$$r = g\,(E, Y) \tag{13.3}$$

Following Dean (1999), equation 13.4 represents the share of pollution-intensive goods in total output. Assume that an increase in output raises income and that clean goods are relatively income elastic. Then S will decrease as Y increases and, therefore, $Z_Y < 0$.

$$S = Z(T, Y) \tag{13.4}$$

For economies that possess a comparative advantage in pollution intensive goods, an increase in trade will lead to a rise in S and hence $Z_T > 0$; while for economies with a comparative advantage in relative clean goods, one expects $Z_T < 0$.

In equation 13.5, trade flows (T) reflect output (Y), FDI, geographic remoteness (R), and a trade policy indicator (t), where $W_Y > 0$, $W_{FDI} > 0$, $W_R < 0$, and $W_t > 0$ if a trade policy is designed to promote trade; Otherwise, $W_t < 0$.

$$T = W(Y, FDI, R, t) \tag{13.5}$$

The FDI determinants considered in equation 13.6 include output (Y), cumulative FDI inflows of the previous year (FDI_{-1}), wage rates (w), infrastructure quality indicators (I), policy indicators (P), and levy rates (r). As shown in equation 13.10, the purpose of separating levy rates from other economic and policy variables is to test whether stricter environmental policies affect FDI inflows.

$$FDI = V(Y, CFDI_{-1}, w, I, P, r) \tag{13.6}$$

Typically, one expects $V_Y > 0$, $V_{FDI\text{-}1} > 0$, $V_I > 0$, $V_P > 0$, $V_r < 0$, while the value of V_w could be positive, zero, or negative

The empirical framework reflects the lack of long environmental and economic time series for China as a whole. Therefore, more attention is paid to model disaggregation to Chinese provinces. The empirical model employs provincial-level panel data, which expand the sample size and improve the efficiency of estimates and permit us to better deal with the effects of missing or unobserved variables (Hsiao 1986).We use two-stage least square regression (2SLS) estimation with the linearized reduced form and employ the White heteroskedasticity consistent covariance matrix estimator to assure a normal error structure. An application of this method and its results, including model validation, appears in Huang and Labys (2004).

DATA AND VARIABLES

Most provincial emissions data are from a province-level panel database constructed by the World Bank. This data set is limited to the industrial sector for the period 1987 to 1995. Other provincial social and economic data are from various *China Statistical Yearbooks* (1987–1999) and from provincial statistical yearbooks (1987–1999). Data sources and variable definitions are reported in Table 13.1, which contains the names, sources, and definitions of the variables, and the values of the variable parameters.

All nominal variables are measured either in 1990 constant RMB yuan or in 1990 constant U.S. dollars. Nominal variables measured in RMB yuan were converted either using Chinese GDP price indexes, price indexes for investment in fixed assets, or general consumer price indexes (obtained from various *China Statistical Yearbooks*), while variables in U.S. dollars were transformed using implicit price deflators for US GDP published in the *Survey of Current Business* (Park 2000).

The data cover 28 of 34 provinces regardless of the levels of their development. Tibet and Hainan are not included because of insufficient data. Chongqing was part of Sichuan before 1997. Taiwan, Hong Kong, and Macao are also excluded. These three regions, however, are among China's major trading partners and FDI sources.

Industrial GDPs include all the values created by the industrial and construction sectors that consist of enterprises of different types of ownerships, such as private, collective owned, and state owned. and various industries, such as textile,

TABLE 13.1 Variable Definitions, Coefficient Assumptions, and Data Sources

Variable Name	Definition	Coefficient Assumption	Source
Endogenous Variable			
Y_{it}	GDP, in 100 million RMB yuan at 1990 constant prices	$b_2>0$, $c_2>0$, $d_2<0$, $e_1>0$, $f_1>0$	Various issues of *China Statistical Yearbook*
E_{it}	Industrial wastewater discharges, in million tons	$a_4>0$, $c_1>0$	China's provincial environmental data set compiled by the World Bank, various issues of *China Environmental Year Book*
R_{it}	The levy rate, at 1990 constant prices, computed as total levy collected on industrial wastewater discharge divided by total amount of wastewater discharge, in cents per ton	$b_1<0$, $f_2<0$	China's provincial environmental data set compiled by the World Bank, various issues of *China Environmental Yearbook*
S_{it}	Share of industrial GDP in total GDP, %	$b_4>0$	*China Statistical Yearbooks*
T_{it}	Total trade flows (exports plus imports), in 10,000 US$ at 1990 constant prices	$a_1>0$, $d_1<>0$	*China Statistical Yearbooks*
FDI_{it}	Foreign direct investment inflows, in 10,000 USD at 1990 constant prices	$e_2>0$	*China Statistical Yearbooks*
Exogenous Variables			
L_{it}	Number of total employed persons, in 10,000	$a_2>0$	*China Statistical Yearbooks*
K_{it}	Cumulative total investment in fixed assets, in 100 million RMB yuan at 1990 constant prices	$a_3>0$	*China Statistical Yearbooks*
SOE_{it}	Share of state-owned firms in industrial GDP, %	$b_5>0$	*China Statistical Yearbooks*
N_{it}	Population, in 10,000	$c_2'>0$	*China Statistical Yearbooks*
C_{it}	Number of pollution complaints per million population	$c_3<>0$	China's provincial environmental data set compiled by the World Bank, various issues of *China Environmental Yearbook*
ED_{it}	Illiteracy and semi-illiteracy rate, %	$c_4<0$	*China Statistical Yearbooks*
PD_{it}	Population density, in number of inhabitants per km^2	$c_5<>0$	*China Statistical Yearbooks*
V_{it}	Investment in fixed assets, in 100 million RMB yuan at 1990 constant prices	$d_4<>0$.	*China Statistical Yearbooks*

(*Continued*)

TABLE 13.1 (*Continued*)

Variable Name	Definition	Coefficient Assumption	Source
R_{it}	Remoteness, computed as the nearest distance between a province's capital and the capitals of China's 15 biggest trading partners, in kilometers	$e_3<0$.	Author's calculation
ER_t	Exchange rate, in RMB yuan per 100 USD	$e_4<>0$	*China Statistical Yearbooks*
TN_t	National total tariff revenues divided by national total imports, %	$e_5<0$.	*China Statistical Yearbooks*
TP_i	1996 provincial ad valorem tariff rates, %.	$e_5<0$	World Bank (1997)
$CFDI_{I(t-1)}$	Lagged cumulative FDI inflows, in 10,000 USD at 1990 constant prices	$f_3>0$	*China Statistical Yearbooks*
TI_{it}	Highway intensity, kilometers per 100 square kilometers	$f_4>0$	*China Statistical Yearbooks*
TAX_{it}	Overall tax rate, tax revenue divided by GDP, %	$f_5<0$	*China Statistical Yearbooks*
$PGDP_{i(t-1)}$	Lagged per capita GDP, in RMB yuan per capita	$f_6>0$	*China Statistical Yearbooks*
D_i	Regional geographic and policy dummy variable, 1 for coastal provinces and Beijing; 0 for other provinces	$d_5<>0$, $e_6>0$, $f_7>0$	
DT_t	Time dummy variable, 1 for 1989, 1990, and 1991; 0 for other years	$e_7<0$, $f_8<0$	

machinery, mining, chemical, electricity, construction material, and fertilizer. The capital variable K_{it} is measured by proxy as cumulative total investment in fixed assets since 1986 with no depreciations. The labor variable L_{it} is measured as the number of total employed persons; their working skills are not accounted for due to the lack of data.

Several environmental variables require some explanation. Since 1993, the levy data available are total levies collected on excess industrial wastewater discharges; the levy rate is approximated as the total levy on wastewater divided by the total discharge of the pollutant. Although this is a rough measure as a price indicator for environmental demand and supply, it does reflect the differentials in strictness of environmental enforcement across provinces. Another variable, national level tariff, is calculated as the national total tariff revenues divided by national total imports. Our calculated tariffs are much lower than those reported by other sources, such as the World Bank (1999). Nevertheless, they are used in this analysis because they capture the decreasing trend of the variable during the study period, and there is no available single source that releases China's tariff data.

MODEL SIMULATION

The simulation of the theoretical model is based on specification adjustments to deal with the panel data set and consists of the equations 13.7 to 13.12 (see Huang and Labys 2004 for more detailed information of model estimation):

$$\log Y_{it} = -1.238 + 0.157 \log T_{it} + 0.345 \log L_{it} + 0.357 K_{it} + 0.137 \log Eit + u_{1it} \quad (13.7)$$

$$\log E_{it} = -5.327 - 0.509 \log r_{it} + 2.406 \log Y_{it} - 0.103 (\log Y_{it})^2 - 0.108 S_{it} + 0.430 \log SOE_{it} + u_{2it} \quad (13.8)$$

$$\log r_{it} = 4.443 - 0.055 \log E_{it} + 0.264 \log IN_{it} - 0.163 \log C_{it} - 0.362 \log ed_{it} + 0.119 \log PD_{it} + u_{3it} \quad (13.9)$$

$$\log S_{it} = 0.223 + 0.006 \log T_{it} - 0.011 \log Y_{it} + 0.915 \log S_{i(t-1)} + 0.023 \log V_{it} - 0.010 \log D_{it} + u_{4it} \quad (13.10)$$

$$\log T_{it} = 10.610 + 0.715 \log Y_{it} + 0.127 \log FDI_{it} - 0.478 \log R_{it} - 0.198 \log ER_{1t} - 0.035 (\log TN_t)(\log TP_i) + 0.542 D_i + 0.033 DT_t + u_{5it} \quad (13.11)$$

$$\log FDI_{it} = -2.212 + 1.010 \log Y_{it} + 0.252 \log r_{it} + 0.358 CFDI_{t(t-1)} + 0.648 \log TI_{it} - 0.197 \log TAX_{it} + 0.389 \log PGDP_{i(t-1)} + 0.395 D_i - 0.827 DT_t + u_{6it} \quad (13.12)$$

To analyze the linkages among trade, environment, and FDI, we examine 10 possible scenarios, as shown in Table 13.2. Deterministic and stochastic simulations are run based on scenarios that involve initial changes in the included endogenous variables. To investigate the effect of these changes on other endogenous variables, the model is solved by excluding the endogenous variables that initiate a change for the entire solution sample. To evaluate the net effect of each scenario, the results of a scenario obtained are compared with its corresponding deterministic or stochastic baseline solutions, based on the percentage changes of the mean average of an endogenous variable relative to that of its baseline solution. In a deterministic simulation, this represents an average of 252 simulated values. In a stochastic simulation, it is the mean of 252,000 simulated values for each of the scenarios analyzed.

The computational algorithm is based on an iterative Gauss-Seidel method embedded in EViews 4, employing a dynamic solution with a convergence criterion of 0.00001. Values for endogenous variables of the model are computed for each observation in the solution sample. Since the solution sample is set to cover 28 provinces and nine periods, each endogenous variable has 252 simulated values.

For deterministic simulations, all equations in the model are solved so that they hold without error during the simulation period, and all coefficients are fixed at their point estimates. That is, the equations of the model are solved so that each of the equations is exactly satisfied. This results in a single path for the endogenous variables that can be evaluated by solving the model once. Although the application of deterministic simulation procedures to econometric models that contain

TABLE 13.2 List of Simulation Scenarios

Scenario	Increase in Endogenous Variables		
	Trade	FDI	Levy Rate
Scenario 1	10%		
Scenario 2	20%		
Scenario 3		10%	
Scenario 4		20%	
Scenario 5			10%
Scenario 6			20%
Scenario 7	10%		10%
Scenario 8	20%		20%
Scenario 9		10%	10%
Scenario 10		20%	20%

nonlinearities in the endogenous variables can generate solution values different from the corresponding historical values even if the econometric model is properly specified, the differences between the simulated and the actual values are systematic and consistent in nature (Howrey and Kelejian 1971).

The purpose of the stochastic error solutions is to assess the interactions between the trade and environmental variables subject to uncertainty. For stochastic simulations, the model is solved for a set of randomly drawn residuals and/or coefficients. That is, the model is solved so that the fitted residuals match randomly drawn errors and/or the coefficients of the model are varied randomly. For each variable and observation of a stochastic simulation, a set of independent random numbers is drawn from the standard normal distribution, then these numbers are scaled to match the estimated variance-covariance matrix of the system calculated from the model equation residuals. Simulation of the model generates a distribution of outcomes for the endogenous variables in every period. This distribution is approximated by repeatedly solving the model using different draws for the random components in the model and then calculating statistics, such as means and standard deviations, over different outcomes. In each repetition, as for the deterministic simulation, each endogenous variable has 252 simulated values.

Therefore, although a stochastic simulation follows a procedure similar to that of the deterministic one, several variations are obtained. First, when binding the variables, a temporary series is created for every endogenous variable in the model. Additional series in the work file are used to hold the statistics for the tracked endogenous variables. Second, the model is solved repeatedly. If coefficient uncertainty is included in a simulation, then a new set of coefficients is drawn before each repetition. During the repetition, errors are generated for each observation in accordance with the residual uncertainty. At the end of each repetition, the statistics for the tracked endogenous variables are updated to reflect the additional results.

RESULTS AND DISCUSSIONS

The means and deviations of the baseline solutions are summarized in Table 13.3.

The impacts of the introduction of error shocks and coefficient shocks on the deterministic baseline solutions are presented in Table 13.4. As Howrey and Kelejian

TABLE 13.3 Means and Deviations of Baseline Solutions in Industrial Wastewater Pollution (IWW) Case

Baseline	Means and Deviations (in parentheses)					
	GDP (13.1)*	IWW (13.2)*	Levy Rate (13.3)*	Industrial Share (13.4)*	Trade (13.5)*	FDI (13.6)*
Actual sample mean (deviation)	809.23	853.99	4.12	43.35	436587.4	61879.1
	(624.44)	(596.28)	(1.73)	(8.81)	(111977.7)	(297739.7)
Trade det. solution	809.09	796.69	3.91	43.33	436587.4	44934.5
Excluding trade with error shocks only	815.62	896.71	4.16	43.36	436587.4	89028.4
	(108.31)	(469.22)	(1.50)	(1.57)	(0.0)	(149588.7)
Excluding trade with error and coef. shocks	816.65	899.99	4.16	43.37	436587.4	90458.3
	(111.02)	(478.57)	(1.54)	(1.58)	(0.0)	(158860.0)
FDI det. solution	807.31	800.49	3.90	43.32	316719.0	61879.1
Excluding FDI with error shocks only	818.20	902.99	4.15	43.35	362892.1	61879.1
	(139.46)	(475.44)	(1.51)	(1.55)	(202833.8)	(0.0)
Excluding FDI with error and coef. shocks	819.48	908.79	4.16	43.35	366493.5	61879.1
	(143.29)	(492.60)	(1.54)	(1.58)	(212256.0)	(0.0)
Levy rate det. solution	806.49	809.75	4.11	43.32	312118.3	43031.7
Excluding levy rates with error shocks only	818.46	902.00	4.11	43.35	358904.5	87797.9
	(146.09)	(451.86)	(0.00)	(1.55)	(204440.2)	(167416.6)
Excluding levy rates with error and coef. shocks	818.83	907.37	4.11	43.35	361261.3	88650.6
	(149.72)	(464.63)	(0.00)	(1.58)	(213816.1)	(148457.5)

(*Continued*)

TABLE 13.3 *(Continued)*

	Means and Deviations (in parentheses)					
Baseline	GDP (13.1)*	IWW (13.2)*	Levy Rate (13.3)*	Industrial Share (13.4)*	Trade (13.5)*	FDI (13.6)*
Levy rate and trade det. solution	807.56	803.35	4.11	43.33	436587.4	45463.3
Excluding levy rates and trade	815.24	892.94	4.11	43.36	436587.4	86805.7
with error shocks only	(113.24)	(433.73)	(0.00)	(1.56)	(0.0)	(137525.1)
Excluding levy rates and trade	816.02	897.03	4.11	43.37	436587.4	90267.8
with error and coef. shocks	(115.74)	(443.39)	(0.00)	(1.58)	(0.0)	(156330.0)
Levy rate & FDI det. solution	805.79	809.69	4.11	43.32	315500.3	61879.1
Excluding levy rates and FDI	817.81	905.39	4.11	43.35	361563.0	61879.1
with error shocks only	(146.39)	(457.67)	(0.00)	(1.55)	(205943.2)	(0.0)
Excluding levy rates and FDI	818.99	906.36	4.11	43.36	365519.4	61879.1
with error and coef. shocks	(149.63)	(463.63)	(0.00)	(1.58)	(213555.2)	(0.0)

*Refers to numbered equation in chapter.

(1971) suggest, the deterministic simulation of a model with nonlinear endogenous variables may provide results that systematically diverge from actual observations. The stochastic baseline results also show such a systematic deviation from actuals (Table 13.3) and from those of the deterministic baselines (Table 13.4).

The stochastic solutions have greater average means and smaller average deviations. Why there exists such a systematic difference between the stochastic and

TABLE 13.4 Deterministic Baseline Solution (DBS) versus Stochastic Baseline Solution (SBS) in Industrial Wastewater Pollution (IWW) Case

	Changes in Endogenous Variables Compared with DBS (%)					
Stochastic Baseline	GDP (13.1)*	IWW (13.2)*	Levy Rate (13.3)*	Industrial Share (13.4)*	Trade (13.5)*	FDI (13.6)*
1. Excluding trade with error shocks only	0.81	12.55	6.34	0.07	0.00	98.13
2. Excluding trade with error and coef. shocks	0.82	12.86	6.40	0.07	0.00	99.82
3. Excluding FDI with error shocks only	1.35	12.80	6.32	0.06	14.58	0.00
4. Excluding FDI with error and coef. shocks	1.51	13.53	6.62	0.05	15.72	0.00
5. Excluding levy rates with error shocks only	1.48	11.39	0.00	0.07	14.99	104.03
6. Excluding levy rates with error and coef. shocks	1.53	12.06	0.00	0.07	15.74	106.01
7. Excluding levy rates and trade with error shocks only	0.95	11.15	0.00	0.06	0.00	90.94
8. Excluding levy rates and trade with error and coef. shocks	1.05	11.66	0.00	0.08	0.00	98.55
9. Excluding levy rates and FDI with error shocks only	1.49	11.82	0.00	0.07	14.60	0.00
10. Excluding levy rates and FDI with error and coef. shocks	1.64	11.94	0.00	0.08	15.85	0.00

*Refers to numbered equation in chapter.

the deterministic solutions requires further examination. Given the nature of error shocks as a combined effect of all missing variables in our system, this combined effect on each of the endogenous variables in the model is positive. Similar to the deterministic simulation case, such systematic differences should not affect the comparisons between the stochastic simulated results of different scenarios and those of the corresponding stochastic baseline solutions.

Results of the deterministic, the stochastic error, and the stochastic error and coefficient solutions are reported in Tables 13.5, 13.6, and 13.7, respectively. These tables report changes in average means of the endogenous variables compared with their corresponding baseline solutions.

In contrast to the deterministic solutions in Table 13.5, the stochastic simulation results (Tables 13.6 and 13.7) are very close to the deterministic ones, except for the results of the FDI variables. A significant difference between the stochastic and the deterministic solution for the FDI variable is not surprising, given that FDI is the most

TABLE 13.5 Deterministic Simulation Results in Industrial Wastewater (IWW) Pollution Case

	Changes in Endogenous Variables (%)					
Scenario	GDP (13.1)*	IWW (13.2)*	Levy Rate (13.3)*	Industrial Share (13.4)*	Trade (13.5)*	FDI (13.6)*
1. 10% increase in trade values	1.71	1.53	0.36	0.04	10.00	1.79
2. 20% increase in trade values	3.30	2.93	0.69	0.07	20.00	3.46
3. 10% increase in FDI inflows	0.25	0.22	0.05	0.01	1.40	10.00
4. 20% increase in FDI inflows	0.47	0.42	0.10	0.01	2.69	20.00
5. 10% increase in levy rates	−0.84	−5.54	10.00	0.01	−0.40	1.58
6. 20% increase in levy rates	−1.60	−10.32	20.00	0.01	−0.76	3.04
7. 10% increase in levy rates and in trade values	0.96	−3.81	10.00	0.04	10.00	3.41
8. 20% increase in levy rates and in trade values	1.85	−7.17	20.00	0.08	20.00	6.62
9. 10% increase in levy rates and in FDI inflows	−0.63	−5.34	10.00	0.01	0.77	10.00
10. 20% increase in levy rates and in FDI inflows	−1.20	−9.96	20.00	0.02	1.47	20.00

*Refers to numbered equation in chapter.

TABLE 13.6 Stochastic Error Simulation Results in Industrial Wastewater (IWW) Pollution Case

	Changes in Endogenous Variables (%)					
Scenario	GDP (13.1)*	IWW (13.2)*	Levy Rate (13.3)*	Industrial Share (13.4)*	Trade (13.5)*	FDI (13.6)*
1. 10% increase in trade values	1.74	1.54	0.41	0.02	10.00	1.42
2. 20% increase in trade values	3.40	3.28	0.80	0.05	20.00	4.36
3. 10% increase in FDI inflows	0.28	0.27	0.11	0.01	1.26	10.00
4. 20% increase in FDI inflows	0.39	0.08	0.08	0.01	2.13	20.00
5. 10% increase in levy rates	−0.82	−5.42	10.00	−0.01	−0.50	−3.73
6. 20% increase in levy rates	−1.55	−9.77	20.00	0.02	−1.21	−3.99
7. 10% increase in levy rates and in trade values	0.91	−3.94	10.00	0.06	10.00	5.32
8. 20% increase in levy rates and in trade values	1.77	−7.54	20.00	0.08	20.00	8.13
9. 10% increase in levy rates and in FDI inflows	−0.58	−5.67	10.00	0.00	1.36	10.00
10. 20% increase in levy rates and in FDI inflows	−1.11	−9.80	20.00	0.02	2.01	20.00

*Refers to numbered equation in chapter.

unpredictable and uncertain endogenous variable in our system, as indicated by the summary statistics of the variables (Huang 2002). In addition, a comparison between Tables 13.6 and 13.7 shows that random draws of the values of coefficients do not generate obvious deviations in outcomes for most endogenous variables, suggesting that the TEM model is reasonably insensitive to coefficient perturbations. That is, the model is relatively robust to changes in the estimated values of the coefficients. Therefore, the averaged outcomes of the three types of simulations (Table 13.8) can be used in the discussion that follows.

IMPACTS OF AN INCREASE IN TRADE VALUES

The averaged simulation results reported in Table 13.8 show that a 10% (20%) increase in trade values might lead to a 1.73% (3.36%) increase in GDP, 1.56%

TABLE 13.7 Stochastic Error Coefficient Simulation Results in Industrial Wastewater (IWW) Pollution Case

	Changes in Endogenous Variables (%)					
Scenario	GDP (13.1)*	IWW (13.2)*	Levy Rate (13.3)*	Industrial Share (13.4)*	Trade (13.5)*	FDI (13.6)*
1. 10% increase in trade values	1.75	1.60	0.58	0.04	10.00	2.64
2. 20% increase in trade values	3.38	2.72	0.77	0.08	20.00	5.56
3. 10% increase in FDI inflows	0.16	0.09	0.00	0.03	1.51	10.00
4. 20% increase in FDI inflows	0.37	0.23	−0.09	0.03	2.40	20.00
5. 10% increase in levy rates	−0.71	−5.60	10.00	0.00	0.22	1.76
6. 20% increase in levy rates	−1.57	−10.46	20.00	0.01	−0.08	2.99
7. 10% increase in levy rates and in trade values	0.80	−4.22	10.00	0.04	10.00	2.84
8. 20% increase in levy rates and in trade values	1.64	−7.94	20.00	0.07	20.00	5.50
9. 10% increase in levy rates and in FDI inflows	−0.60	−5.29	10.00	0.01	1.02	10.00
10. 20% increase in levy rates and in FDI inflows	−1.24	−10.01	20.00	0.02	1.75	20.00

*Refers to numbered equation in chapter.

(2.98%) increase in wastewater discharges, 0.45% (0.75%) increase in levy rates, 0.03% (0.07%) in industrial shares in GDP, and 1.95% (4.46%) in FDI. The results regarding the impact on GDP are close to the findings of an econometric study by Liang (2000), which indicates that an increase of 10% in China's exports would increase its GDP by 1.43% on average.

Since our results suggest that trade would lead to more discharges of wastewater, can it be inferred that China has a comparative advantage in pollution-intensive goods? Careful examination of the results shows that the increase in wastewater discharges is smaller than the increase in GDP. Although trade generates a considerable increase in GDP, it produces a relatively smaller increase in industrial wastewater. In addition, the industrial share in GDP, a measure of output composition, remains almost unchanged, suggesting that trade does not significantly change the composition of output and hence generates little additional emissions through a composition effect. Therefore, the results provide no evident support for the hypothesis that China has a comparative advantage in pollution-intensive goods.

TABLE 13.8 Averaged Simulation Results in Industrial Wastewater (IWW) Pollution Case

Scenario	Changes in Endogenous Variables (%)					
	GDP (13.1)*	IWW (13.2)*	Levy Rate (13.3)*	Industrial Share (13.4)*	Trade (13.5)*	FDI (13.6)*
1. 10% increase in trade values	1.73	1.56	0.45	0.03	10.00	1.95
2. 20% increase in trade values	3.36	2.98	0.75	0.07	20.00	4.46
3. 10% increase in FDI inflows	0.23	0.19	0.05	0.02	1.39	10.00
4. 20% increase in FDI inflows	0.41	0.24	0.03	0.02	2.41	20.00
5. 10% increase in levy rates	−0.79	−5.52	10.00	0.00	−0.23	−0.13
6. 20% increase in levy rates	−1.57	−10.18	20.00	0.01	−0.68	0.68
7. 10% increase in levy rates and in trade values	0.89	−3.99	10.00	0.05	10.00	3.86
8. 20% increase in levy rates and in trade values	1.75	−7.55	20.00	0.08	20.00	6.75
9. 10% increase in levy rates and in FDI inflows	−0.60	−5.43	10.00	0.01	1.05	10.00
10. 20% increase in levy rates and in FDI inflows	−1.18	−9.92	20.00	0.02	1.74	20.00

*Refers to numbered equation in chapter.

Impacts of an Increase in FDI Inflows

The simulation results show that an increase in FDI inflows by 10% (20%) expands GDP and trade by 0.23% (0.41%) and 1.39% (2.41%), respectively, suggesting that FDI inflows in China are more likely to be export oriented and trade promoting. The results also indicate that increases in FDI of this magnitude can lead to a 0.19% (0.24%) increase in industrial wastewater discharges, 0.05% (0.03%) increase in levy rates, and 0.02% (0.02%) in the industrial share in GDP. Since the increase in wastewater discharge arising from FDI inflows is smaller than that in GDP and the impact of FDI on the industrial share is almost negligible, we cannot conclude whether FDI flows into China are pollution intensive or not.

Impacts of an Increase in Levy Rates

Increasing levy rates by 10% (20%) would decrease industrial wastewater discharges by 5.52% (10.18%), suggesting that China's emissions charge system is an effective means of industrial wastewater control. However, higher levy rates have a negative impact on the economy. Table 13.8 shows that GDP and trade would decrease by 0.79% (1.57%) and 0.23% (0.68%), respectively. The simulation results concerning the impact of levy rates on FDI inflows are inconsistent. When levy rates increase by 10%, FDI inflows decrease by 0.13%, but an increase in FDI by 20% may lead to a 0.68 % increase in FDI. This inconsistent result is probably due to the unpredictability and volatility of the FDI variable. The results cannot confirm that an increase in levy rates will have negative impact on FDI inflows. The results show that increases in levy rates have virtually no impact on the industrial share in GDP composition.

Impacts of a Simultaneous Increase in Trade and Levy Rates

While increasing GDP and FDI inflows by 0.89% (1.75%) and 3.86% (6.75%), respectively, a simultaneous increase in levy rates and trade by 10% (20%) could decrease industrial wastewater discharges by 3.99% (7.55%), although the industrial share in GDP could increase by 0.05% (0.08%). That is, if levy rates increase at the same rate as trade, positive GDP growth is possible even when wastewater pollution is reduced. This suggests that to achieve sustainable development, accompanying trade expansion with appropriate environmental policies is the key.

Impacts of a Simultaneous Increase in FDI and Levy Rates

The impacts of a simultaneous increase in levy rates and FDI inflows by 10% (20%) are a GDP decrease of 0.60% (1.18%), an industrial wastewater discharges decrease of 5.43% (9.92%), a trade values increase of 1.05% (1.74%), and an industrial share in GDP increase of 0.01% (0.02%). The increase in levy rates and FDI together reduce not only wastewater pollution but also GDP levels because the positive effect of FDI is overcompensated by the negative effect of levy rates on GDP. Since increasing trade and levy rates together can reduce wastewater discharges and increase GDP simultaneously, trade is essential to achieve coordinated development between the economy and the environment.

CONCLUSIONS

The examination of empirical interactions between trade and the environment requires going beyond econometric interpretation and employing simulation methods for assessing the impacts and simultaneous relationships between major variables. The simulation results show that increased trade can lead to increased GDP, wastewater discharges, levy rates, and FDI inflows. An increase in levy rates, which is a measure of the strictness of environmental policies, may have negative impacts on GDP, industrial wastewater discharges, trade values, and FDI inflows. If levy rates increase at the same rate as trade expands, however, wastewater pollution can be reduced and positive GDP growth achieved. Increasing levy rates and FDI together when trade is not growing can lead to simultaneous reduction in wastewater pollution and GDP levels. In other words, trade is an essential part of a policy aimed at achieving a balance between economic development and an improving environment.

From the modeling perspective, the results indicate that the nonlinear simultaneous equations model and its 2SLS estimation results are relatively robust. Specifically, the deterministic simulation results are consistent with and very close to those derived from comparative static analysis. In addition, the stochastic simulation results indicate that the TEM model is relatively stable vis-à-vis error structure shocks and that the impacts of uncertainty on model performance are generally insignificant. Moreover, the stochastic error and coefficient simulation demonstrates that the TEM model is also relatively robust to changes in the estimated values of the coefficients.

Concerning future research with this type of model, we suggest four points.

1. There is a need for more case-specific empirical studies on trade and environmental issues.
2. Both more theoretical and more empirical studies are required to investigate the impact of environmental degradation on trade and economic growth, that is, on sustainable development. There is a sizable literature on how trade can affect the environment, and there is also a sizable literature on how environmental policies affect international trade. However, our knowledge of the trade and economic consequences of environmental degradation is limited.
3. We could gain insights from studies using industry-level data such as those employed in input-output models and computable general equilibrium models.
4. Theoretical and empirical research is needed that incorporates spatial elements into the investigation of trade and environmental issues. Trade and environmental research often include references to space or location, but in most cases, they are not part of the analysis, mostly because data do not exist. The quality and nature of the modeling effort is always constrained by the available data, or by the time and monetary budget to obtain them.

REFERENCES

Antweiler, W., B.R. Copeland, and M.S. Taylor (2001). "Is Free Trade Good for the Environment?" *American Economic Review* 91.4: 877–908.

Dean, J.M. (1999). "Testing the Impact of Trade Liberalization on the Environment: Theory and Evidence." In P.G. Fredriksson, ed., *Trade, Globe Policy, and the Environment*, World Bank Discussion Paper 402. Washington, DC: World Bank.

Eviews 4.0 User's Guide 1994–2000. Irvine, CA: Quantitative Micro Software.

Fox, M. (1999). "Chinese Cities' Bad Air Imperils Children—Study." Reuters new release, January 2.

Howrey, E.P., and H.H. Kelejian. (1971). "Simulation versus Analytical Solutions: The Case of Econometric Models." In T.H. Naylor, ed., *Computer Simulation Experiments with Models of Economic Systems:* 299–319. New York: John Wiley & Sons.

Hsiao, C. (1986). *Analysis of Panel Data*. New York: Cambridge University Press.

Huang, H. (2002). *Modeling Trade and Environmental Interactions*. Ph.D. Dissertation, West Virginia University, Morgantown.

Huang, H. and W.C. Labys. (2002). "Environment and Trade: A Review of Issues and Methods." *International Journal of Global Environmental Issues* 2.1 and 2: 100–160.

Huang, H., and W.C. Labys. (2004). "Modeling Trade and Environmental Linkages in China," *International Journal of Global Environmental Issues* 4.4: 242–266.

Jha, V., A. Markandya, and R. Vossenaar. (1999). *Reconciling Trade and the Environment.* Northampton, MA: Edward Elgar Publishing.

Liang, Y. (2000). "China's Econometric Model for Project Pair." In L.R. Klein and S. Ichimura, eds., *Econometric Modeling of China*, chap. 4. River Edge, NJ: World Scientific Publishing Co.

NEPA. (1992). *Pollution Charges in China.* Beijing: National Environmental Protection Agency.

———. (1994). *The Pollution Levy System*, Beijing: China Environmental Science Press.

———. (1997). *1996 Report on the Environment in China*, Beijing: National Environmental Protection Agency.

———. (1998). *China Environmental Yearbook 1997.* Beijing: China Environmental Yearbook Press.

Park, T.S. (2000). "Comparison of BEA Estimates of Personal Income and IRS Estimates of Adjusted Gross Income," *Survey of Current Business* 80.2: 12–22.

Qu, G. (1991). *Environmental Management in China.* Beijing: UNEP and China Environmental Science Press.

Seldon, T.M., and D. Song. (1994). "Environmental Quality and Development: Is There a Kuznets Curve for Air Pollution Emissions?" *Journal of Environmental Economics and Management* 27: 147–162.

Shafik, N. (1994). "Economic Development and Environmental Quality: An Econometric Analysis," *Oxford Economic Papers* 46: 757–773.

Tobey, J. (1990). "The Effects of Domestic Environmental Policies on Patterns of World Trade: An Empirical Test," *Kyklos* 43.2: 191–209.

World Bank. (1997). *Clear Water, Blue Skies: China's Environment in the New Century.* Washington, DC: World Bank.

———. (1999). *World Development Indicators.* Washington, DC: World Bank.

Wu, C.H. (2000). "Trade and Sustainability: A China Perspective." Working Paper, World Resource Institute.

Xia, Y. (1995). "Study on China's Control Measures to the Transfer of Foreign Wastes and Pollution Intensive Industries through Trade and Investment." Paper prepared for the Working Group on Trade and Environment, Winnipeg, Canada.

CHAPTER 14

Critical Needs in China's Water Resources

Andres Liebenthal

INTRODUCTION

China is facing a severe water crisis. For years, water shortages and pollution have constrained the sustainability of growth, affected public health, and caused extensive damage to the ecology. Ineffective water resource management and pollution-control institutions and excessive reliance on administrative approaches appear to have been the leading causes. To address the growing water scarcity, China needs to accelerate its move toward increased reliance on market-based approaches, supported by the twin pillars of integrated river basin management and rigorous pollution management.

This chapter reviews the underlying causes of China's emerging water crisis and identifies key elements of a comprehensive strategy for resolving it. The first section discusses the commingling of water shortages and extensive pollution that have created a growing water scarcity crisis. The second section highlights the many technically viable and economically feasible water-saving and cleanup options available to address water scarcity and outlines the potential for the market to accelerate their implementation. The next section discusses the rebalancing of the institutional framework around the integrated river basin management approach needed to support the establishment of a functioning water market. Then we identify key areas of the pollution management system that deserve more attention, including nonpoint source (NPS) pollution, the implementation of payments for environmental services, and the unification of the pollution control planning, monitoring and evaluation framework. This chapter is synthetic in nature and discusses key aspects of an integrated strategy that deserve special attention. More detail on specific issues, as well as the underlying analysis, is available in the referenced reports.

CHINA FACES A SEVERE WATER CRISIS

China's total annual renewable water resources amount to about 2,841 billion cubic meter (m^3), the sixth largest in the world. However, annual per-capita availability was only 2,152 mm^3/person, about one-quarter of the world average and among the lowest for a major developing country. Total consumption withdrawals were 554.8 billion mm^3 in 2004, of which 81.2% were from surface water, 18.5% from groundwater, and 0.3% from other sources. The countrywide exploitation rate of 20% is not alarming compared to the internationally recommended maximum of 40% needed to sustain ecosystems, but the maximum is far exceeded in many regions (Li 2005).

Water is scarce in North China, which accounts for 46% of the population, 44% of gross domestic product (GDP), and more than 60% of farmland but has less than 20% of the national water resources, and where the per-capita availability (about 700 m^3/person[1]) is only one-third of the national average. The scarcity is particularly severe in the Yellow, Huai, and Hai river basins, where exploitation rates reach 67%, 59%, and 90%, respectively, far exceeding the sustainable yield. This overexploitation has resulted in the drying up of lakes and wetlands, the degradation of the dilution and self-purification capacity of the rivers, and the deterioration of riverine and coastal ecosystems. Another impact is the depletion of groundwater, which results in the lowering of water tables and eventual exhaustion of groundwater reservoirs as well as extensive subsidence in many cities in North China. By contrast, the South is relatively water abundant.

The scarcity is aggravated by extensive pollution. In 2004, more than 75% of all rivers and lakes were polluted and 90% of rivers around urban areas were seriously polluted. Of the seven major rivers, 42% of the monitored sections met the Grade I–III surface water quality standard (i.e., water that can be made safe for human consumption after treatment), 30% met Grade IV–V standards (safe for industrial and irrigation use), and 28% failed to meet Grade V and are unsafe for any use (Grade V*). The most polluted rivers are found in North China, where the bulk of river flows consists of wastewater and pollution has worsened over the past few years. Pollution has declined in the South (World Bank 2006a). Figure 14.1 provides a map that shows the geographic distribution of surface water quality in 2000 and 2004.

The most important source of pollution is discharges of municipal wastewater, of about 28.1 billion tons in 2005, which accounted for 52% of organic pollutants (BOD), 69% of nitrogen (TN), and 2% of phosphorus (TP) discharges. Industrial wastewater discharges, of 24.3 billion tons, mostly met discharge standards, and contributed only 11% of BOD, 4% of TN, and 2% of TP. Nonpoint sources of pollution (NPS), primarily related to agricultural activities, including fertilizer and pesticide run-off from farmland and infiltration of livestock waste, also accounted for a major share: 37% of BOD, 27% of TN, and 45% of TP (World Bank 2006a).

The extent of pollution imposes substantial costs on the economy. The most important costs relate to the health risks faced by the two-thirds of the rural population (about 300 to 500 million) who do not have access to piped water and rely on untreated and often polluted surface and groundwater supplies for domestic use. The lack of access to piped water has been associated with a 26% increase in diarrheal disease in children under five years of age (Figure 14.2). In addition, water pollution has also been associated with an increased incidence of cancer in rural China, mostly cancers of the stomach, esophagus, and liver, of about 11%. An estimate of

[1] 1 m^3 holds 264.14 U.S. gallons of water. 1 m^3 = 1 square foot.

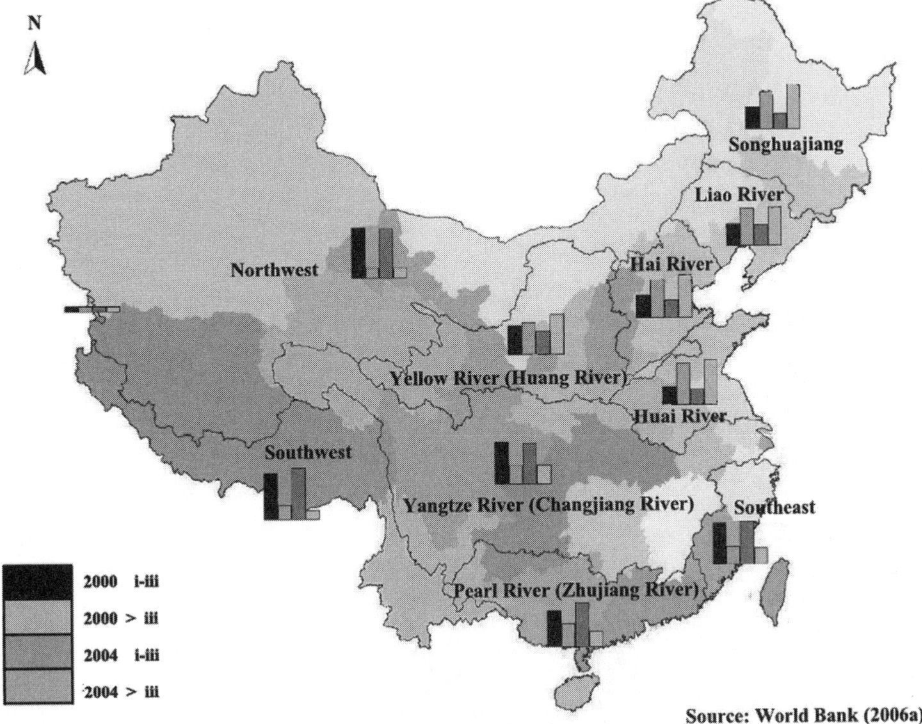

FIGURE 14.1 Surface Water Quality in 2000 and 2004

the economic cost of the disease and deaths associated with the excessive incidence of diarrhea and cancer in rural China, based on 2003 data, is 66.2 billion yuan, or about 0.49% of GDP. This estimate understates the true costs, however, since it does not include many health impacts associated with water pollution for which not enough data are available to determine a dose-response relationship (World Bank 2007a).

Another important cost results when wastewater (water that does not meet Class V standards for irrigation) is used to irrigate crops. About 4.05 million square hectares[2] (ha), or 7.4% of total irrigated lands, mostly (67%) in North China, are irrigated with polluted water. This leads to reduced harvests and poor-quality crops as well as degradation of the quality of the soil. The economic loss attributed to these impacts has been estimated at about 61.3 billion yuan, equivalent to about 0.46% of GDP in 2003. This estimate reflects the fact that large amounts of polluted crops (i.e., produce that fails to meet minimum standards for human consumption due to excessive pollution) have been produced every year. This unsafe produce constitutes a threat to human health and should not be sold in the market (World Bank 2007a).

[2] 1 hectare = 2.47 acres.

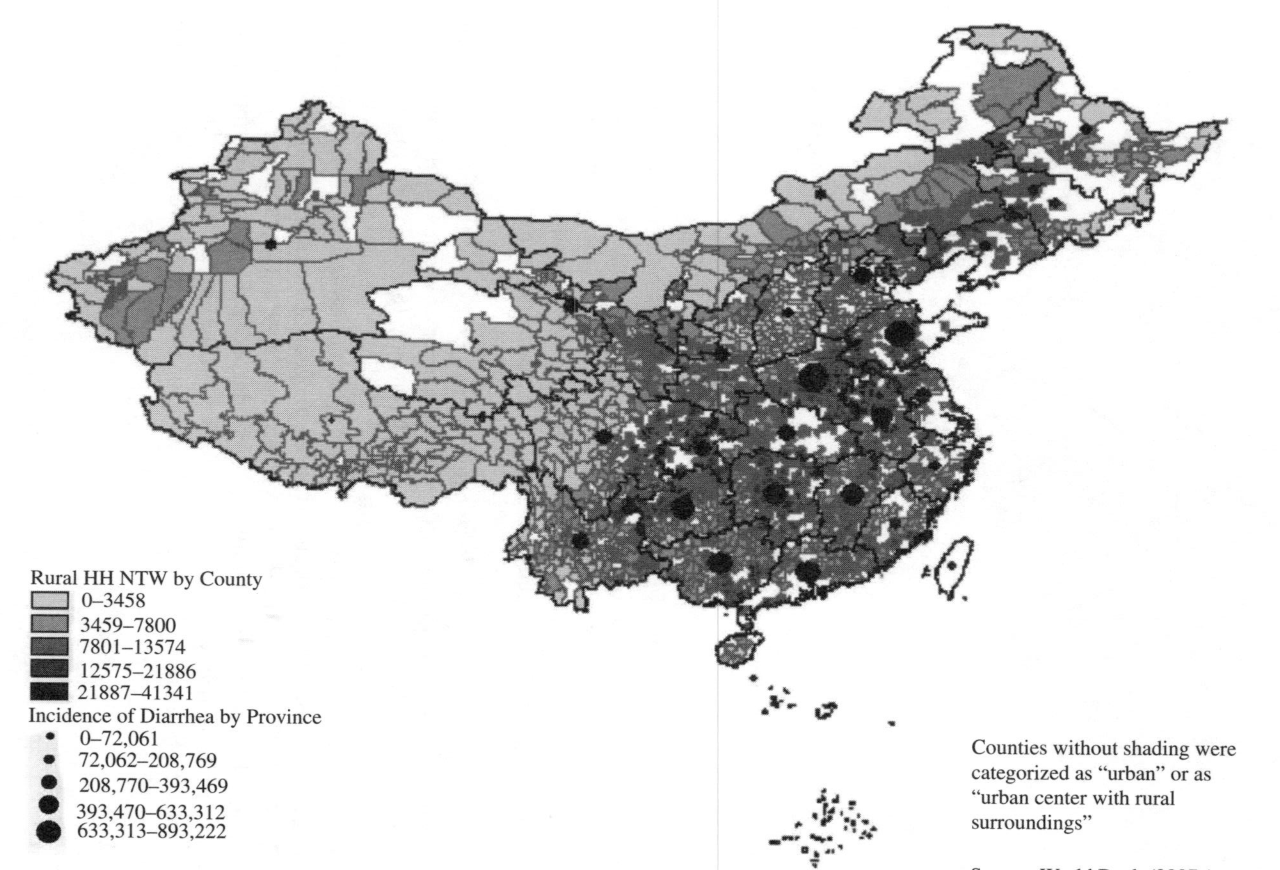

FIGURE 14.2 Rural Households without Access to Piped Water and Diarrhea Incidence in Children Age 5 and Younger, by Province

Water pollution also has an important impact on fisheries. Fishery losses due to acute pollution accidents amounted to over RMB4.3 billion in 2003[3]. While not insignificant (this figure is equivalent to 0.03% GDP), these figures greatly underestimate the total fishery loss due to pollution, since chronic pollution costs are not included in the estimate and are likely to be much higher (World Bank 2007a). There are also major impacts on aquatic and marine ecosystems that are not included in the estimate.

In addition to direct impacts, pollution compounds the scarcity of water. This imposes significant costs on all productive sectors, especially agriculture. China depends on 55 million hectares of irrigated lands for about 80% of total grain output. Of these, about 20 million hectares are suffering from water deficiency and an additional 7 million hectares cannot be irrigated at all, largely because of a shortage due to 25 billion m^3 of polluted water that cannot be used. The economic cost of water held back from supply has been estimated at RMB85.4 billion, or about 0.64% of GDP, based on the scarcity value of water from 2.1 to 5.2 yuan/m^3 (He and Chen 2005).

Excessive pollution also results in groundwater depletion. As much as 24 billion m^3 of water beyond rechargeable quantities is extracted from the ground, leading to lowering of water tables and eventual exhaustion of groundwater reservoirs as well as extensive subsidence in many cities. The economic cost of groundwater depletion has been estimated at 92.3 billion yuan, equivalent to 0.69% of GDP, based on the scarcity value of water (World Bank 2007a).

Overall, water scarcity is constraining the long-term sustainability of development. The estimates just provided suggest that the water crisis is already costing China about 2.3% of GDP, of which 1.3% is attributable to the scarcity of water and 1% to the direct impacts of water pollution. These estimates only represent the tip of the iceberg. They do not include many costs for which not enough data are available to form estimates, such as the avoidance and treatment costs incurred by individual households and enterprises; the ecological impacts associated with the drying up of lakes, wetlands, and rivers; and the loss of amenity value from the absence of clean water in most of China's water bodies.

Climate change is also aggravating the scarcity. China's total water resources of 2805 billion m^3 from surface and groundwater sources are almost entirely dependent on rainfall, which is highly uneven, averaging about 200 to 400 millimeters (mm) in North China and more that 2000 mm in South China. Over the past 100 years, these regional differences have increased, with rainfall gradually declining in North China at rates of 20 to 40 mm per decade and rising in South China at rates of 20 to 60 mm per decade. Average annual air temperatures have also increased by 0.5 to 0.8°C during the past 100 years. As a consequence of climate change, these trends are expected to continue in the future, with precipitation continuing to fall in the North, rise in the South, and average nationwide temperatures increasing by 1.3 to 2.1°C by 2020 and 3.2 to 3.3°C by 2050, as compared to 2000 (National Development and Reform Commission 2007). These trends will certainly worsen the already serious water scarcity in North China.

[3] The renminbi (RMB) or Chinese yuan renminbi (CNY) is the Chinese currency. On April 9, 2008, USD1 exchanged for RMB7.01150. Both abbreviations, RMB and CNY, are common in foreign exchange markets.

TECHNICAL SOLUTIONS ARE AVAILABLE AND ECONOMICALLY FEASIBLE

Although the emerging water crisis is serious, there are good options for addressing it by improving the productivity of water use and reducing pollution. China's water productivity of $2.2/m^3 is low in comparison with the average of middle-income ($3.3/m^3) and high-income ($28.2/m^3) countries (World Bank 2007b). The gap is due to differences in the structure and efficiency of water consumption. The potential for increasing water productivity from the gradual evolution of the sectoral structure of the economy follows from the fact that agriculture, which accounted for 65.0% of fresh water withdrawals, saw its share of GDP decline from 25% in 1989 to 13% in 2005. Over the same period, manufacturing increased its share of GDP from 43% to 48%, and services from 32% to 40%, while consuming only 23.4% and 1.7%, respectively, of water withdrawals. In addition, domestic uses accounted for 8.5% of total water use and ecological uses for the remaining 1.4% (Ministry of Water Resources 2005).

Water productivity in agriculture of only $0.80/m^3 is the lowest of all sectors, due to extensive waste in irrigation systems and suboptimal allocation among crops and between different parts of the same river basin. The extent to which water is wasted is difficult to estimate with accuracy. One estimate is that, due to the poor management of irrigation canals, only 50% of water from primary canals is delivered to the field (Xu 2001). The water that reaches the fields is not used efficiently by local irrigation managers and farmers, and between 20% to 30% is wasted. Overall, only about 40% of water withdrawals for agriculture are used by farmers on their crops (Wang et al. 2005). (See Table 14.1.) Since agriculture accounts for 65% of total freshwater withdrawals, this suggests that 39% of total water withdrawals could potentially be saved.

Water productivity in industry, of 8.09 $/m^3, is also low by international standards. China's paper producers, for example, consume about 400 to 500 tons of water per ton of paper, compared to less than 200 tons of water in Organization for Economic Cooperation and Development (OECD) countries. The largest steel mills use about 60% more water to produce a ton of steel than the average of the United States, Japan, and Germany, while water consumption by smaller firms is as much as five times higher than in those developed countries. This may be due to

TABLE 14.1 Irrigation Efficiency by River Basin (RB) in 2004

	Song Liao RB	Hai RB	Huai RB	Yellow RB	Yangtze RB	Pearl RB	South-east RB	South-west RB	Inland RB
Surface Water (nonpaddy)	0.39	0.50	0.49	0.33	0.40	0.34	0.41	0.35	0.42
Surface Water (paddy)	0.19	0.25	0.23	0.15	0.20	0.17	0.20	0.17	0.20
Ground Water	0.50	0.74	0.67	0.50	0.60	0.49	0.55	0.60	0.58
Conjunctive Water	0.40	0.71	0.62	0.40	0.47	0.47	0.53	0.45	0.45

differences in the structure of production as well as low levels of water reuse. The water recycling level in industry is 40% on average compared to 75% to 85% in developed countries. If China's industry could improve its water utilization efficiency to that level, it could reduce its raw water consumption withdrawals by two-thirds (Policy Research Center for Environment 2006).

China's urban water utility distribution network losses are among the highest in the world, with an average around 50 to 75 m^3/day per kilometer (km) of network, twice the leakage rate in Brazil and Russia and more than 10 times the rate in the United Kingdom. The worst-performing utilities have average leakage rates of around 150 m^3/day/km. Many pipelines are old and need rehabilitation, and many newer pipelines built prior to 1990 were constructed with poor-quality materials and substandard construction methods. A major underlying cause has been the utilities' limited ability to support the maintenance and rehabilitation of these pipelines (World Bank 2006b). The leaks account for about 18% of total urban water supplies on average, or about 1.5% of China's total water withdrawals.

All together, over half of current fresh water withdrawals is wasted and could be saved through the introduction of appropriate measures. The potential for water savings is by far the greatest in the agriculture sector, amounting to about 39% of total water withdrawals. The potential savings from industry amount to an additional 15% of total withdrawals, based on the potential for increased water recycling alone. In addition, the potential for water savings from reducing urban network leakage, substantial for some local utilities, is equivalent to 1.5% of total water withdrawals.

Finally, the cleanup of pollution will contribute substantially to addressing the scarcity of water. As discussed, approximately 25 billion m^3 of polluted water is held back from irrigation, contributing to unmet demand and groundwater depletion. As much as 47 billion m^3 of water that does not meet quality standards is nevertheless supplied to households, industry, and agriculture, with the attendant costs. A further 24 billion m^3 or water beyond rechargeable quantities is extracted from the ground and creates groundwater depletion. Altogether, the cleanup of pollution could make nearly 100 billion m^3/year of additional surface water available for consumption, equivalent to 18% of China's total freshwater withdrawals (World Bank 2007a).

The expanded use of water savings and cleanup options is economically feasible. The scarcity value of water, as estimated from its highest-value uses, was estimated to range from 2.1 to 5.2 yuan/m^3 (He and Chen 2005). The value differs between river basins, with the highest values obtained in the Yellow, Huai, and Hai basins, where water is scarcest. An ongoing study of the Hai basin has found that the economic value of water ranges from 6.6 yuan/m^3 in agriculture to 67.9 yuan/m^3 in industry and 150.0 yuan/m^3 in the services sector (He and Chen 2005).

In comparison to these scarcity values, current water prices are low. There are no extraction fees for the agricultural use of groundwater, and the only payment made is for the cost of the energy for pumping (in the range of 0.08 yuan/m^3 to 0.56 yuan/m^3 in Hebei). In most irrigation districts, water fees are assessed on the basis of the size of a household's irrigated area. When the cost of water is low or unrelated to the quantity used, the benefit from saving water is low. As a result, the current cost recovery approach to water pricing in the agricultural sector has not been effective in providing incentives to save water (Huang et al. 2006).

An adjustment of water prices to reflect water's scarcity value would greatly stimulate the adoption of water-saving techniques. A recent study estimated price elasticities of water demand for the irrigation of grains in the range of –1.7 to –2.8, suggesting that a 10% price increase would lead to a 17 to 28% reduction in water use (Blanke et al., 2006). These savings would largely result from the greater use of water-saving technologies, such as border and furrow irrigation, alternate wetting and drying irrigation, field leveling, minimum tilling, plastic sheeting, drought-resistant varieties, surface and underground piping systems, canal lining, and sprinkler systems. These technologies are familiar in many parts of North China, yet the extent of adoption is quite low, largely due to inadequate appreciation of the scarcity value of water as well as lack of supportive institutional arrangements. Some of these technologies (e. g., plastic sheeting), have been reported to be able to reduce water requirements by up to 90% (Huang et al. 2006).

An increase in the price of water for industry and the domestic sector can also be expected to stimulate an increase in water savings, mainly through higher rates of water treatment to allow for its reuse and recycling. The cost will vary, but a recent survey of 1,000 enterprises and households in 10 provinces has estimated that the treatment cost for of industrial purposes is 4.6 yuan/m^3 and for domestic purposes about 2.6 yuan/m^3, both of which are below the scarcity value of water, at least in North China (Chinese Academy of Environmental Planning 2006).

Overall, a range of water-saving and pollution-abatement technologies is available and has already been adopted in China, to a limited extent. But the rate of adoption has been insufficient to balance the supply and demand of water and to address the water quality issues that have contributed to the emergence of a serious water crisis. Research indicates that the adoption of such technologies by major water-using sectors could be accelerated by using prices that reflect the scarcity value of water. Given the diversity of water users, the creation of basin-wide and local water markets would appear to be an effective strategy for introducing prices that reflect scarcity values and stimulate the adoption of water-saving and cleanup technologies to the extent needed to address the water crisis.

In the absence of water markets, China's current administrative approach has led to major differences in water productivity between sectors and regions. A study of the Hai basin found that the economic value of water in agriculture (6.6 yuan/m^3) was only one-tenth that of the industrial sector (67.9 yuan/m^3) and less than one-twentieth that of the services sector (150.0 yuan/m^3) (Institute of Water Resources and Hydropower Research 2007). A study of the Yellow River basin estimated the scarcity value of water for irrigation use to be up to 20 times higher in the lower stretches of the basin when compared to the upstream areas, mainly due to differences in soil productivity (Heany et al. 2005). A functioning water market, in which water users can sell their water rights to others, can be an excellent mechanism for reallocating water from lower-value to higher-value uses, thus increasing its overall productivity and eliminating water scarcity as a constraint to growth.

CREATING A WATER MARKET FOR THE LONG TERM

Given the objective of building a resource efficient and environmentally friendly society, the government's eleventh Five Year Plan (2006–2010) has set mandatory targets to reduce water consumption per unit of industrial value added by 30% and reduce emissions of water pollutants by 10%. It also set an anticipatory target to increase the effective utilization rate for irrigation water to 0.50 (National Development and Reform Commission 2006). These targets are realistic and achievable, particularly since the plan identified numerous supporting measures. The measures include the promotion and construction of water-savings innovations; raising water consumption performance standards; implementation of financial, fiscal, price and investment policies conducive to resource conservation; strengthening pollution prevention and enforcement; accelerating the process of pollution treatment marketization; strengthening unified management of water resources on a watershed and regional basis; and establishing water rights distribution and transfer systems.

For the longer term, the plan lays the groundwork for a strategic move toward more strongly integrated river basin management and greater reliance on market-based instruments. The establishment of water rights distribution and transfer systems is the key to the creation of a water market. China already has a functioning water rights system, but it lacks a link between the amount of water authorized for use and an overall water resources allocation plan based on water balance analyses at the river basin level. A central problem is that, while local governments administer water rights, the basin-wide water allocation plans are prepared by Water Basin Management Committees (WBMC), where the local governments are not represented. Under the current structure, the WBMCs are technical institutions with limited administrative power. They provide technical direction and guidance to local governments within the basin, while the local governments are responsible for implementation.

A well-functioning water market also requires the full integration of water quality considerations into water allocation planning and water rights administration. This has been a challenge, since quantitative aspects of water resource management are under the responsibility of the Ministry of Water Resources (MWR), while State Environmental Protection Agency (SEPA) and local environment bureaus have the responsibility to supervise and manage the prevention and control of water pollution. In response to growing pollution levels and to provide technical guidance to the WBMCs, in the 1990s, several Water Resources Protection Bureaus (WRPBs) were established. Although the MWR supervises the WBMCs, the WRPBs were put under the dual supervision of the MWR and SEPA. In 2002, SEPA decided to distance itself from participation in the WRPBs and to exercise its regulatory authority through direct SEPA-local government channels (World Bank 2006a).

As a result, the planning process for basin-wide water quantity and quality management has mainly proceeded on two separate tracks, under the supervision of MWR and SEPA, respectively, with the actual implementation in the hands of the local governments. This two-track system is replicated at the local (province, prefecture, county) level, where Water Affair Bureaus (WABs) are responsible for the administration of water rights and the planning and operation of water utilities, and Environmental Protection Bureaus (EPBs) are responsible for zoning of water bodies, issuing pollution permits, controlling pollution, and protecting drinking water sources.

MWR and SEPA are not the only ministries with jurisdiction over water-related issues. The full national-level institutional framework for water resource management is set out in Figure 14.3. Apart from MWR and SEPA, the Ministry of

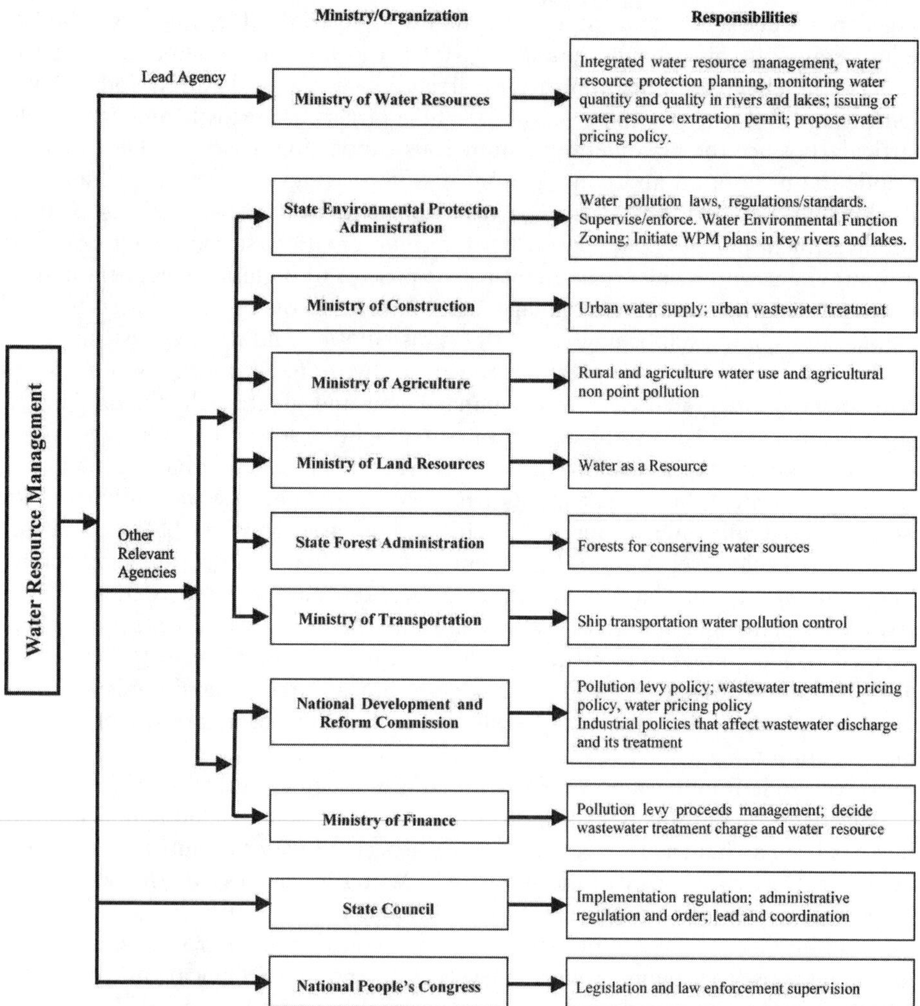

FIGURE 14.3 Ministries and Authorities Involved in Water Resource Management

Construction (MOC) has a leadership role for the planning and regulation of urban water supply and wastewater treatment systems, the Ministry of Agriculture (MOA) has important responsibilities for rural and agricultural water use and non-point pollution, and several other agencies also have important roles. The State Council and the National People's Congress have a coordinating role through the enactment of laws and supervising their implementation, but the complexity of the challenge faced in balancing the quantitative, qualitative, and other aspects of water resource management are evident.

The difficulty of coordinating such a multitrack system is aggravated by differing priorities between the horizontal and vertical dimensions of the water resource management framework. The sector and basin-wide objectives, such as abating pollution, balancing upstream and downstream needs, and protecting aquatic ecosystems, tend to have relatively low priority among local authorities, who have an incentive to meet local needs with local resources. For example, the benefits from pollution abatement and water savings in one province will be felt farther downstream. However, the majority of funding for pollution management and water-saving investments must come from local budgets (user fees or loans), with only a small share contributed by the central government.

There is no universally valid model for the integration of quantitative and qualitative, horizontal, and vertical aspects of water resources management. In more developed economies, the current tendency is to manage water resources in an integrated manner at the river basin level. China is moving in that direction, but implementation has been hampered by the lower standing of environmental agencies relative to the older and more established water resource management and use ministries and by the separation of basin-wide planning responsibility from implementation by the local governments. Although further studies and consultations are required to establish the appropriate structure for balancing all of these aspects, this eight-part structure can be envisaged:

1. MWR will continue with the overall responsibility for the quantitative aspects of water resource management, including hydrological monitoring, water planning, management of distribution, and conservation of water.
2. SEPA will be elevated to a cabinet-ministerial–level institution and to continue with the leading role for water quality and pollution management, including water quality monitoring, definition of water environmental function zones, and relationship with river basin institutions. In these areas, SEPA's responsibilities should cover all issues, from policy formulation and program implementation to law enforcement.
3. WBMCs will be put under joint supervision of MWR and SEPA, with representation of local governments and other relevant line agencies. Their existing mandate should be extended to include full regulatory authority for river basin management. That is, they should have the mandate to coordinate and assess, reward, and punish all levels of local government in relation to their water resource management and pollution control performance.
4. WBMCs will undertake water balance analyses and water resources planning to determine water allocations to subbasins, administrative units (provinces, cities, counties, townships, and villages), sectors (irrigation, municipal water supply, industry), and the environment. Total water allocations should be based on sustainable use of water resources after meeting minimum ecosystem needs and without groundwater overexploitation.
5. Water use rights will be administered by local governments and linked to sustainable allocations. Water use rights need to be specified in volumetric terms and not exceed sustainable allocations.
6. Water rights should also include strict water quality requirements for inflow, return flow, and wastewater discharges, within the framework of the established water quality grades. This will allow the market to transparently factor quality into the setting of prices and provide incentives to reduce pollution and increase conservation.
7. Water use and water quality must be measured and controlled. Water rights must be enforced. This is a major administrative undertaking that needs to be supported with adequate personnel and financial resources.

8. Water rights need to be freely tradable. Rights holders should have the ability to sell to the highest bidder or stay out of the market. This should ensure that farmers will maximize their income and will be no worse off than before.

Pioneering water rights trading schemes already exist in China, such as those between Dongyang and Yiwu cities in Zhejiang, between irrigation districts and a power plant in Ningxia and Inner Mongolia, and between Shanxi and Henan. However, the further expansion of such transactions is hampered by high transaction costs associated with the lack of a supportive legal and regulatory framework to clarify water rights, obligations for buyers and sellers, and established payments criteria (Zheng, Haixi, and Zhang 2007). A particular challenge has been the integration of "horizontal" cooperation between water resources and environmental protection bureaus with "vertical" coordination between central and basin authorities and local jurisdictions.

In light of the complexity of the proposed institutional adjustments, the establishment of a functioning water market needs to be seen as a long-term objective that will take 10 to 15 years to achieve. To develop and demonstrate the specific institutional arrangements required for the establishment of an effective water market, the government, in cooperation with the World Bank, has launched the Hai Basin Integrated Water and Environment Management Project. The project is designed to address the integration of horizontal and vertical coordination through the planning and design of integrated water resource management actions, including water rights and well permit administration, and pollution control measures, and demonstrate their implementation in 10 counties. This project is expected to be completed in 2010 and will serve as a useful model for the implementation of the water market approach (World Bank 2004).

STRENGTHENING POLLUTION MANAGEMENT

The establishment of an effective water market will have to go hand in hand with the strengthening of the pollution management framework. A major rationale for integrated river basin management is that many aspects of pollution control cannot be separated from water resource management, particularly in countries such as China, where scarcity is a problem. Under such conditions, it is essential to look for ways to increase water reuse and recycling in agricultural, industrial, and municipal/domestic applications. The "cascade management" approach should also be considered. This implies that water is used several times and is transferred among different sectors and use categories (municipal, industrial, agricultural, etc.), where treatment is performed only to the level prescribed by the subsequent use. The implementation of such an approach, although consistent with China's current policy of managing its rivers and other water bodies based on functional zones, will obviously influence the design and administration of the water market and pose a challenge to China's pollution management and control framework.

The nature of the difficulty is suggested by the fact that seven major factors affect water quality in rivers and determine its suitability for different functions:

1. Discharges from industrial sources
2. Discharges from urban domestic sources
3. Discharges from agricultural nonpoint sources

4. Regulation of river flows
5. Natural precipitation
6. Background water quality
7. Dilution and self-purification capacity of the river

Among the factors listed, the first four depend on human activities, while the rest are natural conditions. Of the four human factors, the first two are under the purview of the environmental management system; river flows are managed by the WBMCs, while discharges from agricultural NPS are totally out of control. This is an important gap, since NPS account for nearly half of total pollution loads.

NPS of pollution are particularly difficult to address with the standard administrative and market-based instruments. NPS are mainly due to farmers' applying too much fertilizer and pesticide and inappropriate disposal of livestock wastes. The underlying causes are complex and include (China Council on International Cooperation in Environment and Development, 2004):

- Fertilizer application rates that exceed the amount that crops can readily use
- Poor fertilizer application techniques
- Imbalanced fertilizer use
- Excessive use of pesticidesy
- Lack of integration between livestock and crop production, with little processing of animal wastes into organic fertilizers
- Inadequate extension services
- Lack of awareness of NPS by the general public and especially farmers

This taxonomy of causes points to the need for a more appropriate policy framework and institutional mechanisms for informing farmers about NPS and encouraging them to adopt appropriate technologies and management practices to minimize NPS pollution. Based on international experience (World Bank 2006a), four steps should be taken:

1. The first step toward managing NPS pollution is to derive reliable load estimates. This can be done by (a) monitoring the flux of pollutants in watercourses in agricultural areas, or (b) preparing pollution production and retention budgets. Ideally, these two approaches should be used in parallel.
2. The next step should be to develop a strategy for agricultural pollution management, starting with the establishment of a consensus among the relevant parties on the current pollution situation (i.e., the different pollution sources and environmental impacts). Unless a common understanding is reached, it will be difficult to develop a consensus on the required measures.
3. In establishing the aforementioned consensus, the agriculture sector and farmer representatives have to play a primary role. Unless the need for action has support from the agriculture sector and individual farmers, little progress will be seen.
4. Following this assessment, it is necessary to identify different options for pollution reduction related to NPS and prioritize them on the basis of the cost efficiency of each measure.

For the implementation of pollution management actions for NPS, win-win options that will save money for farmers and reduce pollution deserve the highest priority. Examples include fertilizer planning, integrated pest management, and the composting of animal wastes to produce organic fertilizer and biogas. Here again, most of the technical options are already known in China, but their adoption has been slow and could be greatly stimulated through the implementation of appropriate market approaches. A useful instrument to consider is a system of payments for ecological and environmental services (PES).

PES systems are based on the principle that the providers of environmental services (e.g., farmers engaged in the implementation of environmentally and ecologically responsible agriculture, water-saving measures, and watershed conservation) need to be compensated for the incremental costs incurred in providing such services by the beneficiaries (e.g., downstream water users). This approach has recently been endorsed by the government, and several pilot projects have already been implemented, such as controlling NPS and protecting the watershed of Miyun Reservoir, Beijing's main drinking water source, and similar arrangements in Zhejiang and Fujian (Zheng and Zhang 2006).

A recent assessment of these early PES systems has concluded that their implementation has been hampered by issues such as the lack of supporting legislation and policies to clarify water rights, determine payment criteria, and support effective and efficient payment mechanisms (Zheng and Zhang 2006). Four important lessons and recommendations emerge:

1. The lack of a functioning water market, with tradable water rights, clear rights and obligations for buyers and sellers, and established payment criteria, has been a major impediment for establishment of a PES system. The establishment of a well-administered water rights trading system is an essential prerequisite for a PES system.
2. PES systems are not universally applicable, since the willingness to pay for downstream benefits may not be sufficient to cover transaction costs and provide enough incentive to cover the opportunity costs of water conservation to upstream stakeholders. Thus, PES systems are easiest to establish in watersheds where the downstream beneficiaries are relatively affluent and the water scarcity is serious enough for the willingness to pay to cover the transaction costs and provide adequate compensation to upstream service providers.
3. Even where the economics may be feasible, there may not be enough funds to make the PES worthwhile. To generate adequate funds, it will be necessary to raise water tariffs to fully reflect the scarcity value of water as well as the strict implementation of pollution controls and discharge fees.
4. A reliable system for the monitoring and evaluation of water quality and quantity will need to be set up. The data will need to be entered into the watershed information and management system and shared between upstream and downstream stakeholders to underpin the payments system.

The last two requirements are fully consistent with the strengthening of the management framework for point sources of pollution that is already under way.

China's current framework for environmental management has had some success in addressing point sources of water pollution, particularly in the industrial sector. Between 1995 and 2004, the absolute discharge of wastewater decreased from 28 billion m^3 to 22 billion m^3, although the situation has deteriorated somewhat in the last few years. Between 1999 and 2004, the share of industrial wastewater meeting discharge standards increased from 67% to 91%. Target levels for the reduction of industrial discharges of eight of the main water pollutants (mercury, cadmium, chrome, lead, arsenic, cyanides, oil, and chemical oxygen demand [COD]) were achieved over the period 1990 to 2000, but in the 2001 to 2005, period some of the critical water pollution reduction targets were not been achieved (World Bank 2007a). The overall trend for indicates that water quality has become substantially better in the water-rich South but has not improved and may even have worsened in the water-scarce North (Figure 14.4a) (*China Statistical Yearbooks* 1990–2005; *China Environmental Statistical Yearbooks* 1990–2005). Figures (14.4a and b)

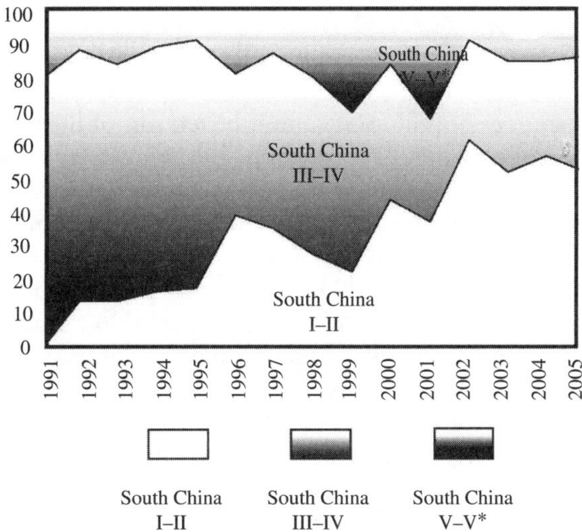

FIGURE 14.4a Water Quality Grades in South China Rivers, 1991–2005

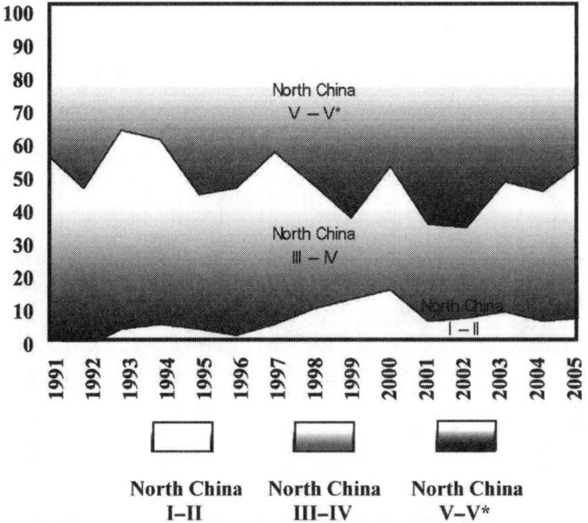

FIGURE 14.4b Water Quality Grades in North China Rivers, 1991–2005

provide an illustration. The information used is from the *China Environmental Yearbooks* (various years).

A recent case study of the Huai River basin, the most heavily polluted in China, identifies a few reasons why the extensive water pollution prevention and control programs of the ninth and tenth Five-Year Plan periods have not achieved their objectives, in spite of substantial investments (Zhong 2006). The study identifies the lack of cooperation and coordination between MWR and SEPA—as evident, for example, from the absence of a common database on water quality information—as a major reason for the disappointing results. Figure 14.5 presents a graphical illustration based on information from the *China Environment Yearbook* (various years) and the *MWR Statistical Yearbook* (various years).

The study recommends the enhancement of the water pollution control planning, monitoring and assessment framework along these five lines:

1. The nonpoint sources of pollution cannot be left out of the water pollution and prevention control plans (WPPCPs). Only by taking NPS sources into account will the WPPCPs be able to target the specific ambient water quality standards for each functional zone, if only by controlling industrial and municipal point sources.
2. Total pollutants discharges should be taken as the enforceable pollution control targets for the WPPCPs. This will avoid confusion and ambiguities caused by the use of ambient water quality targets, which are affected by river flows and self-purification capacity as well as NPS.
3. Total pollutant discharge targets should be directly assigned to the main pollution sources through discharge permits. This will avoid confusion and ambiguity caused by the current practice of allocating total discharge targets to districts or control zones, which are often difficult to relate to basins and subbasins.
4. Water pollution abatement projects should be planned and designed based on total discharge control targets at the basin level.
5. The pollution monitoring capacity of the environment bureaus needs to be strengthened for the effective implementation and enforcement of the discharge licensing system.

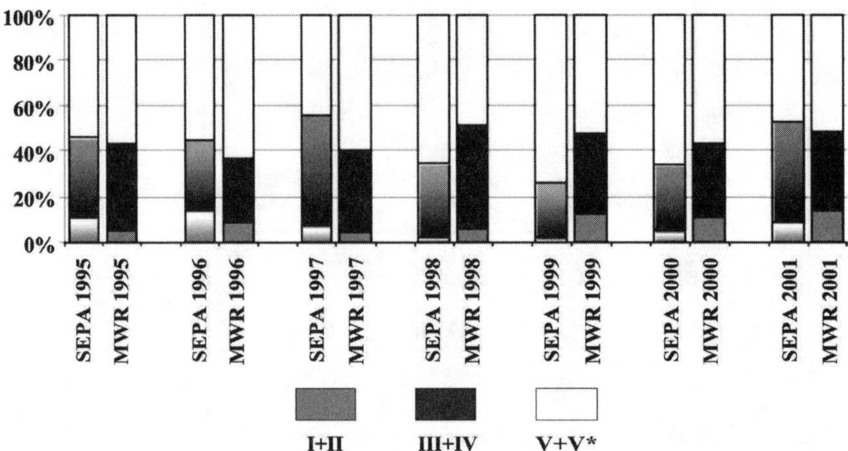

FIGURE 14.5 SEPA and MWR Water Quality Data for Huai River, 1995–2001

Although the evaluation was focused on the Huai River Basin, many of its findings are applicable to other basins in North China, where water scarcity and pollution are most serious, as well as other parts of China, where the environmental management framework is similar. The implementation of these recommendations is essential for the establishment of water markets, where water quality, and the control of pollution, will be central for setting prices and ensuring the tradability of the water rights.

Overall, in order to avoidance an emerging water crisis, China must move toward increased reliance on market-based approaches, supported by the twin pillars of integrated river basin management and rigorous pollution management. In the latter pillar, areas that deserve special attention include nonpoint sources of pollution, payments for environmental services, and the enhancement of the water pollution control planning, monitoring, and assessment framework. Given the complexity of the water resources management problem, its resolution needs to be seen as a long-term objective to be achieved over a 10- to 15-year horizon. The implementation of the recommended measures needs to be approached in a stepwise manner, initially designed for the most critical areas, such as the Huai and Hai River basins, and gradually expand when a wider understanding and general acceptance of the measures has been developed.

CONCLUSIONS

China is facing a severe water crisis. A looming water shortage, aggravated by water pollution, is slowing down the country's development and imposing a significant economic cost on the economy, and poses a health risk to parts of the population. Technological solutions to the problem exist, but price incentives and administrative and legal structures do not encourage their adoption to a socially optimal degree. Therefore, policies and strategies to address the crisis need to deal with both sides of the problem: technical and legal-administrative.

REFERENCES

Blanke, A., S. Rozelle, B. Lohmar, J. Wang, and J. Huang. (2006). "Water Saving Technology and Saving Water in China." Ms., University of California, Davis, and Center for Chinese Agricultural Policy, Chinese Academy of Sciences.

China Council on International Cooperation in Environment and Development, Task Force on Non-point Pollution from Crop Production. (2004). "Policy Recommendations on Reducing Non-point Pollution from Crop Production in China." Beijing, http://eng.cciced.org/cn/company/Tmxxb143/card143.asp?lmid=5220&siteid=1&tmid=864&flbh=143003003.

China Environmental Statistical Yearbook. (1990–2005). Beijing, China: Ministry of Environmental Protection.

China Environmental Yearbook, The. Beijing, China: National Environmental Protection Agency.

China Statistical Yearbooks. (1990–2005). Beijing, China: China Statistics Press/National Bureau of Statistics.

Chinese Academy of Environmental Planning. (2006). Survey Data of Enterprises for the National Survey of Green Accounting and Pollution Cost Valuation in Ten Candidate Provinces, Beijing.

Haixia, Z., and L. Zhang. (2007). "Chinese Practices of Ecological Compensation and Payments for Ecological and Environmental Services and Its Policies in River Basins." Draft background paper for Water Scarcity Analytical and Advisory Assistance Program China. Washington, DC: World Bank.

He, J., and C. Xikang. (2005). "Calculation of Chinese Shadow Price of Water Resources Based on Dynamic Computable Equilibrium Models," *Systems Engineering & Practice* 25.5: 49–54.

Heaney, A., A. Hafi, S. Beare, and J. Wang. (2005). "Water Reallocation in Northern China: Toward More Formal Markets for Water," ACIAR Special Session. International Commission on Irrigation and Drainage Congress, Beijing.

Huang, Q., S. Rozelle, R. Howitt, J. Wang, and J. Huang. (2006) "Irrigation Water Pricing Policy in China." Ms., University of California, Davis, and Center for Chinese Agricultural Policy, Chinese Academy of Sciences.

Institute of Water Resources and Hydropower Research. (2007). *Economic Valuation of Water Resources and Policy Intervention in Hai Basin: Interim Report.*

Li, Y. (2005). *Water Development and Management Strategy in China.* Ministry of Water Resources.

Ministry of Water Resources. (2005). *Statistic Bulletin of China Water Activities*, www.mwr.gov.cn/gb/tj/egbmenu.asp.

National Development and Reform Commission. (2006). *Guidelines of the Eleventh Five-year Plan for National Economic and Social Development.* Beijing, China: State Economic and Trade Commission.

National Development and Reform Commission. (2007). *China's National Climate Change Program.* Beijing, China: State Economic and Trade Commission.

Policy Research Center for Environment and Economy. (2006). "Improving Resource Utilization Efficiency in Key Sectors," Technical Paper for Study on Policies for Promoting Circular Economy in China, Beijing, China: Ministry for Environmental Protection.

Wang, J., Z. Xu, J. Huang, and S. Rozelle. (2005). "Incentives in Water Management Reform: Assessing the Effect on Water Use, Production and Poverty in the Yellow River Basin," *Environment and Development Economics* 10: 769–799.

World Bank. (2004). "China, Hai Basin Integrated Water and Environment Management Project." Project information document, http://web.worldbank.org/external/projects/main?pagePK=64283627&piPK=73230&theSitePK=40941&menuPK=228424&Projectid=P075035.

———. (2006a). "China Water Quality Management—Policy and Institutional Considerations." Discussion Paper, Environment and Social Development, East Asia and Pacific Region, http://web.worldbank.org/WBSITE/EXTERNAL/COUNTRIES/EASTASIAPACIFICEXT/EXTEAPREGTOPENVIRONMENT/0,,contentMDK:21049869~pagePK:34004173~piPK:34003707~theSitePK:502886,00.html.

———. (2006b). "Strategic Directions for China's Urban Water Sector." Ms. (July).

———. (2007a). "Cost of Pollution in China—Economic Estimates of Physical Damages," conference ed., http://web.worldbank.org/WBSITE/EXTERNAL/COUNTRIES/EASTASIAPACIFICEXT/EXTEAPREGTOPENVIRONMENT/0,,contentMDK:21252897~pagePK:34004173~piPK:34003707~theSitePK:502886,00.html.

———. (2007b). *World Development Indicators 2006.* Washington, DC: World Bank.

Xu, Z. (2001). "Study on Increasing Water Use Efficiency," *Journal of China Water Resources* 455: 25–26.

Zhong M. (2006). "Evaluation of the Implementation of Water Pollution Prevention and Control Plans in China: The Case of the Huai River Basin." Ms. for Water Scarcity—Analytical and Advisory Assistance Program China. Washington, DC: World Bank., November.

CHAPTER 15

Public Input in Rural Land Preservation

Modeling Preference Asymmetries in Stated Preference Data

Robert J. Johnston and Kelly Giraud Cullen

INTRODUCTION

Public preferences for land use or other public policies often are elicited using variants of the common Likert scale, such as a scale from 1 to 5, where 1 = strongly oppose and 5 = strongly support (Bateman et al. 2002; Danielson et al. 1995; Kline and Wichelns 1998; Lynne, Shonkwiler, and Rola 1988; Variyam, Jorday, and Epperson 1990). Such scales provide information regarding a respondent's strength of preference beyond a simple referendum, that is, a binary yes-or-no response. However, in return for the ability to model the increased information provided by Likert scales (LS), researchers often accept implicit assumptions not required when modeling binary responses. These include the assumption that respondents choose a cardinal, rather than a more basic ordinal, response on the continuum of the provided scale by reference to a single underlying preference function.

Despite the common use of simplifying assumptions when working with LS data, the literature addressing other choice contexts suggests that responses to such preference scales may be complex. For example, since Likert scales usually allow respondents to express varying degrees of support or opposition, there is the possibility that responses will manifest preference or response asymmetries. Response asymmetries formally imply that different factor weightings determine the extent to which respondents support versus oppose otherwise identical statements, and might cause the determinants of an initial binary choice (e.g., oppose versus support) to differ from determinants of preference intensity (e.g., how strongly do I oppose or support).

The only formal discussion of response asymmetries in the stated preference literature is provided by Johnston and Swallow (1999), who show that asymmetries may occur in more complex, two-stage stated preference questions. An example of a two-stage stated preference question would be one in which respondents are first asked whether they support or oppose a hypothetical policy and then for their strength of support or opposition. In an extension of prior experimental findings in the psychology literature (Shafir 1993; Yamagishi and Miyamoto 1996), Johnston and Swallow (1999) demonstrate that different functions may govern the extent to which respondents support versus oppose hypothetical watershed management plans. Johnston and Swallow demonstrate the existence of response asymmetries in two-stage questions, but they fail to provide a practical modeling alternative that allows for such behavioral patterns. Hence, the analytical and policy guidance provided by their empirical results is somewhat limited.

This chapter assesses whether response asymmetries also exists in the case of much more common single-stage preference questions.[1] The LS rating is a classic example. Specifically, we assess implications of preference asymmetry for cases in which statistical models are used to assess differences in stated preferences associated with demographic or other attributes of individual respondents. For example, one might wish to assess how heterogeneity of the population affects the support for particular land use polices. Heterogeneity usually is measured by attributes such as age, income, and education. Such models typically are estimated using ordered logit or probit, with the LS response as an independent variable (Swallow, Opaluch, and Weaver 2001). A discovery of response asymmetries in such common choice frameworks would represent a significant and perhaps surprising finding, and would imply that even simple ordered preference ratings along a single, continuous preference scale, such as a Likert scale, may involve more complex choice processes than are currently anticipated and modeled in the literature.

When estimating ordered response models of LS data, the typical assumption is that responses are symmetric. In empirical terms, ordered response models presume that the weight given to independent variables, as revealed by estimated coefficients, is approximately constant over the range of possible outcomes, subject to increasing or decreasing returns and/or interactions captured by the chosen functional form. A corollary to this assumption is that respondents choose a LS rating in a single-stage process. However, other choice mechanics are possible. For example, when presented with a LS question regarding support for a land use policy, respondents might, without prompting, first assess whether they support the policy and then assess the strength of their support or opposition. In such cases, LS responses may no longer be symmetric, as explained. Typical ordered response models may then provide improper inferences regarding the impact of the independent variables on policy support or opposition.

In cases where response asymmetries are evident, alternative choice models may reveal behavioral patterns obscured by traditional modeling approaches. To address such possibilities, this chapter presents a model of LS responses that may be applied when preference asymmetries are suspected and contrasts this alternative to a more traditional ordered response approach. This allows formal hypothesis tests for the presence of preference asymmetries as well as assessments of policy implications.

[1] This research was funded by the USDA Fund for Rural America 97-36200-5219. Opinions are those of the authors and do not imply endorsement by the funding agencies or the U.S. Government. Address correspondence to the lead author at rjohnston@canr.uconn.edu.

STANDARD STRENGTH OF PREFERENCE MODEL

Our application concerns the estimation of the relationship between attributes of survey respondents and stated preferences for common land use policy tools. The preference for each tool is measured on a standard LS, in which respondents are asked to rate each policy tool on a five-point scale ranging from "strongly oppose" (1) to "strongly support" (5).

Standard random utility models assume that a respondent's strength of preference for a given policy tool (or statement) is determined by the happiness, or *utility*, that would result from the application of that tool, compared to the utility generated by the status quo or lack of that tool. That is, for each management tool i, the difference in utility resulting from the application of that tool may be specified as:

$$dU_i = dv_i\,(\mathbf{D}) + \theta_i \tag{15.1}$$

where $dv_i(\mathbf{D})$ = deterministic or observable component of the change in utility
$\mathbf{D}$ = a vector of variables characterizing demographic and other characteristics of the individual or household hypothesized to influence management preferences
θ_i = random, unobservable element of the utility difference

Equation 15.1 models heterogeneity in preferences for specific policy tools; it is a function of individual and household attributes.

Ordered response models represent a standard approach to such problems. The approach presumes that the individual assesses the utility difference, dU_i, associated with a particular policy tool and then indicates within which of a set of intervals this utility difference falls. Here each interval corresponds to a specific LS response, represented by a strength of preference indicator variable, L_{ij}, where $j = \{1, 2, \ldots, 5\}$, such that

$$L_{ij} = 1 \quad \text{if} \quad \alpha_{i,j-1} < \mathrm{dU} \leq \alpha_{i,j}; \quad L_{ij} = 0 \quad \text{otherwise} \tag{15.2}$$

For example, if the respondent "strongly opposes" a management tool, then $L_{i1} = 1$, and $L_{i2} = \ldots = L_{i5} = 0$. The α_{ij} in equation 15.2 represent utility thresholds associated with particular values of L_{ij}. These thresholds are unobserved, and the ordered response model treats them as parameters (Maddala 1983).

Assumptions regarding the distribution of θ determine whether the model is estimated as an ordered probit or ordered logit model. Maddala and others provide appropriate likelihood functions. Here we estimate the model using an ordered probit likelihood function. We emphasize that such models estimate parameters defining a single preference function, dv_i, applicable to responses over the entire continuum represented by the Likert scale.

MODEL ALLOWING FOR PREFERENCE ASYMMETRIES

In contrast to the standard approach represented by equations 15.1 and 15.2, models incorporating preference asymmetry allow for judgments of *strength of support* to be determined by a different choice mechanism or component weighting than judgments of *strength of opposition*. In addition, the initial decision to support or oppose is governed by a different choice mechanism from those governing judgments of how strongly to support or oppose. The former are usually modeled as binary choices in which an option is supported or opposed (Yamagishi 1996; Yamagishi and Miyamoto 1996). For example, when faced with the opportunity to rate a policy tool on a continuous LS, a respondent might first make an initial (binary) decision to support or oppose the tool in question. Simultaneously (or perhaps subsequently), the respondent would choose a level of support or opposition. These two choices, however, need not be governed by an identical choice or by identical preference functions.

The model specifies one preference or choice function to govern the initial support-versus-oppose choice,

$$dU_{1i} = dv_{1i}\,(\mathbf{D}) + \theta_{1i} \tag{15.3}$$

where the subscript 1 = choice to support (versus to oppose)

The respondent's choice is represented by the indicator variable L_j, which takes on a value of 0 if the respondent opposes policy tool *i* and 1 if the respondent supports the tool. We denote this as the "first-stage" choice, although it could be simultaneous with the "second-stage" choice that reveals preference intensity.

The second-stage choice reveals a respondent's preference intensity, or strength of support or opposition. We consider that it is made simultaneously with the first-stage choice, although one might also consider it a subsequent choice. The function given in equation 15.4 is assumed to govern preference intensity.

$$dU_{2i} = dv_{oi}\,(\mathbf{D}) + dv_{si}\,(\mathbf{D}) + \theta_{2i} \tag{15.4}$$

where subscript o = opposition
subscript s = support
$dv_{oi}(\mathbf{D}) = 0$ for $L_i = 1$
$dv_{si}(\mathbf{D}) = 0$ for $L_i = 0$

That is, those who support the policy tool in question in the first stage have $dU_{2i} = dv_{si}\,(\mathbf{D}) + \theta_{2i}$. For those who oppose the policy tool in the first stage, the expression is $dU_{2i} = dv_{oi}\,(\mathbf{D}) + \theta_{2i}$.

We assume that a binary choice reveals the strength of support or opposition, represented by the indicator variable S_i. Respondents who support the tool *i* may do so "moderately" ($S_i = 0$) or "strongly" ($S_i = 1$). Respondents who oppose the tool may similarly do so "strongly" ($S_i = 0$) or "moderately" ($S_i = 1$). Note that Si is defined for supporting and opposing contexts such that the directional effect of utility difference on preference strength is preserved. That is, for opposition or support, $S_{ij} = 1$ corresponds to a higher level of utility or preference, dU_{2i}, within each category. One may envision this intuitively as splitting the data (observations) into support (*S*) and oppose (*O*) responses, creating two independent datasets of binary strength of preference responses. The support (*S*) data include all "support" and "strongly support" responses (LS responses 4 and 5); the oppose (O) data include all "strongly oppose" and "oppose" responses (LS responses 1 and 2). The resulting support and oppose datasets are then vertically "stacked" or pooled into a single binary dataset, such that the directional effect of the utility difference on strength of preference is preserved. The result is a pooled dataset, incorporating both the "oppose" and "support" data vertically stacked. For similar data transformations, see Mazzotta and Opaluch (1995) and Johnston and Swallow (1999).

The special case, implied by the standard ordered response model of equations 15.1 and 15.2, is that dv_{1i} (D) = dv_{oi} (D) = dv_{si} (D), allowing the two-component decision governed by equations 15.3 and 15.4 to be collapsed into a single-component decision governed by equation 15.1. However, while it is certainly possible that the same underlying preference or utility function determines support or opposition, strength of support (for supported tools), and strength of opposition (for opposed tools), a preference asymmetry model considers this a hypothesis to be tested. Thus, it is possible that dv_{1i} (D) $\neq$ dv_{oi} (D) $\neq$ dv_{si} (D). The model in equations 15.3 and 15.4 allows for that possibility.

Because of the additional flexibility, models incorporating preference asymmetries allow for possibilities not often considered by the stated preference literature. For example, standard ordered response models assume that each demographic indicator (e.g., age) has a fixed marginal effect on utility difference function and that this single function determines the LS rating of the entire continuum. Implicit in this approach is the assumption that both the magnitude and directional impact (i.e., sign) of each indicator is fixed.

Such behavioral assumptions notwithstanding, there are various other systematic mechanisms through which demographic and other indicators may influence stated preferences. Perhaps the most obvious is that certain demographic attributes may be associated with stronger, or with more moderate, preferences for a given policy choice, regardless of whether that policy choice is supported or opposed. For example, older respondents may have more extreme opinions, stating stronger opposition to disliked policies and stronger support for favored policies than younger respondents, ceteris paribus.

Were such patterns to hold, the marginal directional effect of age on strength of preference (i.e., the sign of the coefficient) would change as we move from the "oppose" to the "support" segment of the LS continuum. Because standard ordered response models of LS data do not allow for this possibility, misspecification of respondents' choice behavior is possible. A typical symptom of such misspecification would be that the model fails to identify a systematic effect of a particular attribute on strength of preference, when in fact a systematic and significant effect exists.

Statistical Model

Although estimation of ordered response models for LS data is well established, to our knowledge, there is little precedent for modeling of preference asymmetries with such data in the literature. Johnston and Swallow (1999) present hypothesis tests that establish the presence of preference asymmetries in two-stage stated preference questions, but they fail to provide a consistent approach to model respondents' choices in the presence of such asymmetries. Moreover, the model characterized by equation 15.3 lends itself to a variety of existing estimation methods, depending on behavioral assumptions and data manipulations. Perhaps the most straightforward approach to this issue would be to apply generalized ordered logit, an approach that relaxes the proportional odds assumption implicit in traditional ordered logit models (U.S. EPA 2002). However, here we apply a bivariate probit model instead, which formalizes the hypothesized two-stage decisions implicit in a preference asymmetry model.[2]

We model the choices implicit in equations 15.3 and 15.4 as simultaneous bivariate decisions with correlated disturbances, in the tradition of seemingly unrelated regressions, where correlation is incorporated by $\rho = Cov\,[\theta_{1i}, \theta_{2i}|\mathbf{D}]$. The first bivariate choice, corresponding to equation 15.3, indicates a respondent's opposition ($L_i = 0$) or support ($L_j = 1$) for a specific management tool i. The second bivariate choice, corresponding to equation (15.4, indicates a respondent's strength of preference ($S_i = \{0,1\}$), where statistical determinants of this choice may differ between those who oppose and support tool i, as noted. Nonindependence between the two choices can be incorporated by assuming a bivariate normal distribution of equation errors, leading to estimation using a bivariate probit likelihood function. Given parameters are estimated using a bivariate probit model. We rely on Greene (2002) and Poe et al. (1997) for the likelihood function for the model.

Model estimation allows for hypothesis tests of various aspects of potential preference asymmetry. We test the null hypothesis H_0: the statistical determinants of the strength of opposition to tool i are not significantly different from those of strength of support. The alternative hypothesis is H_A: the statistical determinants are significantly different. Comparisons of the overall fit and performance of the ordered response and bivariate probit models allow appraisals of each model's ability to characterize respondents' choice behavior.

Treatment of Neutral Responses

Although the bivariate probit approach provides flexibility in allowing for preference asymmetries, it does so at a cost. Specifically, because the model is as a combination of two bivariate decisions, it cannot incorporate neutral responses, described in the survey as "neither oppose nor support." The data of interest is comprised of LS ratings on a five-point scale, where the median score represents a neutral response to tool i. The ordered response model represented by equations 15.1 and 15.2 can deal with such data points, but the bivariate probit model only allows "oppose" or "support" choices, jointly with a binary strength of preference choice. Because it cannot incorporate neutral responses, they are dropped from the data prior to estimation. Hence, information (data) is lost in the bivariate probit model.

As a pragmatic matter, neutral responses make up a small proportion of the Likert scale data in question. However, some data are nonetheless discarded in estimating the bivariate probit model. Johnston et al. (2003) also drop neutral responses in hypothesis tests of preference asymmetries in two-stage stated preference questions. It is important to view the performance of the bivariate probit model in light of the smaller dataset. While the additional information incorporated in the ordered response models should afford additional efficiency and robustness, this advantage may be lost, however, if such models misspecify respondents' behavior. In this chapter, we do not ignore "neutral" responses, but investigate them separately since the bivariate probit model cannot incorporate them.

[2] We thank Scott Shonkwiler for suggesting this alternative approach.

DATA

Data are from the *Rhode Island Rural Land Use* survey, an instrument designed to assess rural residents' trade-offs among attributes of residential development and conservation. Survey development required over 18 months, including background research, interviews with policy makers and residents, and focus groups. Surveys were mailed to 4,000 randomly selected residents of four Rhode Island rural communities following the total survey design method (Dillman 2000). The response rate was 58.2%, reflecting 2,157 responses out of 3,702 deliverable surveys. For additional details on survey research and administration, see Johnston, Swallow, and Bauer (2002) and Johnston et al. (2003).

Survey respondents were asked to indicate their degree of opposition to, or support for, 21 different land use management policy options. The five-point LS ranges from "strongly oppose" (1) to "strongly support" (5). Policy options included zoning changes, fee-based land preservation techniques, tax policies, housing caps, impact fees, and other land use policy tools common in Rhode Island rural communities. Based on the results of focus groups, all policies were described in simple, nontechnical terms. Table 15.1 lists the policy options rated by respondents and the mean support ratings associated with each option. Mean scores above 3.0 indicate that the average respondent supports the policy option, with higher scores indicating greater mean support. Mean scores below 3.0 indicate that the average respondent opposes the policy option, with lower scores indicating greater mean opposition. Diversity in average responses across similar management tools suggests that respondents considered each policy in detail when providing LS responses rather than providing identical ratings of broadly similar policies (e.g., tools 1 and 2; tools 7–9).

EMPIRICAL RESULTS

Empirical models compare performance of the ordered probit (traditional) and bivariate probit (preference asymmetry) approaches, applied to the same LS data. For both models, responses are modeled as a function of an identical set of independent variables. Independent variables include length of residency in the rural community, standard demographic descriptors characterizing age, income, and education, and other indicators such as membership in environmental or business organizations or ownership of a local home (Table 15.2).

We estimate distinct ordered and bivariate probit models for each of the 21 management tools considered by respondents, resulting in 42 estimated models. Table 15.3 summarizes overall model statistics, including the likelihood ratio χ^2 for each model, McFadden's pseudo-R^2 for both models (McFadden 1974) and the likelihood ratio χ^2 for the null hypothesis H_0: the statistical determinants of strength of support are identical to those for strength of opposition in the bivariate probit model. The χ^2 statistic is calculated as –2[LRR–LRU], where LRR is the log likelihood function of the restricted model when $\gamma_{oi} = \gamma_{si}$, and LRU is the log likelihood function of the unrestricted model. All models are statistically significant at better than $p < 0.01$, as indicated by likelihood ratio tests (Table 15.3). Model fit statistics provide support for the bivariate probit model.

TABLE 15.1 Likert Scale Strength-of-Support Ratings for Land Use Policy Options[a]

Option	Description (survey text)	Mean Rating
1.	Attract new commercial development to your town by offering tax incentives	2.49 (1.26)
2.	Attract new residential development to your town by offering tax incentives	1.85 (0.94)
3.	Encourage preservation by reducing property taxes on undeveloped land	4.11 (0.89)
4.	Encourage new development by expending public water and sewer services	2.31 (1.11)
5.	Discourage people from moving into your town by increasing the tax rate	1.98 (0.89)
6.	Revitalize town or village centers using new public funds	3.36 (1.03)
7.	Purchase and preserve undeveloped land with private funds (e.g., land trust donations)	4.08 (0.81)
8.	Purchase and preserve undeveloped land with public funds (e.g., public bond issues)	3.58 (1.05)
9.	Purchase and preserve undeveloped land through a new real estate sales tax	2.68 (1.16)
10.	Collect fees from developers to offset costs of additional public services for new developments	4.16 (0.86)
11.	Collect fees from developers to offset additional environmental damages from new developments	4.28 (0.83)
12.	Encourage residential development by decreasing zoning restrictions	1.79 (0.92)
13.	Encourage commercial development by decreasing zoning restrictions	1.95 (1.04)
14.	Require new developments to preserve some undeveloped land	4.21 (0.76)
15.	Require trees and shrubs between new houses and roads	4.11 (0.82)
16.	Further protect water resources by increasing zoning restrictions	4.08 (0.83)
17.	Further protect wildlife resources by increasing zoning restrictions	4.04 (0.87)
18.	Require new commercial development to occur along major roadways	3.75 (1.01)
19.	Require new commercial development to occur within town or village centers	3.00 (1.09)
20.	Institute a cap on the total number of new homes allowed to be built each year	4.09 (0.93)
21.	Tighten enforcement of existing zoning and subdivision regulations	4.02 (0.86)

[a]Measured on a five-point Likert-scale in which 1 = "strongly oppose" and 5 = "strongly support."
Numbers in parentheses are standard deviations.

Bivariate probit results also show strong evidence of preference asymmetry in strength of preference responses. We reject the null hypothesis at $p < 0.01$ in all cases (Table 15.3), providing strong evidence that determinants of preference strength for opposed tools differ from analogous determinants for supported tools, violating one of the primary assumptions on which traditional ordered response modeling relies. The presence of such asymmetries may help explain the relatively poorer statistical

TABLE 15.2 Variables Included in the Strength of Preference Models

Variable	Description	Units and Measurement	Mean (Std)
Resid_year	Length of residency in the community in which a respondent currently resides	Number of years	16.59 (15.55)
Age	Reported age of survey respondent	Number of years	47.28 (12.44)
Female	Dummy variable distinguishing male and female respondents	Binary (0,1), 1 = female; 0 = male	0.33 (0.47)
House_size	Size of household, including children	Number of individuals	2.93 (1.30)
Own_home	Dummy variable identifying those who indicate that they own their principal residence (versus renting)	Binary (0,1), 1 = homeowner	0.91 (0.28)
Hi_educate	Dummy variable identifying those respondents with at least a four-year college education	Binary (0,1), 1 = four-year college or greater education	0.34 (0.47)
Hi_income	Dummy variable identifying those respondents with reported household income above $39,999 per year	Binary (0,1), 1 = income > $39,999	0.53 (0.49)
Envi_group	Dummy variable identifying those indicating membership in environmental groups (Audubon Society, land trusts, etc.)	Binary (0,1), 1 = environmental group member	0.19 (0.39)
Bus_ group	Dummy variable identifying those indicating membership in business organizations (chambers of commerce, etc.)	Binary (0,1), 1 = business group member	0.20 (0.40)
Neutrals	Number of times respondent expressed neutral preferences toward one of the policy tools	Number of neutral votes	3.59 (3.28)
ToolOppose	Dummy variable indicating a preference in opposition of a policy tool	Binary (0,1), 1 = opposed policy tool	Tool1: 2.50 (1.24) Tool6: 3.34 (1.02) Tool8: 3.56 (1.04)

TABLE 15.3 Model Statistics: Ordered Probit and Bivariate Probit Estimation Results

Model (Policy Tool)	Ordered Probit LR χ^2 (df = 9)[a]	Ordered Probit Pseudo-R^2	Bivariate Probit LR χ^2 (df = 28)[a,b]	Bivariate Probit Pseudo-R^2	LR χ^2 for H_0: $\gamma_{oi} = \gamma_{si}$ (p-value)
1.	93.64	0.017	192.48	0.047	76.00 (0.01)
2.	96.00	0.021	111.96	0.035	38.58 (0.01)
3.	63.65	0.014	163.30	0.048	103.71 (0.01)
4.	101.70	0.019	162.96	0.045	70.96 (0.01)
5.	26.06	0.006	79.00	0.027	43.00 (0.01)
6.	48.77	0.009	173.99	0.054	118.26 (0.01)
7.	97.79	0.023	172.10	0.055	100.92 (0.01)
8.	100.20	0.019	219.37	0.062	117.45 (0.01)
9.	94.13	0.016	206.82	0.055	89.95 (0.01)
10.	39.93	0.009	119.96	0.037	61.83 (0.01)
11.	43.41	0.011	115.92	0.035	54.21 (0.01)
12.	111.55	0.025	110.16	0.034	29.18 (0.01)
13.	115.73	0.024	153.25	0.043	28.82 (0.01)
14.	55.87	0.014	135.56	0.043	63.04 (0.01)
15.	69.84	0.016	150.39	0.051	88.80 (0.01)
16.	44.85	0.010	140.67	0.046	93.87 (0.01)
17.	75.30	0.016	153.47	0.049	92.21 (0.01)
18.	48.92	0.010	135.45	0.040	74.79 (0.01)
19.	51.67	0.009	169.25	0.047	96.63 (0.01)
20.	37.82	0.008	115.89	0.034	67.27 (0.01)
21.	57.71	0.013	146.52	0.049	92.67 (0.01)

[a] All models are statistically significant at $p < 0.01$.
[b] Statistics are for the full bivariate probit model including both equations.

performance of ordered probit relative to the bivariate probit in this context. Hence, while direct specification tests are infeasible, and despite the larger dataset from which the ordered response model is estimated, the general fit of the bivariate probit model of LS responses appears to improve over that of the traditional ordered response approach.

Implications for Heterogeneity in Policy Preferences

Additional insight regarding the policy relevance of such results may be gained by reviewing model results for specific management tools. Given the impracticality of illustrating full estimation results for each of the 42 estimated models, we focus on a subset. Although we emphasize cases in which evidence of preference asymmetry is relatively clear, similar evidence may be found in most estimated models. The evidence suggests that asymmetric responses seem to have considerable and significant impacts on the results of traditional ordered preference models.

For example, Table 15.4 illustrates results for tool 1 and tool 6, including both bivariate probit and ordered probit models. In Table 15.4, tool 1 is described as "attract new commercial development to your town by offering tax incentives."

TABLE 15.4 Ordered and Bivariate Probit Results: Tools 1 and 6[a]

Bivariate Probit: Support/Oppose

	Tool 1			Tool 6		
Variable Name	Parameter Estimate	Std. Error	p > |z|	Parameter Estimate	Std. Error	p > |z|
Resid_year	0.012	0.003	0.001	0.005	0.003	0.045
Age	0.005	0.003	0.067	−0.012	0.003	0.001
Female	−0.189	0.072	0.008	0.272	0.079	0.001
House_size	−0.023	0.026	0.387	0.010	0.030	0.742
Own_home	0.266	0.130	0.041	−0.316	0.140	0.024
Hi_educate	−0.067	0.074	0.364	−0.078	0.079	0.330
Hi_income	0.001	0.073	0.992	−0.001	0.080	0.990
Envi_group	−0.260	0.091	0.004	0.139	0.098	0.156
Bus_group	0.228	0.082	0.005	0.158	0.093	0.088
Intercept	−0.763	0.186	0.001	0.874	0.218	0.001
Bivariate Probit: Strength of Preference[b]						
Resid_year × Oppose	0.009	0.002	0.001	0.009	0.004	0.015
Age × Oppose	−0.008	−0.002	0.001	−0.017	0.005	0.001
Female × Oppose	−0.137	0.068	0.045	0.178	0.117	0.129
House_size × Oppose	−0.016	0.021	0.448	−0.074	0.042	0.076
Own_home × Oppose	0.242	0.121	0.045	−0.322	0.222	0.148
Hi_educate × Oppose	−0.087	0.072	0.225	−0.138	0.108	0.203
Hi_income × Oppose	−0.091	0.071	0.196	−0.018	0.113	0.873
Envi_group × Oppose	−0.249	0.085	0.004	0.158	0.138	0.254
Bus_group × Oppose	0.093	0.082	0.259	0.023	0.125	0.855
Intercept × Oppose	0.853	0.110	0.001	2.157	0.306	0.001
Resid_year × Support	0.003	0.003	0.422	0.005	0.003	0.076
Age × Support	0.011	0.005	0.023	−0.005	0.004	0.267
Female × Support	−0.215	0.120	0.074	0.105	0.092	0.252
House_size × Support	−0.004	0.047	0.933	0.097	0.034	0.005
Own_home × Support	0.293	0.233	0.209	−0.303	0.147	0.040
Hi_educate × Support	−0.009	0.114	0.940	0.056	0.096	0.558
Hi_income × Support	0.011	0.120	0.929	0.067	0.097	0.489
Envi_group × Support	−0.404	0.166	0.015	0.081	0.113	0.476
Bus_group × Support	0.333	0.119	0.005	0.178	0.105	0.091

(Continued)

TABLE 15.4 *(Continued)*

Bivariate Probit: Support/Oppose

	Tool 1			Tool 6		
Variable Name	Parameter Estimate	Std. Error	p>|z|	Parameter Estimate	Std. Error	p>|z|
Intercept × Support	−2.108	0.345	0.001	−1.456	0.267	0.001
ρ	0.999	0.001	0.001	0.998	0.332	0.004
N	1648			1401		
−2 LnL χ^2 (df = 28)	192.48		0.001	173.99		0.001
Ordered Probit						
Resid_year	0.009	0.002	0.001	0.006	0.002	0.001
Age	0.007	0.002	0.003	−0.007	0.002	0.003
Female	−0.083	0.053	0.119	0.193	0.053	0.001
House_size	0.024	0.021	0.243	0.026	0.020	0.207
Own_home	0.142	0.092	0.123	−0.249	0.091	0.006
Hi_educate	−0.065	0.056	0.246	−0.007	0.055	0.894
Hi_income	−0.005	0.055	0.928	0.014	0.055	0.794
Envi_group	−0.224	0.066	0.001	0.049	0.064	0.446
Bus_group	0.163	0.064	0.011	0.127	0.064	0.047
Estimated Cut-Points						
α_1	−0.112			−1.602		
α_2	0.640			−0.904		
α_3	1.085			−0.076		
α_4	2.175			1.281		
N	1886			1899		
−2 LnL χ^2 (df = 9)	93.64		0.001	48.77		0.001

[a]The text describing tool 1 is: "attract new commercial development to your town by offering tax incentives." Tool 6 is described as "revitalize town or village centers using new public funds."

[b]For bivariate probit strength of preference model oppose responses, 0 = strongly oppose and 1 = moderately oppose. For support responses, 0 = moderately support and 1 = strongly support. (See text for additional information.)

Based on likelihood ratio tests, both the bivariate and ordered models are statistically significant at better than $p < 0.001$ for tool 1. The ordered probit model suggests that four attributes influence strength of preference at $p < 0.10$: length of residency (positive influence); age (positive); membership in an environmental organization (negative); and membership in a business group (positive).

The bivariate probit model allows attribute influence to differ, depending on the choice made. For the support versus oppose choice, the bivariate model finds statistically significant influences associated with six attributes, including: length of residency (positive); age (positive); gender (female respondents associated with more negative responses); homeownership (positive); membership in an environmental organization (negative); and membership in a business group (positive).

The results of both models appeal to prior expectations. We are not surprised to find that members of environmental organizations state greater opposition to tax incentives designed to attract commercial development and that members of business groups express greater support. However, the bivariate model is able to discern statistically significant effects, at least in the support versus oppose model, for two additional attributes: gender ($p < 0.01$) and homeownership ($p < 0.05$). Based on the bivariate probit results, these attributes also influence the probability of supporting commercial tax incentives. While the ordered probit p-values for these attributes are close to the generally accepted $p = 0.10$ threshold for statistical significance, we cannot reject the individual null hypotheses of zero influence on LS responses (Table 15.4).

Policy implications of such results are not difficult to envision. For example, if a policy maker were to request information regarding support for commercial tax incentives among local homeowners, the traditional approach to LS data (ordered response modeling) would indicate no statistically significant influence, a result that is important when seeking to identify constituencies for this particular policy option. However, the bivariate strength of preference model suggests that this conclusion may be misleading. Based on bivariate probit results, one would conclude that homeowners are more likely to support such tax incentives (at $p < 0.05$).

The reason for the discrepancy in the finding in this particular case between the two models seems straightforward. The bivariate model indicates that homeownership influences both the probability of supporting commercial tax incentives (*own_home*, Table 15.4) as well as strength of opposition of those respondents who oppose such policies (*own_home* × *oppose*; $p < 0.05$). However, homeownership cannot be shown to influence the strength of support among those who support such policies (*own_home* × *support*; $p = 0.21$). The lack of a statistically significant effect over a *portion* of the LS continuum likely contributes to the failure of the ordered probit model to identify a statistically significant effect of home ownership over the entire response continuum. Recall that the ordered probit model estimates only one parameter per attribute, which applies over the entire continuum of Likert scale responses.

Aside from an improved ability to identify statistically significant attribute effects, the bivariate model also reveals differences in preference determinants among those who oppose and those who support tool 1 (Table 15.4). For example, significant effects on strength of opposition ($dv_{oi}(\mathbf{D})$) are associated with residence duration (positive or *weaker* opposition), female respondents (negative or *stronger* opposition), age (negative), homeowners (positive), and members of environmental groups (negative). In contrast, strength of support ($dv_{si}(\mathbf{D})$) is associated with age (positive or *stronger* support), female respondents (negative or *weaker* support), members of environmental groups (negative), and members of business organizations (positive). Hence, as suggested by the joint hypothesis test in Table 15.3, the bivariate probit model for tool 1 indicates that determinants of strength of support and strength of opposition differ.

Bivariate strength of preference results for tool 1 also reveal a characteristic incidence of preference asymmetry associated with the variable *age*. As noted, older residents who oppose tool 1 reveal stronger opposition at $p < 0.01$ (*age* × *oppose* < 0; Table 15.4). However, older residents who support tool 1 reveal stronger support at $p < 0.03$ (*age* × *support* > 0). Combining these results leads to the conclusion that increasing age is associated with stronger preferences for commercial tax incentives, both in support and in opposition, a classic representation of response asymmetry associated with a demographic attribute.

Similar results are evident for tool 6 (Table 15.4). To streamline discussion of these results, Table 15.5 provides a simplified illustration of statistically significant effects identified by each model, with "plus" and "minus" signs indicating positive and negative statistically significant impacts. As shown in Table 15.5, the signs of statistically significant effects in the bivariate support/oppose model are identical to those found in the ordered probit model, a sign that both models are identifying similar patterns in LS responses. However, among various symptoms of response asymmetry manifest in the bivariate strength of preference model for tool 6, Table 15.5 provides another archetypal illustration of preference asymmetry and its potential implications.

The identified preference asymmetry is associated with the attribute *house_size* (the number of people in the household). The results do not show household size to influence the probability of supporting the "revitalization of town centers using public funds" (tool 6). However, for those respondents who support tool 6, larger household sizes are associated with stronger support at $p < 0.01$ (Tables 15.4 and 15.5). In contrast, for those respondents who oppose tool 6, larger household sizes are associated with stronger opposition at $p < 0.08$. Standard ordered response specifications cannot capture such patterns. Despite the statistical significance of such patterns identified by the bivariate model, the ordered probit model shows *house_size* to have an insignificant effect on LS responses.

Once again we find a pattern of potential relevance obscured by the ordered response framework: Members of larger household tend to express stronger preferences regarding revitalization of town centers. Those who oppose such policies will oppose more strongly, and those who support them will support them more strongly. Aside from indicating patterns of heterogeneity in policy support, these results also have potential implications for the implicit weight given to respondents from larger households in the analysis of LS responses. The tendency of such

TABLE 15.5 Summary of Statistical Results: Tool 6[a]

	Bivariate Probit			Ordered Probit
Variable Name	Support/Oppose	Strength of Preference Support	Strength of Preference Oppose	
Resid_year	+	+	+	+
Age	−		−	−
Female	+			+
House_size		+	−	
Own_home	−	−		−
Hi_educate				
Hi_income				
Envi_group				
Bus_group	+	+		+

[a]+ indicates a statistically significant positive effect. − indicates a statistically significant negative effect.

respondents to provide more extreme (or outlier) responses may provide them with a greater-than-average influence on statistical results.

A look at the responses concerning tool 8 provides a final illustration of response asymmetries. The survey describe tool 8 as "purchase and preserve undeveloped land with public funds." Table 15.6 provides a summary of statistically significant effects. As in Table 15.5, for simplicity we emphasize only the direction (sign) of statistically significant effects.

The ordered probit model identifies preference heterogeneity associated with only three out of nine attributes: *age*, *hi_educate*, and *envi_group*. In contrast, the bivariate probit model, including both the support/oppose and strength of preference models, identifies statistically significant impacts of six out of nine attributes: *age*, *female*, *house_size*, *hi_educate*, *envi_group*, and *bus_group*. Here the ability to distinguish attribute effects on the support/oppose choice versus the strength of preference choice allows the identification of additional sources of response heterogeneity, in this case associated with household size, gender, and membership in business organizations. The results indicate a negative effect of household size on the probability of supporting the purchase and preservation of undeveloped land ($p < 0.05$). The statistical significance of this effect is not apparent in the ordered response model. For policy makers or researchers interested in forecasting referendum support for proposed policies among different demographic groups, such patterns would be of considerable relevance.

Similar patterns exist to varying degrees in models addressing LS responses for all 21 management tools considered. Results strongly support the hypothesis that response asymmetries occur, thereby refuting a primary assumption on which standard ordered response models rely. Perhaps more important, the results show that alternative choice models in the bivariate probit specification are able to identify behavioral patterns obscured by traditional ordered response models when analyzing

TABLE 15.6 Summary of Statistical Results: Tool 8[a]

	Bivariate Probit			Ordered Probit
Variable Name	Support/Oppose	Strength of Preference Support	Strength of Preference Oppose	
Resid_year				
Age	−		−	−
Female		+		
House_size	−			
Own_home				
Hi_educate	+	+		+
Hi_income				
Envi_group	+	+	+	+
Bus_group			−	

[a]Tool 8 described as "purchase and preserve undeveloped land with public funds (e.g., public bond issues).

\+ indicates a statistically significant positive effect. − indicates a statistically significant negative effect.

LS data. These findings illuminate aspects of preference heterogeneity that may be of considerable importance in policy analysis contexts, as our analysis and examples illustrate.

Investigation of Neutral Responses

As mentioned earlier, the bivariate probit model cannot deal with neutral responses. Referendums generally allow voters to respond "yes," "no," but voters can also choose to enter a blank. The political process often ignores blanks, but it is useful to see if or how socioeconomic attributes predict those more likely to have a neutral response (vote a "blank" or choose the middle value on the Likert scale). To obtain a broader representation of preferences for land use policies, we examine three tools in Table 15.7: Tool 1 supports new commercial development, tool 6 supports revitalization of existing retail development, and tool 8 supports land preservation.

Identifying attributes of residents who are likely to have neutral responses (or choose not to vote) can be a useful tool, for example, if planners wish to target education programs and decrease neutral responses. Using a basic probit model to estimate the relationship of the attributes and the presence of a neutral versus stated preference yields interesting results. Table 15.8 shows the parameters and tests for goodness of fit. The models perform relatively well for cross-sectional data, with significant likelihood ratio statistics and pseudo-R^2s from 0.1723 to 0.42. In this model, we look at the how the variables relate to the probability that a respondent would choose a neutral stance on an issue. In Table 15.7, variable with significant positive coefficients denote a tendency to be neutral on that issue as that variable increases. Variables that were positive and significant for $p < 0.05$ for at least one tool include gender, belonging to an environmental group, and a pattern of voting neutral on other policy tools. If a variable is negative and significant, there is an indication that there is less of a tendency to have neutral feelings for a policy tool as

TABLE 15.7 Summary of Statistical Results: Neutral Responses

	Probit: Neutral/Preference		
Variable Name	Tool 1	Tool 6	Tool 8
Neutrals	+	+	+
Resid_year	–	–	
Age	–		
Female	+		
House_size			
Own_home		–	
Hi_educate			
Hi_income			
Envi_group	+		–
Bus_group	–	–	
ToolOppose			

+ indicates a statistically significant positive effect. – indicates a statistically significant negative effect.

TABLE 15.8 Neutral Response Probit Results: Tools 1, 6, and 8

Variable Name	Tool 1 Parameter Estimate	Tool 1 Std. Error	Tool 1 p > |z|	Tool 6 Parameter Estimate	Tool 6 Std. Error	Tool 6 p > |z|	Tool 8 Parameter Estimate	Tool 8 Std. Error	Tool 8 p > |z|
Neutrals	0.103	0.013	0.000	0.084	0.010	0.000	0.155	0.012	0.000
Res_year	−0.008	0.003	0.008	−0.010	0.002	0.000	−0.002	0.003	0.564
Age	−0.011	0.004	0.011	0.006	0.003	0.069	−0.005	0.003	0.117
Female	0.227	0.097	0.020	−0.087	0.070	0.216	0.127	0.075	0.091
House_size	−0.026	0.039	0.504	−0.011	0.028	0.683	0.003	0.030	0.917
Own	0.271	0.172	0.115	−0.286	0.124	0.021	0.117	0.125	0.348
Hi_educate	−0.051	0.105	0.629	−0.087	0.075	0.246	0.016	0.080	0.847
Hi_income	−0.069	0.102	0.496	0.017	0.073	0.813	0.017	0.079	0.827
Envi_group	0.428	0.124	0.001	0.138	0.087	0.112	−0.546	0.105	0.000
Bus_group	−0.449	0.122	0.000	−0.215	0.088	0.014	−0.160	0.096	0.097
ToolOppose	−9.425	8145906	1.000	−7.879	270290	1.000	−8.884	580160	1.000
Intercept	0.041	0.286	0.886	−0.602	0.204	0.003	−0.869	0.222	0.000
N	1948			1948			1948		
−2 LnL χ^2 (df =11)		802.54	0.001		413.11	0.001		448.48	0.001
Pseudo R^2		0.429			0.172			0.213	

the variable increases. Variables that are negative and significant include age, number of years residing in the town, and homeownership.

It seems logical that individual who tend to have neutral preferences for other policy tools would also more likely feel neutral about tools 1, 6, and 8. The variables indicating that this is so are positive and significant in all three models. It also seems logical that the longer a person lives in a town, the less likely that individual is to be neutral about land use tools. *Resid_years* is significantly negative for tools 1 and 6, which both deal with development, either encouraging new commercial development or revitalizing current town or village centers. This variable was insignificant for tool 8 (preserving undeveloped land). Age was significant and negative in tool 1, showing that older respondents were likely to have a definite preference for commercial development. Female respondents were more likely to be neutral about encouraging commercial development. Homeownership was significant and negative only for downtown revitalization. Homeowners are more likely to want to see their downtowns revitalized.

Interestingly, members of environmental groups were more likely to have neutral preferences for commercial development. As expected, they are not likely to have neutral votes for open space preservation. Preceding models also show that membership in an environmental organization correlates with strong preferences for conservation policies. Finally, members of business groups were more likely to have a stated preference for commercial development and for town center revitalization.

The only characteristics consistent across all neutral respondents were that the more neutral responses people had on other policy tools, the more likely they were to be neutral about the three tools just discussed.

CONCLUSIONS

If one is solely interested in calculating mean policy support over a sample of respondents, then findings of preference asymmetry in LS responses may be of little relevance. However, if one wishes to characterize heterogeneity in support for management tools or assess statistical determinants of LS responses, then the potential for such patterns may be of critical importance. In this chapter, we show that the assumption of response symmetry implied in traditional ordered response models conceal potentially significant influences on strength of support or opposition and prevent their detection. The results from our modeling efforts support the potentially surprising conclusion that statistically significant response asymmetries are both common and policy relevant, even in relatively straightforward LS ratings applied over a single ordered preference scale.

Besides showing the existence of response asymmetries in our LS data, our findings indicate that preferences for land use tools are potentially more complex than is typically assumed. For example, bivariate probit specifications of our LS data frequently reveal differences among the variables influencing the decision to support or oppose particular land use policies and the variables influencing strength of preferences for supported or opposed policies. Moreover, while certain universal and intuitive patterns are apparent (e.g., environmental group membership is almost universally associated with stronger support for pro-environment policies and stronger opposition to pro-development policies), the effect of other attributes varies considerably. Such patterns suggest caution in making general statements concerning heterogeneity in preferences for particular types of land use policies.

Although the current analysis provides evidence that response asymmetries occur in simple LS questions (e.g., decisions to be made in a single stage. questions to be answered at once, and the answer to be indicated on a LS scale) and discusses potential policy implications of such patterns, there is much left for future research. For example, researchers often use principal component factor analysis of the response correlation matrix to estimate latent factors that capture a high degree of variation in LS responses. Resulting factor scores then guide the inclusion of either independent or dependent variables in statistical models (e.g., Variyam et al., 1990). Implications of response asymmetry (in the raw LS data) on derived factor scores, and on statistical models incorporating these scores, have yet to be explored.

Additional areas of future research include alternative approaches to data incorporating response asymmetries. Bivariate probit models represent only one potential means of modeling response asymmetries. Variants of Heckman-type sample selection models or nested choice models (e.g., nested logit) are other potential approaches. The exploration of such potential alternatives to LS data analysis was beyond the scope of this study, but such as-yet-undeveloped approaches might provide superior means to model LS response asymmetries of the type identified here. For example, alternative approaches might be able to able to model response asymmetry but be able to retain "neutral" responses. Regardless the promise of potential alternatives, the results presented in this chapter suggest that models allowing for response asymmetries in LS data may provide insight over and above that provided by traditional ordered response models.

REFERENCES

Bateman, I.J., R.T. Carson, B. Day, M. Hanemann, N. Hanley, T. Hett, M. Jones-Lee, G. Loomes, S. Mourato, E. Ozdemiroglu, D.W. Pierce, R. Sugden, and J. Swanson. (2002). *Economic Valuation with Stated Preference Surveys*. Northampton, MA: Edward Elgar.

Danielson, L., T.J. Hoban, G. Van Houtven, and J.C. Whitehead. (1995). "Measuring the Benefits of Local Public Goods: Environmental Quality in Gaston County, North Carolina," *Applied Economics* 27.12: 1235–1243.

Dillman, D.A. (2000). *Mail and Internet Surveys: The Tailored Design Method*. New York: John Wiley & Sons.

Greene, W.H. (2000). *Econometric Analysis*, 5th ed. Upper Saddle River, NJ: Prentice Hall.

Johnston, R.J., and S.K. Swallow. (1999). "Asymmetries in Ordered Strength of Preference Models: Implications of Focus Shift for Discrete Choice Preference Estimation," *Land Economics* 75.2: 295–310.

Johnston, R.J., S.K. Swallow, and D.M. Bauer. (2002). "Spatial Factors and Stated Preference Values for Public Goods: Considerations for Rural Land Development," *Land Economics* 78.4: 481–500.

Johnston, R.J., S.K. Swallow, D. Marie Bauer, and C.M. Anderson. (2003). "Preferences for Residential Development Attributes and Support for the Policy Process: Implications for Management and Conservation of Rural Landscapes," *Agricultural and Resource Economics Review* 32.1: 65–82.

Kline, J.D., and D. Wichelns. (1998). "Measuring Heterogeneous Preferences for Preserving Farmland and Open Space," *Ecological Economics* 26.2: 211–224.

Lynne, G.D., J.S. Shonkwiler, and L.R. Rola. (1988). "Attitudes and Farmer Conservation Behavior," *American Journal of Agricultural Economics* 70.1: 12–19.

Maddala, G.S. (1983). *Limited Dependent and Qualitative Variables in Econometrics.* Cambridge: Cambridge University Press.

McFadden, D. (1974). "The Measurement of Urban Travel Demand," *Journal of Public Economics* 3: 303–328.

Poe, G.L., M.P. Welsh, and P.A. Champ. (1997). "Measuring the Difference in Mean Willingness to Pay When Dichotomous Choice Contingent Valuation Responses Are Not Independent," *Land Economics* 73.2: 255–267.

Shafir, E. (1993) "Choosing Versus Rejecting: Why Some Options are Both Better and Worse than Others," *Memory and Cognition* 21: 546–556.

Swallow, S.K., J.J. Opaluch, and T.F. Weaver. (2001). "Strength-of-Preference Indicators and an Ordered Response Model for Ordinarily Dichotomous, Discrete Choice Data," *Journal of Environmental Economics and Management* 41.1: 70–93.

Variyam, J.N., J.L. Jorday, and J.E. Epperson. (1990). "Preferences of Citizens for Agricultural Policies: Evidence from a National Survey," *American Journal of Agricultural Economics* 72.2: 257–267.

Yamagishi, K. (1996). "Strength of Preference and Effects of Valence in the Domains of Gains and Losses," *Organizational Behavior and Decision Making Processes* 66 (June): 290–306.

Yamagishi, K., and J.M. Miyamoto. (1996). "Asymmetries in Strength of Preference: A Focus Shift Model of Valence Effects in Difference Judgments," *Journal of Experimental Psychology* 22: 493–509.

CHAPTER 16

African Women in Mining Partnerships

Brigitte Bocoum

INTRODUCTION

In a variety of ways, high costs have been found to be associated with the low participation of women in the economic sphere. Yet the traditional paradigm still limits the recognition that women need greater flexibility to play multiple roles as mothers, wives, workers, and citizens, to maximize family welfare. Meanwhile, few families in Africa and most other parts of the world are affluent enough to live comfortably on one income, whereas it has become common knowledge that gender inequality holds back a country's economic performance. Barriers, in whatever form, that reduce open competition impede a country's ability to draw on its best talents, and ultimately undermine economic growth and productivity. The need has now thus become urgent to look to alternative models of growth and development.

It is worth recalling the importance of the mineral sector for at least 23 of Africa's 53 nations (Bocoum-Kaberuka 1999a). Also, the fact that mining has not yet generated the kind of socioeconomic development one would expect is an important consideration. So are the availability of sizable deposits of great variety, the several revisions of development policies and large investments granted over time, but most important here is the fact that mineral exploitation is not new on the continent. It is thus believed that the situation calls for rethinking the development strategy for the sector. It is further suggested that this process urgently puts great emphasis on the need to involve a wider spectrum of stakeholders to include women with the aim to better guide policy and perform mining business for development purposes. The chapter highlights the importance for any policy reformulation process to seriously reconsider the existing gender imbalances and prevailing unsuitable approaches to women's integration in the mining of Africa's resources. Suggestions are also offered to fully integrate both the concept and the practice of increased female participation in mining business and related activities with its associated impact in promoting sustainable socioeconomic development on a much larger scale on the continent.

The proliferation of new mining partnerships across the globe offers unique opportunities to mainstream gender equality into the mining sector of Africa. These partnerships through mining networks are a viable channel through which we can create sustainable economic growth and development (Bocoum 2003). They aim at establishing close ties between all constituents with a commitment to the sustainable development of the abundant, diversified, and still mostly untapped mineral resources of the continent (Bocoum 2006; Bocoum-Kaberuka 1999b). An increasingly significant number of knowledgeable women are involved in all aspects of mining in several countries. However, any increase in female recruiting generally starts from a very low base. This, as well as current conditions surrounding women and their low level of involvement in the mining industry of Africa, matches neither the need and aspirations of women nor the realities and needs of the region. Similar mining networks should be be created or strengthened among women wishing to contribute substantially to the socioeconomic development of Africa (Bocoum-Kaberuka 1999a). The ultimate aim is to create an enabling environment for the successful integration of women as key partners for mineral development.

There is no doubt that the makeup of the mining labor force is changing and will continue to evolve. The most urgent needs lie in the participation of women in decision making and in insuring that gender is mainstreamed in the mining industry without discrimination. As time goes by, there will be a growing need to involve more people from nontraditional sources, reconciling the experiences and seeking the most effective approaches that meet the specific needs of women in mining in an efficient and lasting way.

WOMEN'S INVOLVEMENT IN MINING

Available statistics point to huge discrepancies in both the degree and levels of involvement between men and women in the mining sector of Africa. Mining and many other industries traditionally are viewed as a male domain, and the integration, advancement, and retention of women in this sector have been slow to nonexistent. In the job market, there is ample evidence that employers in the field prefer to hire and work mostly with men. Empirical analyses conducted to explain such phenomena have shed light to the significant detrimental influence caused by the general belief that men's income is more important to their families (Farrell 2005; Rognerud 2006). Also, the demand for female labor has been found more tied to the level and state of economic growth than the demand for male labor, which does not induce much for Africa. Greater details are available on this topic elsewhere in the literature (World Bank 2003). This chapter mainly focuses on female labor force constraints in the mining sector, to ensure that inefficiencies and distortions that affect much of the increasingly growing and capable workforce are better addressed in the future.

Natural resource endowments are used in another preferred underlying theory to explain the causes of retardation of women's involvement in the mining sector of Africa. The theory advances that higher levels of unearned income, such as natural resource rents, reduce the need for earned income, which in turn is thought to reduce the supply of female labor in general. Resource-poor economies tend to rely more heavily on labor-intensive development and so have depended more on women's economic participation, with rates of female labor force participation closer to their potential. Labor-abundant, resource-rich countries like Nigeria and South Africa (10,500 women miners total, i.e., 2.6% of the workforce in 2004; Onstad 2006 and Hinton et al. 2002) tend to have slightly lower rates of female labor force participation than labor-abundant, resource-poor African economies. This is valid of most countries, albeit with a few exceptions.

Other analyses have placed greater emphasis on the direct link that exists between the discouraging support infrastructure and the degree of women's participation in the mining sector. This has also been termed "the lack of right-enabling environment." The analyses underline the fact that women are more constrained than men by their immediate physical environment. A woman's horizon could be greatly expanded by investments in standard infrastructure, such as better transport, water, and telecommunications as well as expansion in market services, acquisition of skills, and education for the provision of vocational and lifelong learning opportunities. Indeed, the matching of competency standards across gender is an essential link between marketable employment requirements and systems. Directly linked to this concept are learning programs, education, and training. When isolating specifically the issue of training, the need to maintain a properly skilled workforce has led the mining industry to place strong emphasis on on-the-job training and to develop multiskilled jobs, formal skill development programs, and payment systems based on available skill use. In developed mineral economies such as Australia, about three-fourths of work organization systems in the mining industry reflect these developments. However, in Africa, very few such programs include let alone benefit women.

Based on actual figures concerning employment rates and working conditions, the gaps between men and women in the mining sector of Africa are even more substantial. The proportion of women in the workforce was computed by the International Labor Organization (ILO 2000) on a sample of 15 countries out of which 3 were from Africa. In those, female employment stood at 21%, 7%, and 2.5%, respectively, for Kenya, Mauritius, and South Africa. Typically, female employment in the mining sector is below 10% on the continent. The data made available here further evidence four points:

1. In most countries and mining companies, the average remuneration of women in mining is below that of men.
2. The representation of women in senior management positions is less than that of men.
3. The proportion also declines with the introduction of longer working hours and compressed shifts, which tend to have a disproportionate effect on women because of their family responsibilities.
4. There is no difference between female employment in mining in developing or developed countries.

Mismanagement of the workplace environment also plays a major prohibitive role. The example of South Africa is worth mentioning, where there have been noticeable cases of decline in female employment since 1995, mainly due to a substantial decrease in the number of women mineworkers in underground production in poor conditions, such as exposure to dust, heat, and noise.

Thus, despite the huge potential for women to significantly increase their contribution to mining development, actual rates of participation in Africa remain among the lowest in the world. In most cases, the lack of the required specialized skills renders difficult the recruitment of women. This is worsened by the fact that the mining industry is also an employer of predominantly full-time workers (women increasingly need flexibility in work hours to adjust to child care demand), an increasing number of whom are contractors, including in development, production, and maintenance. Age also seems to be a discouraging factor for women because, on average, the age of the mining labor force is considerably above that of the industry as a whole. Regarding the type of activities conducted, available global statistics for the region reveal no restriction, apart from the different operational levels, beginners and medium scale included. In terms of representation, African women in mining are present in the industry as full-time professionals, miners, mining company owners, jewelry store owners, manufacturers, and traders. Concerning the specific sectors of intervention, their involvement range from the exploitation of a number of minerals—gold, silver, diamonds, rubies, emeralds, aquamarines, tin, malachite, cobalt, copper, industrial minerals, talc, gypsum, dimension stones, granite, marble, limestone, and so on—to broad policy making, academia, and project finance. On the ground, women are concentrating mainly on small-scale mining and have had to experience the typical major issues having to do with the subsector, like illegal trading (where sales are not transparent and smuggling is rife, benefits are lost to the community, and, in most cases, the commodities pass through several hands at discounted prices before reaching the formal market. Often this translates into artisanal miners receiving less than half the market value of their production). Other issues include health and safety; environmental mismanagement (pressure on the environment as well as on worker health is particularly strong with respect to gold mining because of the use of mercury); and taxation; in addition to gender discrimination.

Environmental hazards are worth mentioning since gold and gemstones are the main substances extracted by women small-scale miners in sub-Saharan Africa, particularly since few women miners have formal mining skills and most have acquired experience on the ground. Moreover, they are generally not organized. However, both training and organization into small groups is starting to occur in places. In Africa, women represent only a small proportion of the mining force; but because of extended families in many countries and a small multiplier effect, their socioeconomic impact could be as substantial as that of large-scale mining development. However, any increase in involvement by women in order to be efficient ultimately will depend on the approach taken to restructuring—from the planning stage—which will entail adequate vision and willingness/openness on the part of the people and the decision-making body involved in the process.

Further from a socioeconomic standpoint, the mining industry remains the main sector, beside agriculture, that can hire large numbers of unskilled workers. The industry is, therefore, in a unique position to contribute substantially, at least in the short to medium term, to the development of the country's human capital, including women. However, it is imperative that enlightened and committed gender planners be involved in the process. Indeed, when performed efficiently, gender planning enables development workers to have the effect they want on women as well as men. Gender planning is supposed to promote gender equity so that women's roles are equally supported as those of men and so that benefits from the mining industry accrue more equitably by gender.

In actual practice, a growing number of measures are being taken, either voluntarily or imposed by institutional pressure groups or as a result of legislation, to counter these imbalances (Bocoum 1997, 2004). But their inefficient implementation accompanied by poor monitoring is a problem and is resulting in mounting dissatisfaction. In addition, it is expected that, with time, all these measures will rely less heavily on equal opportunity and affirmative action policies. Rather, eventually they will be based more on economic and social rationales. To that effect, current efforts should concentrate on initiatives aimed at opening the way forward. It is hoped that this would result in more appropriate policy development as well as the establishment/strengthening of all the causal links and partnerships needed to find working solutions to the problem.

FACTORING IN WOMEN INTO GLOBAL PARTNERSHIPS

Most substantive reforms achieved to date aimed at promoting sustainable development in Africa's mining sector could not have been achieved without the strong participation of a multidisciplinary consortium to ensure that all key aspects were addressed. Using the mining sector as one of the most important channels forward translates into the need to develop the necessary strategic partnerships to ensure that the minerals and mining sector is identified as a vehicle for poverty eradication in Africa. Today, mining actors everywhere are placing great emphasis on the development of partnerships with all stakeholders having a similar strategic orientation and with whom partnership can lead to constructive division of labor and benefits from synergies. Partnerships are being sought everywhere and at all levels, with two broad (and sometimes conflicting) purposes in mind: (1) provide stability; and/or (2) create a better life for all. A snapshot of some of the most recent partnership-building efforts in the mining sector offers a better background picture. Bocoum (2003) offers a comprehensive review of initiatives outside the continent. The underlying argument is threefold:

1. There is a direct link between poverty eradication and the ability to build adequate institutional capabilities and synergies among key regional partners.
2. As past experience has shown, potential additional negative future development impacts and increased sector vulnerability could result from such global initiatives where Africa does not play an active role.
3. No body similar to such global initiatives as the Global Mining Initiative (GMI) and the Collaborative Group on Artisanal and Small Scale Mining (CASM) exists to represent the local sector's interests. A weakening of the local sector would have eroded the continent's effectiveness at guiding mineral policy and worsened the quality of operations over time. It is worth noting the important role played by these global partnership initiatives. There is an urgent need for consolidation at all key levels in African mining. Due to the industry's economic importance, it warrants a similar level of institutional organization and high-power consultation on the part of all actors and institutions involved in the development of mining activities on the continent.

In a similar attempt to share good practices for generating mineral resources based sustainable development in Africa, the MINTEK Institute in South Africa has recently established a partnership with the United Nations Economic Commission for Africa (ECA). Other important global mining initiatives with an African focus have been established, such as the African Mining Network (AMN) at the ECA headquarters in Addis Ababa in February 2003. Meanwhile, the African Millennium Initiative on Science and Technology (AMIST) hosted by UNU/INRA, an initiative of Africa scholars launched by the African diaspora in 2000, will continue to assist Africa in its development path by integrating mining activities in the near future. In 2002, the African Mining Partnership (AMP) was launched at the World Mines Ministries Forum in Toronto (WMMF) following recommendations made by the New Partnership for Africa's Development (NEPAD) Mining Chapter and the Special Conference of African Ministers of Mining and Energy, which called for the immediate establishment of a forum for high-level consultations and consensus building, which was held in Ouagadougou in December 2000. The creation of AMP had been supported by the African mining ministers who met in Cape Town, South Africa, in February 2003 to discuss issues of common interest, particularly those considered strategic in the NEPAD. AMP is seen as a potential vehicle to implement the minerals and mining chapter of NEPAD with a view to harnessing Africa's mineral wealth to promote socioeconomic development (Bocoum 2003).

Notwithstanding the critical role of mining to the well-being of so many African economies, the evidence is that women, despite their growing involvement in mining, have not received the same kind of attention as other cross-cutting issues such as the environment, for example. Today the mining sector's overall contribution to the region's gross domestic product does not exceed 4% and its net contribution to socioeconomic progress is insignificant. In this chapter, we take these five premises/understandings as givens:

1. The economic well-being of a population—including consumption of food, housing, healthcare, and other market-based goods and services—is determined not only by how much each working person earns but also by what proportion of the population works.
2. Importantly in Africa, each employed person supports more than two nonworking dependents, and women often support nearly all their children.
3. Africa's achievements in many areas of women's well-being compare favorably with those of other regions. Indicators such as female education, fertility, life expectancy, and per capita income show that Africa's progress over the last decades has been substantial.
4. Africa falls considerably short on indicators of women's substantive participation in key economic activities.
5. It is commonly agreed that African economies must look to new models of growth and development relying more heavily on more productive use of human capital. Women remain a largely untapped resource in the region, making up 53% of the population and in some countries the majority of enrolled university students, but only a small proportion of the active labor force (FAO 2006).

In all situations, individual champions are a prerequisite for success and for building capacity to foster change. This is an important starting point. However, the societal poverty reduction process mostly entails a multifaceted partnership; strong support from knowledgeable resource persons, including practitioners, public and private institutions, as well as supporting services is critical. In this context, research could play a significant supporting role in assessing the evolution of key measurement parameters, such as involvement/employment levels, levels of poverty, salary rates and income-generation capabilities, social and environmental problems, education and job levels, socioeconomic contribution capacity, and empowerment.

The first official regional Association of African Women in Mining Network (AFWIMN) was launched in Elmina, Ghana, in September 2003 at the third annual meeting of CASM. It took off with the initial technical and financial assistance of the United Nations Development Fund (UNIFEM), the SADC Gender Program from CIDA Canada, the Minerals Commission of Ghana, the World Bank Group through the CASM initiative, and experts in the area. This has been achieved with some difficulties: getting all the member states to sign (SADC, ECOWAS, COMESA, etc.) and refining its overall purpose, as time evolves. The ultimate aim of AFWIMN (2003) is "to set a vibrant and transparent sector where gender imbalances do not exist and access and control of resources from the mining industry are equally distributed." AFWIMN proposes to achieve its objectives by making visible the participation of women in mining through gender mainstreaming, growth, innovation, and increased productivity for the economic empowerment of women, poverty reduction, and employment creation of all. Recently some momentum has gathered. It is hoped that AFWIMN will grow not only in membership but also in terms of net impact/contribution. Its impact will depend on the network's ability to adjust on the spot to the ever-changing realities of the sector, to rely on clear definitions of targets and objectives based on consensus and enlighten knowledge of the requirements embodied in growth, to true commitment on the part of all designated representatives, to the search for collective gain as well as a dynamic and multidisciplinary approach to resolving the challenge of achieving sustainable development in the mining sector of Africa.

TRUE FOCUS REMAINS SUSTAINABLE DEVELOPMENT

Mining on all scales—small scale, industrial scale, trade, and so on—can contribute to poverty reduction in a variety of ways, mostly through generating income as well as creating opportunities for growth for different categories of businesses. As stated, discrimination against segments of a population on the basis of gender, race, ethnicity, and/or religious background influences a country's larger social climate and reduces development prospects, good governance, and the effectiveness of society's institutions. Studies show that inclusiveness and diversity of perspectives improve decision making about resource allocation (Wente 2002). Women tend to have different perspectives than men about issues of importance in the public domain and decision making. Women's presence in the key economic and public arenas and their influence on public policy are still limited in Africa.

The third of the Millennium Development Goals agreed between all members of the United Nations aimed at promoting gender equality and empowering women. Nowadays, girls are staying longer in school. Across the region, more than one in four girls now enrolls in tertiary education, and women outnumber men in colleges and universities in several countries of the region. Also, girls who stay in school tend to outperform boys. By investing increasingly in women's education and training and integrating women in economic activities that are key most for the continent, Africa is increasing women's economic potential and their capacity to earn incomes and to participate in decisions. Paradoxically, the very low levels of active female participation in the labor force and/or women's representation at the decision-making level mean that the region is not capturing a large enough part of the return on this investment. Add to that the proven higher rates of return, in general, to empowering women, and it becomes clear that increased female labor force participation and surrounding women with the right enabling environment in the workforce would raise the returns to education and training throughout the economy and would improve national living standards as well as institutional functioning.

Selected Parameters for Women's Contribution to Sustainable Development in the Mining Sector and in Mining-Related Activities

- **Budget and Finance Related.** Agree and obtain a budget and/or business plan as well as mobilize funding per target activity.
- **Institutional Matters.** Establish specialized agencies, pressure groups, or thematic partnerships if needed.
- **Government/Institutional Support.** Seek and obtain support at the highest possible levels.
- **Data Related.** Gather specific quantitative figures to back up and substantiate the facts.
- **Market Related.** Assess all specificities and define all requirements in the surrounding environment.
- **Social Dialogue.** Develop efficient means and strengthen channels to address specific prioritized issues of interest.
- **Education and training.** Acquire all necessary sound basic skills to ensure efficient involvement and long-term employment opportunities.
- **Technology Related.** Value the acquisition of technological know-how and the need to master technical processes.
- **Environmental Matters.** Support the provision and practice of appropriate standards.
- **Removal of Gender Barriers.** Seek the acquisition of power in order to influence decision making.
- **Communication Frontiers.** Access all modern means of communication and expand knowledge frontiers.
- **Poverty Reduction.** Adopt a voluntary approach to the issue of contributing to development and encourage involvement in self-generating development promotional activities; make poverty reduction a strategy.
- **Global Sustainability.** Encourage involvement in activities and forums with global scope.
- **Research and Development.** Develop the means to conduct research, further functional capability, and improve on existing operational tools.

The benefits of enhanced female participation in the labor force have been found to be positive on sustainable development. Besides, low female labor participation has proven to have a high cost to the economy and to the family. Simulations, although not specific to the mining sector—although the latter could yield even higher results—have shown that increasing female labor force participation from their actual rates to predicted rates could boost average household earnings by as much as 25%. For many families, this is a ticket for greater comfort in life. Analyses based on cross-country data have also suggested elsewhere that as countries progress to higher levels of per capita income, increased female labor force participation results in significantly faster income growth. If female participation rates had been at predicted levels, per capita gross domestic product growth rates might have been at least 1.0% higher during the last decade.

Today, the traditional male-breadwinner model is increasingly out of date, with economic pressures leaving many households without a choice: A growing number of women now need to work outside the home to help support their families. The correct assessment of the socioeconomic realities have created everywhere a generation of young women who are increasingly on a par with their male counterparts and expect the same opportunities and rewards. This is also true of the key economic activity, which represents the mining sector. Change, however, will need to be led from the top and supported at the grassroots level. The responsibility lies in the hands of women but also with the state and institutions. Gender equality will remain an abstraction unless a substantial number of women believe that they must do something to exercise their rights. Of course, they will have to rely/work on the improvement of institutional frameworks to achieve that purpose. In mining, the challenge for women ultimately lies in how to integrate themselves successfully in light of the prevailing constraints.

Several key ingredients to ensure the successful integration as well as the sustained involvement of women in mining activities in Africa are highlighted in the list above. It is clear that nearly all of these activities will require the building of strong partnerships, whether at the individual, national, regional, or international levels.

CONCLUSIONS

Calls for gender equality are often seen as claims to share power and control or undermine existing systems. Common perception sees such calls as threats to social order and an erosion of the established power structure, the latter perhaps with some justification. Yet gender equality has been broadly recognized as important for improving economic growth, creating productive employment, and reducing poverty. Past policies of growth strategies left fewer opportunities for women outside of traditional female jobs. As the region adopts new development models that are oriented more toward global impact, the demand dynamics for female labor will evolve.

African women in mining still face significant disadvantages today, often working under suboptimal conditions that afford them little potential for growth. Subtle forms of discrimination against women take place through a host of nonwage employment benefits; labor laws themselves do not explicitly discriminate against women. In fact, such laws clearly stipulate that women should receive equal compensation for work and skills of equal value while stressing the need to understand that recognition, respect, and promotion are natural requirements and are not included in the compensation package. It remains valid to date, however, that the benefits granted by these laws tend to remain unattainable, since they are weakly enforced and the potential beneficiaries lack recourse or information. Significant responsibility hence lies on networks such as AFWIMN and its ability to expand its scope of activities in the future. This expansion should include the promotion of large-scale development and the involvement of women in nontraditional activities, such as industrial minerals development, the provision of technical assistance, advisory and policy-related work, and dissemination of information on best practices in fostering the integration of African women in the mining field. Once fully operational, the network should join efforts with key regional institutions and partners, such as the NEPAD Secretariat and the ECA, to insure that significant benefits accrue to the local community and the economies of the African countries while factoring in the substantive impact of women in the mining sector.

It has become evident that great benefits—including income generation, local community development, and the mitigation of health, environmental, and sociocultural risks—would be reaped from furthering and in particular sustaining women's involvement in mining activities. This chapter has also highlighted the importance of the need for active participation by all key constituencies and the consolidation of partnerships in order to all achieve sustainable development in the mining sector of Africa. Finally, the promising challenges offered by NEPAD and the dynamism embodied in globalization offer a unique opportunity to mainstream the issue of women in mining on the continent. Greater attention should, however, be given to improving family welfare, social and community uplifting, and labor laws in mineral development. The creation of a new paradigm for better integration of women into broader socioeconomic development goals at national and regional levels is also paramount. The ultimate challenge remains one of men and women joining forces in order to encourage understanding and strengthen collaboration among all stakeholders who have a similar strategic orientation and with whom partnerships can lead to constructive division of labor and benefits from synergy; to avoid further waste of valuable and scarce human resources; and to finance development projects, design and/or implement carefully selected programs capable of optimizing the socioeconomic linkages generated by mining-related activities, and thus promote sustainable growth and poverty eradication on the continent.

REFERENCES

African Women in Mining Network (AFWMIN). (2003). Mandate Definition, opening speech at launch ceremony, September 7–10, Elmina, Ghana.

Bocoum, B. (1997). "The New Mining Legislation of Côte d'Ivoire: Some Comparative Features," United Nations Conference on Trade and Development Discussion Paper 125, Geneva, Switzerland.

———. (2003). "NEPAD and Mining Partnerships: A Challenge for the ADB," African Development Bank, *ADB Bulletin* 6.2.

———. (2004). "Harmonization of Mining Policies, Standards, Legislative and Regulatory Frameworks in Southern Africa." United Nations Economic Commission for Africa, Southern Africa Office. Gaborone, Botswana: Southern African Development Community.

———. (2006). "Mines ces richesses que l'Afrique laisse échapper." Interview by Frédéric Maury, *Jeune Afrique*, 2377 (July 30–August 5, 2007).

Bocoum-Kaberuka, B. (1999a). "An Assessment of Industrial Minerals Development Levels in Africa," *Southern and Eastern African Mineral Centre (SEAMIC) Newsletter* 3.1.

———. (1999b). "The Significance of Mineral Processing Activities and Their Potential Impact on African Economic Development," *African Development Review* 11.2: 233–264.

FAO. (2006). "Women and Sustainable Food Security." Prepared by the Women in Development Service, FAO Women and Population Division, Sustainable Development Department, Rome, Italy: Food and Agriculture Organization.

Farrell, W. (2005). "Why Men Earn More: The Startling Truth Behind the Pay Gap and What Women Can Do About It," AMACON (American Management Association), Washington, DC.

Hinton, J.J., M.M. Veiga, and C. Beinhoff. (2003). "Women and Artisanal Mining: Gender Roles and the Road Ahead."In G. Hilson, ed., *The Socio-Economic Impact of Artisanal and Small-Scale Mining in Developing Countries*, chap. 11. The Netherlands: A.A. Balkema, Swets Publishers.

Määttä, P. (2000). "Equal Pay Policies: International Review of Selected Developing and Developed Countries," Social Dialogue, Labour Law and Labour Administration Department, Geneva, Switzerland: International Labour Organization. www.ilo.org/public/english/dialogue/ifpdial/publ/infocus/equalpay/3_2.htm.

Onstad, E. (2006). "South African Women Push for Top Spots in Mining," *Mail & Guardian* online, December 18. www.mg.co.za/.

Roguerud, M.A., and P.-H. Zahl. (2006). "Social Inequalities in Mortality: Changes in the Relative Importance of Income, Education and Household Size over a 27-year Period," *European Journal of Public Health* 16: 62–68.

Wente, B. (2002). "It's the Women Who'll Save Africa," *Globe and Mail*, December 14.

World Bank. (2003). "Gender and Development in the Middle East and North Africa: Women and the Public Sphere," *World Bank Report*, September.

EPILOGUE

Conclusions and Perspective

Walter C. Labys

These conclusions attempt to elucidate the major findings of the chapters in this book and to provide a perspective for future problem solving and research. The authors' contributions reflect the efforts of a group of the many doctoral students and colleagues with whom I have collaborated over the years. The quality of their research demonstrates their outstanding expertise and abilities. The subjects covered help close the gap on current and future economic problems surrounding commodity markets and constitute extensions and applications of state-of-the-art methods for analyzing and modeling the dynamic behavior of these markets and their interactions with the economy and the environment. Of significance is the balance they provide between theoretical and empirical research. The chapters presented here also reflect the research directions that I have taken during my career; I will say more about this later.

These chapters are grouped into four parts according to the issues they address. Part One analyzes the dynamic behavior of commodity prices in terms of their nonlinear chaotic and cyclical properties. This behavior is then considered in a multivariate context in terms of price comovements, business cycles, and other influencing variables. The latest time-series tests are presented and applied to the commodity price series of interest. In Part Two, commodity inventory adjustments are introduced to the price framework. The authors have compiled new inventory data, permitting a more in-depth analysis of inventory-price adjustments than was possible before. Again the latest time-series methods are employed to model the relationship between these variables. In Part Three, innovative modeling methods are applied to supply and demand aspects of commodity markets as a multivariate equilibrating mechanism. Here emphasis shifts from time series to mathematical programming and input-output methods. Energy applications dominate with concentration on the problems of coal industries and markets. In Part Four, these modeling efforts are expanded beyond direct market phenomena to include the interactions between commodities, other forms of resources, and the environment. Pollution impacts are analyzed, as well as needs for fresh water and land preservation. The results and related analyses illustrate how applications of these methods can inform policy making in corporate business, government, and international institutions.

Part One goes beyond research that I performed at the beginning of my career. The publication of *Speculation, Hedging and Commodity Price Forecasts* (1970) with

Clive Granger provided new insights into the use of spectral and autoregressive-moving average (ARMA) methods to identify the underlying time-series behavior of commodity price fluctuations. My doctoral students have continued to develop and to apply these methods in a number of new directions, as proven here. Some of these directions have been published earlier in *Univariate Tests for Time Series Models* (with J. Cromwell and M. Terraza, 1994), *Multivariate Tests for Time Series Models* (with J. Cromwell, M. Terraza, and M. Hannan, 1994), and in *Modeling and Forecasting Primary Commodity Prices* (2006).

Chapter 1 accordingly introduces new estimation methods for structuring nonlinear time-series models that have special memory processes. The mentioned ARMA models do not accurately describe situations where the long memory component of the impulse-response coefficients is predominant. Of course, long memory could be approximated well with a suitably large-order ARMA representation, but this is of little help for the special case of the small samples modeled here. Instead, Armand Sadler, Jean-Baptiste Lesourd, and Vêlayoudom Marimoutou propose a truncated version of the fractionally integrated model that has the advantage of being easily estimable and that parsimoniously captures the growth pattern of slow-decaying processes. They consistently estimate the model's parameters, using Monte Carlo experiments. In their applications to forecasting annual steel consumption, they found evidence of stochastic cycles, including some correlations between consumption, prices, and business cycles. Their work with small samples will improve forecast performance in this area.

Chapter 2 deals with time-series advances that relate the dynamics of commodity price cycles more directly to business cycles. Although falling commodity prices imply recessionary behavior and can precede downturns in industrial activity, rising industrial activity increases demand pressure on primary commodities and can raise their prices. Over long- and short-run movements in the business cycle, commodity prices generally coincide with those movements and can be procyclical or acyclical. Ahmad Afrasiabi expands on recent procyclical tests that would regress commodity prices on business cycle variables by employing a sophisticated spectral process to filter the times-series behavior of a group of commodity price series. Some of the baseline coefficients were negative or insignificant. The removal of longer-term variations, often longer than typical business cycle durations, made the coefficients positive and significant. The sole exceptions to his conclusion are the countercyclical prices of gold and the acyclical prices of sugar. As a contribution to the record of "stylized facts," the cyclical comovements of agricultural, mineral, and energy prices with industrial output seem to have the same significance as does the procyclicality of wages with this and other business cycles. His findings should help researchers evaluate alternative business cycle theories in light of their capacity to predict these comovements correctly.

Chapter 3 analyzes these same dynamics, but this time a more thorough nonlinear analysis is made just among the prices themselves. Catherine Kyrtsou investigates the possibility of nonlinear feedback between inflation in the United States and several metal and energy price series, including crude oil. The application of tests for nonlinear feedback causality, recently developed by Hristu-Varsakelis and Kyrtsou, reveals the presence of nonlinear interdependencies and unidirectional nonlinear causality between the given commodity price series and inflation, including bidirectionality in the case of crude oil. The results confirm the findings of previous studies of an influence of inflation and other business cycles on crude oil prices. They also have two important implications for policy:

1. Policy makers in the United States should no longer neglect the impact of crude oil prices on inflation by relying excessively on monetary policy to resolve the problem.
2. Employing asymmetric versions of nonlinear causality tests should provide help policy makers with information that helps them refine their understanding of commodity price fluctuations in upturns versus downturns.

In Chapter 4, Sadek Melhem and Michel Terraza provide an updated analysis of the relationship between the U.S. dollar exchange rate and the world oil price. While exports of the OPEC countries are denominated in dollars, their imports come mainly from the zones denominated in the euro and the yen. The devaluation of the dollar against the euro and the yen directly affects their economies and incites them to maintain their purchasing power by increasing oil prices. The fact that global oil imports are denominated in U.S. dollars raises the question of the extent of the correlation between exchange rates and oil prices. The authors thus address the question of whether changes in the impacts of oil prices are the reason for or the result of the changes in the nature of relationship between oil prices and exchange rate. They also examine the nature of the influence of monetary policy on this relationship and the predominant response of exchange rate policies relative to oil price behavior. Cointegration and causality tests are used to study the sources of the relationship between the oil price and the U.S. dollar exchange rate over the period from 1999 to 2007. These tests also evaluate the relation of the dollar bilateral real exchange rate against a basket of five currencies: euro, Swiss franc, British pound, Canadian dollar, and Japanese yen. Their results suggest that a depreciation of the dollar could lead to an increase in oil prices in the long run, although there are differences in sensitivity in the relationship between exchange rates and oil prices. They explain such differences by the nature of the exchange rate regimes in each of these currencies and by an oil exporter's location relative to the United States. Proximity influences trade patterns, and the larger the percentage of imports denoted in U.S. dollars, the smaller the effect of a dollar depreciation.

Part Two advances research in an area that I began with Clive Granger concerning how short-term inventory adjustments can be modeled to provide a more comprehensive explanation of commodity price movements. In addition to the inventory research we provided for Unilever Ltd., the commodity modeling and market stabilization studies I prepared for the United Nations (Geneva) appeared in *Dynamic Commodity Models* (1973). Further modeling efforts of a number of commodity markets culminated in *Commodity Models for Forecasting and Policy Analysis* (with P. Pollak, 1984). Related studies include *Quantitative Models of Commodity Markets* (1975), *Commodity Markets and Models—An International Bibliography* (1987), *International Commodity Market Models* (with O. Guvenen and J.B. Lesourd, 1991), and *Politiques Economiques et Marches Internationaux des Matieres Premieres* (with O. Guvenen and J.B. Lesourd, Paris, 1991). Similar inventory issues appear in *Le Vin* (Paris, 1994), which dealt with the dynamics of international wine markets (the text was translated into French thanks to my collaborator, Pierre Spahni).

New directions in inventory-price research occur here because of a larger-scale effort to obtain more detailed inventory data. In Chapter 5, Irene Xiarchos explores potential primary and scrap price relationships with inventories by applying multivariate time-series methods to aluminum, copper, lead, and zinc data. A production-smoothing model that relates the ratio of primary and scrap prices to levels of primary metal stocks was also evaluated. The results show that even though long-run equilibrium between primary and scrap prices exists, dynamic shocks lead to an unstable relationship in the short run. The model furthermore helps to explain how inventory levels affect the primary and scrap price spread. With low inventories, the spread between primary and scrap prices becomes smaller, whereas ample inventories mean wider spreads between primary and scrap prices. Although the production smoothing results describe a short-run phenomenon, the long-run equilibrium found between inventories and price ratios for zinc and aluminum suggests possibilities for the future investigation of other forces that lead to this relationship.

In Chapter 6, the emphasis shifts to investigating the influence of commodity futures or derivative markets on the price-inventory relationship. Paul Crompton evaluates the underlying supply of storage theory for metal contracts traded on the London Metal Exchange. Polynomial regression analysis has been applied to spot and futures price spreads as a function of inventory holding. However, only weak empirical evidence was found to confirm the existence of the supply of storage curve. Copper and lead provide the most impressive confirmations, while aluminum and zinc are less supportive. His results question the empirical rigor of this theory for metals and suggest that most of the explanatory power rests among stock, cash, and futures price levels, not their spreads. Based on cointegration and causality tests among these variables along with a corresponding Granger error correction model, inventories were found to cause price movements rather than the reverse. The strongest results of this analysis suggest that consumer inventories drive price movements, with no bidirectional links in the case of aluminum, copper, and zinc.

Chapters 7 asks whether the inventory-price relationships of Chapter 5 and 6 should be considered in an asymmetric context. Eugene Kouassi investigates temporal asymmetry in the metal price-stock relationship based on threshold cointegration and asymmetric noncausality tests. Asymmetric causality tests also indicate a feedback link between prices and stocks for the four metals under consideration. He further discovers that negative changes for both prices and stocks have stronger effects than positive changes. Several theoretical explanations of asymmetry rationalize the findings. An important futures market trading implication of his results is that the commodity demand function for bears is steeper than the demand function for bulls. The results also indicate that expectations are stabilizing in a bull market but destabilizing in a bear market.

Chapter 8 extends the analysis of the inventory-price relation to the case of wine markets. Globalization and the expansion of world wine trade have caused a wine boom that together with agricultural subsidies have made fluctuations in wine inventories a more critical issue. In the case of domestic and international wine markets, little is known about intertemporal inventory adjustments and how they relate to prices. James Bukenya investigates possible dynamic relations between these variables by assembling several national wine inventory and price series and using cointegrating and vector autoregressions to analyze them. The shapes of the impulse functions estimated from the vector autoregressions confirm the proper negative relationship between positive stock changes and falling prices and negative stock changes and rising prices. These results are strongest for wine markets in Argentina, Australia, France, Italy, and Spain, and weakest in Germany. Policy makers could utilize this approach to better understand how wine producers and traders can achieve better financial stability.

Part Three moves from the dynamics of price and inventory analysis to the dynamics of market supply and demand adjustments as a whole. Now the modeling emphasis moves in the direction of mathematical programming and input-output analysis. My own research after 1975 shifted somewhat in the direction of modeling commodity supply and demand adjustments in a regional or spatial context. My collaboration with Takashi Takayama confirmed the need to study commodity trade and transportation flows as spatial equilibriums. Bill Miernyk and Adam Rose taught me how regional market problems could be studied using input-output analysis. At the same time the energy crisis of the 1970s had struck the United States. My research efforts in this direction led to the publication of *Quantitative Methods for Market-Oriented Economic Analysis over Space and Time* (with T. Takayama and N. Uri, 1989), and my efforts to expand energy modeling, including my collaboration with David Wood at MIT, finally appeared in updated form in *Modeling Mineral and Energy Markets* (1999). Of particular importance are the contributions that these findings have for analyzing problems and policies in today's energy markets.

Chapter 9 advances methods of mathematical programming by using a quadratic programming algorithm that enables engineers to blend coals with different chemical characteristics to meet client specifications, for example, heat and ash. Bruce Bancroft has developed and implemented a dynamic-feedback mathematical model to blend coal to meet barge specifications by employing a proportional-integral-derivative controller. Such a controller utilizes nuclear analyzers to obtain real-time feedback of the quality of a blended product and produces a given quality at a fast rate. The blended product typically controls the properties of two sources of coal: one that has a quality higher than the target quality and one that is lower than the target quality. Each coal has different costs. The innovations brought to the blending model depend on the two sources being autocorrelated in time with stochastic measurement errors. The proportions of the sources adopted can now be adjusted more accurately by using the probabilistic measurement errors.

Chapter 10 features the adaptation of a mathematical spatial equilibrium programming model to evaluate how prices react to pollution taxes in coal markets. Chen Wei-Yang implements a rent-minimization spatial equilibrium model using a price specification to explain coal supply and demand behavior in the United States; he then uses the model to evaluate the possible application of pollution taxes on coal shipments outgoing from the supply regions. His results suggest that use of conventional pollution taxes and price controls could possibly lessen the volumes of interregional coal shipments. In addition, the imposed taxes could lead to lower efficiency levels because of increased economic rents. Geographically, the Midwest market could to a large extent be taken over by the eastern Appalachian coal-producing regions rather than by western coal-producing regions, because of lower transportation costs. Although the total coal supply could be much lower except for the eastern Appalachian regions, a reduction or termination of pollution-causing coal mines could be beneficial to the environment, despite the increased economic rent on inefficiency. The results suggest that a suitable pollution tax policy would not be possible without some overall considerations of its impacts on the economic activities of other regions as well. This finding suggests that a variety of means are needed to correctly formulate tax policies to control coal emissions. It is believed that such environmental policies could be effectively analyzed by the further use of models of this type.

In Chapter 11, Ukar Soelestijo employs a techno-modeling approach to assess possibilities for interim coal substitution in Indonesia. Given the failure of oil and gas reserves in Indonesia to meet growing domestic energy demands, plans to increase the utilization of domestic coal resources are under way. Such plans include both the direct utilization of coal as fuel and its indirect utilization in processed forms such as coal briquettes, bio-coal, upgraded brown coal, and coal gasification and liquefaction. The use of coal as a direct fuel is anticipated in steam-generating power plants, while coal as bio-coal and briquette would help industrial production. Coal liquefaction could help meet the growing demand for diesel fuels in transportation. Coal gasification or coke making also possesses definite opportunities, for example, in iron casting, because coal is much cheaper than imported coke. Based on existing coal resources in Indonesia of around 61 billion tons, the study forecasts that coal should be able to supply energy for as long as 100 years (assuming 75% recovery), given a production level of 400 million tons of coal per year. In the long term, coal utilization can also be envisioned as a feedstock for the chemical industry.

Chapter 12 looks at how structural changes have occurred in materials demands. Adam Rose and Chia-Yon Chen show how input-output–based structural decomposition analysis (SDA) represents a major advance in forecasting intensity-of-use patterns in the materials industries. Prior work by the authors also shows that is able to overcome the major limitations of the basic, static input-output model, including the fixed coefficient requirement. The authors demonstrate that SDA is capable of yielding results comparable to those derived from two-tier KLEM (capital, labor, energy, and materials) models based on flexible functional forms, yet with much less demanding data requirements. They apply SDA to analyze changes in materials demand and to illustrate the workings of the methodology in the case of the United States.

Part Four reflects some of the research I conducted with students and colleagues on the interaction of commodity markets with the environment, human resources, world trade, and economic development. Much of this research has been conducted in an international context and has resulted in three books: *Market Structure, Bargaining Power and Resource Price Formation* (1980), *Commodity Exports and Latin American Development: A Modeling Approach* (with M.I. Nadiri and J. Nunez del Arco, 1980), and *Industrial Development and Environmental Degradation* (with Se-Hark Park, 1998).

Chapter 13 examines how international trade and resource usage in China increases land, water, and air pollution. Haixiao Huang uses a simulation approach to examine interactions between trade and the environment based on a simultaneous econometric trade and environment model. The robustness of the model's coefficients is assured, using a unique nonlinear two-stage least-squares algorithm. Although the deterministic simulation results are consistent with and very close to those derived from a comparative static solution, the stochastic simulation results indicate that the model performance is reasonably stable when subjected to uncertainty shocks. The empirical results suggest that trade can be harmonized with economic growth and the environment. In particular, increased trade can lead to increased wastewater discharges and levy rates but also greater gross domestic product (GDP) and foreign direct investment inflows. An increase in levy rates, a measure of the strictness of environmental policies, was found to need careful regulation in order to prevent negative changes in GDP, trade values, and foreign direct investment inflows. If levy rates increase and foreign direct investment expands at the same rate, wastewater pollution can be reduced and positive GDP growth can also be achieved. Concerning future research with this form of model, there is a need to expand our knowledge of how international trade can lead to environmental degradation. Further application of the present modeling approach in China and elsewhere depends on obtaining better-quality data so that impact forecasts and policy analysis can be improved.

Chapter 14 evaluates a related environmental problem by assessing how the combination of growing water shortages and water pollution has created a substantial water scarcity crisis in China. Andres Liebenthal analyzes this problem and identifies key elements of a comprehensive strategy for resolving it. China is advised to accelerate its increased reliance on market-based approaches, such as integrated river basin control and rigorous pollution management. The rebalancing of the institutional framework around an integrated river basin management approach is needed to support the establishment of a functioning water market. Key areas of the pollution management system that deserve more attention include nonpoint source pollution, the implementation of payments for environmental services, and the unification of pollution control planning, monitoring, and management. The implementation of the measures Liebenthal recommends needs to be approached in a stepwise manner over a 10- to 15-year horizon, first for the most critical areas, such as the Huai and Hai River basins, and then elsewhere to generate a wider acceptance of water management policies.

In Chapter 15, Robert Johnston and Kelly Cullen evaluate the importance of including rural opinion inputs in making land preservation decisions. Public preferences for land use or other public policies have often been assessed using variants of the Likert Scale method. Their work shows that the given assumption of opinion response symmetry, implied by common ordered response models, may prevent the detection of potentially significant influences on the strength of support or opposition to land use, as revealed by Likert data. They confirm this by showing that significant response asymmetries are both common and policy relevant, even when relatively straightforward Likert ratings are applied over a single-ordered preference scale. Although the study provides evidence that response asymmetries occur in simple Likert questions, the authors advise that researchers can use principal component analysis of response correlation matrix form to estimate latent factors that capture a higher degree of variation in Likert responses. Resulting factor scores can then be used as either independent or dependent variables in statistical models. Implications of response asymmetry on factor scores and on derived statistical models are suggested as a next stage of research in opinion evaluation.

Chapter 16 is devoted to the mining industry in Africa and focuses on the important role of women in mining partnerships. Brigitte Bocoum analyzes gender equality as being important for improving economic growth, creating productive employment, and reducing poverty, despite arguments that it could erode local power structures. Sustaining women's involvement in the difficult area of mining activities has been shown to foster a number of benefits, including local community development and the reduction of health, environmental, and sociocultural risks. Efforts are required to finance development projects and to implement carefully selected programs capable of optimizing the socioeconomic linkages generated by mining-related activities and thus promoting sustainable growth and poverty eradication. Ultimately men and women are advised to join forces in order to encourage understanding and strengthen collaboration among all stakeholders who have a similar mining orientation. Partnerships of this nature can lead to the constructive division of labor and its benefits.

Where do we go from here? These chapters are promising because they point to new ways in which the dynamic, if not unstable, nature of commodity markets can be dealt with, not only in terms of individual market activity but also in terms of their interactions with the economy and the environment. Most recently we have rediscovered the severe consequences of resource exhaustion, environmental damage, and market instability. However, the illumination of these problems has been with us for more than two centuries. Many studies have been performed to make the world aware of the impacts of both commodity price instability and the exhaustion of a variety of natural resource commodities ranging from petroleum and hardwoods to marine species and fresh water. Other destabilizing factors being analyzed range from multinational market power and forced government policies to international economic and financial transmission and feedback effects. Also of importance are the studies related to environmental damage caused by producing and consuming commodities as well as related industrial processes and their global warming effects.

This book has also provided a perspective on the application of a variety of econometric, programming, and related modeling methods that would help us to analyze, predict, and provide policy to deal with these economic and environmental problems. The chapters in Part One, featuring time-series and econometric methods developed for analyzing and forecasting financial market and price movements, deals with short-term issues. One basic assumption underlying price behavior is that commodity markets are efficient at some scale so that the resultant price series are considered to be stochastic or possibly chaotic. This means that price behavior has been found not to follow linear but rather nonlinear processes. The present research points to a shift from autoregressive and moving average models to the nonlinear integrated fractional, autoregressive, and moving average processes, where the order of integration plays an important role in stationarity assumptions. Various time-series methods have been developed to incorporate nonlinearity, including the threshold autoregressive models for the conditional mean employed here as well as the family of autoregressive conditional heteroscedastic and generalized heteroscedastic models. Although these models emphasize nonlinearity in price means, modeling based on nonlinearity in price variance or volatility has continued in the form of the variety of autoregressive hetereoscedastic models.

The chapters in Part Two deal with the multivariate relations not only between prices and inventories but also between prices and business cycles. Recall that some studies evaluate the impact of commodity prices on the macroeconomy while other ones examine these linkages in the reverse direction. The structural relations that are thought to exist between such variables typically are explained using underlying micro- and macroeconomic theories. Multivariate time-series analysis helps with the investigation of such theories using not only cointegration and causality analysis but also cross-spectral density measures of coherence and phase. In addition, variables that have common changing conditional means in the form of co-integration imply Granger-causality in at least one direction and generally do not drift too far from each other. They can be analyzed using vector autoregressive and vector error correction models. Assessing how some structural relations in the market move in and out of phase has considerable impact on the timing of price signals with regard to movements in key economic indicators.

The chapters in Part Three advanced multivariate analysis not only at the level of markets over time but also simultaneously and across activities or space. This includes resource exhaustion and interactions with the environment. A better theoretical and statistical understanding of resource commodity market behavior requires that we improve the specification, estimation, and simulation of structural commodity models in which simultaneity and feedback again play a role. Programming, computable general equilibrium, and input-output methods help us to deal with economic activities of a regional or global spatial nature, because of difficulties in the correct specification of multiequation, nonlinear dynamic econometric systems for commodity markets. The importance of the programming studies included here is that they help us to recognize the need to model commodity markets as a mechanism, if not part of a global network. Today, more than ever, commodity market behavior is intertwined with an international economic mechanism that includes globalization and expanded trade as well as interactions with developed and developing macroeconomies, including related financial institutions. Each of these chapters suggests new frontiers of research in this area.

The chapters in Part Four provide a different perspective on economic globalization and increased international trade that includes environmental and social impacts. The four chapters contribute models, methods, and policies to increase the benefits from resource extraction, use, and trade

All of this research requires improved sources of data. Today no current estimates are available of commodity demand and supply elasticities for most commodities, because practical commodity data compilations have been neglected. The stock or inventory data available today are not as complete as those archived 20 years ago, because of the decreased public and private expenditures on basic data collection and publication. That is why the inventory data collected for the chapters in Part Two shed new light on the study of price-inventory relations. Other intransigent commodity data problems need to be conquered, such as short-length series, missing observations, measurement error, and stochastic noise.

Finally, I appreciate how the chapters in this book contribute to the continuity of resource commodity research. I have participated in research organized by or on behalf of my mentors and colleagues, including Clive Granger, Alf Maizels, and Jerry Adams. It is thus encouraging that many of my colleagues and former students carry on with the work of these pioneers. This continuity reflects the importance of solving the difficult economic problems that, unless tended to, can only grow more severe in their effects.

List of Contributors

Dr. A. Behrooz Afrasiabi earned a Ph.D. at West Virginia University. He has been a faculty member at Allegheny College in Meadville, Pennsylvania, for the past 21 years. His research interests include time-series analysis, especially as applied to mineral resource markets. He has also published articles on the applications of input-output analyzes to regional and energy issues.

Dr. Bruce A. Bancroft is Group Director in the Applied Improvements Department, Coal Operations, of CONSOL Energy Inc., the largest producer of high-Btu bituminous coal in the United States. His educational background includes a Ph.D. in mineral economics and an M.S. in statistics from West Virginia University. Active areas of interest include simulation, geostatistics, process control, mathematical programming, machine vision, and wireless sensor networks.

Dr. Brigitte Bocoum was with the African Development Bank until Spring 2008. She is now with the World Bank's Mining, Oil, Gas and Chemicals Department. With a background in engineering and economics, she specializes in strategy development and development economics. She is an insightful writer who has authored numerous publications. Dr. Bocoum is an advocate of sustainable socioeconomic development in Africa. She understands the long-term importance of judicious finance for development and the urgent need for Africa to generate endogenous wealth. Over the years, she has established a reputation for her research on the proper integration of natural resources in national and regional economic development planning and has become an influential speaker at international forums.

Dr. James O. Bukenya is Associate Professor of Agricultural Economics at Alabama A&M University. His primary research interests are in rural and economic development and related issues in labor markets, human capital, and quality-of-life issues. Secondary interests are in time-series analysis, spatial analysis, and geographical information systems. He has authored and coauthored over 20 publications in peer reviewed scientific journals. As principal and coprincipal investigator, he has secured over $3 million in research grants in the past five years. His list of professional recognitions include the B.D. Mayberry Young Scientist Award by the Association of Research Directors for outstanding achievement in research among 1890 Land Grant Colleges and Universities and the prestigious E. B. Carmichael Award from the Alabama Academy of Science for best peer reviewed publication. Dr. Bukenya has twice been recognized as Outstanding Researcher of the Year by Alabama A&M University.

Dr. Chia-Yon Chen is a professor in the Department of Natural Resource Engineering at the National Cheng Kung University in Taiwan. He specializes in mineral and energy economics and plan evaluation. In his research, he employs input-output methods, sometimes combined with econometric methods for impact analysis. In energy modeling, he has conducted research with so-called gray forecasting models, which rely on fuzzy logic when knowledge is limited and uncertain. The results of his research have been widely disseminated in refereed journals and at international meetings. Dr. Chen earned the Ph.D. in Mineral and Resource Economics at West Virginia University.

Dr. Paul Crompton is a member of the Business School (Economics) of the University of Western Australia. He specializes in mineral and energy economics and general equilibrium modeling. He has published three books and numerous articles in journals such as *Energy Economics* and *Resources Policy*. In 2006 the Curtin Business School of the Curtin University of Technology appointed him to a panel of external experts on that university's Oil and Gas Management project as an area of research excellence. Dr. Crompton earned his Ph.D. at the University of Western Australia. His research has focused on the steel industry in East Asia and its upstream connection with the Australian iron ore industry, and he has served as a consultant for Hamersley Iron and BHP Billiton on forecasting steel consumption and iron ore demand.

Dr. Kelly Giraud Cullen earned her M.S. in Agricultural and Resource Economics at West Virginia University and her Ph.D. in the same field at Colorado State University. She has taught at the University of Alaska Fairbanks and is currently an Associate Professor and program coordinator of Community and Environmental Planning at the University of New Hampshire. Dr. Cullen's main areas of interest are nonmarket valuation, real estate markets, and green building trends.

Dr. Haixiao Huang is a research assistant professor at the University of Illinois at Urbana-Champaign. He previously held a similar position at West Virginia University. He also served on the faculties in civil engineering and economics at Shandong University of Science and Technology, as a visiting scholar in the Institute of Chemical Engineering, Fuel and Environmental Technology, Vienna University of Technology, Austria, and a postdoctoral research associate at University of Illinois at Urbana-Champaign. His research interests include alternative fuel economics, energy demand and supply modeling, carbon sequestration modeling, environmental and agricultural economics, and the relationship between trade and the environment. He is the author of more than 30 articles in journals and proceedings. He received a B.Sc. in Mine Construction and an M.Sc. in Mining Systems Engineering from Shandong University of Science and Technology in China and his Ph.D. in Natural Resource Economics from West Virginia University.

Dr. Ming-Jeng Hwang obtained his Ph.D. degree in economics from Texas A&M University and has held a faculty position at West Virginia University since 1974. His research interest includes microeconomics, spatial economics, regional economics, and energy economics. He has published a total of more than 30 papers in refereed journals such as *American Economic Review*, *Econometrica*, *Journal of Regional Science*, *International Economic Review*, *Southern Economic Journal*, and *Energy Economics*.

Dr. Robert J. Johnston is Associate Professor of Agricultural and Resource Economics and Associate Director of the Sea Grant College Program, University of

Connecticut. He holds a B.A. in economics from Williams College and a Ph.D. in environmental and natural resource economics from the University of Rhode Island. Dr. Johnston is the Vice President of the Marine Resource Economics Foundation and is on the Board of Directors of the Northeastern Agricultural and Resource Economics Association. He also serves on the editorial board of the Agricultural and Resource Economics Review. He is an internationally recognized expert in the valuation of nonmarket resources and ecosystem services, management of coastal and marine resources, and the economics of land use and preservation.

Dr. Eugene Kouassi is Professor of Statistics and Econometrics at the University of Cocody, Ivory Coast. He previously served as a Visiting Professor at West Virginia University, Ivory Coast, Post-Doctoral Fellow at the University of Montreal, and Visiting Scholar at the African Economic Research Consortium in Kenya. He has also conducted research for the World Bank and earned a Ph.D. in Statistics and Econometrics from the University of Montpellier, France.

Dr. Catherine Kyrtsou is Assistant Professor of Economics at the University of Macedonia in Greece. She is also Visiting Professor at the Greek Open University and the University of Montpellier I in France. She holds degrees from the University of Macedonia (B.A. in Economics), and the University of Montpellier I (DEA and Ph.D. in Economics). Dr. Kyrtsou's work has appeared in numerous publications including *Empirical Economics*, *Computational Economics*, *Physica A*, *Journal of Macroeconomics*, *Energy Economics*, *Economic Modelling*, and *International Journal of Applied and Theoretical Finance*. She is editor and co-editor of three special issues on the applications of nonlinear analysis in macroeconomics and finance in the *Journal of Macroeconomics*, *Energy Economics*, and *Brussels Economic Review*, respectively.

Dr. Walter C. Labys is Benedum Distinguished Scholar and Professor Emeritus in the Agricultural and Resource Economics Program at West Virginia University. He also holds the position of Gunnar Myrdal Scholar at the United Nations Economics Commission for Europe and has been Faculty Research Associate of the Group on Applied Econometric Research at the University of the Mediterranean (Aix-Marseille) in France. Over the past 30 years, Dr. Labys has pioneered in the development and application of econometric methods important for analyzing commodity price behavior; the modeling of agricultural, mineral, and energy markets; and the impact of commodity markets on the stability and growth of surrounding developing economies. He has published numerous articles in leading journals of agricultural, energy, and resource economics as well as international trade. Among his best-known books are *Speculation, Hedging and Commodity Price Forecasts* (with C.W.J. Granger), *Dynamic Commodity Models*, and *Modeling and Forecasting Primary Commodity Prices*.

Dr. Jean-Baptiste Lesourd is an applied economist at the University of the Mediterranean in Marseille, France, where he is Professor in the School of Journalism and Communication of Marseille and is conducting research with the Research Group on Media, Information and Communication (MédiaSic). Previously he was a Research Professor with GREQAM (Groupement de Recherche en Economie Quantitative d'Aix Marseille). He serves on the editorial board of *Frontiers in Finance and Economics*. He is an expert on international commodity markets and a past chair of the Applied Econometrics Association chapter on commodities. His research on commodities covered such diverse markets as electricity and wine. His coauthored books, *International Commodity Trading* (2001) and *The Environment in Corporate Management: New Directions and Economic Insights* (2003), are well known in the English-speaking world.

Dr. Andres Liebenthal is an international environmental and energy consultant. He recently retired after 27 years in the World Bank, where he worked on environmental policies and safeguards, energy economics and institutions, and ex-post evaluation. His most recent assignment was as environment and social development coordinator at the Beijing office, where he provided technical leadership and quality control for environment-related activities and oversaw the implementation of environment and social safeguards policies for all of the World Bank's projects in China. He was the country coordinator for China and Mongolia. Dr. Liebenthal has traveled extensively, particularly in Latin America and East Asia regions, managing and contributing to a wide range of environmental and energy projects and reports. He also held positions in the Independent Evaluations Group, where he produced major evaluations of the bank's overall portfolio of dam projects, its environmental performance, and its extractive industries portfolio. Prior to joining the World Bank, Dr. Liebenthal worked as an energy economist for the General Electric Corporation and TRW, Inc. Dr. Liebenthal has a BA in Asian studies from Pomona College and a Ph.D. in economics from West Virginia University.

Dr. Vêlayoudom Marimoutou is a Professor of Economics at the University of Aix-Marseille, France, and a member of the GREQAM (Groupement de Recherche en Economie Quantitative d'Aix Marseille) research group. He also serves as deputy director in charge of Social Sciences and Humanities in CNRS (Centre National de la Recherche Scientifique). He is a coauthor of *Econometric Modeling and Inference* with J.P. Florens and A. Peguin Feissolle and has published numerous articles in the field of theoretical and applied econometrics.

Mr. Sadek Melhem is a doctoral student in econometrics at the University of Montpellier, France, where he is employed in the Laboratoire Montpelliérain d'Economie Théorique et Appliquée (LAMETA).

Dr. Adam Rose is Research Professor in the University of Southern California's (USC) and coordinator for economics at UCS's Department of Homeland Security Center for Risk and Economic Analysis of Terrorism Events (CREATE) and Acting Director of USC's new Energy Institute. He received his Ph.D. in economics at Cornell University and has taught at Cornell, the University California-Riverside, West Virginia University, and Pennsylvania State University, where he served as professor and head of the Department of Energy and Environmental Economics prior to joining the faculty at USC. The emphasis of Dr. Rose's research is on the economics of energy and climate change, with particular regard for the design of policy instruments. He is the recipient of a Woodrow Wilson Fellowship, East-West Center Fellowship, American Planning Association's Outstanding Program Planning Honor Award, Earthquake Engineering Research Institute Special Service Recognition Award, and Applied Technology Council Outstanding Achievement Award. Since arriving at USC less than three years ago, Dr. Rose has received external research support from the National Science Foundation, U.S. Department of Homeland Security, American Petroleum Institute, Center for Climate Strategies, and National Biodefense Analysis and Countermeasures Center.

Dr. Armand Sadler studied economics at the University of Liège, Belgium. In 1974 he joined ARBED SA and worked mainly as a forecaster of apparent and real steel demand. Later he obtained his doctorate in mathematical economics and econometrics at the University of the Mediterranean in Aix-Marseille, France, with a dissertation on international demand of steel. In 2001 he was appointed Chief Economist of Arcelor, the world's largest steel company. He retired in 2007. He served as Chairman of the Medium Term Forecasting Group of the International Iron and Steel Institute, chairman of the Forecast Review Group and, since 2008, is working as a consultant for the institute.

Dr. Peter Schaeffer is Professor of Economic Policy at West Virginia University. Previously he served on the faculties of the University of Illinois at Urbana-Champaign, University of Colorado at Denver, as a visiting professor at the Swiss Federal Institute of Technology, Zurich, and as a visiting scholar at the International Labour Organization in Geneva. He has consulted on regional economic development in the United States, Switzerland, Norway, and the People's Republic of China. Dr. Schaeffer is a past chair of the North American Regional Science Council and president of the Southern Regional Science Association, 2008–2009. He studied economics at the University of Zurich and the University of Southern California.

Dr. Ukar W. Soelistijo was educated in Indonesia as a mining engineer and earned a Ph.D. in Mineral and Energy Resource Economics from West Virginia University. In his doctoral research, he analyzed the mineral and energy resource allocation in the Indonesian economy, and published several articles in major resource economics journals. After returning to Indonesia, he began working for the national Ministry of Energy and Mineral Resources. He eventually rose to the rank of director of research of the ministry's Research and Development Center for Mineral and Coal Technology (tekMIRA). In this role, he made many valuable contributions to the Indonesian mining industry. Upon retirement, he became a Professor of Mining and Oil Engineering at the Institute of Technology, Bandung. He is also a member of the Faculty of Engineering, Department of Mining, Bandung Islamic University.

Dr. Michel Terraza is Professor of Economics at the University of Montpellier, France, where he also holds a research appointment in and serves as director of the Program in Applied Econometrics at the Laboratoire Montpelliérain d'Economie Théorique et Appliquée (LAMETA). His research focuses on behaviors of commodity markets, and he has published over 100 scholarly papers on these and related topics in applied econometrics. He was previously a faculty member and associate dean at the University of Perpignan, France.

Dr. Irene M. Xiarchos is a natural resource and environmental economist in the Office of the Chief Economist in the U. S. Department of Agriculture (USDA), where she works in the area of renewable products and energy and examines public instruments for supporting innovation. She also is implementing a federal preferred procurement program and a labeling program for biobased products. Additionally she teaches economics and policy in the USDA Graduate School. Her research has extended from commodity markets to environmental markets and sustainable development.

Dr. Xiarchos holds a BS degree in economics from the Athens University of Economics and Business and an MS in agricultural and natural resource economics and Ph.D. in natural resource economics from West Virginia University.

Dr. Chin W. Yang is Professor of Economics at Clarion University of Pennsylvania. His research interests include spatial equilibrium models, taxation, and applied econometrics. He has published papers in *Operations Research*, *Journal of Regulatory Economics*, *Public Finance Quarterly*, *Quarterly Review of Economics and Statistics*, *Southern Economic Journal*, *Journal of Comparative Economics*, *Defense and Peace Economics*, *The Manchester School*, *Journal of Real Estate Finance and Economics*, *Energy Journal*, *Energy Economics*, *Asian Economic Journal*, *Atlantic Economic Journal*, *Eastern Economic Journal*, and *Annals of Economics and Finance*.

Index